ESSAYS IN
SOCIAL ANTHROPOLOGY
AND ETHNOLOGY

Fred Eggan

ESSAYS IN SOCIAL ANTHROPOLOGY AND ETHNOLOGY

Fred Eggan

*Harold H. Swift Distinguished
Service Professor Emeritus of
Anthropology, University of Chicago*

The University of Chicago Studies in Anthropology
Series in Social, Cultural, and Linguistic Anthropology, No. 1

Published by the Department of Anthropology,
The University of Chicago

1975

Burg
GN
304
·E33

c. 2

Library of Congress Cataloging in Publication Data

Eggan, Frederick Russell, 1906-
    Essays in social anthropology and ethnology.

    (Series in social, cultural, and linguistic anthropology;
no. 1) (The University of Chicago studies in anthropology)
    CONTENTS: Introduction.--Kinship and social organization:
The Maya kinship system and cross-cousin marriage. The Cheyenne
and Arapaho kinship system. Historical changes in the Choctaw
kinship system. The Hopi and the lineage principle. Northern
woodland ethnology. [etc.]

    1. Ethnology--Addresses, essays, lectures. I. Title.
II. Series. III. Series: Chicago. University. Dept. of
Anthropology. The University of Chicago studies in anthropology.
GN304.E33   301.2
ISBN 0-916256-00-6
75-37810

The University of Chicago Studies in Anthropology
are available from:
Department of Anthropology
The University of Chicago
1126 East 59th Street
Chicago, Illinois 60637
    Price: $6.00 list; $4.00 series subscription

CONTENTS

iii

ILLUSTRATIONS

INTRODUCTION

I

The collected essays included in this volume range over some forty years and cover both kinship and social organization and method and theory. I have restricted the papers--with one or two exceptions-- to those dealing with the American Indian, and have left my reports on the Philippines to some other occasion. The field research on American Indian groups was carried out primarily in the 1930's, though I have continued to visit the Hopi Indians and their neighbors as often as possible, and most of my theoretical studies have grown out of this field research. While I spent a prewar year with the Tinguian of Abra Province, Philippines, I didn't return to the Mountain Province until 1949-50 and the field data gathered in these and subsequent shorter periods is only partially published.

Professor Evans-Pritchard has estimated that an intensive study of a single primitive society and the publication of its results takes about ten years, when one is engaged in teaching or administration. For various reasons my own work has been more extensive than intensive, particularly with regard to the American Indians, and I have not been able to keep to Evans-Pritchard's prescribed schedule. What I have written, however, appears to conform to a general pattern, and the essays reinforce one another in varying ways.

Rereading these essays involves reliving one's intellectual and emotional history. In "Among the Anthropologists" (*Annual Review of Anthropology*, Vol. 3, 1974) I have provided an informal account of my anthropological education at the University of Chicago, of which the present series of papers is one product. I had begun with an interest in archeology and culture history under the tutelage of Fay-Cooper Cole, Edward Sapir, Robert Redfield, and Leslie Spier but had shifted to social anthropology under the influence of A. R. Radcliffe-Brown, and throughout my career I have tried to integrate historical and social anthropological points of view in a single synthesis.

My first published paper came about by accident. I stopped in to see Redfield one day in the fall of 1933 and found him engaged

with some sheets of kinship data. "Here," he said, "you take these
and see what you can do with them. I can't make head or tail of
these Maya terms." Thus challenged I took the terms which J. Eric
Thompson had gathered from the Motul Dictionary and proceeded to analyze them. "The Maya Kinship System and Cross-Cousin Marriage" was
the result and with it I became interested in cross-cousin marriage
in North America and its relation to varying social systems.

A few months earlier I had spent the summer, first among the
Choctaw of Mississippi and then with the Cheyenne and Arapaho in western Oklahoma. Both studies were written up in draft form in 1933,
but were not revised for publication until I returned from the Philippines in the fall of 1935. "The Cheyenne and Arapaho Kinship System" was published in a volume in honor of Radcliffe-Brown, as he
left Chicago for Oxford, and represents my first demonstration of
what I later called the method of controlled comparison. Kinship
terminology was seen in relation to other social groupings and compared with the behavior between relatives in terms of the life cycle.
Special attention was paid to respect and joking relations, for which
a socio-psychological interpretation was provided, and the nature of
social integration in the Plains was described. Two major types of
kinship systems were outlined for the Plains area and related to different styles of life. When *Social Anthropology of North American
Tribes* was enlarged in 1955, I added a chapter on "Social Anthropology: Methods and Results" which expanded the analysis of the Plains
area to encompass other North American regions and problems. Here
I was able to draw on the work of graduate students, as well as on
colleagues, and to extend various historical hypotheses and generalizations.

For the Southeast I was able to utilize information on the
Choctaw to see what had happened to matrilineal systems and Crow type
kinship under acculturation from White missionaries and government
agents during the nineteenth century. Here I was fortunate to find
documentary evidence for my hypotheses; later Alexander Spoehr studied the Creek, Seminole, Choctaw, and other groups in Oklahoma and
found confirmatory evidence for the changes I had outlined, and some
further evidence that any marked functional inconsistencies in social
systems tend to induce change.

I had earlier studied Crow type kinship systems among the
Hopi Indians and their western Pueblo neighbors for my doctoral thesis in 1933, but *The Social Organization of the Western Pueblos* was
not published until 1950--after I had spent several additional seasons among the Hopi. In the meantime I prepared a condensed version

of "The Hopi and the Lineage Principle" for a volume edited by Meyer
Fortes as a tribute to Radcliffe-Brown on his retirement from Oxford.
With regard to the Hopi I have depended particularly on the researches
of Mischa Titiev and John Connelly, and also on the important studies
of the Hopi-Tewa by Edward Dozier, himself a Tewa from the Rio Grande.
Here I have been concerned with structural principles of an intermediate level and with an understanding of the factors involved.

The complex relations between the Western Pueblos and the
Eastern Pueblos have resulted in variant interpretations and considerable controversy. Robin Fox in *The Keresan Bridge: A Problem in
Pueblo Ethnology* (1968) has proposed an alternative solution, utilizing some of Professor Lévi-Strauss's formulations, but the questions are not as yet settled. In the meantime, Alfonso Ortiz has
written *The Tewa World* (1969), which provides the first definitive
account of Tewa culture and cosmology, and suggests that the origins
of Pueblo culture are more complicated than we formerly thought.

In "Northern Woodland Ethnology" I return to some of the
problems originally developed with regard to the Cheyenne and Arapaho
in connection with the Northern Algonkian peoples of Eastern Canada.
Here I have considered the pioneer work of Frank Speck and Father
John Cooper, and the problems raised by the family hunting territory
and cross-cousin marriage, utilizing data provided by A. I. Hallowell, Ruth Landes, W. D. Strong, and Eleanor Leacock, among others.

II

The papers on method and theory have in part grown out of efforts to
make sense out of ethnographic data or to investigate the relations
of social anthropology to other disciplines. I include an unpublished paper on "Culture History Derived from the Study of Living
Peoples," one of a series of lectures by the anthropology department
in 1936, to show something of the flavor of theory in those long gone
days. With both Radcliffe-Brown and W. Lloyd Warner on the depart-
mental staff, most of my teaching in the 1930's centered on ethnology
and culture history, and I gave ethnographic courses on all the major
regions of the world except for Europe.

In 1941 John Collier became interested in a pilot study of
food and nutrition in order to prepare a plan for the larger study
of highland South America, and I was asked to direct it. We decided
on a study of Southwestern communities--both Indian and Spanish-
American--and our study group was hard at work when Pearl Harbor was
bombed. We finished up the field research and prepared a series of
studies for publication but the proposed volume was a casualty of

wartime disruptions. "Some Problems in the Study of Food and Nutrition," written with Michel Pijoán, M.D., provides an outline of our
procedures which may be of interest in connection with recent activities in this field.

My earlier interest in archeology is reflected in "The Ethnological Cultures and Their Archeological Backgrounds," prepared for
a volume in honor of Fay-Cooper Cole. I had originally planned a
doctoral thesis on the ethnological interpretation of archeological
cultures and this paper includes some of the ideas I might have developed with regard to the eastern United States. In the Southwest
I had spent the summers of 1939 and 1940 with the Peabody Museum-
Awatovi Expedition, under the leadership of J. O. Brew, and was much
interested in the development of Hopi culture as seen in the archeological record.

"Social Anthropology and the Method of Controlled Comparison"
is my first major statement of what I have been trying to do and the
methods I prefer to employ. Edward Bruner made the suggestion that
I write up what I had been doing, and the paper was published at a
time when there was considerable discussion of the "comparative method" and its advantages and disadvantages. The Wenner-Gren Conference
on Anthropology Today had just been published and the competition between British social anthropology and American cultural anthropology
was at its height. In this paper I give my own prescription of how
we should proceed but in retrospect I was mainly writing for myself.

"Social Anthropology and the Educational System" was written
for a symposium in *The School Review,* Autumn, 1957. Here I tried to
make educators aware of the differences in various cultures and what
might be learned by observing the Hopi Indians or the Igorots in the
Mountain Province of the Philippines. Jules Henry has carried these
studies much further in the classrooms of ghetto schools in Saint
Louis and other cities, and "Anthropology and Education" is now a
flourishing enterprise, though it is having great difficulty keeping
up with the political scene.

I had been introduced to Lewis H. Morgan in different ways
by Leslie Spier and Radcliffe-Brown and had utilized *Systems of Consanguinity and Affinity of the Human Family* (1871) in my early studies of North American kinship systems. I returned to Morgan's *Systems* in writing "Lewis H. Morgan in Kinship Perspective" for a volume
in honor of Leslie A. White, utilizing the *Indian Journals* of Morgan
which White had just edited. A few years later I expanded some of
the conclusions here reached in the Morgan Lectures for 1964 at the
University of Rochester, later published under the title *The American*

Indian: Perspectives for the Study of Social Change (1966). "Lewis
H. Morgan and the Future of the American Indian" is a by-product of
these lectures and provides a view of Morgan that is not always appreciated. More recently, as a result of the revived interest in
Morgan in connection with the Centennial of *Systems*, I prepared "Lewis
Henry Morgan's Systems: A Reevaluation" for the Anthropological Society of Washington's Centennial celebration.

I had utilized the concept of "cultural drift" in an early
interpretation of the changes I found in Tinguian society and returned
to the problem in "Cultural Drift and Social Change" prepared in hon-
or of Melville J. Herskovits. Cultural drift represents an historical process and I have illustrated it with an analysis of the variations in social institutions in the Mountain Province, Philippines,
utilizing ecological and acculturative factors as explanatory tools,
but the concept has a wider relevance.

In "Alliance and Descent in a Western Pueblo Society" I return to the Hopi data to provide a preliminary evaluation of the significance of these currently controversial concepts for Western Pueblo social integration. And, finally, in "From History to Myth: A
Hopi Example" I attempt an analysis of the ramifications of an event
taking place in the 1850's on the social organization and belief system a century later.

As I reach "retirement" age I find most of these enterprises
are still unfinished and there is much to do, particularly with the
Philippine materials which are only partially published. In recent
years I have begun to analyze the Basin Shoshonean backgrounds to
Hopi society and culture, as well as to prepare a further analysis
of the Hopi dreams which Dorothy Eggan collected but didn't live to
interpret in published form. Reading over the essays included in
this volume I still find them relevant to social anthropology and I
hope they will be of interest to a wider audience.

I would like to thank the members of the Department of Anthropology for recommending publication of these essays, and especially Ralph Nicholas for overseeing the preparation of this volume.
Amy Arnett Knoespel is responsible for the typescript and a grant
from the Marian and Adolph Lichtstern fund has provided for the
printing.

PART I. KINSHIP AND SOCIAL ORGANIZATION

1

THE MAYA KINSHIP SYSTEM
AND CROSS-COUSIN MARRIAGE

1934

INTRODUCTION[1]

Although considerable is known about certain aspects of the culture
of the ancient Maya, information now available concerning their
social organization is extremely unsatisfactory. In regard to kinship only a few partial lists of terms have been presented and these
have hardly sufficed to give any clear picture of the nature of
their kinship system. The available information concerning social
structure, descent, marriage, etc., is even less satisfactory.
Landa[2] has only a few paragraphs relative to these subjects, while
Tozzer[3] indicates some possible survivals among the Lacandones.

    With the recent publication of the Motul dictionary,[4] how-
ever, a considerable amount of new material has been made available
to the ethnologist, including a much more complete set of kinship
terms and applications which throws new light on the nature of the
kinship system and the probable type of marriage which prevailed
among the ancient Maya.

    The importance of the kinship system in relation to the
social organization and marriage practices has been underestimated
by the majority of American ethnologists. This relationship has
been emphasized recently by Lowie:

> Relationship terms are studied by the Anthropologist not
> merely as so many words inviting philological analysis and com-
> parison, but as correlates of social custom. Broadly speaking,
> the use of a specific kinship designation, e.g., for the maternal
> as distinguished from the paternal uncle, indicates that the
> former receives differential treatment at the hands of his
> nephews and nieces. Further if a term of this sort embraces a
> number of individuals, the probability is that the speaker is
> linked to all of them by the same set of mutual duties and
> claims, though their intensity may vary with the closeness of

    Reproduced by permission of the American Anthropological
Association from the *American Anthropologist* 36:188-202, 1934.

the relationship. Sometimes the very essence of social fabric may be demonstrably connected with the mode of classifying kin. Thus kinship nomenclature becomes one of the most important topics of social organization.[5]

It is of course highly desirable that this relationship be actually observed, for as Professor Radcliffe-Brown has pointed out,

. . . the way in which relatives are classified for social pur-poses, although this is correlated with the terminology, cannot be inferred with any certainty, and in any detail, from the terminology.[6]

Actual observance of the ancient Maya kinship system being no longer possible, it seems desirable to analyze the existing mate-rial in an attempt to arrive at some tentative conclusions which may be of value, both in the interpretation of Mayan social organization and in the further study of other Central American groups.

In this connection it is perhaps pertinent to recall that Rivers[7] long ago pointed out the possibility of cross-cousin marriage among certain of the Cree groups on the basis of the kinship termin-ology, that Hallowell[8] independently came to similar conclusions, and that, later, Strong[9] actually found cross-cousin marriage among the northern band of Naskapi.

Analysis of the Mayan kinship terms, in regard to their various applications, strongly indicates a marriage system of the bilateral cross-cousin type. In view of the reported rarity of this type of marriage in North America, along with its occurrence in northern South America and brief references to its occurrence in Central America, any new evidence is important. This evidence will also have significance in regard to recent views advanced by Ralph Beals[10] concerning the nature of Mexican social organization.

The following list of Maya terms and applications is taken from the Motul[11] and Beltrán[12] dictionaries. These two sources agree quite well, although the former gives a much more complete set of terms. Terms given by Beltrán alone are marked with a B. The varied nature of the applications makes it difficult to arrange the terms systematically. The arrangement selected is based primarily on generation; where terms are repeated they are marked with an asterisk and the complete applications given the first time only. Several terms, particularly those for affinal relatives, are com-pounded by the use of a descriptive word.

MAYA KINSHIP TERMS AND THEIR APPLICATIONS

Ego's Generation

zucun (reciprocal: idzin), older brother; man's father's father; man's second cousin (if older).

cic (reciprocal: idzin), older sister; man's mother's brother's daughter (if older); man's son's wife's mother.

idzin (reciprocals: zucun; cic), younger brother; younger sister;
     man's son's son; man's son's daughter.

mam (reciprocal: mam), man's mother's sister's son; man's father's
     brother's son; man's mother's father; man's daughter's son.

ca zucun,[13] older male cousin ("second elder brother") (B); wife's
     older sister's husband; greatgrandfather.

ca cic, older female cousin (B); woman's mother's mother.

ca idzin, younger male or female cousin (B); man's son's son;
     greatgrandchild.

zucun cabal, husband's older sister's husband; woman's daughter's
     husband's father; woman's son's wife's mother.

cic bal, wife's brother's wife (if brother is older).

chich, wife's brother's wife; man's mother's mother; man's daughter's
     son's wife.

idzin cabal, wife's younger sister's husband; wife's younger
     brother's wife; man's daughter's daughter's husband; husband's
     younger brother's wife; husband's younger sister's husband.

hachil, wife's brother; man's sister's husband; father-in-law
     (non-voc.).

hauan, husband's sister; woman's brother's wife; woman's son's
     wife's mother; woman's daughter's husband's mother; husband's
     mother; wife's mother.

muu, wife's sister; man's brother's wife; husband's brother;
     woman's sister's husband.

baal, wife's brother; man's granddaughter's husband; wife's grand-
     father.

bal, man's son's wife's father; man's daughter's husband's father;
     wife's father's father.

icham, husband.

atan, wife.

Parents' Generation

yum[14] (reciprocal: mehen), father.

mahan yum,[15] step-father.

dze yum (reciprocal: mehen), father's brother; step-father's
     brother; mother's sister's husband.

na (reciprocal: al), mother.

mahan na, man's step-mother.

dze na[16] (reciprocal: al), man's mother's sister; man's father's
     brother's wife.

acan (reciprocal: achak), man's mother's brother; man's step-
     mother's brother; man's father's sister's husband; man's

mother's grandfather.

han, man's mother's brother; wife's mother's brother; man's daughter's husband; wife's brother's son; wife's father; man's
   mother's sister's husband; woman's daughter's husband.

ix cit (reciprocal: mehen), man's father's sister; man's step-
   father's sister; man's mother's brother's wife.[17]

noh yum,[18] husband's father; woman's father's sister's husband.

ix han, wife's mother (B).

*hauan, wife's mother; woman's husband's mother.

*hachil, father-in-law (non-voc.).

Grandparental Generations

*zucun (reciprocal: idzin), man's father's father.

*ca zucun (reciprocal: ca idzin), man's greatgrandfather (father's
   father's father?).

*mam (reciprocal: mam), man's mother's father.

ca mam, mother's grandfather; daughter's son's son.

mim (reciprocal: camehen; i), father's mother; mother's grandmother.

*chich,[19] man's mother's mother.

ca cic,[19] woman's mother's mother.

ca icham, woman's grandfather; woman's granddaughter's husband.

ca atan, woman's mother's mother; man's grandson's wife.

ca yum, woman's father's grandfather.

*acan, man's mother's grandfather.

*baal,[20] wife's grandfather.

*bal,[20] wife's father's father.

Children's Generation

mehen,[21] man's son; man's brother's son; woman's brother's son;
   woman's sister's children; woman's sister-in-law's children.

ix mehen,[22] man's daughter.

al, woman's child; woman's sister's child.

xiblal,[23] woman's son.

achak (reciprocal: han; acan), man's sister's son; man's wife's
   brother's son.

ilib, wife's brother's daughter; man's son's wife.

ilbal, woman's son's wife.

*han, man's daughter's husband; wife's brother's son; woman's
   daughter's husband.

Grandchildren's Generations

ca mehen, man's grandson.

*idzin, man's son's children.

*ca idzin, greatgrandchild; man's son's son.
*mam, man's daughter's son.
 i, woman's son's children.
 abil, woman's daughter's children.
*idzin cabal, man's daughter's daughter's husband.
*ca icham, woman's granddaughter's husband.
*baal, man's granddaughter's husband.
*ca atan, man's grandson's wife.
*chich, man's grandson's wife.
 ox mehen, man's greatgrandson.
*ca mam, man's daughter's son's son.
 ca al, woman's daughter's daughter's children.

The applications of these terms are considered in the following pages. An analysis of these applications, besides throwing some light on the type of marriage practiced by the ancient Maya, also gives some basis for tentatively completing the kinship structure.

The Maya kinship system is of the "classificatory" type in that the father is classed with the father's brother and the mother with the mother's sister. The tendency to generation stratification is rather strongly marked, but is complicated by a tendency to link alternate generations through the use of the same or similar terminology. Sexual differentiation is stressed; practically all the important terms in ego's generation and above (except idzin) indicate the sex of the relative, while in the descending generations the sex of the speaker is indicated. In many cases the sex of the connecting relative is also stressed. Seniority is emphasized in ego's generation only, but is extended to a group of special relatives by marriage. The large number of terms in the Maya system is partly brought about by the fineness of the distinctions made among various affinal relatives. It may be noted that certain affinal relatives are designated by compounding sibling terms while others have independent terms.

The extensions of the kinship system are not clear, but relatives seemed to have been recognized to the third or fourth cousin at least. There is evidence in the literature to indicate a further extension to relatives in the father's line by means of the naming system, while certain relatives of the mother were not considered as "related," for marriage purposes at least (see below).

The Mayan terms, as given by Beltrán, have been analyzed and compared with other terminologies for aboriginal Mexico from Kroeber's[24] "psychological" point of view by M. H. Watkins.[25] He found that the "Maya system consists of more primary terms than any other" in the region concerned, and that in regard to the expression of Kroeber's principles there was much general uniformity throughout the area.

A preliminary study of the Maya kinship terminology by the writer suggested the possibility of a cross-cousin marriage system. The following analysis of the terminology is designed to marshall the evidence in favor of this possibility. Much of the apparently random nature of the kinship applications disappears when such a marriage is assumed. This check of internal consistency, while indirect, is nevertheless very important. The information available in the literature for both the ancient Maya and for modern Central American groups will be noted.

In the grandparents' generations there are four terms used by a male ego, while a female ego classifies the mother's father with the father's father. The terms used, zucun, mam, chich or cic, ca icham, and ca atan, also serve to link alternate generations. Great-grandparents are designated by the qualifying word ca ("second"), or by the use of other terms such as acan ("mother's brother") or mim.

In the parents' generation the classifying of parents with their siblings of the same sex has been noted. The classification of the father's brother with the mother's sister's husband, and the mother's sister with the father's brother's wife is consonant with both cross-cousin marriage and the sororate and levirate. Since this classification of relatives may be found in tribes having none of these institutions, it is possible that other more basic factors are involved.[26]

Two terms are given for the mother's brother, acan and han, the former perhaps being primary.[27] Under a system of cross-cousin marriage the mother's brother (acan) would normally be the father's sister's husband (acan). The father's sister would likewise be the mother's brother's wife (ix cit). A man's mother's brother (han) would also be his wife's father, and under certain circumstances (such as a pair of brothers marrying two sisters who stand in the relation of cross-cousin) the mother's sister's husband would be the wife's mother's brother. The extension of acan to the mother's grandfather represents a linking of alternate generations.

The terms for parents-in-law would also fit a cross-cousin marriage system. Noh yum, "great father," classes together a woman's husband's father and her father's sister's husband. The term ix han, "wife's mother," is interesting in view of the applications of the term han to a man's wife's father and to the mother's brother, and suggests the possiblity of a mother's brother providing his daughter as a wife for his sister's son.

The limited application of the mother's brother-sister's son terms suggests a special relationship between these two relatives. The use of mehen ("child") as a reciprocal term to ix cit ("father's sister") suggests that the latter was perhaps considered as a "female parent." The alternate classification of her husband as a "great father" is additional evidence.

In ego's generation the terms for siblings are the same for both a male and female ego. The older brother and older sister are distinguished while the younger brother and sister are classed together. This emphasis on seniority is observed in the extensions of the sibling terms to alternate generations and to affinal relatives.

The deficiencies of the Motul in regard to terms for parallel and cross-cousins is surprising in view of the presence of so many affinal terms. Only mam, "male parallel cousin," and cic, "man's mother's brother's daughter" (if older), are specifically given by the Motul. Watkins' study of Beltrán indicates that sibling terms were used for cousins.

> A cousin is designated by adding a prefix, according to the degree of remoteness, to the corresponding sibling: e.g.,
> caa zucun, older male cousin (second older brother)
> caa cic, older female cousin (second older sister)
> caa idzin, younger cousin (second younger sibling)
> ox zucun, older male second cousin (third older brother)
> can zucun, older male third cousin (fourth older brother).
> A man's father's brother's son is also called mam and this sort of cousinship is called mam bil.[28]

The use of sibling terms for cousins is indicated for neighboring groups by Fuentes y Guzman.[29] The significance of the additional differentiation for male parallel cousins is not clear since practically nothing is known of the kinship behavior of the ancient Maya. Under a system of cross-cousin marriage it would be desirable to be able to distinguish parallel from cross-cousins.

The extension of the sibling terms to certain of the siblings-in-law is of considerable significance from the standpoint of the marriage system. If relatives by marriage are to be differentiated in a cross-cousin marriage system, one solution is the extension of the pre-marital terms for such relatives.

An analysis of the sibling terms and their extensions yields considerable insight into the nature of the kinship structure and the marriage system. The term zucun serves to link the father's father and the elder brother. Used for cousins (ca zucun, etc.) it serves to differentiate degrees of relationship in regard to "brothers." In regard to affinal relatives a wife's elder sister's husband (ca zucun) would be an older brother under a system of cross-cousin marriage where an eldest son married his eldest cross-cousin, etc. Zucun cabal fits a cross-cousin marriage system in that a woman's son's wife's father, her daughter's husband's father, and her husband's elder sister's husband may all be the same person.

The term cic likewise serves to link the mother's mother and the elder sister. Under a cross-cousin marriage system a man's elder sister may, in certain cases, also be his son's wife's mother; in other cases his mother's brother's daughter may be his son's mother-in-law. A man's wife's brother's wife (cic bal) would also be a sister under cross-cousin marriage where exchange was involved. The term chich, which seems to be closely related to cic, is subject to the same analysis.

The term idzin shows applications and extensions to younger relatives which parallel those for zucun and cic. Under a cross-cousin marriage system a man's wife's younger sister's husband (idzin cabal) might be his younger brother, his wife's younger brother's wife would be his younger sister, and his daughter's husband might very well be his son's son (idzin). Further, a woman's husband's younger sister's husband (idzin cabal) would be her younger brother, and her husband's younger brother's wife would be a younger sister.

It seems evident from the above analysis that the distinctions made on the basis of relative age among the affinal relatives are consonant with similar distinctions made among the siblings involved. It may be noted that sibling terms are involved only in one particular type of relatives-in-law. This evidence points to a marriage system in which the eldest child marries the eldest cross-cousin, etc. Since the terminology for the new relatives is based on the sibling terms, it is probable that Beltrán's analysis of the "cousin" terminology is substantially correct.

The use of the term mam as an alternate designation of male parallel cousins may have served to differentiate parallel from cross-cousins where necessary. The term, which is self-reciprocal, also serves to link the mother's father with these parallel cousins.

The other terms for siblings-in-law are all of the pattern "spouse's sibling." Under cross-cousin marriage a man's wife's brother (hachil) would be his sister's husband. The terms hauan, muu, and bal may be similarly analyzed. These siblings-in-law, under a system of cross-cousin marriage, would be cross-cousins before marriage. If the assumption of such a marriage is correct, it is evident that the Maya have chosen to extend the sibling terms, as outlined above, and to modify the previous cross-cousin terminology ("second siblings") by using new terms, hauan, muu, baal, and bal. This procedure retains the socially closer relationships (siblings)

This procedure retains the socially closer relationships (siblings) and avoids too great confusion among the affinal relatives. The failure of the Motul dictionary to give a complete set of "cousin" terms, while furnishing a detailed list of affinal relatives, is partially intelligible from the above analysis.

Separate terms are used for the husband and wife. These are extended to the grandparents' and grandchildren's generations by means of the qualifying word ca, "second." Here, again, alternate generations are linked by means of the terminology since separate terms are used for the children's spouses.

In the children's generation separate terms are used by men and women for their children. A man classes his brother's children with his own but has a special term for his sister's son. A woman classes her sister's children with her own, but also uses the term mehen for her sister's and brother's children.

The terms for son-in-law and daughter-in-law reflect a cross-cousin marriage system. The term han refers to a man's daughter's husband and his wife's brother's son. A man's son's wife (ilib) would normally be his wife's brother's daughter.

The terms for children's parents-in-law, bal, zucun cabal, and hauan likewise may be analyzed from the standpoint of cross-cousin marriage. The term bal equates a man's son's wife's father and his daughter's husband's father. If the term baal is considered as an equivalent term, the man's wife's brother would also be the son's wife's father. Zucun cabal has been analyzed in another connection, while hauan may be similarly analyzed.

In the grandchildren's generations separate terms are used by men and women. A man may call his grandchildren ca mehen, "second children," or alternately, class them with his younger brother (idzin), or use the reciprocal term mam. Greatgrandchildren are either ox mehen ("third children") or ca mam. A woman uses a separate set of terms for grandchildren.

The terms for grandchildren-in-law reflect the tendency to link alternate generations by means of the terminology, rather than having any reference to cross-cousin marriage. Under such a system of marriage the relatives listed under baal would have similar positions, conceptually, in the resulting kinship structure.

CONCLUSIONS

In the foregoing pages the kinship terminology of the ancient Maya has been analyzed from the hypothesis of a system of cross-cousin marriage. It is now desirable to see what alternative hypotheses there are that might account for the same phenomena, and what evidence exists in the literature for one or the other of these hypotheses. The validity of the above analysis must rest on evidence found in the literature, information from surviving Maya groups, and on the internal consistency that is achieved within the kinship system.

If the kinship terminology may be considered as classifying relatives for social purposes, the possible purposes which might be correlated with a terminology of the Maya type are as follows:[30]

1. Cross-cousin marriage;
2. Exogamous moieties (or clans);
3. Daughter exchange by households.

These three possibilities are not mutually exclusive or incompatible with one another, in fact the three are often found together. Hence it is difficult to select any one of them on the basis of the terminology alone, since any series of terms which fits a cross-cousin marriage system will also fit a "moiety" organization. A system of exogamous clans or moieties with reciprocal daughter exchange by households is theoretically possible in regard to the ancient Maya. However, the number of terms for affinal relatives, the extension of sibling terms to certain of these relatives, and the fineness of the distinctions made, argue for a system of bilateral cross-cousin marriage. Terms for certain relatives do not seem to fit a "moiety" division in that these relatives may be in different divisions; the following terms may be cited: mam, cic, zucun, mehen, han, hauan, etc. The fact that apparently random and meaningless applications and extensions of terms become intelligible when cross-cousin marriage is assumed is perhaps the best evidence available from the terminology alone.

Proposed Maya Kinship Structure

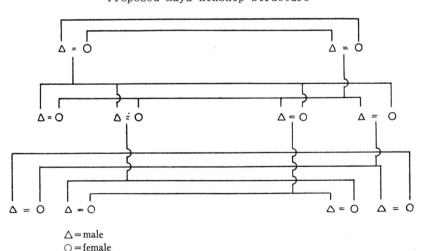

△ = male
○ = female

The basic kinship structure resulting from such a marriage system would be as follows:

If the applications of the various kinship terms given above are analyzed in connection with this chart, the apparently random and complex usages will be found to be organized into a simple and coherent system; one which holds together the resulting structure and at the same time differentiates the units where necessary.

With a bilateral system of cross-cousin marriage related households will tend to exchange daughters. The new relationships set up by such marriages may be ignored or recognized. The Maya seem to have differentiated the new relatives by extending the sibling terms to them, at the same time modifying the terms to indicate the nature of the relationship.

Under such a system a man normally looks to his mother's brother and his father's sister ("mother's brother's wife") to supply him with a wife. It is probable that this social function may be related to the restricted mother's brother-sister's son terminology, and it is consonant with the view advanced concerning the position of the father's sister and mother's brother as "parents."

From the standpoint of holding together the social structure as outlined, the linking of alternate generations through the terminology is an important integrative factor. Within the same generation a similar integrative function is performed by the extensions of sibling terms.

The question of an unilateral social organization among the Maya has been recently raised by Ralph Beals[31] on the basis of information given by Landa.[32] Since this information has considerable bearing on the present discussion it is presented as translated by Beals:

> They were careful to know the origin of their lineages, especially if they come from some house of Mayapan. The names of the fathers remain always with the sons and not with the daughters. They always call their sons and daughters by the name of the father and mother. In this way the son of Chel and Chan is called Na-Chan-Chel, which is to say, the son of such ones, and this is the cause that those of one name are said to be relatives and are treated as such and for this, when one arrives in some place where he is unknown and is in need, he immediately makes known his name and if there is any one of this name he is immediately received and treated with all kindness and thus no man or woman marries with one of the same name because it is for them a great disgrace. The Indians do not permit the daughter to inherit with the sons except by charity . . . the sons divide equally, except to him who most notably has helped gather the estate is given an equivalent return, and if all are daughters, the brothers inherit. . . . If one married one's brother's wives it was considered bad. They do not marry with step-mothers, nor their wives' sisters, nor their mother's sisters, and if someone did so it was considered bad; with all

other relatives on the mother's side they could marry, even though they were first cousins.[33]

According to Beals this "only makes sense if we assume a sib system."[34] While the evidence is suggestive of an unilateral organization it is not conclusive.

It is evident that in Landa's time marriage was permitted with the mother's brother's daughter and other relatives on the mother's side. Whether marriage with the mother's sister's children was barred is not clear. While both the sororate and levirate were condemned according to Landa, it is uncertain whether this referred also to marriage with the widow or widower of a deceased sibling.

Landa's information seems to indicate patrilineal, named groups which had duties in regard to marriage, inheritance, and assistance, and which were not localized. While it is not necessary for a cross-cousin marriage system to be correlated with an unilateral organization, the association is frequently found. An analysis of the terms for affinal relatives in regard to a possible "moiety" organization indicates that, except for two terms (han and hauan), they fall consistently into one division or the other. Regardless of whether or not unilateral institutions are shown to be present among the ancient Maya, the social structure based on cross-cousin marriage seems to be the primary structure.

Further information, referring probably to the Quichés or Cakchiquels, is given by Fuentes y Guzman:

La mujer que enviudaba, si quedaba moza no había de quedar libre, y suelta de aquel yugo que se contraía por el género de sus matrimonios, porque el marido la casaba de su mano cou hermano o pariente cercano de el, y los hijos de estos casaban con los parientes de la madre, juzgando que, porque ella salío de la casa de sus padres, ya no era parienta de aquel calpul; y hasta hoy en sus proprios parentescos, no saben hacer distinciones, y generalmente todos los del calpul se llaman hermanos, sin explicar otro grado.[35]

While the significance of this paragraph is not entirely clear, several points are of interest in connection with this paper. After marriage a woman apparently broke the kinship ties which held her in her own calpul and contracted new ties with the members of her husband's calpul. These latter ties were continued after the death of her husband by means of marrying his brother or other near relative. Further, sons of the mother by these men could marry back into the mother's household, or relatives, since she was no longer considered as being "related" to them.[36] Within the calpul all were called "siblings" without any other distinction (presumably within the same generation). While the structure of the calpul in this region is not known, it was evidently based upon kinship ties and maintained

by marriage back into the mother's calpul, by a modified form of the
levirate, and by patrilocal residence. Whether this marriage took
place between parallel cousins as well as cross-cousins is not clear.

There is undoubtedly further material in the literature concerning the nearby and related tribes of which the writer is not
aware. Breton[37] gives a list of kinship terms for various tribes
gathered from the literature but these are too fragmentary for comparative purposes in regard to the problems dealt with in this paper.

Supporting evidence for cross-cousin marriage is to be found
in some of the recent ethnographic field work in the region. Conzemius has the following statement concerning marriage restrictions
among the Miskito and Sumu Indians of Honduras and Nicaragua:

> The children of two brothers or of two sisters are considered
> real brothers and sisters and they are not allowed to marry each
> other. . . . Upon the death of his wife a man generally married
> her sister; similarly if a woman has lost her husband she was
> taken in marriage by her brother-in-law. . . On the other hand
> the children of a brother and sister [cross-cousins] are not
> considered blood relatives, and a union between such cousins is
> the common and originally perhaps the only marriage allowed.
> Unions of this kind are still encouraged today, for it is felt
> that family ties are strengthened thereby. . . . The children
> are sometimes engaged by their respective parents while still in
> early infancy . . . when she arrives at puberty he takes her as
> his wife. The man is considered a member of his wife's family
> and he goes to live in the house of his parents-in-law. When the
> family enlarges he will build a house of his own nearby.38

It is evident that cross-cousin marriage is the proper marriage
among these tribes. Unfortunately Conzemius does not give the kinship terminologies so that it is not possible to compare the kinship
structures with that of the Maya.

Among the Chorti of Guatemala[39] a person loses relationship
to the household members and rights of inheritance upon moving out
at marriage. Individual families are referred to by animal "nicknames" and there is a feeling, on the part of some at least, that
marriage should not take place between persons having the same family
"nickname." Tozzer[40] found named groups among the Lacandones with
patrilineal descent and some tendency to exogamy, but apparently
found no evidence of cross-cousin marriage. The present day Maya
of Yucatan[41] seem to have adopted the Spanish kinship system, though
still using the native terms in many cases. The only feature which
is not clearly European is the disposition to use the old Maya sibling terms and extend them to siblings-in-law.

The tentative conclusions concerning the type of marriage
which occurred among the ancient Maya, based on an analysis of the
kinship terminology, finds some support in the literature. It is
possible that a social structure, based on cross-cousin marriage,

was rather widespread in Central America, and perhaps northern South America.[42] It is hoped that further material from the early literature will come to light, and that current field work in Central America will yield additional evidence which may support or modify the tentative conclusions reached in this paper. Some knowledge of the types of social organization of the Mexican and Central American groups seems desirable in any attempt to understand the history of this area. The presence of cross-cousin marriage among peoples as culturally and geographically separated as are the Maya, the Tlingit[43] and Haida,[44] the Woods Cree,[45] the Chipewyan,[46] the Naskapi, the Miskito and Sumu, and some of the tribes of northern South America offers further problems which are outside the scope of this paper.

NOTES

[1]This study was initiated by Dr Robert Redfield and greatly aided by Mr J. Eric Thompson who gathered the kinship terms as part of a page-by-page study of the Motul dictionary. Prof A. R. Radcliffe-Brown made valuable suggestions and criticisms, and Dr Manuel J. Andrade cleared up several linguistic difficulties. The writer is greatly indebted to these men.

[2]Diego de Landa, Relacion de las Cosas de Yucatan (Paris), 1864.

[3]A. M. Tozzer, A Comparative Study of the Mayas and Lacandones (New York), 1907.

[4]Diccionario de Motul, Maya Español, atribuido a Fray Antonio de Ciudad Real. . . . edición hecha por Juan Martinez Hernandez (Merida, Yucatan), 1929.

[5]R. H. Lowie, Relationship Terms, Encyclopaedia Britannica (14th ed.), 1929.

[6]A. R. Radcliffe-Brown, The Social Organization of Australian Tribes, Oceania Monographs, no. 1:12-13 (note), 1931.

[7]W. H. R. Rivers, Kinship and Social Organization (London), 1914.

[8]A. I. Hallowell, Was Cross-Cousin Marriage Formerly Practiced by the North Central Algonkian?, ICA 23 (New York), 1928.

[9]W. D. Strong, Cross-Cousin Marriage and the Culture of the Northeast Algonkian, AA 31:277-88, 1929.

[10]Ralph Beals, Unilateral Organizations in Mexico, AA 34:467-75, 1932.

[11]Diccionario de Motul. *op. cit.*

[12]Pedro Beltrán, Arte del Idioma Maya (2nd ed., Merida), 1857. The date of the composition of the Motul dictionary is uncertain. Juan Martinez Hernandez, the editor of the edition used, says (p. xvii) "it was written in the last quarter of the sixteenth century because the author, under the word 'budz-ek' mentions a tailed comet which he observed in the year 1577." Beltrán says in the grammar which bears his name, and from which Pio Perez extracted and published the vocabulary used, that he dictated his work in 1742. It was first printed in 1746.
A summary of the Beltrán terms is given by P. Radin in AA 27:100-102, 1925. A more complete list from Beltrán is given by M. H. Watkins, Terms of Relationship in Aboriginal Mexico (master's thesis, University of Chicago, 1930).

[13]Second cousins are designated by prefixing the word ox, "third," and third cousins by prefixing can (Beltrán). Beltrán and the Motul vary somewhat in the applications of these terms.

[14]There were also non-vocative terms: yumbil, "father;" hach yum, "legitimate father," etc., the latter probably due to Spanish influence. There were similar non-vocative terms for other relatives.

[15]The terms for parents are extended by means of descriptive qualifiers: mahan, "borrowed," and dze, "little."

[16]The terms for parents, uncles, aunts, and siblings are the same, in general, for both male and female egos.

[17]The Motul gives "father's brother's wife." This seems to be an error in view of the applications of acan and dze na.

[18]Noh means "big."

[19]It is probable that chich and cic are related or similar terms.

[20]It is probable that bal and baal are similar terms.

[21]Mehen also means "semen" at present.

[22]Ix probably means "woman" or "female." It is so used in related languages.

[23]Xib refers to "male" or "man." Al refers to "being heavy with child" also.

[24]A. L. Kroeber, The Classificatory System of Relationship, JRAI 39:77-84, 1909.

[25]M. H. Watkins, *op. cit.*, 41 ff.

[26]Professor Radcliffe-Brown (*op. cit.*, 96-99), has proposed the principle of the "equivalence of brothers" as the general principle underlying both the "classificatory" system of terminology and the sororate and levirate.

[27]It is possible that the term, han, is used after marriage has taken place since most of its applications are to relatives by marriage.

[28]M. H. Watkins, *op. cit.*, 44. There is some difference between the Motul and Beltrán in the use of the qualifiers ox, ca, etc.

[29]See quotation below.

[30]Cf. R. H. Lowie, Relationship Terms, Encyclopaedia Britannica (14th ed.).

[31]Ralph Beals, Unilateral Organizations in Mexico, AA 34, 1932.

[32]Diego de Landa, Relacion de las Cosas de Yucatan (Paris), 1864, pp. 134-40.

[33]Ralph Beals, *op. cit.*, 471-72.

[34]*Ibid.*, 472.

[35]Fuentes y Guzman, Historia de Guatemala (1695) I, chap. IV:32 (Madrid), 1882. (Reference furnished by J. Eric Thompson.)

[36]There is also a long reference in Torquemada, Book XIII, chapter 7, which indicates that relatives on the mother's side were not considered to be related (J. Eric Thompson). Whether "related" refers to marriage purposes or to kinship extensions is not clear.

[37]A. C. Breton, Relationship in Central America, Man, 1919, pp. 188 ff.

[38]Eduard Conzemius, Ethnographic Survey of the Miskito and Sumu Indians of Honduras and Nicaragua, BAE-B 106:146-47, 1932.

[39]Personal communication from Charles Wisdom.

[40]A. M. Tozzer, A Comparative Study of the Mayas and Lacandones, Arch. Inst. of America (New York), 1907, pp. 40-41.

[41]Communication from Robert Redfield.

[42]Cf. T. A. Joyce, South American Archaeology (New York), 1912, p. 22.

[43]K. Oberg, Manuscript on the Tlingit Indians, 1933.

[44]G. P. Murdock, The Kinship System of the Haida Indians (Manuscript), 1933.

[45]E. S. Curtis, The North American Indian, 18:appendix, 1928.

[46]*Ibid.*

2

THE CHEYENNE AND ARAPAHO KINSHIP SYSTEM[1]

1937

CONTENTS

Reproduced by permission of the University of Chicago Press, Chicago, from *Social Anthropology of North American Tribes; Essays in Social Organization, Law, and Religion,* Fred Eggan, editor (1937), pp. 35-95.

INTRODUCTION

The Cheyenne and Arapaho, along with the related Gros Ventre, offer an excellent opportunity to study certain problems connected with the kinship system, both in its internal relations, its relation to other aspects of social organization, and in terms of wider historical and conceptual problems. These problems may be concerned with the nature of the kinship system at a given period, or with the changes which may occur over a given period of time.

The Cheyenne and Arapaho[2] have occupied a central position in the Plains area in historic times and are considered in many ways to be the most typical tribes of the region. There is some evidence, however, that this central position is rather recent. In early historic times the Cheyenne are reported living in permanent villages in southwestern Minnesota, planting corn and other crops and engaging in a summer hunt. Pressure from the Assiniboine, Ojibway, and Dakota forced the Cheyenne out onto the plains around the beginning of the nineteenth century where they become nomadic buffalo hunters. After crossing the Missouri River, the Cheyenne encountered the Suhtai who spoke a closely related dialect; around 1830 the latter became incorporated into the Cheyenne tribe and contributed several important ceremonies to the Cheyenne ritual.

The early history of the Arapaho is not so well known. While there is indirect evidence that they were once agricultural and resided farther to the east, they are first reported (in 1789) in the northern plains above the Missouri River, from whence they moved southward into the western plains. The most northerly group of the Arapaho remained north of the Missouri River and became known as the Gros Ventre or Atsina; except for a brief sojourn with the Arapaho in 1818-23, their closest associations have been with the Blackfoot.

Sometime after the Cheyenne moved out onto the plains they met the Arapaho; henceforth the two tribes lived in close alliance although each tribe maintained its individuality. Together they controlled eastern Colorado and southeastern Wyoming, but ranged widely over the plains. A division into a northern and a southern group[3] gradually took place in both tribes, but the divisions maintained close associations and kept their tribal unity. No accurate

estimate of the size of these tribes is available for the early periods, but in 1890 the Cheyenne numbered 3,654, the Arapaho 2,157,
and the Gros Ventre about 850. The earlier populations seem to have
been larger.

Both the Cheyenne and the Arapaho are somewhat divergent
members of the Algonkian linguistic stock. Kroeber considers the
Arapaho language more specialized than the Cheyenne, indicating a
more recent connection of the latter with Ojibway and other Central
Algonkian languages.[4] The Gros Ventre seems sufficiently differentiated from the Arapaho to indicate a separation of more than two
centuries.[5] These conclusions are consonant with what we know of
the historical relations of these tribes.

The Cheyenne and Arapaho possessed the typical culture of
the western plains, which centered around the buffalo and war. Culturally the two tribes are quite close, as we might suspect from their
long and intimate contact, but important differences persisted, particularly in social organization. Differences between the Arapaho
and the Gros Ventre are less marked in general.

Both the Cheyenne and the Arapaho are divided into named
"bands" which occupied definite positions in the camp circle. These
bands are difficult to describe or classify; they are not composed
exclusively of kindred nor are they exogamous. The feeling concerning descent is bilateral, or even slightly patrilineal at present,
but matrilocal residence led to the identification of children with
the mother's band, for the most part. Each band was composed of a
group of extended households based on matrilocal residence, and as
such was a self-sufficient economic unit. But a change of band
affiliation was possible, and the family might return to the husband's band or join another one. The Cheyenne[6] in later years had
about ten divisions or bands of this character which hunted and
camped independently for most of the year under the leadership of
a band chief. While definite territories did not exist, each band
had one or more favorite spots in which it spent the winter. With
the coming of summer the bands joined together and formed a camp
circle, preliminary to the annual hunt and tribal ceremonies. The
Arapaho[7] band organization has long disappeared; originally the Arapaho were divided into four subtribes (plus the Gros Ventre), and
four bands are remembered for one of these tribes which had definite
positions in the camp circle. The Gros Ventre[8] "bands" differed
from the Arapaho in that they tended to be patrilineal and exogamous,
and to occupy more definitely marked-off hunting territories. These
patrilineal clans likewise came together in the summer and occupied
definite positions in the camp circle.

These three tribes were further divided into a series of societies which had military, social, and ceremonial functions, and which operated only when the tribe was united. The Cheyenne[9] had six societies restricted to males (except for honorary female members); these were co-ordinate and followed the same general pattern. Membership was by invitation, but usually a man joined his father's society. The Arapaho[10] had eight such societies, arranged in a graded structure through which successive groups of men passed. The ceremonies of these societies increased in importance, the highest society, composed of the old men, supervising the ceremonial life of the tribe. The women had a single society which paralleled the men's organization. The Gros Ventre[11] system is basically similar to the Arapaho, but each grade was divided into a series of companies which were named and perpetuated.

The Cheyenne had a highly developed political organization in comparison with other Plains tribes. Secular affairs were in the hands of a council of forty-four chiefs, selected every ten years by the retiring group. In theory four were selected from each band, while four were re-elected to serve as head chiefs or executives. The Arapaho had a much simpler system; the government of the tribe was in the hands of four chiefs, apparently representing the earlier subdivisions, and these held office for life. In recent times they were replaced from among one of the graded societies. Little is known of Gros Ventre political organization, but apparently each of the eight or ten clans had a chief, and these chiefs made up the tribal council.[12]

The ritual head of the Cheyenne was the keeper of the sacred Medicine Arrows, but the Sun Dance and other ceremonies were largely controlled by the warrior societies. Among the Arapaho the Sun Dance and other ceremonies were definitely associated with the societal structure; this was probably true for the Gros Ventre as well, though definite information is lacking.

These various aspects of social organization are not independent entities but are related to one another in varying ways. One way of gaining insight into their interrelations is to examine them from the standpoint of social structure,[13] which may be defined as the sum total of the social relations of the individuals making up the social group. These social relations are composed largely of social usages-- customary ways of behaving--which are abstractable from the actual behavior of individuals. Since these social relations persist, in many cases, from one generation to another, they can be viewed as a structure and analyzed from that point of view.

Among the Cheyenne and Arapaho the most characteristic social relations are those between kindred. Kinship relations not only prevail in everyday life but ramify through the other aspects of social organization as well, so that an analysis of social structure might well start with the kinship system. But while the Cheyenne and Arapaho have been excellently described in most respects, there are no satisfactory accounts of their kinship system. This has not been due to any difficulty in securing material, since the kinship system usually survives the breakdown of other aspects of social structure, but rather to the preoccupation of ethnologists with other problems.

The importance of studying kinship has been apparent since Morgan, but his emphasis on terminology led to linguistic and psychological analyses; the recognition of terminology as a part of the kinship system, and of the latter as an integral and important part of the social organization, is more recent.

One of the important problems facing the ethnologist is to be able to explain the social organization of a given tribe. One type of explanation is historical, and considerable effort has been expended in reconstructing histories of various types of social organization. An alternative method of achieving insight into the nature of social organization is by means of a comparative study of the correlated phenomena in a series of tribes. In order for this procedure to be valid it is necessary to make comparisons within a class or type, to begin with; hence the first problem is adequately to classify social organizations.

Ideally such a classification should be based on the total social structure, but for practical purposes (since the social structure is known in detail for only a few tribes) a preliminary classification may be made on the basis of related criteria. Professor Radcliffe-Brown has suggested that the function of the social structure is to achieve social integration, and hence there is a correlation between the range and complexity of the social horizon and the social structure of the group. On this hypothesis he sets up as indices such factors as the size of the social group, the density of its population, the territorial arrangement, the sex and age divisions, the kinship system, and the various formal organizations which the group may take.

Of these indices, the kinship system has proved the most useful index of social integration; in some cases the kinship system represents practically the total social structure of the group. A kinship system consists of all the social usages--or patterns of behavior--between relatives in a given community and therefore includes the linguistic usages or terminology. These relations originate in the domestic family but are largely socially determined;[14] the kinship system provides rules of behavior which are consistent and which result in a minimum of conflict. The terminology represents one means of organizing these social relations between kindred. From this point of view the social usages, rather than the terminology, represent the most important aspect of the kinship system, and the traditional emphasis on the terms of relationship is not justified. Such a system may be assumed to have some degree of functional consistency, and a fairly close correlation is usually found between the terminology and the social behavior of relatives. Hence in the absence of information concerning social usages some insight into the kinship system may be obtained by a study of the way in which relatives are classified terminologically.

By an analysis and comparison of kinship systems a limited number of structural principles has been worked out which seem to derive from the relations existing in the elementary family and which lie behind both the social behavior and the terminology. These principles are found in varying proportions in different kinship systems and may serve as a basis for their classification, as well as for the explanation of the particular correlated features which are found.

The present paper is concerned primarily with the nature of the kinship system of the Cheyenne and Arapaho, and with the relations of the kinship system to other aspects of the social organization. In addition it seems desirable to indicate the significance of the data in relation to various historical and sociological problems, with a view to testing theories or generalizations which have been advanced. The paper may likewise serve to define the type of social integration which is present in these tribes. This is of particular importance since the Cheyenne and Arapaho represent a basic type of social organization for the western plains and thus furnish a convenient starting point for classification and comparative studies.

In the following presentation, description and interpretation will be kept separate, so that the materials may be utilized for other purposes or for different interpretations.

THE KINSHIP SYSTEM

The Cheyenne and Arapaho kinship systems may be conveniently described by an analysis of their terminological structure, the behavior of reciprocals, and the individual life-cycle. The materials for this study were gathered among the Southern Cheyenne and Arapaho[15] on

their reservation in western Oklahoma, and supplemented by published
materials on these two tribes and the Gros Ventre. The problem of
presenting the data for these tribes in compact form is rather difficult, but since the Cheyenne and Arapaho systems are similar in many
respects, they will be presented together; Gros Ventre variants will
be noted wherever information is available.

Terminological Structure

The following diagrams (Figs. 1-3) illustrate the basic terminological structures for the Cheyenne and Arapaho. Kroeber's material
indicates that the Gros Ventre structure is essentially the same as
the Arapaho.[16] For convenience in analysis English terms will be
used, but these terms should be understood in reference to their
native meanings which are determined by the applications and the
social behavior involved. Table 1 gives the Cheyenne, Arapaho, and
Gros Ventre equivalents for the English terms.

The Cheyenne and Arapaho kinship systems are of the "classificatory" type in that collateral and lineal relatives are classed
together. The father's brother is classed with the father and the
mother's sister with the mother, while separate terms are used for
the mother's brother and father's sister. Grandparents are distinguished according to sex, and grandparental terms are extended to
their siblings and spouses. In ego's generation older brothers and
older sisters are distinguished, while younger siblings are classed
together; these terms are extended to both parallel and cross-cousins.
The children of brothers are "sons" and "daughters," male speaking,
or "nephews" and "nieces," female speaking; the children of sisters
are the reverse. All children of sons, daughters, nephews, and
nieces are called "grandchildren." For consanguineal relatives,
therefore, the Cheyenne and Arapaho have precisely the same basic
terminological structure, despite differences in the actual terms
used. The Gros Ventre have a similar structure, their terms being
cognate with the Arapaho for the most part.

In regard to the system of affinal relatives, however, there
are certain important differences between the Cheyenne, on the one
hand, and the Arapaho and Gros Ventre, on the other. The Cheyenne
classify the father-in-law with the grandfather and the mother-in-
law with the grandmother, the children-in-law being classed with the
grandchildren, though special terms are available to avoid ambiguity.
In ego's generation a man's wife's siblings are classed with his
siblings' spouses as "brothers-in-law," or "sisters-in-law," whereas
the wife's sister's husband and the wife's brother's wife are called
"brother" and "sister," respectively, and their children classed

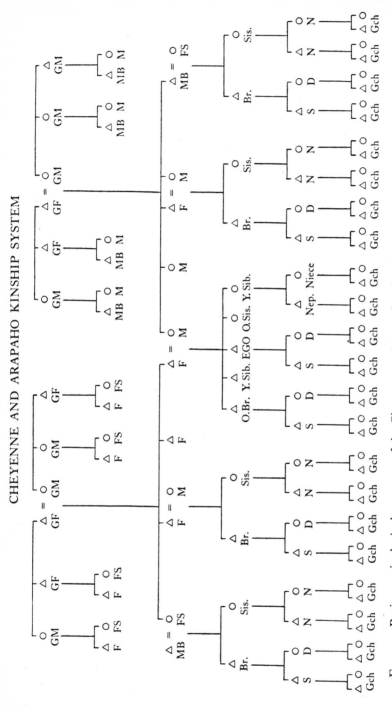

Fig. 1.—Basic terminological structure of the Cheyenne and Arapaho. In this chart the abbreviations *F, M, FS, MB, GF,* etc, refer to father, mother, father's sister, mother's brother, grandfather, etc. For the native equivalents see Table 1. Ego = male. When ego = female, the terms remain the same except that her sister's children are "son" and "daughter," and her brother's children are "nephew" and "niece," respectively. △ = male and ○ = female.

CHEYENNE KINSHIP SYSTEM

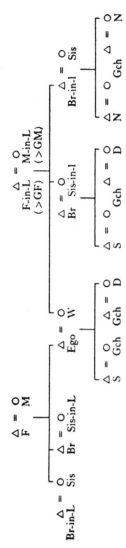

Fig. 2.—Cheyenne affinal structure. Ego=male. Reciprocal terms are used when ego= female. > = "derived from." For the native equivalents see Table I.

ARAPAHO KINSHIP SYSTEM

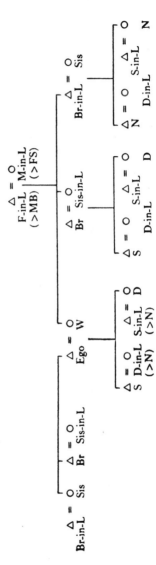

Fig. 3.—Arapaho affinal structure. Ego=male. Reciprocal terms are used when ego= female. For the native equivalents see Table I.

TABLE 1

CHEYENNE, ARAPAHO, AND GROS VENTRE KINSHIP TERMS

English Term	Cheyenne*	Arapaho†	Gros Ventre‡
Grandfather (GF).......	namcim̀	nɛbɛ'si·wa·'	näbeseip
Grandmother (GM)......	nicji''·ɛ·'	newa'; nȩíbeˣᵃ'a	niip'
Father (F)............	nihu''·ɛ·'	ne·sa'na;nexa'	niiçinǫ
Mother (M)...........	na'go'·ɛ·'	na'a·'; néna'	neinǫ
Father's sister (FS).......	nahań; na·'ɛ'	nɛhéha'; nɛhȩí	nähei
Mother's brother (MB)...	naxań	nesha'; nɛsi'	nis'
Older brother (O.Br).....	na'níha	nä·'sä'hä'ä	nääçahää
Younger brother (Y.Sib)..	na·'sima	nä·'häbä'xä'ä	näⁿhäbyⁱ
Older sister (O.Sis).......	nam̀han	nɛbiha·''; nɛbi'	nibyᵉ
Younger sister (Y.Sib)....	na·'sima	nä·'häbäxä'ä	nǫ häbyⁱ
Son (S)................	na·'; na·ᵃha'	ne·'; ne·hä'	neih'ä
Daughter (D)...........	na·'ts; na·'tona	na'ta·'; nata·nɛ	natan
Nephew (N)............	nats; natsínut	nɛ'thɛ' ɛ'thɛ	nêt'êt
Niece (N)...............	na'ᵃham	nǫ·sɛbi	nääçibyⁱ
Grandchild (Gch).......	nixa	ne·śiǫ	niisä
Father-in-law (F-in-L)....	namcim̀; tséhemcímit	nɛsíthɛ'	nêsit
Mother-in-law (M-in-L)...	nicji'ɛ·'; tséheɣisjimiτu	nɛhȩíhä'	näheihä
Son-in-law (S-in-L).......	nixa; tséheɣixahaiτu	nɛthɛ'äxʋ	nataos
Daughter-in-law (D-in-L).	nixa	nǫsɛʙɪ	nääçibyⁱ
Brother-in-law [m.s.] (Br-in-L)....·.......	nitówɪ	ya·'; neya·'	nayaǫ
Brother-in-law [f.s.] (Br-in-L)...............	nitäm	ne·thɛ·'bi'	niitibyⁱ
Sister-in-law [m.s.] (Sis-in-L)...................	nitäm	ne·thɛ·'bi'	niitibyⁱ
Sister-in-law [f.s.] (Sis-in-L)	naxa'ɛm§	sä·'; nato'u	natou
"Parents-in-law" (P-in-L).	na'Dowam̀	na'tanǫτɪ	nätänaké (M)
Husband (H)...........	naįhäm	nä·s	näse (M)
Wife (W)..............	na'si'im	nätäsihä'ä	nätiçää
"Friend"...............	ni'sima	bä·'; ne·tɛʰᵉi	....

* The Cheyenne terms are derived from field notes. Where two forms are given, the second is usually nonvocative. In the case of father-in-law, etc., where direct conversation is restricted, the second form is used for clearness of reference. The phonetic symbols follow the Smithsonian convention.

† The Arapaho terms listed are derived from field notes. Kroeber (*The Arapaho*, I, 9) gives a similar list, with one or two exceptions.

‡ The Gros Ventre list of terms is given in Kroeber (*ibid.*) except for those taken from Morgan (*Systems*, No. 56) and marked "M."

§ May be used as a general term for "sister," male speaking.

accordingly. A woman classifies her husband's relatives in parallel fashion. The two sets of parents of a·couple refer to each other by a reciprocal term ("parents-in-law").

The Arapaho and Gros Ventre, on the other hand, seem to classify the parents-in-law with the mother's brother and father's sister, and the children-in-law reciprocally, since these pairs of terms appear to use the same stems but different suffixes.[17] In regard to other affinal relatives the Arapaho and Gros Ventre make the same distinctions as the Cheyenne.

The terms recorded by earlier writers reveal essentially the same terminological structure. Morgan[18] recorded a set of terms, furnished by a French trader who had married into the Cheyenne tribe, which agrees except for cross-cousins. Since his informant could not recall a word for "cousin," Morgan assumed they were probably classed as "uncle" and "nephew" or "mother" and "daughter."[19] This, of course, does not take into account the possibility that cousins were classified as siblings.[20] Grinnell[21] classes cousins as "siblings" but his terms are not complete. For the Arapaho and Gros Ventre Morgan[22] gives a Gros Ventre schedule which shows several inconsistencies but indicates that cross-cousins were classed as siblings. Curtis[23] classifies the father's brother with the older or younger brother for both the Cheyenne and the Arapaho.

This brief survey indicates a high degree of stability for the basic kinship structures of the Cheyenne and Arapaho over a considerable period, extending back into the pre-reservation period. Further, if the early separation of the Arapaho and Gros Ventre be considered, their terminological structure probably extends back into aboriginal times.

The extensions of kinship among the Cheyenne, Arapaho, and Gros Ventre show some important differences. The Cheyenne and Arapaho extend their terminological pattern bilaterally, as far as can be conveniently remembered. There is no unilateral emphasis, or any marked distinction between the parental groups of relatives in the terminology. The siblings and spouses of relatives are classed as relatives. Among the Gros Ventre this simple extension is modified by a unilateral extension based upon the patrilineal clan--"all the members of both the father's and mother's clan being considered relatives."[24] At marriage a new set of relations is established among the Cheyenne and Arapaho; these are extended to the siblings of the new relatives as well. The use of sibling terms for the spouses of siblings-in-law has been mentioned above. Special terms for stepparents exist, but their use depends on the age of the children at the time of remarriage. Adoption is common; any relationship may be established by the proper procedure, and kinship terms are employed.[25]

The extension of kinship for ceremonial purposes is more varied. The Cheyenne may call a fellow-society-member "friend" or "brother," though the former seems to be preferred. The Arapaho, who have a series of graded societies, relate the members of alternate societies as "older brother" and "younger brother," while the instructors and novices use "grandparent-grandchild" terms. According to Kroeber,[26] the members of the highest society were also called "grandfather" during ceremonial periods. In the Sun Dance and other tribal ceremonies instructors were called "grandfather" by their pupils in both tribes.

An institution of ceremonial friendship is found among both the Cheyenne and the Arapaho. Two men in such a relationship call each other "friend" rather than "brother," but the relationship is felt to be similar to the latter in many respects, and the children of "friends" often use kinship terms.

A ritual extension of kinship to certain aspects of the natural environment occurs among both tribes, but there is considerable individual variation in such applications at present. There is a general application of kinship terms to the earth, the sky, the sun, and perhaps one or two animals, particularly in ceremonies. Individuals also apply kinship terms to certain objects or animals on the basis of personal experiences.

The various methods of extending kinship for social purposes make it possible for a Cheyenne or Arapaho to be related to a good proportion of his tribe, in one way or another,[27] and to extend relationships beyond the tribe into other groups and to various aspects of nature. These extensions occasionally result in cases where two or more kinship terms are applicable; in such cases the blood-relationship is preferred, even though another relationship, by marriage, might seem closer. In certain cases of adoption the original relationships are kept in order to maintain the system.

This brief survey of the Cheyenne and Arapaho terminological structures shows them to be simple and balanced systems of classifying relatives which are extended in a logical way without any formal limits. Both structures are organized on a strict principle of generation; within the range of consanguineal relatives this principle is not violated. In regard to descent the lineal and collateral relatives are almost completely merged, and there is a definite bilateral character to the structures. In practically all relationships there is a sex differentiation involved, but relative age is important only in one's own generation. Affinal relatives are only partially separated from consanguineal, the Cheyenne and Arapaho differing somewhat in their classification, particularly in regard to parents-in-law and children-in-law. The Gros Ventre have essentially the same terminological structure as the Arapaho, but the extensions are partially determined by clan limits.

Kinship Behavior: Reciprocals[28]

The Cheyenne and Arapaho kinship systems have been surveyed from the standpoint of the classification of relatives and the extent to which these relationships are socially recognized; it is now desirable to see how the behavior of relatives is organized in Cheyenne and Arapaho life. The various reciprocal duties and obligations which exist between relatives play an important part in social integration. The basic relationships are those between members of the immediate family, but because of conditions of residence certain relationships of a more distant order are likewise important. In the following pages an outline of the general pattern of behavior prevailing between each pair of relatives is presented.

Parent-child.--The relationship of parents to their children is an important one in Cheyenne and Arapaho life. Parents are primarily responsible for the care and education of their children, but in this regard, as in many others, there is a rather strict division on the basis of sex. A father is responsible for the training of his sons but has almost nothing to do with the education of his daughters, though he must help take care of them throughout their lives. The mother, on the other hand, is responsible for her daughter's training, particularly in regard to household duties, and with the father's sister teaches her how to conduct herself in the presence of young men, but has little to do with the training of her sons. In particular any disciplinary measures are referred to the father.[29]

Children, in return, are expected to respect and obey their parents; if they do not, it reflects back on the grandparents who are considered to have neglected their duties in regard to their children. A boy is "sort of afraid" of his father, while a girl is careful to obey her mother; the relation to a parent of the opposite sex is more affectionate but never one of familiarity. It is the duty of children to look after their parents when they get old. The relations between parents and children at the various periods of the life-cycle will be summarized in a following section.

The extension of behavior to classificatory parents and

children is on the same pattern; these "parents" have the same duties and obligations toward their "children," but their opportunities may be limited by circumstances. The father's brother may become a stepfather; the mother's sister, because of matrilocal residence and the sororate, is very close to her sister's children, so that often there may be little difference in the social position of a mother and her sister. For more distant "fathers" and "mothers" both the Cheyenne and the Arapaho emphasize the extension of attitudes rather than of behavior.[30]

Sibling-sibling.--The relations between siblings are fundamental to many activities in Cheyenne and Arapaho life. Between siblings of the same sex there is a close and intimate bond. Two brothers work and play together, protect each other from danger, and revenge each other. An older brother helps look after a younger brother; the latter should heed his brother's advice. There is no formality between brothers; they may tease one another in a mild fashion but not roughly. Two sisters likewise work and play together and help each other at all times. Frequently they remain together all their lives, holding property in common and often being married to the same man.

The relationship of a brother and sister is modified by differences in sex and age. An older sister will help take care of her younger brother, but an older brother will have little to do with a younger sister. When puberty is reached, their behavior is considerably restricted. A brother is required to respect his sister very highly and is not supposed to be alone with her, gossip, or talk obscenely in her presence. On the other hand, he is vitally interested in her welfare and largely controls her marriage. The sister is subject to similar restrictions but expresses her affection for her brother by looking after his needs and interests.[31]

Among the Cheyenne and Arapaho the attitudes and behavior existing between siblings are extended to all relatives classed as "brother" or "sister," but the intensity of the relationship varies with circumstances. Distant "brothers" might take advantage of their rights in regard to "sisters-in-law" and provoke a quarrel; close "brothers" would ordinarily not do this.[32] Two men who marry sisters call each other "brother," and vice versa. Such men have common duties toward the household and each other's children. Among the Arapaho the "older brothers" in the societies are treated like own brothers; in addition to helping one another during the ceremonies they might play tricks on one another, such as painting the other's horses a different color.

Husband-wife.--The relationship of husband and wife among
the Cheyenne and Arapaho is rather hard to define, but certain tendencies seem clear. The social separation of the sexes is difficult
to overcome, particularly where the marriage has been arranged, and
the husband and wife are frequently shy and restrained for a while.[33]
The husband also feels a stranger in his wife's camp and may frequently visit his own home. The activities incidental to rearing a
family rapidly create new bonds, however. Michelson's Cheyenne narrator remarks: "We had our first child after we had been married a
year. It was at that time that I began really to love my husband.
He always treated me with respect and kindness."[34] The Arapaho
method of allowing the son-in-law to work and live in the father-in-
law's household before marriage tended to adjust matters somewhat,
also.

The economic and social activities of the husband and wife
are regulated by the division of labor. This division is rather
strict and is so organized that the activities of each are complementary, not only in household activities but in many ritual activities as well. The men supply the meat food and protection; the
women are responsible for the household activities and the moving of
camp. In both tribes the wife is included in any ceremonial pledge;
among the Arapaho a woman is considered to have gone through the age-
societies in accordance with the rank of her husband.[35]

Father's sister-brother's child.--The relationship of a
father's sister to her brother's child is one of affection and help-
fulness. Before birth she makes a cradle for her brother's child,
and later she watches over its welfare. If the child is a girl, she
may give it her name and aid the mother in training her. If she
neglects her obligations to her brother's children, other women in
the family will criticize her, saying: "Your heart is bad--you don't
love your brother--you don't help his children."

A father's sister may tease her nieces and nephews in a mild
way; a nephew is not supposed to joke very much in return, but a
niece may tease her aunt. The father's sister feels closer to her
niece, and they have more in common, than does an aunt and her nephew.
Brother's children may take their aunt's property, if necessary.
Gift exchanges frequently occur; among the Arapaho the niece is not
required to make a return--"everything comes to the niece." The
father's sister also has special duties at marriage, death, and other
occasions.

Both the Cheyenne and the Arapaho equate the mother's brother's wife with the father's sister as far as social behavior is con-

cerned. While the real father's sister has certain duties which are not shared by the mother's brother's wife or more distant "aunts," similar attitudes are extended to all.

Mother's brother-sister's child.--The relation of a mother's brother to his sister's children parallels, in many respects, that outlined for the father's sister, taking into account the differences in sex. A mother's brother feels a great affection for his nephews and nieces and helps protect and look after them for the sake of his sister. He has duties toward his nephew at various ceremonial occasions and may talk to him if he violates customs but will not punish him.

A mild joking or teasing relationship exists between a mother's brother and his nephews and nieces. The relationship is closest with the nephew, who can take his uncle's property but is expected to make an equivalent return in the future. A niece seldom exercises this privilege but may carry out gift exchanges through the mother's brother's wife.

The father's sister's husband has similar duties and obligations to his "sister's" children; more distant "uncles" feel the same general affection for their "nephews" and "nieces" but have fewer opportunities to express it.

Grandparent-grandchild.--The relation of grandparent to grandchild is likewise characterized by affection and aid. Grandparents usually spoil their grandchildren; if the parents are too harsh with their children, the grandparents will stand up for the latter and threaten to bring them up themselves. In return a grandchild looks up to his grandparents, treating them with deference[36] because of their age and knowledge but being pretty much on a footing of equality. A grandfather often teaches his grandson the stories and myths and the ritual observances. A grandmother aids in the domestic training of her granddaughters but also takes an interest in her grandsons. Both sets of grandparents come together at birth, the father's parents having the privilege of looking after their new grandchild for the first ten days, but the mother's parents normally have more to do with the grandchildren because of conditions of residence.

There is a mild joking or teasing relationship; grandparents may pour water on a grandchild to wake him up early or run him around the camp, and the grandchild may retaliate. Among the Arapaho, in particular, they are considered "sort of equals" who belong together, and special terms may sometimes be applied to grandchildren while they are young. A grandfather may jokingly refer to his granddaughter as "youngest wife" and his grandson as "brother-in-law," while a grandmother may call her grandchildren "husband" and "sister-in-law."[37] These terms do not refer to marriage but are terms of affection; they likewise emphasize equality in terms of generation.

Both the Cheyenne and the Arapaho extend the basic attitudes toward grandparents to more distant "grandfathers" and "grandmothers." An Arapaho summed up the relationship in classifying the sun as "grandfather" because it is "so distant and old and yet so near and attached to us." Ceremonial "grandfathers," however, have to be much more highly respected; among the Arapaho, in particular, there are various restrictions on behavior. It is not permissible to gamble with them, pass in front of them, or take any liberties with them under pain of supernatural sanction.[38] "This 'grandfather' business is dangerous," say the Arapaho.

Parent-in-law-child-in-law.--The relationships between parents-in-law and children-in-law assume a special importance among the Cheyenne and Arapaho. Because of general matrilocal residence a man is in a somewhat different position toward his parents-in-law than is his wife. A man is required by custom to work for his wife's parents; in return a father-in-law looks out for his interests,[39] and a mother-in-law cooks for her son-in-law and makes moccasins and robes for him. A father-in-law may talk with his son-in-law when necessary but is not supposed to remind him of his duties directly. A mother-in-law and son-in-law must honor and respect each other very highly, but must never speak, look at, or be in the same room with each other. If they should accidentally meet, the son-in-law covers his head; if they need to communicate, they do so through the wife.[40]

The relation of a woman to her parents-in-law is not nearly so restricted. A father-in-law must be respected, but he may talk to his daughter-in-law, if necessary, and be in the same room with her. Between a mother-in-law and a daughter-in-law there are no such restrictions; they should treat each other in the "best way," but they may talk freely together. Among the Arapaho they may even argue over the rearing of the children and joke with each other a little. Among the Gros Ventre, Kroeber mentions the restrictions which exist between a mother-in-law and a son-in-law but states that there was "no father-in-law taboo."[41]

Among the Cheyenne a man may publicly present a fine horse to his mother-in-law, who, in return, may make a beaded tipi. They then have the right to talk to one another, if necessary, and the ceremonial exchange is felt to make them less strangers.[42] Among the Arapaho this same custom holds but does not seem so well developed.

The daughter-in-law makes moccasins for her father-in-law, who returns dresses or ornaments through his wife.

The extension of kinship terms to the siblings of parents-in-law and children-in-law is paralleled by an extension of social attitudes and behavior among all three tribes, though not necessarily to the same degree. The relationship of parents-in-law to children-in-law is thus fundamentally the same among the Cheyenne and Arapaho, although the terminology used differs in an important way.

Sibling-in-law-sibling-in-law.--The relationships of siblings-in-law among the Cheyenne and Arapaho, despite the variety of combinations, may all be characterized as "rough" joking relationships. In all of them, likewise, there seems to be a combination of conflict and mutual help. Two brothers-in-law are bound closely together and must work together and help each other. A man is supposed to help his wife's brother--"it is his duty"--and a wife's brother has the right to use his sister's husband's property when necessary. Each must respect the other when he is not present, but when they are together in public, they are expected to joke "roughly" with each other, play tricks on each other, and call each other various uncomplimentary names.[43] Both should take such joking in good spirit and not get angry; in fact, an exchange of presents is essential to a full exercise of this privilege. A man will also make fun of his brother-in-law if the latter doesn't carry out his duties and obligations. Two brothers-in-law may quarrel over the husband's treatment of his wife, and the brother may take her away and force the husband to pay an indemnity. On the other hand, if a wife runs away, the husband has a claim against her brother.

The relationship of two sisters-in-law is parallel in many respects. They are supposed to help each other and exchange gifts; they respect each other but must joke and play tricks on each other when together. A sister keeps watch over her brother's wife and attempts to protect his interests.[44]

The relationship of a brother-in-law and sister-in-law is quite the opposite from that of a brother and sister. They may joke "roughly" with each other, make obscene remarks, and indulge in sexual play.[45] In both tribes the levirate and sororate make brothers-in-law and sisters-in-law potential husbands or wives. The Cheyenne recognize this, saying: "The sister-in-law is like a wife." Among the Arapaho, younger sisters might be promised to exceptional warriors before they were mature; "they would let them know that they were their wives and joke with them."[46]

The social behavior outlined is extended to all siblings-in-

law, particularly the joking aspect. The spouses of siblings-in-law,
however, are classed as siblings and treated as such.

Parents-in-law-parents-in-law.--The relationship of the husband's parents to the wife's parents is one of mutual respect and
honor. While they help one another and come together occasionally,
"there is something in between them," and they don't talk very much
or joke with one another.[47] Their common interests lie in their
grandchildren, and they keep up the general pattern of exchange as
long as their children's marriage lasts. It is considered bad form
to marry any of the children-in-law's relatives; people would talk
about such a marriage. This social behavior extends to the siblings
of these relatives and to the parents of the spouses of nephews and
nieces.

"Friend"-"friend."--The relationship of "friends" takes several forms in the Plains. Among the Cheyenne it was customary to
select some nonrelative to pierce the ears of one's child; this
might start a reciprocal friendship which continued for several generations. "Friends" usually have little direct contact; they must
respect one another and act quite formally, never joking or being
familiar with one another--"they are kind of shy." Yet in other
respects the relationship is like that of "brothers," and their children often use kinship terms on that basis. In the old days this
institution was associated with the warpath and the warrior societies.[48]

The Arapaho do not have this institution developed to the
same degree as the Cheyenne, and some Arapaho say they have borrowed
it from the latter. Former husbands of the same wife, and former
wives of the same husband, may call one another "friend," though
different terms are used. In the old days if, when on the warpath,
a man didn't stop to pick up a fallen lodge-comrade and the latter
escaped, he would ever afterward call the man and his brothers
"cowards" and joke with them in public; if the man did pick up his
fallen comrade, he and his brothers could joke with the fallen man.
This relationship is like that of brothers-in-law as far as the joking is concerned.

Kinship Behavior: The Life-Cycle
In the previous section the general attitudes and behavior patterns
prevailing between pairs of relatives have been outlined, but most
social activities involve a more complex set of relations. Some
insight into the actualization of these attitudes and behavior patterns may be gained through a brief survey of the Cheyenne and Arapaho life-cycles. Since general accounts of the more important

events in the life-cycle are available in the literature, it will be sufficient for our purposes to indicate the duties and obligations of relatives at these times.

Marriage and the household.--Marriage is perhaps the most important social event among the Cheyenne and Arapaho[49] and involves practically all the close relatives of the couple. In addition, each gets a new set of relatives--"it is good to get more relatives"-- and a whole new set of relationships is established between the relatives of the husband and the relatives of the wife.

While there are several variant methods of getting married, the duties and obligations of relatives are essentially the same. The regulation of marriage in both tribes is by kinship; blood-relatives, no matter how distant, should not marry.[50] Since the extension of kinship is bilateral, the range of restriction need not coincide with the band, although it may cover the latter more or less completely. Furthermore, it is customary to marry within one's own generation. Among the Gros Ventre, marriage was regulated both by kinship and by clan exogamy--marriage was not allowed with known blood-relatives or in the father's and mother's patrilineal clan groups.[51]

While the majority of marriages in both tribes are elopements at present, the more honorable form is that of purchase. Courtship was formerly a rather difficult procedure, because of the separation of the sexes and the care with which girls were watched by their mother's and father's sisters, but it has become much bolder in recent years, particularly among the Cheyenne. A girl who respected her parents and remained virtuous would be sought after as a wife, and a young man would send his mother, sisters, or father's sisters to ask for her hand. The decision rested primarily with the girl's brother or, if he were not present, with her mother's brother. The girl would usually assent to her brother's decision--"My brother, I have no right to decide--I am your property--I belong to you. If it is all right with you, I am satisfied."[52]

The marriage is validated by an exchange of goods between the families of the bride and the families of the groom. The male relatives of the groom (particularly his "fathers," "older brothers," and "mother's brothers") furnish horses and equipment, while his female relatives bring dresses, shawls, cloth, moccasins, and food. These are taken to the bride who usually selects her brother (or mother's brother) as sponsor. The latter distributes the horses and equipment among the girl's male relatives, while his wife distributes the dresses, shawls, and other articles among the female relatives.

The girl's mother and father's sisters prepare a feast for the husband's relatives, the men eating apart from the women, as usual. The
parents, or an old medicine woman, may give advice. The men who have
received horses now return other horses, while the women who received
dresses, etc., return tipis, quilts, beds, and other household furnishings, and the girl is sent with these gifts to the young man's
camp. There his sisters and aunts carry her into the lodge, give
her presents, and make her feel at home, while the return gifts are
distributed among the groom's relatives in payment for their original
gifts. In the meantime the girl's mother and father's sisters have
erected a lodge for the couple outside the camp circle; here they
reside for a short time before removing to the vicinity of the girl's
parents' lodge where a lodge is provided for them in the girl's camp,
the first lodge going to the husband's parents.

A variant form of this marriage, more common among the Arapaho,[53] took place when a promising young man would be accepted as
a prospective son-in-law and would work for his father-in-law for
several years before marriage. The work was considered the equivalent of the "gift" of horses. Among the Gros Ventre, horses were
given to the relatives of the bride "for the honor of the act"; sometimes a man would give his daughter to a young man in order to obtain
his aid and services. At marriage the man received a lodge and
household furnishings, usually from his parents-in-law, and apparently
resided near them.[54]

While parents desired their children to have an honorable
marriage and usually attempted to arrange one, the young men preferred to elope with the girl of their choice; otherwise their
friends might laugh at them.[55] If a young man could persuade a girl
to elope with him, they would usually run off to the camp of his
older brother or mother's brother. The brother would consider this
an honor, and he and his wife would take charge of the marriage, the
procedure being much the same as outlined above.

The general custom of matrilocal residence gave rise to an
extended domestic family among the Cheyenne and Arapaho, consisting
of a man and his wife, their married daughters and husbands, their
unmarried sons, their daughters' children, and any adopted or dependent relatives. The Cheyenne called such a group a "camp" and usually
named it after the male head of the family. While each elementary
family in the camp occupies a separate lodge, the camp represents an
economic unit. The sons-in-law assist in the hunting and work; food
is prepared in the mother's lodge, each daughter taking her share to
her own lodge where each elementary family eats as a unit.[56] Such

an arrangement lasts as long as the sons-in-law carry out their duties.

In former times polygyny was possible, and both the sororate and the levirate were practiced. Younger sisters were potential wives, becoming second wives on reaching puberty or taking their sister's place in case of death. Likewise a brother of a deceased husband might marry his widow. These institutions were not compulsory, but if a wife died, her family would usually want the husband to continue as a son-in-law, and the wife's brother would arrange to furnish a younger "sister" from the camp.[57] If a husband died, his family would want to keep the children close to them, and a younger brother would often take his place. In the old days it was common for households to exchange brothers and sisters in marriage, and for brothers to marry wives who were sisters, real or classificatory. Such marriages were considered a good thing, as bringing the families closer together, but there was no definite regulation.

Divorce seems to be fairly common among both the Cheyenne and the Arapaho. If a wife runs away with a lover, the latter must settle with the husband through an intermediary (usually the latter's ceremonial "grandfather") or be subject to retaliation.[58] If the husband accepts horses and smokes, the incident is closed, but he may demand his wife back and punish her in various ways. A husband has control over his wife, but if he treats her badly, her brothers may interfere and take her away until an indemnity is paid. Where separation is permanent, the children usually remain with the mother's household.

The system of gift exchanges which is instituted at the time of marriage continues as long as the marriage lasts. This exchange, which is practically identical among the Cheyenne and Arapaho, centers around the married couple and follows the rules previously indicated.[59] The initiative comes from the husband's side, in keeping with the view that his side should look after the wife's, and exchanges usually take place between persons of the same sex. When gifts are made across sex lines, the spouse usually makes the return gift. A person who receives a gift is supposed to make a suitable return and may enhance his prestige by returning a larger amount.

Birth and naming.--The birth of a child is an important event among the Cheyenne and Arapaho, and both sets of relatives assemble for the occasion. The women see to the delivery, taking care of the child and putting it into its cradle.[60] It is the duty of the husband's sister to make this cradle for her brother's child; usually she receives a horse in return. The husband's mother and other female relatives are in charge of the child for the first ten days; friends who bring presents are repaid by the husband and his male relatives.

Naming takes place a few days after birth and is in charge of the husband's relatives. A boy is usually named after the father's brother or some older male relative; a girl after her father's sister or grandmother. Among the Gros Ventre[61] a man might receive his father's name at birth, or take it after the father's death. It is considered an honor to have one's name chosen for a child; such a person gives a present to the child and helps look after it until the child reaches maturity, taking, in turn, a name from among his father's relatives. The names, themselves, usually refer to different activities or characteristics, or to various animals or objects.

The aboriginal beliefs concerning conception are difficult to discover. The Cheyenne seem to have a belief in spirit children which enter the mother; these may be long-dead children or old people who wish to return as a child. Sometimes two spirits travel together and decide to go into the same mother. Children belong mainly to the mother because they come from her; a husband "really has no part in the child, but it is his child because he is the husband."[62]

Training and initiation.--While both sets of relatives contribute to the training of the child, there is some specialization involved. The husband's relatives usually take charge of ceremonial events; in addition to naming, they sponsor the piercing of the child's ears[63] and later his ceremonial haircut. Among the Arapaho these symbolize war activities; among the Cheyenne the father's sisters and other female relatives yell during the piercing. Among the Gros Ventre ear-piercing was not a ceremonial performance.

The mother and her relatives are largely responsible for the behavior of a child around the camp, and particularly for the economic training of girls. A boy had the honored position in the lodge. For a boy there was no particular ceremony at puberty, but sometime after this period he would begin to wear a blanket, avoid his sisters, and act in a grown-up manner. For a girl the period of puberty was an important one. Among the Cheyenne her father might publicly announce the event and give away horses. The girl was painted red and incensed with smoke before retiring with her grandmother to a separate lodge, where she had to remain four days and observe certain restrictions. The Arapaho were not so strict, but a woman was considered "dangerous" during her menstrual periods and the family might move out of the lodge temporarily, except for the mother.[64] In both tribes a "protective rope" was worn by girls after puberty, any violation of which was punished by her relatives.

Among the Cheyenne the first buffalo hunt and the first war party were the occasions to which a boy looked forward. The father celebrated his son's return from his first successful hunt by giving away horses. The return from his first war party marked the achievement of adult status, and if the young man had achieved any notable deed, his sisters and father's sisters would yell and dance, and the youth would receive a new name.

In both tribes individual fasting, as a result of a vow or to obtain power, might be performed at any time after puberty but was not compulsory. Among the Gros Ventre the situation was similar, men going out to fast "with the intention of becoming doctors, or receiving miraculous powers."[65]

The age and conditions for entrance into the warrior societies varied among the three tribes. According to Grinnell,[66] boys from thirteen to sixteen years of age might elect to join one of the Cheyenne societies. Usually a boy joined his father's society, and ordinarily he remained in that society, but he might leave and join another. Horses and other gifts had to be given away at the first dance, but otherwise there was no special ceremony. Among the Arapaho[67] the young men around sixteen to eighteen years of age would be formed into a society which performed a dance; this group would then progress through the various dances or societies in order. The Gros Ventre had several companies for each society or dance, which remained as units throughout the series.[68]

Death and mourning.--If a person is sick, close relatives call a doctor and the father's relatives come. When death occurs, the near relatives will wail and mourn. Among the Cheyenne the members of the household give away everything they own, saying: "We have lost one of our flesh--we can accumulate horses and goods again, but we can't bring back our relatives." If a man were killed in war, the female relatives would gash their legs; otherwise they might only cut off their hair. Among the Arapaho mourning was much the same, except that a man's brothers came and took most of his property.[69] Among the Gros Ventre a man might cry on the prairie for a brother, father, or son; a sister would gash herself and cry for a brother, while parents who had lost an only child would give away their property.[70]

Mourning continued for a year or more, the mourners camping outside the camp circle. Finally someone would come and comb their hair and end the mourning; among the Cheyenne a "friend" would usually do this, among the Arapaho some stranger was usually appointed. After mourning was over a surviving spouse might remarry. If a child had been lost, a chum of the same age and sex might be adopted in its place; such a child would use kinship terms for its adopted parents and spend part of its time with them.

In case of murder within the tribe the relatives of the deceased attempted to take revenge, especially the fathers, brothers, and mother's brothers. A murderer was outlawed and had to leave the tribe. Among the Cheyenne the relatives of a murderer might intercede through a chief and pay an indemnity; if successful, the murderer might return and camp near by.[71]

CONCLUSIONS AND INTERPRETATIONS

It is now possible to get some insight into the nature of the Cheyenne and Arapaho social structure by examining the relationship of the various aspects of the kinship system to one another and to other aspects of the social organization. Since rather detailed information on respect and familiarity was secured, an analysis of these relationships will be presented as a basis for further comparative studies. The position of the Cheyenne and Arapaho kinship system in the Plains will be outlined, and an analysis of the types of kinship systems, and their relation to certain historical and sociological problems in the Plains and near-by areas, will be presented.

The Kinship System

If we consider the Cheyenne and Arapaho kinship systems as a whole, there is a rather close correlation between the kinship terminology and the social behavior of relatives. The kinship system classifies relatives into socially recognized groups, on the one hand, and regulates their social behavior, on the other; toward each class of kindred there is a fairly definite relationship, expressed in terms of duties, obligations, and attitudes, which serves to order social life with a minimum of conflict. Within each class of kindred the intensity varies with the "social closeness" of the relative. The Gros Ventre parallels, in both terminology and social behavior, indicate, so far as they go, that this correlation is rather fundamental and that the kinship system of the Arapaho, at least, is relatively stable.

The Cheyenne and Arapaho kinship system is of the "classificatory" type in that there is a merging of lineal and collateral relatives and in its general aspects--terminology, behavior, and extensions--is bilateral. Within consanguineal relationships, the kinship systems are organized on strict principles of generation[72] and sex and, within one's own generation, on the basis of relative age. There is an important distinction made in attitude and behavior between consanguineal and affinal relatives, though certain of the latter are partially assimilated to consanguineal relatives in terminology. In

both tribes there is a basic reciprocity to the kinship system, contradictory terms or modes of behavior not being used between relatives.
These features result in a definite symmetry to the systems as a whole.
Among the Gros Ventre the extensions of kinship are modified somewhat
in accordance with the patrilineal clan groups, but the latter seem
to have exerted no important effects on the central core of the kinship system.

In certain cases the correlation between the terminology and
the social behavior of relatives doesn't hold. There are differences
between the Cheyenne, on the one hand, and the Arapaho and Gros Ventre,
on the other, in regard to the classification of parents-in-law, without any important differences in the general social behavior of such
relatives. Furthermore, there are important differences in the behavior of a man and his wife toward certain of their affinal relatives,
particularly the parents-in-law, which seem to be related to the organization of the matrilocal household situation but which are not
expressed in the terminology.

This lack of correlation between the terminology for certain
affinal relatives and their social behavior is in contrast to the rest
of the system and needs to be explained in one way or another. It is
possible to consider these variations, from a historical standpoint,
as examples of "cultural lag," and from what is known of Arapaho and
Cheyenne history there is some evidence for this view. A comparative
study of other Central and Northern Algonkian tribes throws some light
on the problem. Certain of the Northern Algonkian tribes classify
parents-in-law with the mother's brother and father's sister in the
Arapaho manner, while many Central Algonkian tribes classify them
with the grandparents in the Cheyenne manner. It is possible, therefore, that the Cheyenne and Arapaho have maintained old forms of
classification relatively unmodified, despite the changes incidental
to Plains life. It is important to note in this connection, however,
that the Arapaho do not seem to be aware of the similarity between
the linguistic forms for parents-in-law and the linguistic forms for
uncles and aunts and consider them separate terms.[73] The Cheyenne
are aware of the linguistic similarities but differentiate these relatives in terms of the form of address (vocative and nonvocative).
This difference between the tribes is in accord with the relative
length of time they have been in the Plains area. It is also possible
that the extended family situation serves to differentiate parents-
in-law sufficiently, so that a tendency to maintain a symmetrical terminology does not result in too much conflict,[74] particularly as there
are special terms available. These problems will be considered later

in relation to the changes which seem to have occurred among some of the Algonkian tribes with reference to social organization.

The possibility of explaining the kinship system of a tribe as the result of various social institutions, and, in particular, of various forms of marriage, has long intrigued students of social organization. Lowie[75] has outlined the correlations to be found in North America between the classification of relatives, on the one hand, and the clan and various forms of marriage, on the other, and has suggested a causal relationship between them. Lesser has discussed the Dakota kinship type as it occurs among the Siouan tribes in the Plains area and says: "The system itself shows no emphasis which can be correlated with unilateral descent or group exogamy, but rather direct effect of levirate and sororate marriage, both of which occur extensively among the Dakota tribes."[76]

Such attempts at explaining particular features of a social system by reference to other particular features seem methodologically unsound. In the first place, there are always exceptions which have to be explained. Thus the Cheyenne, Arapaho, and Gros Ventre all use a similar classification of relatives and have the sororate[77] and levirate, while the Gros Ventre alone have unilateral descent and exogamy. Second, a decision has to be made as to which is the causal factor, and in the absence of historical data that decision is not always easy. But, more important, such explanations never explain the presence of the causal factor, which is an equally important question.

In an attempt to remedy this situation Radcliffe-Brown has suggested a systematic comparison of social systems, not with reference to superficial similarities and differences, but with reference to the most fundamental or general similarities and differences which can be discovered. This requires a procedure by which each system may be described in terms of a limited number of structural principles.[78] Certain of these principles have been formulated by an analysis of the basic structure of the elementary family and thus have some general significance. It is desirable to see the relative importance of these principles and the forms they take among the Cheyenne and Arapaho, and to evaluate their significance for an understanding of the kinship system.

The principle[79] of the "equivalence of siblings" is one of the basic principles for kinship systems of the Cheyenne and Arapaho type; it is reflected in the classification of a man with his brother and a woman with her sister, and in the strong bonds which are exemplified in their behavior. This principle is especially evident in marriage and the household organization--the sororate and levirate and the matrilocal household all reflect the social equivalence of brothers and of sisters. The important differentiation of sex modifies, but does not obscure, the sibling relationship; a brother and a sister use the same terminology for each other's relatives, for the most part, and there is clear evidence of their strong regard for each other despite the social separation. This is particularly expressed in the control of marriage by the brother and in the mutual obligations toward each other's children. In this connection it is interesting to note that younger siblings are classed together in the terminology regardless of sex, an older sister commonly looking after her younger brothers and sisters without discrimination.

The Cheyenne and Arapaho make a sharp distinction in terminology and behavior on the basis of sex, particularly with reference to older relatives. In practically every aspect of life there is a differentiation according to sex, but this is usually so organized as to provide for co-operation and hence helps hold the family organization together.

Despite the emphasis on sex differentiation, the Cheyenne and Arapaho make no sharp distinction between relatives through the father and relatives through the mother, terminology and behavior patterns being extended bilaterally on the basis of the equivalence of siblings and the distinction of sex, primarily. There is a general equivalence of the two parental groups of relatives, both in terminology and in behavior, although certain duties and obligations belong to one side or the other. This relationship is particularly apparent in the system of gift exchange which serves, in part, to bind these two groups together.

Among the Cheyenne and Arapaho the principle of the "relationship of generations" plays an important role in the kinship system. This principle involves not only the cycle of reproduction but the transmission of the social heritage from one generation to another as well. In both tribes the kinship terminology is organized on the basis of generations, with the parental generation maintaining authority over, and exacting obedience from, the children's generation. Between alternate generations, however, there is a different relationship to be found. Grandparents do not have any particular responsibilities for training their grandchildren and exert no rigid authority; they are rather friendly and familiar relatives who are almost "equals." The distinction of sex, so important elsewhere in the system, becomes less significant in these relations, perhaps because of the differences in age.

The principle of reciprocity, which is necessarily involved to some degree in every kinship system, is important among the Cheyenne and Arapaho. For the most part complementary terms and behavior are used by relatives; only siblings-in-law of the same sex and the two sets of parents-in-law use verbally reciprocal terms, and in these instances the behavior patterns are symmetrical also. There is some tendency to reciprocity in marriage through household exchange, but this does not seem to have become organized. The system of economic exchange described above also illustrates this principle.

On the other hand, the lineage principle, which looms large in kinship systems of the Omaha and Crow types where it results in the overriding of the generation principle, plays practically no part in the Cheyenne and Arapaho systems. Here it enters in the organization of the extended household which is based on matrilocal residence, but it is not formally organized in either terminology or behavior. In the Gros Ventre this principle finds formal expression, along with that of the equivalence of siblings, in the formal clan organization but is not apparent in the central core of the kinship system.

These principles are of value to the extent that they furnish insight into the kinship system and indicate further problems which may be solved or hypotheses to be tested. The principle of the equivalence of siblings, for example, seems to underlie not only the classification of relatives but the sororate and levirate and the various extensions of kinship as well. If this is so, the problem becomes, not to explain one of these in terms of the other, but to determine the nature of the "active agent" behind the descriptive principle and the factors or conditions determining the particular forms it takes. Since the relationship of brothers is a very important one throughout the Plains area, a comparative study of this relationship in the various Plains tribes should throw some light on this problem.

Sex differentiation, organized to some extent by most peoples, is highly developed among some of the Central Algonkian tribes such as the Sauk and Fox, Menominee, and others. The use of the "marriage blanket" to prevent physical contact between the newly married couple in some of these tribes seems an extreme form of the more moderate sexual separation of the Cheyenne and Arapaho. Here, again, a comparative study might be very illuminating, in indicating both the variety of forms and the factors which may bring them about. The differentiation of relatives through the father and the mother also takes a variety of forms in the Plains area. Some tribes arrange them in terms of generation and a bilateral extension, others group them in terms of lineages, and still others assimilate them to ego's generation. The kinship system of a tribe such as the Crow can best be understood as in a process of transition from one form to another.

The principle of generations is another one which takes varying forms in the Plains area. In some tribes, such as the Kiowa and Kiowa-Apache, it is highly developed, three or four ascending generations being recognized in the terminology. In other tribes, such as the Omaha and Crow, the generation principle is overriden to a considerable extent, but even so the relationships between generations have much in common. An understanding of the nature of the relationships between various generations seems essential if we are to account for certain shifts in generation such as are found in the Cheyenne classification of parents-in-law with grandparents.

A principle of reciprocity seems inherent in every system, but the precise forms it takes and their correlations need to be studied. Verbal reciprocity looms large in systems such as those of the Mescalero and Chiricahua Apache but gradually diminishes in importance as one moves northward into the Plains area. A comparative study of a series of such tribes would indicate whether there is a correlation of such terminology with symmetrical behavior patterns, as well as give some insight into the nature of reciprocity as such.

The lineage principle gives us a more precise measure of the extent to which unilateral groupings are utilized in the social group. The clan among the Gros Ventre, Crow, Mandan, and Omaha, for example, varies greatly in its significance and relative importance; this can be determined more accurately by seeing the extent to which a lineage principle is involved in the social systems of these tribes. Such a study would, of course, illuminate the correlations with other factors and the conflicts with other principles.

This brief survey suggests the possibility that it may be profitable to deal with observed correlations between various aspects of social organization, not by considering one aspect as caused by another, but by considering them as variant manifestations of some more general factor or principle. Such principles are descriptive, to begin with, and are abstracted from social usages by analysis. But they seem to stand for active forces or factors which are as yet little understood; these factors seem to interact in varying ways in different social situations but often give rise to similar manifestations in widely separated regions. In the Plains area there is a series of tribes with similar patterns of terminology and behavior, though the actual terms used and the behavior content may be quite different. In the case of tribes such as the Cheyenne and Arapaho the similarities are perhaps attributable in part to diffusion, or rather interaction through intermarriage. But the Kiowa-Apache and Kiowa likewise have similar patterns of terminology and behavior, as do the Teton Dakota and some of the northern tribes, though with greater variation. Here the contacts do not seem to have been strong enough to have affected the pattern of grouping relatives, which is, after all, an abstraction of which the Indian is seldom aware. Further, such groups as the Crow Indians seem to be in the process of changing from a more highly organized kinship system to a more diffuse type represented by the Cheyenne and Arapaho systems. It seems likely that the conditions of Plains life (as yet only vaguely defined) favored such systems in comparison with the more highly organized systems which the sedentary village-dwelling Mandan and Hidatsa had developed, and the Crow, in adapting to these new conditions, gradually modified their social structure in the direction of their neighbors, borrowing some aspects and developing others. The development of patrilineal clans among the Gros Ventre has an important bearing on this question. Lowie[80] ascribes this development to ideas borrowed from the Blackfoot, but the accounts of the latter's social organization indicate that the Gros Ventre system is more highly developed, and hence it is probable that borrowing is not the sole factor involved. In this area there are more definite hunting territories and smaller groups; the increase in band solidarity brought about by these factors may well have tended toward a more formal organization of the bands.[81]

Boas has stated that "each cultural group has its own unique history, dependent partly on the peculiar inner development of the social group and partly upon the foreign influences to which it has been subjected."[82] While there is evidence that both of these factors may be important in the development of a social system, a precise definition of their contribution is not essential to the problems we have just considered. In dealing with the interrelations found in a social system, or the adaptations exhibited, a borrowed trait is just as good as one which is independently developed. Any information we may get as to the past history of social usages is valuable, particularly where processes of change occur, but a knowledge of this past history is not essential in dealing with synchronic problems.

Respect and Joking Relationships

The social usages involving restrictions on behavior or privileged familiarity are well developed among the Cheyenne and Arapaho, practically every relative being involved in one category or the other. Thus a man must respect his parents, sisters, and children-in-law's parents, and must "avoid" his parents-in-law, particularly his mother-in-law. On the other hand, he may joke "mildly" with his father's sisters, mother's brothers, grandfathers, and brothers, and must joke "roughly" with his brothers-in-law and sisters-in-law. A woman has parallel respect and joking relationships, except for her parents-in-law where avoidance is not involved.

Lowie has furnished a foundation for further studies of these social usages by reviewing the available data in the light of various theories. He finds ample evidence for a correlation "between social and sexual taboos, and between social license and the possibility of sex relations," but is aware that "this by no means explains all the phenomena."[83] He is skeptical of any all-inclusive theory and sets down as a principle of method:

> The regulations in any particular locality should rather be viewed in conjunction with the whole culture, ... whatever interpretations appear from such an inquiry may then be compared with corresponding results from other regions.[84]

The social usages centering around avoidance and joking have attracted a good deal of theoretical attention, particularly in terms of sex. In the following analysis a more inclusive formulation of these social usages will be attempted, based on a study of the social situations in which they occur and utilizing the descriptive principles outlined above. This will furnish a preliminary interpretation, which can then be compared with others, and eventually may result in a general formulation with regard to joking and respect.

Respect and joking relationships seem to represent mutually exclusive forms of social behavior which stand at opposite poles of conduct.[85] Each of these relationships may vary in intensity. Thus avoidance seems to represent an intensification of the respect relationship, while "rough joking" seems to be an extreme form of the "mild joking" relationship. We may state our problem as follows: Is there any correlation between the categories of joking and respect relationships and the social situations which exist in Cheyenne and Arapaho life, which will throw light on the classification of relatives in one or the other of these categories?

Among the Cheyenne and Arapaho (as elsewhere) respect relationships seem the more fundamental and involve the members of the elementary family as well as parents-in-law. The parents are responsible for transmitting the social heritage; this transmission involves authority on the part of the parents and obedience and respect on the part of the children.[86] The marked social differentiation on the basis of sex is another factor; the brother must respect his sister at the same time that he looks out for her welfare, and vice versa. The relation of a man to his parents-in-law is more complex. By the general rule of matrilocal residence he must reside in his parents-in-law's camp and must help support them economically, though to begin with he may feel an intruder. The mother-daughter relationship is a respect relationship; this respect is intensified in the case of the son-in-law by the difference in sex. There is a further factor in the rivalry of the mother-daughter and husband-wife relationships; in order that the affairs of the camp may run smoothly, the son-in-law and the mother-in-law avoid each other completely, though manifesting the highest respect for each other. It is significant, in this connection, that the restrictions may be removed when a satisfactory adjustment has been reached by a public exchange of gifts. The relation of a son-in-law and father-in-law is not so restricted. The factor of sex differentiation is absent, and there is the necessity for economic co-operation between the father-in-law and his son-in-law; while there is a reserve felt, there is no avoidance.

A daughter-in-law, on the other hand, has a different relation to her parents-in-law. Normally she is not in close contact with them, unless they should happen to belong to the same band. A daughter-in-law must respect her husband's father because he is of the opposite sex and in the generation above, but there is no avoidance. The mother-in-law, on the other hand, is of the same sex and has an active interest in her son's and daughter-in-law's children; the daughter-in-law may speak freely with her mother-in-law and may argue with her and even tease her mildly--a privilege which is reciprocal.[87] Two sets of parents-in-law are of the same generation, usually, and are related only through the marriage of their children.

All these relationships, centering largely about the domestic household, involve the possibility of social conflict, and in the case of the son-in-law the conflict of interests is inevitable. In certain of these relationships, also, there is a social necessity for avoiding or minimizing conflict if the household organization is to function properly. In these cases the conflict situation seems to be solved largely by suppressing the possibility of conflict.

Joking relationships among the Cheyenne and Arapaho obtain between more distant relatives in general. Mild joking relationships occur between consanguineal relatives, for the most part, and are not obligatory. Between brothers there is a feeling of equality and an absence of any particular restraint, which results in an attitude of familiarity and which allows mild teasing and joking.[88] Grandparents are in a somewhat similar position, except for the difference in age which introduces an attitude of respect to some extent, but they have no specific duties in regard to the transmission of the social heritage. The father's sister and the mother's brother are in the parental generation, and hence represent authority, but are not directly concerned with the training of their nephews and nieces. On the other hand, their affection for each other manifests itself in their behavior toward each other's children, a father's sister being particularly close to her niece and a mother's brother to his nephew. These relationships involve some conflict in attitudes but no particular conflict in interests. A conflict situation which develops seems to be adjusted by establishing a mild joking relationship which regulates its expression in a socially desirable manner.

These joking relationships take a more extreme form among siblings-in-law, where they become obligatory and involve horseplay, practical jokes, satire, and sexual play. The relationship of siblings-in-law is not affected by differences of generation but is by differences of sex. A man must work in close co-operation with his wife's brother, yet since a husband has control over his wife and a brother over his sister, conflict is almost inevitable. A woman is in a parallel position in regard to her husband's sister; they are supposed to help each other and never show any jealousy in public, but there is a similar rivalry and conflict of interests. A man's relations to his wife's sisters and a woman's relations to her husband's brothers represent apparent exceptions to the general restriction in behavior between members of the oppsite sex. But the husband-wife relationship is the one socially recognized exception to the general rule; since sisters are socially equivalent, the wife's sister seems to be brought into the range of the husband-wife relationship and may actually become a second wife, of course. But here, also, there is the possibility of conflict between the husband-wife relationship and the sister-sister relationship. The relationship of a woman to her husband's brother is parallel; she may marry him if her husband dies, but there is a similar possibility of conflict of interests. The behavior of siblings-in-law of the opposite sex centers around obscene jests and sexual play, in addition to ordinary joking.

The relations of siblings-in-law thus involve fundamental conflicts which are inevitable in view of the household organization and the social relations of siblings and spouses. These conflicts must be regulated in some way if the social order is to operate smoothly; respect as a device for suppressing these conflicts is not possible, since there are no generational differences involved and the factor of sex difference is socially nullified, but obligatory joking seems to serve quite well. Essentially it seems to be a device for organizing hostility in socially desirable ways; such relationships not only make an adjustment to an ambivalent situation but create a definite bond between the relatives as well.

Thus respect and joking relationships seem to be part of a single system of social behavior.[89] We may summarize this brief survey of these relationships among the Cheyenne and Arapaho as follows:

1. *Respect relationship*--where there is some possibility of conflict and the social necessity for avoiding it.

2. *Mild joking relationship*--where there is some possibility of conflict but no particular social necessity for avoiding it.

3. *Avoidance relationship*--where the conflict situation is inevitable, where there is the social necessity of avoiding it, and where generation differences are present.

4. *Obligatory joking relationship*--where the conflict situation is inevitable, where there is the social necessity of avoiding it, but where no differences of generation are involved.

Some insight into the nature of respect and joking relationships may be gained from this survey. They seem to be correlated with conflict situations and to represent alternate ways of adjusting social conflicts. Respect seems to be the more fundamental relationship, based as it is on the necessity of transmitting the social heritage and on the differentiation of sex. Where respect is not involved, the relationship tends to be one of equality and familiarity, other things being equal. Conflicts are inevitable in any social system, and each social group must regulate them, either by suppressing them or by organizing them in socially desirable ways. The kinship system deals with the conflicts which arise in the elementary family largely by establishing a relationship of authority and obedience among its members, and also by limiting the possibility of conflict in the sexual sphere. With the enlargement of the elementary family through the marriage of the children (or otherwise), new conflict situations arise for which there has been little preparation on the part of the adult individuals concerned. These new relationships are more complex in that they usually involve indirect relationships by way of a third relative and also involve ambivalent attitudes. New relatives are brought into a new social group in one sense and excluded in another, so that they are in an uncertain social position. Where marriage creates a separate household group, these conflicts, except those between husband and wife, may not cause too great disruption. But when larger households are created by marriage, these conflicts must be regulated if the household is to operate efficiently. In systems of the Cheyenne and Arapaho type the regulation seems to be by establishing a relationship of extreme respect

or avoidance, on the one hand, or of obligatory joking, on the other.[90]
Which of these is chosen depends on several circumstances: the nature
of the situation, the generation and sex differences involved, and
the social necessity for a solution. Avoidance relationships usually
involve generation and sex differences and a situation in which an
immediate solution is essential, but since avoidance operates by
eliminating social relations, it is not very satisfactory in terms
of the social structure. Where generation differences are not involved, obligatory joking relationships are likely to be utilized.
The latter furnish a standardized way of behaving in socially uncertain situations as well as a release of emotional tensions. Also
they establish bonds between such relatives which gradually bind them
together. In regard to the relationships between relatives in different households the same factors seem to be involved, but the conflict situations are normally less numerous and less important, and
their regulation is less rigid. The importance of the household
structure is evident in these various relationships.

The widespread distribution of respect and joking relationships among the Plains tribes indicates that they are important in
this area, but except for Lowie's pioneer account of these relationships among the Crow,[91] there is little comparative material available in the literature. The papers in the present volume will remedy
this deficiency to some extent, and the data presented on these
relationships among the Kiowa-Apache, the Fox, Cherokee, and Southern
Athabaskan groups may be utilized to test and modify the tentative
correlations here advanced on the basis of the Cheyenne and Arapaho
materials. An adequate classification of these various tribes is
essential before comparative studies can take place, however, since
the conflict situations vary according to the social structure of the
group. There is nothing directly comparable in the Cheyenne and Arapaho system, for example, to the Crow joking relationships between
children whose fathers belong to the same clan, since neither tribe
emphasizes the lineage principle or has a clan organization. They
are comparable in more general terms, however, since this Crow relationship is an example of an indirect relationship through the men
of the father's clan who are considered as a unit. When comparative
studies between the Plains types have been carried out, the results
can be compared with those of other regions, and a more general formulation of respect and joking may then be possible.

Social Integration

The nature of social integration is one of the important problems of
social life; the possibility of using the type of social integration
as an ultimate basis for classifying social structure has been mentioned in the Introduction. If we look at social systems from the
standpoint of an "adaptive mechanism," there are two main aspects:
(1) the internal adaptation which "is seen in the controlled relations
of individuals within the social unity,"[92] and (2) the external adaptation of this social structure to the natural environment. Certain
interrelations have been pointed out in considering the kinship system, but it is desirable to consider briefly the whole social organization from this standpoint.

The Cheyenne and Arapaho have a series of social units--the
elementary family, the extended household, the band, the society,
and the tribe--each of which has a definite organization and definite
functions in terms of integration. Each unit has a solidarity based
on kinship as well as economic, ritual, or other ties, and on social
opposition to other units; at the same time each unit is related to
the others in such ways that the whole system continues to exist, and
there is a definite cohesion and unity to social life.

The elementary family normally exists as a subdivision of the
extended matrilocal family; this group of father, mother, and children usually occupies a single tipi and eats together. Within this
group are found the strongest kinship ties and the responsibility
for transmitting the social heritage. This group may be enlarged by
means of sororal polygyny and is maintained in case of death by the
sororate and levirate.

The extended household is the primary economic unit and com-
bines families of orientation with families of procreation by means
of matrilocal residence. The household is concerned with subsistence,
the men securing meat and hides and the women gathering vegetable
products and carrying out other activities. While the families of
such a household occupy several lodges, these camp together, and food
is cooked in the oldest woman's lodge and carried by her daughters
to their own lodges for consumption. The size of the household group
varies greatly between the limits of the elementary family and the
band, but probably averages somewhere between fifteen and twenty-five
individuals.[93] A household is connected by marriage with the households of the husbands and wives of the men and women born in the
household; these ties are maintained and strengthened by the series
of exchanges which take place and by the duties and obligations of
relatives mentioned above.

Such an extended household was well adapted to the rather uncertain Plains life. Several hunters were available for each household, and in case of a large kill there were enough women to prepare the meat and hides. The death of a spouse did not break up the organization, while the household would take care of the children in case of a divorce.[94]

The band among the Cheyenne was composed of a series of extended families, or households, and represented a definite unit. Each band had a name, usually referring to some peculiarity, and each operated as a political and economic unit for much of the year, under the leadership of a band chief. While there were no definite hunting territories, a band usually had favorite winter quarters to which it returned each year.

The band was something of an amorphous social group, difficult to describe in definite terms but operating efficiently under the conditions of Plains life. Because of the general regulation of marriage and residence, the women in a band would normally be born there while their husbands might come from that band or from others. But a man retained his own band affiliation and might rejoin the band in which he was born, or even another one, if the prospects were better. Band affiliation was therefore less of a bond than that of the household.

Rivalry between the bands was quite strong since the power of a band chief was roughly determined by the number of relatives and followers which he controlled. Mooney states that matrilocal residence led the chiefs to encourage endogamy in order to keep up the strength of the band.[95] From the standpoint of tribal integration, however, it was desirable to enforce kinship exogamy and thus to compel band exogamy for the majority. The camp circle was an objective expression of tribal unity--each band had a definite position in the circle and the whole symbolized one large family.

Information concerning Arapaho bands is scanty since their band system disintegrated at an earlier period, but the available evidence points to an organization similar to that of the Cheyenne. The Gros Ventre had patrilineal clans which were exogamous, but unfortunately we do not know whether they were localized. There is some evidence that the household unit of the Gros Ventre was based on matrilocal residence; if this were so, the patrilineal clans must have been nonlocalized segments. Such an organization would tend to increase the tribal integration by uniting the various local groups more firmly, since the scattered clansmen could maintain their relationships more easily. On the other hand, if the patrilineal clan

represented the local group or band, the men would remain in the same
group after marriage. The smaller size of the Gros Ventre clans,[96]
under such conditions, would make it easier to trace kinship in the
local group. Also, more definite hunting territories would lead to
a closer local integration and perhaps an increased patrilineal emphasis.[97]

In olden times, according to some of Grinnell's best informants, the Cheyenne bands were matrilineal and strictly exogamous;
each group was supposed to be a body of kindred descended from a
common ancestor, and each group had its own ceremonies and taboos.[98]
While Mooney and other investigators have denied that the Cheyenne
have a clan system, it is probable that the earlier organization was
less amorphous. The conditions of Plains life demanded a local group
small enough to subsist by hunting and gathering but large enough to
furnish protection against hostile war parties and raids. The extended family was adequate for the first condition but was at the
mercy of any war party; the tribe, on the other hand, was too unwieldy
to act as an economic unit for very long. The band proved an adequate
compromise; this is perhaps the most important reason for its almost
universal presence in the Plains area.

The societies of the Cheyenne, Arapaho, and Gros Ventre were
briefly described in the Introduction. Among the Cheyenne these
societies were co-ordinate, and a young man usually joined the society of his father or other close male relative. The relations of
societies to one another were a mixture of rivalry and co-operation,
and during the tribal gatherings they completely dominated the band
organization. In recent times one of the bands was absorbed by the
"Dog Soldier" society which took its place in the camp circle as a
local group, but for the most part the societies cut across the band
system.[99] Among the Arapaho and Gros Ventre the societies were graded on the basis of age and confined to males, except for a co-ordinate
woman's society. Between the different societies there was a complicated relationship involving purchase, the ceremonial surrender of
wives, and ritual kinship. Alternate societies seem to have a close
bond in contrast to their common antagonism to the intermediate group,
the members of which sell their positions to the lower group and purchase new positions from the higher society.[100] On certain occasions,
such as the Sun Dance, there is evidence that alternate societies
represent opposition units in much the same fashion that Freshmen
and Juniors unite against Sophomores and Seniors in our high schools.
"Grandfathers," who are responsible for the ritual training and initiation, were selected from the next highest society, or occasionally

from the members of the third higher society; these "ceremonial grand-fathers" must be highly respected. The Gros Ventre societies were further divided into a series of co-ordinate companies, each with a name and the privilege of performing the dance of that particular age grade, but the details are not very clear.

The society systems of these three tribes represent segmentary organizations which are relatively independent of the band organization. These societies are primarily associations for men and were concerned with the important activities of protection and war, the tribal buffalo hunt, and the tribal ceremonies. Each society is associated with objects or animals which symbolize these activities. The organization of the Arapaho and Gros Ventre society systems is more complex and highly integrated than that of the Cheyenne, and among the Arapaho, at least, the societies seem to have survived longer than the bands.

The tribal organization of the Cheyenne and Arapaho is compounded of the above elements, but there were additional factors which increased tribal solidarity. The tribe, as we have seen, operated as a unit only during the summer; it was at this time that the tribal ceremonies were performed and the annual hunt carried out. During the period that the tribe was assembled the bands were organized in the camp circle,[101] and the society organization came into operation. The Cheyenne ceremonies involved the presence and co-operation of the whole tribe and were largely concerned with tribal welfare and growth. The most sacred of these ceremonies concerned the Medicine Arrows on whose condition the welfare of the Cheyenne tribe depends. Murder, for example, would stain the arrows; until they were wiped clean and "renewed," the tribe as a whole suffered. Usually this ceremony was performed annually by the keeper, who was the ritual head of the Cheyenne tribe, as the result of a vow undertaken by some individual. During the ceremony every family had to be represented in the camp circle which was policed by the warrior societies; after "renewal" all the males of the tribe assembled to inspect the arrows which were hung outside the Medicine Lodge.

The Sun Dance was much the same among the Cheyenne and Arapaho though the native meanings varied.[102] Among the Cheyenne the Sun Dance was usually held annually as a result of a pledge and involved the co-operation of all former pledgers and the warrior societies, under the general control of the society of the pledger. Kinship relations were established between the pledger and his instructor, and between the dancers and their sponsors, and a definite system of exchange was involved. Another important tribal ceremony was the *Massaum*, or Animal Dance, which seems to have been primarily related to hunting. The Arapaho had parallel ceremonies, though the tribal symbols often differed considerably. The entire ceremonial organization, including the Sun Dance, the society ceremonies, and the woman's society ceremony, was considered to be a single unit and was called by a special name.[103] The Gros Ventre system seems to have been similar but less highly organized.

The secular activities were in the hands of the council of chiefs, assisted by the warrior societies. This group acted as a unit only when the tribe was united. When the tribe was at war or engaged in the summer hunt, the warrior societies seem to have had more authority, but this probably led to little conflict since the society chiefs might also be members of the council.[104] The annual hunt was formerly an important occasion for the tribe. A successful hunt enabled the collection of a surplus of hides and meat; during the hunt the warrior societies maintained rigid discipline and severely punished any infractions which would jeopardize the success of the hunt.

This brief survey has shown something of the complexity of the interrelations of the various units of Cheyenne and Arapaho social organization and some insight into the nature of the bonds holding these units together. Perhaps the most important factors in holding these various groups together and linking them to one another are the bonds of kinship; even local solidarity and ritual relations tend to be expressed in terms of kinship. Included in these bonds are the ties maintained by the system of exchange between relatives. The organization of the household and band may be seen in relation to the conditions of Plains life, particularly in terms of subsistence and protection. The larger tribal organization is reflected in the camp circle but finds its integration primarily in ceremonial and symbolic terms. The band system, which was primarily an economic organization, dominated most of the year, but when the tribe came together, the society organization, composed of males, was pre-eminent and overshadowed the band organization. The importance of the tribal ceremonies in social integration can hardly be overestimated. Today the Sun Dance is perhaps the most important single factor in keeping these tribes from complete disintegration.[105] The symbolic factors in tribal organization are likewise important. Mooney is the only writer on the Cheyenne who has attempted to get at the symbolic basis of Cheyenne social organization. On the basis of a study of the band system, the camp circle, the society organization, and the council arrangement, he came to the conclusion that "Cheyenne tribal life was organized, not on a clan system, but on a ceremonial geographic basis, as determined by the four cardinal points."[106] This conclusion throws considerable light on both ritual practices and symbolism, as well as on social integration and organization.

Kinship in the Plains Area

In order to investigate problems by the comparative method it is necessary to classify a series of tribes in terms of their similarities and differences. While there are not sufficient data available to make an adequate classification of Plains tribes in terms of social integration or social structure, a preliminary classification of their kinship systems should be valuable in formulating various problems and in securing some insight into the important aspects of Plains life.

The majority of the tribes in the Plains area are organized on the basis of a camp circle composed of bands. Most of these tribes have a kinship system which is a variant of what might be called a "Generation" type--a type which is found in its simplest form among the Cheyenne and Arapaho. In the eastern Plains, mainly along the Missouri River, is found another type of social organization which is largely based on the village and clan. The tribes in this area emphasize the lineage principle in the classification of kindred and have variants of the Omaha and Crow types of kinship systems. None of these types is restricted to the Plains area, however; as we leave the Plains, a gradual series of changes takes place, leading eventually to systems based on different principles of classification and social behavior. These series are of considerable value in the study of historical and processual problems and in the study of correlated variations.

In the present paper we shall be primarily concerned with systems of the "Generation" type. The Omaha and Crow types (which I consider as two variants of the same type which might be called "Omaha-Crow") have been dealt with to some extent by both Lowie[107] and Lesser,[108] and will be considered only incidentally in this survey. The "Generation" type, as found in the Plains area, is characterized by a simple and coherent organization in which generation is emphasized, lineal and collateral relatives are merged, the range of relationship is rather wide but indefinite, the duties and obligations between relatives are organized (largely in terms of familiarity and respect), and marriage is outside the circle of blood-relations. In most of the tribes having this general type of kinship organization, the domestic or household group is an extended family based on matrilocal residence.

The Cheyenne and Arapaho kinship systems represent the simplest, and perhaps basic, form for the "Generation" type in the Plains;
the Gros Ventre varies only in that it has organized the range of relationships by means of formal clans and the family and local organizations have been modified somewhat. In the southern Plains, groups
such as the Kiowa-Apache and Kiowa seem to vary only slightly from
the Cheyenne and Arapaho pattern, differing mainly in their recognition of additional generations above and below the grandparental and
grandchild generations and in their greater use of self-reciprocal
terms and behavior. Otherwise the kinship systems are surprisingly
alike, both in terminology and in social behavior, and the households
are also organized largely in terms of matrilocal residence.[109] The
terminologies of the Wichita and Caddo in the southeastern Plains
suggest a kinship system much like that of the Kiowa-Apache, although
the Wichita, in particular, show some variation toward a "Hawaiian"
type. The Comanche kinship system is reported to be quite different
from the general Plains pattern, which is in keeping with its Plateau
affiliations.[110] The Southern Athabaskan tribes have been shown by
Opler[111] to have two main types of kinship systems which merge into
each other. The Lipan and Kiowa-Apache form one type with the Jica-
rilla, the latter varying somewhat toward a type represented in the
Chiricahua and Mescalero systems, in which generation is still emphasized and descent is still bilateral but lineal relatives are set
off from collateral ("non-classificatory"), the range of relationships
seems narrower, and the terminology and behavior patterns tend to be
self-reciprocal. These contrasting types are connected by a series
of intermediate systems, however, and all the tribes have an extended
family based on matrilocal residence and marry outside of blood-
relations.

Another variation on the "Generation" type is found among
the Dakota tribes. The kinship terminologies of the Dakota have been
considered as a basic type but are perhaps best viewed as variants
of the Cheyenne system. The Teton system, which is the best known,
differs terminologically in that cross-cousins are given separate
terms, but they are treated as if they were siblings. The cross-
cousin terms likewise seem fairly recent since Lesser[112] shows that
they are derived from the terms for siblings-in-law. The household
group seems based on an extended bilateral family, which varies in
size and composition, and the larger groupings are somewhat more
amorphous than the Cheyenne bands, but the kinship system, aside from
the terminological differences, matches the Cheyenne almost point
for point.[113] While we know less about the kinship systems of the

other Dakota tribes, including the Assiniboine, there is some probability that they had a similar kinship system. In the northern Plains
the Plains-Cree, Plains-Ojibway, and possibly the Blood and Sarsi
had terminologies which suggest the Dakota type. The Piegan, on the
other hand, seem to have had a kinship terminology which was intermediate between the Cheyenne and Arapaho system and the Plateau systems; here lineal relatives were separated from collateral (except
for the mother's sister), but all collateral relatives in ego's generation, and in the first ascending and descending generations, were
classed as "older" or "younger siblings."[114] Residence tended to be
patrilocal among the Blackfoot, and there was some tendency to patrilineal clans which represented local groups, as far as the men were
concerned.

To the northeast, the Ojibway, Montagnais, Naskapi, and various Cree groups had kinship systems based on cross-cousin marriage
in varying degrees.[115] While these systems still emphasize generation and bilateral descent, the range of relationships is much reduced, the elementary family is isolated in terminology and represents
the household group, and the social behavior of relatives is more
intensely organized and integrated than in the Plains. Here, again,
there seem to be intermediate types; the Plains-Cree and Plains-
Ojibway, and perhaps also the Dakota, form a bridge between the cross-
cousin marriage systems and systems of the Cheyenne and Arapaho type
in which marriage is outside the range of relationships. The variations of the "Generation" type in the Plains, along with a suggested
classification of the Omaha and Crow types,[116] are summarized in
Table 2.

From this brief survey certain problems emerge more clearly.
In the first place, diffusion as an explanation of similarities in
Plains kinship is inadequate; patterns of terminology and social
behavior do not diffuse very easily. Furthermore, the series outlined above end eventually in kinship systems based on quite different principles, in part at least. Our understanding of the factors
determining the choice of alternate principles of classification and
social behavior may very possibly grow out of an analysis of series
which can be controlled in one respect or another. But from the
standpoint of the Plains area it is perhaps more significant that
tribes coming into the Plains with *different* backgrounds and social
systems ended up with *similar* kinship systems. It seems probable that
the conditions of Plains life favored a rather amorphous and mobile
type of social organization which could vary to meet changing conditions.

TABLE 2

A PRELIMINARY CLASSIFICATION OF PLAINS KINSHIP SYSTEMS*

I. *"Generation" type*

   A. *Cheyenne subtype*
     1. Cheyenne
     2. Arapaho
     3. Gros Ventre

   B. *Kiowa-Apache subtype*
     1. Kiowa-Apache
     2. Kiowa
     3. Lipan (?)
     4. Jicarilla (transitional)
     5. Caddo (?)
     6. Wichita (?)

   C. *Dakota subtype*
     1. Dakota tribes
       a) Teton
       b) Yankton
       c) Assiniboine
       d) Etc.
     2. Plains-Cree (transitional)
     3. Plains-Ojibway (transitional)
     4. Blood (?)
     5. Sarsi (?)

   D. *Piegan subtype*
     1. Piegan (transitional)

II. *"Lineage" type*

   A. *Omaha subtype*
     1. Central Siouan tribes
       a) Omaha
       b) Ponca
       c) Kansa
       d) Osage
       e) Iowa
       f) Oto
       g) Winnebago
     2. Central Algonkian tribes
       a) Menominee
       b) Sauk
       c) Fox
       d) Kickapoo
       e) Illinois
       f) Etc.

   B. *Crow subtype*
     1. Mandan
     2. Hidatsa
     3. Crow (transitional)
     4. Pawnee (transitional)
     5. Arikara (?)

---

*This classification is a revision of Morgan (*Systems of Consanguinity*) and Spier (*Distribution of Kinship Systems*). Dr. Spier's classification was based primarily on the terminology for cross-cousins; the present classification attempts to enlarge the criteria used.

Certain of these conditions have been indicated above--the uncertain character of subsistence and the need for protection. Leadership was also of uncertain and varying quality. Perhaps the outstanding adjustment to these conditions in the Plains is seen in the tremendous importance of the relationship of brothers. Everywhere in the Plains brothers formed the most dependable and solid group; among the Dakota "if a man has no brothers or cousins (and this was possible in the days of wholesale death from war parties) he says, 'I am related to nobody.'"[117] Here is a basis for the wide recognition which brotherhood receives in the kinship system. The Cheyenne and Arapaho extend the relationship to all cousins, and fictitiously extend it through the institution of "friends" and by means of common society affiliations. The Kiowa and Kiowa-Apache do likewise, a group of brothers assuming special importance among the Kiowa. We have seen that the Dakota consider cross-cousins as "brothers," even though they are segregated in the terminology, and there is some evidence that the Plains-Cree and Plains-Ojibway likewise attached more importance to the concept of "brothers" than did their relatives to the northeast. The Piegan have carried this principle even farther, so that all collateral relatives, not only in ego's generation but in the first ascending and descending generations as well, are considered "brothers" (or "sisters"). The Crow Indians furnish a crucial instance. Fundamentally, their system of kinship seems to have been in the process of changing from a pure Crow type, such as their close relatives the Hidatsa possess, to a "Generation" type, such as the Cheyenne and Arapaho have developed.[118] Part of this process was the extension of the sibling relationship to cross-cousins. Both the Crow and the Hidatsa also extended the term for brother to the mother's brother and sister's son, though the Mandan preferred to use separate terms.

It is possible, therefore, that the relationship of brothers, because of its importance in Plains life, was one of the factors modifying kinship systems in the direction of a "Generation" type. If this is so, this factor and others may be the important agents in bringing about observed uniformities, and hence it seems worth while to look for and isolate them, rather than to attribute the uniformity to simple diffusion.

Another important set of problems is concerned with the Northeastern Algonkian tribes. The Naskapi have a functioning cross-cousin marriage system, as do certain of the Cree and Ojibway bands. The Plains-Cree and Plains-Ojibway keep the same system of marriage but marry more distant cross-cousins. The Cheyenne and Arapaho marry completely outside of the range of blood-relationships. Here is a series in which there is a progressive widening of relationships by marriage. Dr. Hallowell has suggested that this may be the result of acculturational influences--undoubtedly an important factor. But in a wider context there is some evidence that the conditions of Plains life encouraged a wider integration and gradually brought it about, regardless of the influence of missionaries or traders. If this may be accepted as a working hypothesis, it has some bearing on the Dakota system. It seems probable that the Dakota kinship system was formerly based on cross-cousin marriage,[119] but that under the influence of Plains life (and contacts) it was shifting to a "Generation" type, as exemplified by the Cheyenne. The use of "brother-in-law" terms plus affixes for the cross-cousins, while behaving toward them as if they were "brothers," is intelligible on this basis.

These few examples indicate that it is possible to gain con-

siderable insight into both the historical and the social aspects of
kinship by means of a controlled comparative approach. Working hypotheses can be set up and tested against field work, since it is
still possible to get detailed information on kinship for many tribes.
Where historical data are available for earlier periods, studies of
social change and the factors involved may be made.[120] While such
an approach does not answer all the problems we are interested in,
it does give us insight and information on many of them.

NOTES

[1]The following paper represents a revision and condensation of a
report on field work carried out among the Southern Cheyenne and Arapaho in Oklahoma during the summer of 1933, as part of a project in
North American social organization directed by Professor A. R. Radcliffe-Brown. Funds were provided by the department of anthropology
of the University of Chicago, for which grateful acknowledgment is
made.

[2]The following brief account of the early history of the Cheyenne
and Arapaho is summarized from Grinnell, Mooney, Scott, Swanton,
Kroeber, and Curtis (see Bibliography for references).

[3]This division was based partly on facilities for trade and partly
on preference.

[4]Kroeber, *The Arapaho*, I, 4-5.

[5]Kroeber, *Ethnology of the Gros Ventre*, p. 145.

[6]Cf. Grinnell, *The Cheyenne Indians*, I, 90-93, and Mooney, *The
Cheyenne Indians*, pp. 408-10.

[7]See Kroeber, *The Arapaho*, I, 5-8.

[8]See Kroeber, *Ethnology of the Gros Ventre*, pp. 147-48.

[9]Cf. Grinnell, *op. cit.*, II, 48-87; Dorsey, *The Cheyenne*, I, 15-
30; and Lowie, *Plains Indian Age-Societies*, pp. 894-902.

[10]Cf. Kroeber, *The Arapaho*, III, 153-54; Curtis, *The North American Indian*, Vol. VI, Appendix.

[11]Cf. Kroeber, *Ethnology of the Gros Ventre*, pp. 227 ff., and
Lowie, *op. cit.*, pp. 933 ff.

[12]Curtis, *The North American Indian*, Vol. V, Appendix.

[13]I am primarily indebted to Professor A. R. Radcliffe-Brown for
the conception of social structure which follows.

[14]Compare Radcliffe-Brown, *Social Organization of Australian
Tribes*, p. 11, and Linton, *The Study of Man*, chap. vii.

[15]The kinship system is still in operation among the older people
so that it is possible to get rather detailed and accurate information about the terminology and social usages. Independent accounts
were secured from Kish Hawkins and his mother, John Otterby, Coyote
Barelegs, and Mrs. Bird White Bear for the Cheyenne; and from Bird
White Bear and Jessie Rowlodge for the Arapaho.

[16]Kroeber, *The Arapaho*, I, 9-10.

[17]The differentiation between the term for daughter-in-law and
the term for niece is particularly subtle but was quite definite in
the minds of my informants. Kroeber (*ibid.*) makes no distinction
between these terms for either the Arapaho or the Gros Ventre;
Michelson (*Some Arapaho Kinship Terms and Social Usages*, p. 137)

found a similar distinction but considers the terms to have different stems.

[18]*Systems of Consanguinity*, Tables, No. 53.

[19]*Ibid.*, p. 215.

[20]Such a classification is suggested by Morgan's classing of the father's sister's son's wife as "sister-in-law." Segar, who knew the Cheyenne in their early reservation days, says: "They regard cousins the same as brothers and sisters and they distinguish them from their own brothers and sisters by calling them their 'far' brother or 'near' brother" (in Perry [ed.], *The Indians' Friend, John H. Segar*, p. 862).

[21]*Op. cit.*, I, 157-58.

[22]*Op. cit.*, Tables, No. 56.

[23]*Loc. cit.* Curtis is apparently referring to the northern divisions. This classification is characteristic of the Piegan and may therefore be the result of interaction.

[24]Kroeber, *Ethnology of the Gros Ventre*, p. 147.

[25]When children are adopted, "parent" and "child" terms are usually employed, but if a wife's brother's or husband's sister's child is adopted, "nephew" and "niece" terms must be employed "to keep the relationship right."

[26]*The Arapaho*, III, 160. In both tribes it is also common to call any old man "grandfather," even though no relationship is known to exist.

[27]At a Sun Dance encampment one of my Arapaho informants claimed relatives in practically every family group present.

[28]The necessity of condensing this paper makes it impossible to give much illustrative material. However, Grinnell, Mooney, Kroeber, and Dorsey supply scattered illustrations of kinship behavior, and Michelson's *Narrative of a Southern Cheyenne Woman* and *Narrative of an Arapaho Woman* are exceedingly valuable in this respect and supplement the material here presented.

[29]Physical punishment is seldom employed. "Someone on earth-- whoever gave you your child--is watching you. If you hurt the child he may take it back" (Cheyenne woman).

[30]"For distant 'fathers' the feeling is the only important part-- they don't have much to do--they can help you at marriage," explained a Cheyenne informant. An Arapaho, after outlining the attitude of respect for the father, indicated that "it was just the same for distant 'fathers,' when you see them you have that thought."

[31]The affection of brothers and sisters for one another is largely expressed in their relations to one another's children.

[32]According to Michelson (*Some Arapaho Kinship Terms*, p. 139), if a younger brother does have intercourse with his older brother's wife and the latter finds out about it, he will do nothing, saying that the younger brother can do what he likes with her.

[33]According to Grinnell (*op. cit.*, I, 145), "After a girl had been married . . . . she might still make use of the protective string for a period of from ten to fifteen days. The husband would respect the string for that length of time but usually not longer." Sexual relations were also surrounded by a number of restrictions.

[34]*Narrative of a Southern Cheyenne Woman*, p. 8.

[35]For the relations of husband and wife in regard to polygyny, adultery, separation, mourning, etc., see the next section.

[36] Kroeber (*Arapaho*, I, 18) mentions the custom of young people going around with drinking water for the elders.

[37] Michelson (*Some Arapaho Kinship Terms*, p. 139) states that grandparents may talk vulgarly to their grandchildren, especially the grandson.

[38] The modern peyote cult conflicts in part with the older ceremonial organization because its requirements involve a disregard for the rules regulating behavior toward ceremonial "grandparents," particularly in regard to passing in front of them.

[39] The Arapaho say: "The father is a closer relation than the father-in-law--you can disappoint a son but not a son-in-law."

[40] This relationship is still maintained to a considerable extent under present reservation conditions.

[41] Kroeber, *Ethnology of the Gros Ventre*, p. 180.

[42] Cf. Grinnell, *op. cit.*, I, 147-48.

[43] According to Kroeber (*The Arapaho*, I, 11) they may not talk obscenely to each other. This may be true for the Cheyenne also.

[44] Because of the brother-sister restriction a sister can't say much to her brother's wife in his presence, but the brother's wife is under no such handicap.

[45] Informants vary as to the extent to which this was carried, but in the old days sexual intercourse was probably permitted. During the Sun Dance in particular there was a period of license in which such relations took place between brothers-in-law and sisters-in-law (*ibid.*, p. 15).

[46] Michelson, *Narrative of an Arapaho Woman*, p. 596 n.

[47] Michelson's Cheyenne narrator mentions that her mother watched over her conduct after marriage in order to prevent her husband's people from gossiping (*Narrative of a Southern Cheyenne Woman*, p. 7).

[48] See the accounts in Grinnell, *op. cit.*, I, 150, and Mooney, *op. cit.*, p. 416. Grinnell indicates that a sister was often given to a "friend" as a wife.

[49] See the detailed accounts in Kroeber, *The Arapaho*, I, 12-15, and *Ethnology of the Gros Ventre*, pp. 180-81; Grinnell, *op. cit.*, I, 127-58; and Michelson, *Narrative of a Southern Cheyenne Woman*, pp. 5-7, and *Narrative of an Arapaho Woman*, pp. 602-4.

[50] Segar (*Cheyenne Marriage Customs*, pp. 298-301) indicates the range as extending as far as sixteenth cousins for the Cheyenne, but this would vary. Kroeber (*The Arapaho*, I, 16) says the Arapaho were not strict about distant relatives, providing the relationship was not discovered until after the marriage.

[51] Since kinship is extended to clans, the regulation is still essentially by kinship.

[52] This is a Cheyenne statement. Grinnell (*op. cit.*, I, 130) indicates that elopements were rare in the old days, especially if a girl had been given to her brother to dispose of. Michelson (*Narrative of an Arapaho Woman*, p. 602) indicates a similar situation among the Arapaho.

[53] Michelson's narrator (*Narrative of an Arapaho Woman*, p. 603) intimates that this was the usual Arapaho marriage, but the other types occur also. Some of my informants indicated that this form was rather rare.

[54] Kroeber, *Ethnology of the Gros Ventre*, p. 180.

[55]At present this is the commonest form of marriage, but modern conditions have disturbed parental control.

[56]Kroeber (*The Arapaho*, I, 12-13) intimates that this is because the daughters do not know how to cook yet. At large gatherings the men of the camp, along with their guests, eat apart from the women.

[57]The Cheyenne say that they do not give distant "sisters" in such cases because they are in a different camp.

[58]A whole series of customs has developed around this situation. Kroeber (*ibid.*, pp. 13-14) indicates that the husband can't enter the tent where his wife and her lover are because he might harm them. A Cheyenne husband could destroy some of the lover's property. Also, among the Cheyenne, in case a husband did not get full return in the marriage exchange, he had a claim on the wife's family. A chief, however, was expected to ignore his wife's running away.

[59]Male relatives-in-law exchanged similar products; female relatives-in-law exchanged clothing for household furnishings. There is also another important series of exchanges connected with the Sun Dance.

[60]Among the Cheyenne the father fastens the afterbirth, the "human part" of the child, in a tree; among the Arapaho this seems to have been done by a female relative of the mother.

[61]Kroeber, *Ethnology of the Gros Ventre*, p. 182.

[62]The above statements were obtained from a single informant and could not be verified as a general belief. Twins had a special position among the Cheyenne, being considered powerful and riding jackrabbits for horses. The Arapaho had a vague belief that twins were powerful and must be treated alike.

[63]A Cheyenne father would invite a "friend" to pierce the ears ceremonially, paying him a horse in return. The "friend" had to be qualified through counting a coup, or else had to delegate the job to someone who was so qualified.

[64]Kroeber, *The Arapaho*, I, 15.

[65]Kroeber, *Ethnology of the Gros Ventre*, p. 221.

[66]*Op. cit.*, II, 49. Certain societies selected four girls as honorary members.

[67]Kroeber, *The Arapaho*, III, 151-226. Women had a single parallel society.

[68]Kroeber, *Ethnology of the Gros Ventre*, p. 232. The Gros Ventre had a woman's society.

[69]According to Kroeber, *The Arapaho*, I, 11.

[70]Kroeber, *Ethnology of the Gros Ventre*, p. 181.

[71]The Medicine Arrow ceremony formerly was performed in order to wipe away the stain of a murder from the tribe.

[72]One Cheyenne informant explained that the kinship system was "just like three horizontal lines."

[73]Linguistic authorities such as Sapir and Michelson do not agree on the reconstructions for these terms; hence a linguistic analysis does not throw much light on the situation at present.

[74]A similar situation seems to exist in several tribes in the Plains and adjoining areas, and a comparative study of these might throw some light on the problem.

[75]*Primitive Society*, pp. 162-66, also p. 114.

[76]*Some Aspects of Siouan Kinship*, p. 571.

[77]The sororate is not specifically mentioned for the Gros Ventre but can be inferred from some of the myths, and probably was practiced.

[78]"These principles are not to be regarded as causal agents, but any investigation of general causal processes, as distinct from what are sometimes called causes in history, cannot be undertaken without a classification of social systems on such a basis" (personal communication from Professor Radcliffe-Brown).

[79]For an analysis of these principles for another type of kinship system see Radcliffe-Brown, *op. cit.*, Part III.

[80]*Primitive Society*, pp. 125-26.

[81]Lowie (*ibid.*, pp. 157-66) has pointed out that the sib may grow out of types of residence, but in the case of the Gros Ventre this is not likely because the evidence favors matrilocal residence.

[82]*Methods of Ethnology*, p. 317.

[83]*Primitive Society*, p. 104.

[84]*Ibid.*, pp. 101-2.

[85]Tax has suggested, on the basis of Fox material, that psychologically respect may take two forms: (1) a "teacher-student" relationship in which social distance is emphasized and (2) a "shame" relationship between blood-relatives of different sex. Joking represents a release from an emotionally uncertain situation, in part, and involves the psychology of laughter.

[86]The father is primarily responsible for the training of his son and hence usually exacts more obedience from the son than he does from a daughter; the mother, vice versa.

[87]It is interesting in this connection to note that among the Teton Dakota, who had an extended bilateral family organization, the daughter-in-law avoided her father-in-law and, to a lesser extent, her mother-in-law, to the same degree that a man avoided his mother-in-law and father-in-law (cf. Mead, *Cooperation and Competition among Primitive Peoples*, pp. 391, 394, 401).

[88]There is some slight conflict involved between their "social equivalence" and the actual differences in age which give some authority to the older brother.

[89]The Cheyenne and Arapaho have also organized the satirical sanction around the relationship of siblings-in-law for purposes of social control, but this involves another system (see Provinse's paper on "The Underlying Sanctions of Plains Indian Culture" in this volume for an analysis of the sanction systems of the Plains).

[90]Where the structural arrangement of the social group is quite different, as among the Western Pueblos, for example, the regulation may be accomplished in quite different ways (viz., Eggan, *The Social Organization of the Western Pueblos*).

[91]*Social Life of the Crow Indians*, pp. 204-6, 213-15.

[92]Radcliffe-Brown, *Andaman Islanders*, p. ix. I am indebted to Professor Radcliffe-Brown for this conception of social integration.

[93]In 1862 the Arapaho were reported to have had 380 lodges and a population of 2,800 which averages 7 to 8 persons to a lodge. A household would normally have 2 or more lodges.

[94]Grinnell reports this as the native explanation for matrilocal residence (*op. cit.*, I, 91).

[95] *Op. cit.*, p. 410. The Suhtai generally married among themselves, even after incorporation into the tribe. In recent years, when the "Dog Soldiers" coalesced with one of the bands and thus obtained a place in the camp circle, they tended to intermarry, provided they were not relatives (according to Grinnell, *op. cit.*, II, 63).

[96] The Cheyenne bands average around 300 to 350 members, and the Arapaho were probably about the same. The Gros Ventre clans, on the other hand, were much smaller, averaging only about 100 members in 1885.

[97] The important problem of the relation of the local group to the clan among the Gros Ventre can perhaps be settled by further field work. The correlation elsewhere in America of patrilineal local groups and definite hunting territories is important in this connection.

[98] Grinnell, *op. cit.*, I, 90-91. There is no strong evidence for a former clan system, however, and it is possible that his informants were rationalizing the past.

[99] The integrative effect of the society system is thus very much like that of a nonlocalized patrilineal clan system, as far as males are concerned.

[100] The use of "older brother" and "younger brother" terms between the members of alternate societies is consonant with this situation. Lowie (*Plains Indian Age-Societies*, p. 951) finds no relationship between kinship usages and societal relationships among the Arapaho, in contrast to the Hidatsa, but my evidence, while incomplete, indicates that the Arapaho system was much the same as the Hidatsa in this respect.

[101] Among the Cheyenne the camp circle was "likened to a big tipi with the entrance facing east," according to Dorsey (*op. cit.*, II, 62). This symbolic conception of the tribe as one large family has many expressions, particularly in the ceremonies.

[102] There are excellent accounts of the Sun Dance in Dorsey, Kroeber, and Grinnell (see Bibliography).

[103] Kroeber, *The Arapaho*, III, 151.

[104] The Cheyenne council was composed of a body of forty-four chiefs representing the various bands in the camp circle. The Arapaho and Gros Ventre political organizations are not so well known but seem to have been much simpler. Dr. Opler informs me that Cheyenne society chiefs resigned upon their election to the council.

[105] Recently the Sun Dance has stimulated interest in the old organizations, so that in 1933 the Cheyenne attempted to revive the council of chiefs and increased the membership of the warrior societies.

[106] *Op. cit.*, p. 411. The points are northeast, northwest, southeast, and southwest.

[107] *The Omaha and Crow Kinship Terminologies*, pp. 103-8.

[108] *Op. cit.*, pp. 563-71. Both Lowie and Lesser attempt to explain the kinship terminologies in terms of associated factors such as clans and types of marriage.

[109] See McAllister, "Kiowa-Apache Social Organization," in this volume. I am indebted to Donald Collier for information concerning the Kiowa.

[110] Dr. Ralph Linton is preparing a report on the Comanche.

[111] *The Kinship Systems of the Southern Athabaskan-Speaking Tribes*, pp. 620-33.

[112] *Op. cit.*, p. 564.

[113]Cf. the excellent account in Mead, *op. cit.*, chap. xii.

[114]Michelson, *Notes on the Piegan System*, pp. 320-34.

[115]Dr. Hallowell has kindly sent me a manuscript dealing with this area, Strong has outlined the Naskapi system (*Cross-Cousin Marriage and the Culture of the Northeast Algonkian*), and Ruth Landes has summarized the Ojibway in Mead, *op. cit.*, pp. 87-126.

[116]The problem of the Crow and Omaha types will be taken up in another paper; the relation between these types and the "Generation" types is an important but difficult problem. For a discussion of the Omaha type see Tax's paper on the Fox system in this volume.

[117]Mead, *op. cit.*, p. 394.

[118]An analysis of the Crow material suggests that the Crow pattern persists in the nonvocative terminology, whereas the vocative terminology tends to be bilateral in character. The importance of a wide comparative study is clear in attempting to understand such transitional systems.

[119]This assumption has been made before by Rivers and others; in terms of this analysis it seems a useful working hypothesis.

[120]See Hallowell, *Recent Changes in the Kinship Terminology of the Abenaki*, and Eggan, *Historical Changes in the Choctaw Kinship System*, for examples of such studies.

BIBLIOGRAPHY

The following abbreviations are used:

AA — American Anthropologist
AAA-M — American Anthropological Association, Memoirs
AMNH-AP — American Museum of Natural History, Anthropological Papers
AMNH-B — American Museum of Natural History, Bulletin
FMNH-PAS — Field Museum of Natural History, Publications, Anthropological Series
ICA — International Congress of Americanists
JAFL — Journal of American Folklore
SI-CK — Smithsonian Institution, Contributions to Knowledge
SI-MC — Smithsonian Institution, Miscellaneous Collections

Boas, Frans. The Methods of Ethnology (AA, n.s., 22, 1920, 311-21).

Curtis, E. S. The North American Indian (Cambridge, 1909-11, Vols. V-VI).

Dorsey, George A. The Cheyenne, I: Ceremonial Organization (FMNH-PAS, 9, 1905, No. 1).

————. The Cheyenne, II: The Sun Dance (FMNH-PAS, 9, 1905, No. 2).

Eggan, Fred. The Kinship System and Social Organization of the Western Pueblos with Especial Reference to the Hopi (Ph.D. thesis, University of Chicago, Chicago, 1933).

————. Historical Changes in the Choctaw Kinship System (AA, n.s., 39, 1937, 34-52).

Grinnell, George B. The Cheyenne Indians (New Haven, 1923, 2 vols.).

Hallowell, A. Irving. Recent Changes in the Kinship Terminology of the St. Francis Abenaki (ICA, 22, 1928, 97-145).

Kroeber, A. L. The Arapaho, I: General Description (AMNH-B, 18, 1902, part 1).

————. The Arapaho, III: Ceremonial Organization (AMNH-B, 18, 1904, part 3).

—————. Ethnology of the Gros Ventre (AMNH-AP, 1, 1908, part 4).

Lesser, A. Some Aspects of Siouan Kinship (ICA, 23, 1930, 563-71).

Linton, Ralph. The Study of Man (New York, 1936).

Lowie, R. H. Social Life of the Crow Indians (AMNH-AP, 9, 1912, part 2).

—————. Plains Indian Age-Societies: Historical and Comparative Summary (AMNH-AP, 11, 1916).

—————. Primitive Society (New York, 1920).

—————. The Omaha and Crow Kinship Terminologies (ICA, 24, 1930, 102-8, reprint).

[McAllister, J. Gilbert. Kiowa-Apache Social Organization. In Social Anthropology of North American Tribes, Fred Eggan, ed. (Chicago, 1952, pp. 99-169).]

Mead, Margaret (ed.). Cooperation and Competition among Primitive Peoples (New York, 1937).

Michelson, T. Notes on the Piegan System of Consanguinity (Holmes Anniversary Volume, 1916, pp. 320-34).

—————. The Narrative of a Southern Cheyenne Woman (SI-MC, 87, 1932, No. 5).

—————. The Narrative of an Arapaho Woman (AA, n.s., 35, 1933, 595-610).

—————. Some Arapaho Kinship Terms and Social Usages (AA, n.s., 36, 1934, 137-39).

Mooney, James. The Cheyenne Indians (AAA-M, 1, 1907, part 6).

Morgan, Lewis H. Systems of Consanguinity and Affinity of the Human Family (SI-CK, 17, 1871).

Opler, Morris E. The Kinship Systems of the Southern Athabaskan-Speaking Tribes (AA, n.s., 38, 1936, 620-33).

Perry, D. W. (ed.). The Indian's Friend, John H. Segar (Chronicles of Oklahoma, 11, 1933, No. 2).

[Provinse, John H. The Underlying Sanctions of Plains Indian Culture. In Social Organization of North American Tribes, Fred Eggan, ed. (Chicago, 1952, pp. 341-74).]

Radcliffe-Brown, A. R. The Social Organization of Australian Tribes ("Oceania" Monographs, No. 1, Melbourne, 1931).

—————. The Andaman Islanders (Cambridge, 1933, 2d ed.).

Scott, H. L. Early History and Names of the Arapaho (AA, n.s., 9, 1907, 545-60).

Segar, J. H. Cheyenne Marriage Customs (JAFL, 7, 1898, 298-301).

Strong, W. D. Cross-Cousin Marriage and the Culture of the Northeast Algonkian (AA, n.s., 31, 1929, 277-88).

Swanton, John R. Some Neglected Data Bearing on Cheyenne, Chippewa, and Dakota History (AA, n.s., 32, 1930, 156-60).

[Tax, Sol. The Social Organization of the Fox Indians. In Social Organization of North American Tribes, Fred Eggan, ed. (Chicago, 1952, pp. 243-82).]

3

HISTORICAL CHANGES IN THE CHOCTAW KINSHIP SYSTEM[1]

1937

I

The Southeast furnishes an interesting field for studies in social
organization. Here is to be found a bewildering array of unilateral
institutions, territorial groupings, and social classes which cross-
cut one another in various ways. Most historical and comparative
studies have concerned themselves with these more formal groupings,
largely ignoring the underlying kinship systems.

The importance of kinship systems, particularly in relation
to other aspects of social organization, is beginning to be apparent.
The present paper, while presenting an instance of historical change
in the field of kinship which has important theoretical implications,
also attempts to furnish the basis for a preliminary classification
of Southeastern kinship systems.

One of the important problems in social organization is an
adequate classification of kinship systems according to types. Such
a classification seems essential for either historical or comparative studies of social organization. Dr Leslie Spier has worked out
a preliminary classification of kinship systems for North America
into eight types, largely on the basis of the terminology used for
cross cousins. In regard to two of these types he finds the terminology indicative of a more comprehensive classification of relatives:

> Cross cousin terminology also offers a clue for the discrim-
> ination of the Omaha and Crow types. The first class together
> the mother's brother and his descendants through males: their
> daughters are always called mothers. The paternal cross cousins
> are then conceptual equivalents. Similarly systems of the Crow
> type class the father's sister with her female descendants
> through females and their sons with the father. Again, equiva-
> lent forms are used for the maternal cross cousins. That is,
> both systems ignore differences of generation in one or the
> other type of unilateral descent.[2]

If we look at the distribution of the Crow and Omaha types we find it to be somewhat irregular, though within rather widely scattered areas the distribution tends to be continuous.[3] Furthermore, if we examine various Crow and Omaha kinship systems we find a series of variations on each pattern, so that often there is some difficulty in deciding whether a given kinship system is a Crow type or something else.

II

A preliminary survey of Southeastern social organization indicated such a situation in regard to the various kinship systems studied. While Spier has classified the Choctaw, Chickasaw, Creek, Cherokee, Timucua, and (less probably) Yuchi as belonging to the Crow type,[4] an inspection of the source materials led to some preliminary doubts as to the correctness of this classification.

The formal social organization of the Southeastern tribes seems to have been based on the matrilineal clan, but otherwise few generalizations may be made at present. The Choctaw,[5] for example, had matrilineal exogamous moieties divided into non-totemic clans, a territorial division into three or four groups of "towns," and four social classes. The Chickasaw,[6] close linguistic relatives of the Choctaw, had matrilineal totemic clans with a dual-division which was not exogamous, along with various local groupings. The Creek,[7] just to the east, in addition to the "Upper" and "Lower" tribal divisions, had numerous matrilineal totemic clans grouped into phratries and moieties, with a further dual-division into "red" and "white" towns, associated with "war" and "peace," respectively. The Cherokee[8] had a simpler organization: matrilineal totemic clans which were exogamous, and possibly grouped into seven phratries. The Yuchi[9] had matrilineal totemic clans which were exogamous and which varied in rank; these were cut across by a patrilineal division of the men into "chiefs" and "warriors," associated with "peace" and "war," respectively. This dual patrilineal organization tended toward endogamy in that a "chief" preferred his daughter to marry other "chiefs." The Natchez[10] apparently combined a matrilineal clan system with a system of social classes, the whole regulated by definite rules of marriage. In addition the Natchez had a dual organization of "red warriors" and "white warriors." The Chitimacha seem to have had totemic clans and endogamous classes which approached true castes.

The kinship systems of the Southeastern tribes are all "classificatory" in that the father's brother is classed with the father, and the mother's sister with the mother, as far as terminology is concerned. In the following chart (fig. 1) we have outlined the kinship structures of the Southeastern tribes for which there is adequate data, in terms of the patterns of descent from the father's sister. The Crow type (A) is well known. Both Spier[11] and Lowie[12] agree that its essential characteristic is the classification of the father's sister's female descendants through females with the father's sister, and their sons with the father, thus giving a definite descent pattern.[13] Lowie considers this classification an "overriding of the generation principle in favor of the clan or lineage principle."[14]

If we now examine the kinship structures of the Southeastern tribes with special reference to the pattern of descent from the father's sister, we find some interesting variations. In the Choctaw kinship system[15] (B), for example, the pattern seems to be "turned around." Here the father's sister's son and *his* descendants through *males* are classed as "fathers," whereas the children of the father's sister's daughter (who is classed with the father's sister) become "brothers" and "sisters." Morgan is quite explicit on this point:

> My father's sister's son is my father, *Ah'-kĭ*, whether *Ego* be a male or female; his son is my father again; the son of the latter is also my father; and this relationship theoretically continues downward in the male line indefinitely. The analogue of this is to be found in the infinite series of uncles among the Missouri nations, applied to the lineal male descendants of my mother's brother.16

This is clearly something quite different from the typical Crow pattern of descent.

There are some interesting variations in the other tribes. The Chickasaw pattern of descent (C) as given by Morgan[17] is identical with that of the Crow type, except for the minor variation of "little father" for the father's sister's daughter's son. Swanton,[18] however, gives "father" as an alternative to "brother" for the father's sister's son's son. The Creek kinship structure[19] (D) furnishes another pattern of descent. Here the descendants of the father's sister, in *both* the male and female lines, are classed as "father" or "grandmother." Hence the children of the father's sister's son are called "father" and "grandmother" rather than "brother" and "sister," as in the normal Crow pattern. The Cherokee kinship structure[20] (E) gives a pattern of descent from the father's sister much like that of the Chickasaw, except that the father's sister's son's son is regularly classed with the father, as are his male descendants through males. Information concerning the Yuchi kinship system (F) is difficult to interpret. We have no early accounts, but Speck[21] indicates that the father's sister was classed with the

A. "CROW" TYPE

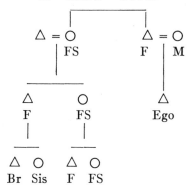

B. CHOCTAW PATTERN

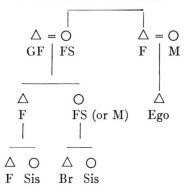

C. CHICKASAW PATTERN

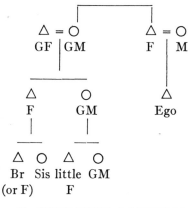

D. CREEK PATTERN

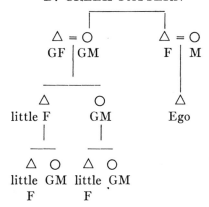

E. CHEROKEE PATTERN

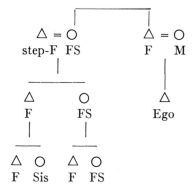

F. YUCHI PATTERN

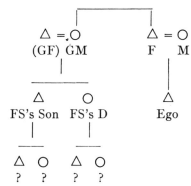

Fig. 1. Kinship Structures in the Southeast. Δ is male and o is female; Ego is male in each case. The equal sign indicates marriage. English equivalents are used for the native terms: F, M, GF, GM, FS, Br, Sis, etc., standing for father, mother, grandfather, grandmother, father's sister, brother, and sister, respectively. For sources see the text.

grandmother, while her children were called by descriptive terms.
Recent information[22] indicates an Omaha pattern of descent, the mother's brother's children being classed as "mother's brother" and "little mother," with the father's sister's children, reciprocally, being
"nephew" and "niece," male speaking, or "little son" and "little
daughter," female speaking. Information concerning the kinship systems of the Natchez and other Gulf Coast tribes is too fragmentary
to be of much value. The Natchez, according to Swanton,[23] classified
the father's sister with the grandmother. While no information is
available concerning the terminology employed for her descendants,
other features of the system, e.g., the classification of the brother's children as "children," male speaking, and "grandchildren,"
female speaking, and the sister's children as "nephew" and "niece,"
male speaking, and "children," female speaking, closely resemble
those found in the tribes mentioned above.[24]

III

On the basis of this preliminary survey it is possible to formulate
some of the problems involved. One of the important problems is:
do these patterns of descent represent new fundamental types of kinship systems or are they simply variations from a Crow type? If
they are fundamental types they are unique; the writer is not aware
of other kinship systems with these patterns of descent. If we examine the variants we find it possible to arrange them in a series
between the Crow and Choctaw types: the Chickasaw have practically
a pure Crow type, the Cherokee vary slightly, the Creek are intermediate, while the Choctaw have an almost completely reversed line
of descent. All of these tribes had a similar culture, resided in
the same area, were removed to Indian Territory under similar conditions, and were subjected to similar influences while there. This
suggests that the variations found may represent historical changes.
A further problem may be set up: if these are variants from a Crow
type, do they represent a series brought about by the action of some
common acculturation process, or are they merely "random," the separate results of unrelated circumstances?

These wider problems grew out of an interest in the Choctaw
kinship system. On the basis of a preliminary study the writer had
come to a tentative conclusion: the Choctaw system probably represented a pure Crow type which had altered under the stress of missionary and governmental activities. To *prove* this it would be necessary to find the older kinship system in operation in some relatively uninfluenced region, or to find an earlier account of the kinship system.[25] Morgan thought highly of his Choctaw schedules. The

Reverends Byington and Edwards collaborated on one, Copeland furnished the other; these missionaries had long resided among the Choctaw and knew their language and customs. Furthermore the two independent schedules checked remarkably well. Hence they must be accepted as basic data--as representing the Choctaw kinship system as it was in 1860.[26]

In 1933, on the advice of Dr John R. Swanton, the writer visited the old Choctaw country in an attempt to find some traces of the assumed older kinship system among the Bogue Chito and other groups which had remained in Mississippi following the general removal of the Choctaw to Indian Territory in the 1830's. This quest was completely unsuccessful, though a considerable body of contemporary material was gathered. The results, where they had any bearing, merely confirmed those presented by Morgan and Swanton.

Later in the summer, while studying Cheyenne and Arapaho social organization, the writer found in the "Chronicles of Oklahoma" the text of a speech which John Edwards made to the students of the University of California about 1880, outlining the *earlier* social organization of the Choctaw.[27] This is the same Edwards who collaborated with Byington in furnishing the basic schedule for Morgan; when the Civil War broke out in the next year he was forced to leave and went to reside in California. In this speech (edited by Dr J. R. Swanton) we find the following statements concerning the older Choctaw kinship system:

> A third important principle was that kinship was not lost by remoteness. This involved a very peculiar system of nomenclature. For instance, with them, my father's brothers are all my fathers, and my mother's sisters are all my mothers, and their children are my brothers and sisters; but my mother's brother is my uncle, and his sons and daughters are mine; and my father's sister is my aunt, her son is my father, her daughter is my aunt, and *her* daughter is my aunt, and *her* daughter is my aunt, and so on, as far as it is possible to go. This is what they call *aunts* in a row. The farthest removed of one's kindred by consanguinity are aunt, uncle, nephew, and niece. The line of relationship, after turning aside thus far, returns into the direct line, and becomes that of father to son, or grandfather to grandson. To us it seems a very complicated system.[28]

Here is clear, unequivocal, documentary proof that the Choctaw formerly had a Crow type of kinship system.

There is good evidence, then, of a definite change in the Choctaw kinship system from the time of removal in the 1830's to the time when Morgan collected the schedules in 1860. Can the influences affecting the Choctaw from the time of removal to the Civil War be historically controlled? Fortunately this question may be answered in the affirmative; Grant Foreman[29] and Miss Debo[30] have both assem-

bled and surveyed the available documentary evidence for precisely
this period, 1830-1860.

The Choctaw were subjected to longer and more intensive acculturational influences than were the Chickasaw, Creek, or Cherokee.
Missions were established among them as early as 1819. They were the
first tribe from the Southeast to be removed to Indian Territory;
they set up a new system of government on the model of our territorial governments; they early established a school system and encouraged education. Their leaders were more friendly to attempts to al-
ter the old ways of life in favor of white ways.

There are many statements in Foreman[31] indicating the efforts--
and success--of missionaries, teachers, and government agents in
changing the mode of life of the Choctaw. The fact that women worked
in the fields and that a father (in accordance with the matrilineal
system of inheritance) failed to provide for his own children, particularly worried the missionaries. There were introduced new regulations in regard to land which emphasized the position of the man as
head of the family; by others leaders no longer represented the clan
but the male membership of the district, being elected by adult male
voters. Marriage was regulated by law, and widows were entitled to
a dower and children to inherit their father's estate.[32]

For our purposes these statements indicate a change from a
matrilineal emphasis to a *patrilineal* emphasis; though the missionaries and others concerned were not aware of the significance of the
changes they were bringing about. The effect on the social organization of the Choctaw was to break down the clan structure and emphasize the territorial tie. In the later periods the clan structure
became largely a memory, many individuals not knowing their own
clans.[33] Specifically, this change seems to have affected the kinship structure by "turning around" the pattern of descent from the
father's sister, making "fathers" descend in the male line, rather
than "father's sisters" in the female line, as Edwards indicates for
the old Choctaw system.

This conclusion, if it is of any value, should also "explain"
the changes which have taken place in the kinship systems of the other
tribes in the Southeast who were subjected to similar influences.
Foreman presents evidence to indicate that the Chickasaw and Creek
were considerably behind the Choctaw in "progress." The Chickasaw[34]
in particular were backward. They were a smaller tribe, less sedentary, and more warlike. Their removal to Indian Territory took place
later than that of the Choctaw and under less favorable circumstances.
They were settled on the western portion of the Choctaw reservation,

where they led a restless and unsettled existence, continually ha-
rassed by the unpacified Plains tribes. Attempts to merge them with
the Choctaw were resented by both tribes, and delayed their advancement. Missionaries and schools were much later in influencing them;
in 1847 there were no preachers or schools in their territory, schools
not getting started until after 1850. Hence the Chickasaw retained
their aboriginal customs to a greater degree, and for a longer time,
than did the Choctaw. The Creek,[35] on the other hand, made more
rapid "progress" than the Chickasaw. The first few years, after the
removal of the majority of the Creek in 1836, were taken up with a
continuation of the quarrel between the Upper and Lower Creek. They
were suspicious and resentful of the efforts of missionaries to change
their customs; in fact they expelled them from the Creek Nation in
1836 with the injunction, "Go teach your white men!" The missionaries returned in 1842, however, and their influence gradually increased. After a measure of tribal unity was restored, some interest
was taken in schools, there being a few schools by 1841. The Lower
Creek settlements advanced faster than those of the Upper Creek,
abandoning compact town settlements and communal cultivation at an
earlier date. By 1844 chiefs were beginning to be elected, but in
general they were prejudiced against the whites because they felt
their authority to be lessened. By 1850-60 many changes were in
progress: new laws were replacing old customs, property was being
inherited according to legal provisions, schools were well established,
men were doing the agricultural work, and missions were expanding.

On the basis of Foreman's material it is possible to arrange
the Choctaw, Chickasaw, and Creek in a rough series, in so far as
the *general* degree of acculturation is concerned. The Choctaw were
subjected to the greatest influence, the Chickasaw the least, while
the Creek were intermediate.

The Chickasaw had a Crow type in Morgan's time; the Choctaw
earlier. There is good reason to believe the Creek formerly had a
Crow type of kinship structure also. An early writer makes the following statement:

> All the men of the father's clan or family are called their fa-
> ther, the women are generally called their grandmother, all the
> men of the mother's family older than themselves are their uncles,
> being their mother's brothers. All of their own age and under
> are called brothers, and all the old women of their mother's clan
> are called grandmother or aunt.[36]

Swanton agrees to this but says:

> In spite of the emphasis which Stiggins places on clans in deter-
> mining the application of terms of relationship, an examination
> of the usages assigned to them shows that all the terms not indi-
> vidual cut across, or at least may cut across, the lines of the
> exogamous groups.[37]

The writer would like to suggest, in view of the above analysis, that both Stiggins and Swanton were right; that the Creek have changed the applications of terms to the descendants of the father's sister. Their early institutions and behavior patterns, so far as we know them, seem to be consistent with such an assumption.*

If we may tentatively assume that the Creek system represents a variant from a Crow type, we thus have a series of variations which corresponds with the series worked out with reference to the general degree of acculturation. If this be so we have an "explanation" for certain discrepancies which exist in the source materials. In regard to the Choctaw, for example, Reverend Copeland's schedule gives "mother" as the term for the father's sister's daughter. If the Choctaw system were in a process of change, the term "mother" might be considered more suitable than "father's sister," since the children of the father's sister's daughter were called "brother" and "sister" in both schedules. This variation apparently was not popular for long, but the earlier process of shortening the line of aunts continued: thus Swanton found that the term for father's sister "sometimes extends to the father's sister's daughter."[38] The Chickasaw material furnishes us with an illustration of the first steps in this change. In Morgan's time the father's sister's son's son was classed as a "brother," but Swanton later reports both "brother" and "father" being used for this particular relative. The Creeks apparently have reached a relatively stable state in which the matrilineal and patrilineal emphases are more or less balanced.[39]

The Cherokee furnish an additional group against which our conclusions may be tested. They belong to a different linguistic stock and have a different early history. On the other hand they were removed to Indian Territory and subjected to much the same acculturational influences that affected the other tribes, though if we may judge by Foreman's account,[40] these influences were less intensive than for either the Choctaw or Creek. During the first period after removal there was considerable trouble between the "Western" Cherokee, who had voluntarily migrated to Arkansas early in the 19th century and then had moved to Indian Territory in 1828, and the "Eastern" Cherokee, who were subjected to a forcible removal ten years later. Again white influence gradually brought about a change in the sentiments relating to females, a new division of labor, new laws and government, but these did not become well developed until

---

[*Also the fact that the Seminoles had a Crow type is additional evidence. F. E.]

after 1850. A national school system was established in 1841 and gradually grew as the leaders perceived the advantages of education.

A small group of Cherokee refused to be removed to Indian Territory and remained in the hills of North Carolina, where they still reside on the Eastern Cherokee Reservation. This group, numbering at present less than 2,000 persons, has been studied recently by Dr W. H. Gilbert, Jr.[41] He found them relatively uninfluenced in many respects, particularly in regard to social organization. He was fortunate enough to find the old kinship system in operation; his account of the terminological structure and the accompanying social behavior of relatives gives us our first relatively complete picture of the kinship system of a Southeastern tribe.

The system, as far as the pattern of descent is concerned, represents a pure Crow type. Relatives are recognized in four clans: one's own matrilineal clan, one's father's clan, one's mother's father's clan, and one's father's father's clan. In each of these, relatives are classified on a "lineage" principle. In the father's matrilineal lineage (and clan), for example, all men are "fathers," their wives "mothers" or "stepmothers," their children "brothers" and "sisters;" all women of the father's generation and below are "father's sisters," those above being "grandmothers" or "father's sisters," all husbands of these women are "grandfathers," all children are "father's sisters" and "fathers."[42]

We have, then, existing among the Cherokee, the situation which the writer had hoped to find among the Choctaw. The evidence suggests that the Cherokee formerly had a Crow type of kinship structure, but that influences affecting the portion of the tribe in Oklahoma have modified the descent system in the same direction as in the other Southeastern tribes considered, so that the father's sister's male descendants through males are classed as "father."[43]

These acculturational influences are of course not completely lacking in North Carolina, but seem to have been much less intensive. Gilbert mentions the loss of political power of clan heads, the gradual decline in family control, particularly in regard to marriage. Also:

> The mother's brother is no longer a power in the family and the transmission of family names for the last three generations through the father's line has tended to shift the emphasis in lineality to the paternal ancestry.[44]

This shift in emphasis from the matrilineal to the patrilineal line among the Cherokee still residing in North Carolina should result eventually in similar changes intthe pattern of descent, assuming other factors remain the same. Our hypothesis may therefore be verified, or modified, by future investigations of these groups.

The Yuchi furnish a separate and more complicated problem; they are considered partly to illustrate the value of our historical analysis, and partly to extend our survey of Southeastern tribes.[45] Speck studied the Yuchi in Oklahoma in 1904-5; they then resided in three scattered settlements in the northwestern corner of the Creek Nation. The Yuchi had belonged to the Creek confederation in the later period and were removed to Indian Territory with the Creek. In Speck's time they seldom mixed with the Creek, but were friendly with the Shawnee and Sauk and Fox.[46]

We have outlined the kinship structure above, as far as it relates to the pattern of descent (fig. 1, F). In describing the kinship system Speck notes that

> The family, in our sense of the word, as a group is of very little political importance in the tribe. The father has a certain individual social standing according to his clan and according to his society. The woman on the other hand carries the identity of the children, who may be said to belong to her. The bonds of closest kinship, however, being chiefly reckoned through the mother, it would appear that the closest degrees of consanguinity are counted in the clan.[47]

It seems probable that by Speck's time (1904-5) the kinship system had already been considerably modified. The use of descriptive terms for the father's sister's children is unique in this area, and suggests a breakdown from some other pattern.[48] The classification of the father's sister as a "grandmother" is suggestive of a Crow type of system, especially when coupled with a matrilineal clan system.

This is mere conjecture, based on probabilities. We will never know precisely what the earlier system was unless new historical evidence is discovered. On the other hand we have evidence of important changes since Speck's visit. Dr Wagner has recently completed a linguistic study of the Yuchi and was kind enough to furnish me with a list of the current kinship terms. These, interestingly enough, seem to represent an Omaha type of structure. The father's sister is now called "little mother," her children are "nephew" and "niece," male speaking, or "little son" and "little daughter," female speaking. The children of the mother's brother are, reciprocally, "mother's brother" and "little mother." That the shift of the term for father's sister is recent is further indicated by the fact that the father's sister's husband is still called "grandfather."

In connection with this shift there are several factors which must be considered. Within the aboriginal Yuchi system there was a patrilineal emphasis through the "War" and "Peace" societies, which were confined to males and definitely patrilineal in membership.[49] Secondly, the same factors influencing the Creeks since their removal in 1836 have necessarily affected the Yuchi, though probably in a

varying degree. Finally we have evidence of close contact with the
Shawnee and the Sauk and Fox in recent years, both of whom have an
Omaha type of kinship system. The Yuchi, then, possibly have gone
through the whole sequence of changes from a Crow to an Omaha type
of descent, though we have definite evidence for the last series of
changes only.

IV

The immediate conclusions which may be drawn from this survey of historical changes in Southeastern kinship structures can be briefly
summarized. (1) The evidence indicates that a Crow type of kinship
structure was widespread over the Southeast.[50] The Choctaw, Chickasaw, Creek, and Cherokee all seem to have had such a system in historic times; the evidence for the Yuchi is inconclusive but favorable.
Even the Natchez may have had a Crow type of kinship structure.
(2) These kinship structures, originally Crow in type, were progres-
sively modified by being subjected to varying degrees of the same
acculturational process. For the Choctaw, Chickasaw, and Creek there
seems to be a precise correlation between the degree of general acculturation and the degree of modification of the pattern of descent.
The evidence available for the Cherokee and Yuchi confirms this correlation.

These conclusions have a firm foundation in documentary and
other evidence. Further, they have a definite value; they make possible the reconciliation of inconsistencies between accounts for
different periods, and thus afford a foundation for preliminary classifications and comparative studies, whether historical or generalizing.[51]

These conclusions also raise a whole series of problems which
have implications for both acculturational studies and studies in
kinship theory, though many of these problems require the analysis
of much more material than is here presented. Since Hallowell,[52]
in a study of recent changes in the kinship terminology of the Abenaki,
came to conclusions concerning certain of these problems which differ
to some extent from those which the above material suggests, it seems
worthwhile to examine some of these problems briefly.

The solid distribution of the Crow type in the Southeast is
important. Lowie has pointed out that this is a characteristic feature of the two main regions in North America where the Omaha type
occurs, and suggests that "there is only one conceivable explanation
of the distributional data--historical connection within each of the
two areas."[53] In the Southwest we also find a solid block of Crow
types in the western Pueblos,[54] though the other occurrences of the

Crow type in North America are rather isolated. In general the Crow
and Omaha types occupy geographically separate areas; only in California and the Southeast do we find the two occurring side by side.
For the Yuchi we know the change to the Omaha type to be relatively
recent. While Lowie utilizes historical connection to explain the
distribution within an area he finds no indication of any borrowing
between areas.[55] Furthermore, borrowing as a *complete* explanation
of the distribution within an area breaks down in the case of California where one of the Pomo subdivisions, as well as the Wappo, have
a Crow type system in the midst of Omaha types.[56] The case of the
Yuchi has some bearing on this problem. Superficially we might consider that the Yuchi have borrowed the Sauk and Fox kinship system
through contact. But obviously a *pattern* of grouping relatives is
not borrowed, particularly when the actual terms are not taken over,
and the languages are not even mutually intelligible. I have attempted above to indicate some of the factors which have influenced this
change among the Yuchi; borrowing is only one. If the situation were
reversed in California, i.e., if there were one or two Omaha types
among a large number of Crow types, we might suspect an acculturational factor such as we find in the Southeast.

In this study we have not been concerned primarily with kinship terminology, but rather with the patterns and principles which
may be abstracted from native usage. In the systems of the tribes
considered there have been few lexical changes; terms have changed
primarily in regard to their applications.[57] Thus we find different
patterns for grouping relatives at different periods. Kinship terminology and the kinship pattern may vary independently: the terms
may change without affecting the pattern, as when a simple substitution occurs, or the pattern may change without affecting the terminology, or both may change. From this standpoint the traditional
dispute over whether linguistic factors or social factors are involved
in the kinship system has little point. One or the other may be
dominant in different situations. Hallowell,[58] for example, found
new terms replacing old ones among the Abenaki, as well as shifts in
application; in the Southeastern tribes considered, the latter change
seems more important.

From the standpoint of acculturation we have here an instance
of culture change which is reflected to a certain extent by specific
changes in the kinship pattern. While the acculturational process
has not been adequately analyzed, its effects on the social organization seem to have been in the direction of emphasizing "patrilineal"
tendencies at the expense of "matrilineal." The precise way in which

the social factors affected the kinship pattern is an important problem. Even in this preliminary study a "causal" relationship of some
sort is indicated, direct or indirect. It does not seem likely that
these social factors have operated directly on the kinship pattern,
which as we have indicated is an abstraction. Other aspects of the
social organization have changed concurrently. Among the Choctaw,
for example, the moiety and clan organizations gradually broke down
under the impact of acculturational influences. The close correlation of the Crow type with matrilineal clans has been pointed out by
Lowie;[59] in his earlier papers he attempted to explain kinship terminology as far as possible in terms of the clan. While it is possible
that the acculturational process operated through the clan organization, the nature of the changes taking place in the Choctaw system
does not make this hypothesis very likely. The clan organization
apparently gradually disintegrated; the kinship system, on the other
hand, developed a new type of organization which did not directly
reflect the clan system.[60]

One important effect of the acculturational process was to
modify the attitudes and behavior patterns which existed between various relatives. The patrilineal emphasis brought definite changes
in the roles of males and females in the family and in the local
group. The relation of a father to his children, in particular, was
changed, largely at the expense of the relations between the child
and the mother, and the child and the mother's brother. Specifically
the relation of father and child was strengthened; the father gradually took over control of his children, became responsible for their
education and training and for their behavior and marriage. Property
came to be largely owned by the father and inherited by his children.
Such changes must have influenced social attitudes toward relatives,
as well as weakening matrilineal descent. It is this change in behavior patterns and attitudes which seems to be the medium through
which the kinship patterns were modified. This is consonant with
recent studies of kinship systems where a close correlation has been
observed between the terminological structure and the social behavior
of relatives. The changes in behavior patterns and attitudes seem
to operate through affecting the choice of alternate principles of
classifying relatives.

Hallowell, studying the historical changes in the Abenaki
terminology, came to the conclusion that there was no precise correlation between the kinship nomenclature and social institutions.

The major lexical changes, as well as the readjustments in the
usage of terms (pattern changes), were found to be most satisfactorily explained as "contact phenomena," resulting from the

influence exerted upon Abenaki speakers by those of related Indian languages and Europeans.[61]
But Hallowell had no data indicating possible changes in social behavior except those inferable from the family hunting territory complex and the levirate.[62] He partially agrees with Speck that the
kinship terminology is in agreement with the social structure in earlier times, but fails to see how the specific changes in relationship
terms can be directly connected with the gradual disintegration of
the family hunting band.[63]

These conclusions do not necessarily conflict with those
reached in the present study. Hallowell was forced to infer the nature of the changes resulting from the contact phenomena: "local
differences and custom must have been remoulded to some extent under
these new conditions."[64] In the Southeast there is more evidence
for these changes. On the basis of our analysis it seems likely that
acculturational factors affect the kinship system through influencing social behavior and attitudes, rather than directly affecting
the terminology.

Changes in social organization presumably may go on at different rates among different tribes. The rapidity of the changes
reported for the Southeast is significant in indicating the sensi-
tiveness of the kinship system to certain social influences, and
raises some doubts as to "survivals" in kinship structures. A more
important problem is concerned with the nature of the changes which
have been described for the Southeastern tribes. Here a *similar*
change seems to have taken place in most of the tribes considered.
These changes vary in extent but may be arranged in a series (from
a Crow type to a Choctaw type, and perhaps even to an Omaha type),
and this series is correlated with the degree of acculturation. This
suggests that we may have here a *general* type of change. If so we
might expect other Crow systems, under similar acculturational influences, to undergo a similar series of changes.[65]

The fundamental problem of the explanation of the kinship
system in terms of correlated social institutions is too complex to
be considered in any detail in this paper. In a future paper on the
Southeast the writer proposes to bring together the relevant material
and indicate its bearing on this problem. Lowie attempts to bolster
the lack of preciseness in the correlations of matrilineal and patrilineal organizations with the Crow and Omaha systems by reference to
special forms of marriage, though he points out that these are in
many instances logical rather than empirical explanations.[66] More
fruitful, in my opinion, is Lowie's insistence that "the more spe-

cific matrimonial arrangements are themselves a function of the rule of descent."[67] It should be possible to go even further and consider them both as functions of some factor or principle which they have in common. Incidentally, the levirate as a causal factor in kinship systems receives a setback in Hallowell's study. He finds, for example, an increase in the number of equations which might reflect the influence of the levirate during the period that the levirate is declining as an institution.[68]

Finally we might point out that in the present study, at least, it seems possible to unite "functional" and "historical" points of view without doing too much violence to either. In studies of acculturation both would seem essential: we need to know something of the interrelations of social institutions before we can deal adequately with cultural change. Without the concept of a *kinship system*, for example, the changes recorded in terminology for the Southeastern tribes have very little meaning. On the other hand, without the historical analysis the kinship structure of the Southeast remains blurred. This analysis must be based on documentary evidence, however, since at present we have no satisfactory technique for reconstructing such changes as have been outlined. In terms of an ultimate interest in systematic general "laws" we have here an instance supporting the general hypothesis that "that any marked functional inconsistency in a social system tends to induce change."[69] The kinship systems of the Southeastern tribes seem to have partially recovered their internal consistency by means of a series of similar changes.

NOTES

[1]This paper is a rather unexpected outgrowth of a research project concerned with North American social organization under the direction of Professor A. R. Radcliffe-Brown. The field work was made possible by the Department of Anthropology of the University of Chicago, for which grateful acknowledgment is made. I would also like to acknowledge my indebtedness to Dr John R. Swanton. Subtract his studies from the material published on the Southeastern tribes and there is an unbridgeable gap. In using his materials as the basis for this study I have been continually impressed by his accuracy and clarity. I suspect he has foreseen many of the conclusions which I have reached in this paper. The paper has benefited from the criticism of Professors Radcliffe-Brown, Robert Redfield, and R. H. Lowie.

[2]Leslie Spier, *The Distribution of Kinship Systems in North America* (University of Washington Publications in Anthropology, Vol. 1, No. 2, 1925), p. 72.

[3]R. H. Lowie, *The Omaha and Crow Kinship Terminologies* (Proceedings, Twenty-fourth International Congress of Americanists, Hamburg, 1930), pp. 102, 105.

[4]Spier, *op. cit.*, pp. 73-74.

[5]J. R. Swanton, *Source Material for the Social and Ceremonial*

Life of the Choctaw Indians (Bulletin, Bureau of American Ethnology, 103, 1931). The moieties went out of existence in historic times, the clans taking over the functions of exogamy, etc.

[6]J. R. Swanton, *Social and Religious Beliefs and Usages of the Chickasaw Indians* (Forty-fourth Annual Report, Bureau of American Ethnology, 1928).

[7]J. R. Swanton, *Social Organization and Social Usages of the Indians of the Creek Confederacy* (Forty-second Annual Report, Bureau of American Ethnology, 1928).

[8]W. H. Gilbert, Jr., *Eastern Cherokee Social Organization* (Ph.D. thesis, ms., University of Chicago, 1934).

[9]F. G. Speck, *Ethnology of the Yuchi Indians* (Anthropological Publications, University Museum, University of Pennsylvania, Vol. 1, No. 1, 1909).

[10]J. R. Swanton, *Indian Tribes of the Lower Mississippi Valley* (Bulletin, Bureau of American Ethnology, 43, 1911). See also J. DeJong, *The Natchez Social System* (Proceedings, Twenty-third International Congress of Americanists, New York, 1930).

[11]Spier, *op. cit.*, pp. 73-74.

[12]Lowie, *op. cit.*, p. 105.

[13]While we are not here concerned with the nature of the terminology itself, it may be pertinent to mention one or two points. The Chickasaw and Creek classified the father's sisters with the grandmother. The Choctaw had a separate term for father's sister, male speaking; the women used the term for grandmother. In the Sixtowns division of the Choctaw we find the term for grandmother used by both sexes for the father's sister.

[14]Lowie, *op. cit.*, p. 103. While Lowie specifically refers to the Omaha type, the same principle obviously holds for the Crow. This seems to be a basic principle for the classification of kinship systems. If this is so the Omaha and Crow types might be considered sub-types of a more fundamental "Crow-Omaha" type. The extent to which this principle operates can best be illustrated by constructing "lineage diagrams."

[15]Cf. L. H. Morgan, *Systems of Consanguinity and Affinity of the Human Family* (Smithsonian Contributions to Knowledge, Vol. 17, 1871), Table II, 28, 29; Swanton, *Source Material for . . . the Choctaw Indians*, pp. 84-90.

[16]Morgan, *op. cit.*, p. 191. The last sentence is probably responsible for much of the confusion which exists in regard to the Choctaw kinship system. Structurally this pattern of descent is not *analogous* in the way that the Crow and Omaha are. J. Kohler (*Zur Urgeschichte der Ehe*, Zeitschrift für vergleichende Rechtswissenschaft, Vol. 12, 1897, pp. 187-354) almost forty years ago considered the Choctaw system as analogous to the Omaha (tribal) system, and attempted to explain both on the basis of certain types of secondary marriages, types which had to be assumed for the Choctaw.

[17]Morgan, *op. cit.*, Table II, 30.

[18]Swanton, *Social and Religious Beliefs and Usages of the Chickasaw Indians*, pp. 185-86.

[19]Morgan, *op. cit.*, Table II, 31; Swanton, *Social Organization . . . of the Creek Confederacy*, p. 85-86.

[20]Morgan, *op. cit.*, Table II, 32, 33. Two schedules are given, gathered by missionaries in Oklahoma. The Cherokee (32) and Mountain Cherokee (33) divisions correspond with the "Western" and "Eastern"

groups, according to Gilbert, *op. cit.*, pp. 50-56. Both were residing in Oklahoma but were differentiated in regard to time of removal and location on the reservation. (Cf. Grant Foreman, *The Five Civilized Tribes*, Norman, Okla., 1934, Book V.)

[21]Speck, *op. cit.*, p. 69.

[22]Communication from Dr Günter Wagner.

[23]Swanton, *Social Organization . . . of the Creek Confederacy*, pp. 94-95.

[24]A feature not noted in other systems reported for this region is the classification of the father's brother as "father" *or* "father's brother," and the mother's sister as "mother" *or* "mother's sister." Swanton inclines to the view that the use of a separate term for the father's brother is ancient, but this is possibly the result of the contact: I found evidence of a similar change among the Mississippi Choctaw.

[25]The comparative analysis outlined above might serve as partial proof. Actually, however, the writer did not see the implications of such an analysis for the Southeastern area until the Choctaw problem had been worked out.

[26]Morgan, *op. cit.*, p. 190. These schedules appear to represent the current kinship system at the time the schedules were gathered: 1860. The differences between the schedules will be considered later.

[27]John Edwards, *The Choctaw Indians in the Middle of the Nineteenth Century* (Chronicles of Oklahoma, Vol. 10, Oklahoma City, 1932, pp. 392-425).

[28]Edwards, *op. cit.*, pp. 400-401. The italics are Edwards. This is a precise and excellent statement of the Choctaw kinship structure, and one which is consistent with what we know of other aspects of early Choctaw social organization.

[29]Grant Foreman, *op. cit.* The following account is based primarily on Foreman.

[30]Angie Debo, *The Rise and Fall of the Choctaw Republic* (Norman, Okla., 1934). This volume was not available to the writer, but Swanton in reviewing this and Foreman's volume, considers that it supplements the latter, giving a much larger mass of material on the Choctaw in the form of a vertical monograph (John R. Swanton in American Anthropologist, Vol. 37, 1935, pp. 675-76).

[31]Foreman, *op. cit.*, Book I: *Choctaw*.

[32]Foreman, *op. cit.*, pp. 84-85. Foreman is here referring to an account written for the "New York Evangelist" in 1852 by the Rev Cyrus Byington.

[33]The Mississippi Choctaw today, where they know of the old clan system, usually characterize it as patrilineal.

[34]Foreman, *op. cit.*, Book II: *Chickasaw*.

[35]Foreman, *op. cit.*, Book III: *Creek*.

[36]Swanton, *Social Organization . . . of the Creek Confederacy*, p. 87, quoting from the Stiggins ms., no date.

[37]Swanton, *loc. cit.* He is concerned here primarily with the fact that the Creeks classify the descendants of the father's sister in *both* male and female lines as "father" and "grandmother." Hence it is not a clan (or lineage) classification exclusively.

[38]Swanton, *Source Material for . . . the Choctaw Indians*, p. 87. In Mississippi the writer found only one or two elderly informants who extended the term for father's sister to the father's sister's daughter.

[39]Most of the material on kinship has been gathered with the view of illustrating the aboriginal systems. Hence changes may have gone on which have been largely ignored in the ethnological presentations.

[40]Foreman, *op. cit.*, Book V: *Cherokee*.

[41]Gilbert, *op. cit.* The following account is summarized from this study.

[42]This kinship structure is best seen when put in the form of "lineage diagrams." The Hopi kinship structure has an almost identical pattern, except that kinship is not extended to the father's father's clan. These two systems might well be considered as type structures for the Crow type, since the system of the Crow tribe is somewhat anomalous. If "lineage diagrams" are made for the Omaha (J. O. Dorsey, *Omaha Sociology*, Third Annual Report, Bureau of American Ethnology, 1884, pp. 205-370) the similarity of the Crow and Omaha types is apparent.

[43]It may be noted that this pattern (fig. 1, E) is very close to that for the Creek (D).

[44]Gilbert, *op. cit.*, p. 278.

[45]My own point of view toward the Yuchi system has changed radically with the working out of this historical analysis. Without it Speck's and Wagner's kinship systems cannot be reconciled. (See below.)

[46]F. G. Speck, *op. cit.*, p. 11.

[47]Speck, *op. cit.*, pp. 68-69.

[48]The father's lineage might be expected to break down before one's own lineage in a matrilineal society.

[49]Speck, *op. cit.*, p. 68. Also we have the statement that both men and women labored together in the fields (p. 18).

[50]This conclusion, of course, is in keeping with previous classifications, though as I have attempted to show, not directly deducible from the available source materials. Spier relied on a communication from Swanton for his classification; it is probable that Swanton had arrived at conclusions similar to the ones here presented.

[51]Unfortunately they also indicate that Morgan's schedules cannot always be accepted as representing the aboriginal kinship systems unaffected by white contact.

[52]A. I. Hallowell, *Recent Changes in the Kinship Terminology of the St. Francis Abenaki* (Proceedings, Twenty-second International Congress of Americanists, Rome, 1928, Vol. 2, pp. 97-145), pp. 144-45.

[53]Lowie, *op. cit.*, p. 102.

[54]Fred Eggan, *The Social Organization of the Western Pueblos* (Ph.D. thesis, ms., University of Chicago, 1933).

[55]Lowie, *op. cit.*, pp. 102-103.

[56]Cf. Spier, *op. cit.*, pp. 73-74 and map.

[57]This, of course, changes the "meaning" of a term. Thus the term "father" has a different meaning among the Choctaw when the applications change.

[58]*Op. cit.*, p. 144-45.

[59]Lowie, *op. cit.*, p. 108.

[60]Compare Hallowell's conclusions, which are given below.

[61]Hallowell, *op. cit.*, p. 145.

[62] *Ibid.*, p. 138.

[63] Hallowell, *op. cit.*, p. 140. Compare this with the conclusion reached above in regard to the disintegration of clans in the Southeast.

[64] *Ibid.*, p. 143.

[65] Such a hypothesis is not necessary for the conclusions reached for the Southeast, since the latter rest on empirical materials. If verified, however, it would have considerable bearing on kinship theory.

[66] Lowie, *op. cit.*, p. 106-107.

[67] *Ibid.*, p. 108.

[68] Hallowell, *op. cit.*, pp. 141-42.

[49] See A. R. Radcliffe-Brown, *Kinship Terminologies in California* (American Anthropologist, Vol. 37, 1935, pp. 530-35), pp. 533-34.

4

THE HOPI AND THE LINEAGE PRINCIPLE

1949

STRUCTURAL ANALYSIS

One of the most significant advances in the study of kinship systems
in modern times has been Professor A. R. Radcliffe-Brown's method of
structural or sociological analysis, by which a limited number of
structural principles have been isolated by comparative study of diverse systems and shown to underly a variety of social and cultural
phenomena. In two recent Presidential Addresses[1] before the Royal
Anthropological Institute Professor Radcliffe-Brown has summarized
his conception of the study of social structure and illustrated the
results which may be achieved in the field of kinship. He conceives
the major task of social anthropology to be the study of social structure: the network of actually existing social relations between the
members of a social group. The kinship system is an important part
of the social structure; in analysing kinship systems as organized
wholes he holds as a working hypothesis the view that there is a complex relation of interdependence between the various features of a
particular system. By a comparison of diverse systems he has isolated such important structural principles as the solidarity of the sibling group, the distinction of generation, differentiation according
to sex and age, and the solidarity and unity of the lineage group.[2]

In the most recent of these addresses, 'The Study of Kinship
Systems,' Professor Radcliffe-Brown has referred to my unpublished
analysis of the social organization of the Hopi Indians[3] as exempli-
fying the principle of the unity of the lineage group. Since this
study was made originally under his direction, and since publication
of the results, which are part of the study of the *Social Organization of the Western Pueblos*, has been delayed by various events in-

Reproduced by permission of the Oxford University Press,
Oxford, from *Social Structure: Studies presented to A. R. Radcliffe-
Brown*, Meyer Fortes, editor (1949), pp. 121-44.

cluding the war, I feel that it is appropriate to present a summary
and interpretation of Hopi kinship in this volume.

The Hopi are one of the few groups of Indians in North America who maintain their social structure and culture in something approximating its aboriginal form; they offer, therefore, an excellent
opportunity to study a Crow type of 'lineage' system of kinship in
operation. Since they possess a majority of features associated with
the classic Crow type, the Hopi may well become the type group for
this important class of systems, thus furnishing a better basis for
classification and comparison. Further, the differential influences
of White and other contacts on various of the Hopi villages and the
long archaeological and historical record offer an opportunity to
study social and cultural change under relatively controlled conditions. [4]

THE HOPI KINSHIP SYSTEM

The Hopi Indians, the most western and isolated of the Pueblo groups
of Arizona and New Mexico whose distinctive mode of life is so well
known, live in villages on a series of mesas in north-eastern Arizona.
Their territory is part of the arid and dissected Colorado Plateau,
which here averages some 6,000 feet in height. The Hopi are dry
farmers, depending directly or indirectly on rainfall; rain is scarce
and variable, averaging only some 10 inches per year. [5] The need for
water, vital for agriculture, profoundly influences the social and
ceremonial life as well.

While a specifically Hopi culture cannot be identified beyond
the beginning of Pueblo IV times (c. A.D. 1300), peoples with Pueblo
cultures have been living in the region for a much longer period.
At the time of Coronado's visit in 1540 there were some seven villages on four mesas, but after the Pueblo Rebellion in 1680 important
changes took place in village location. In recent years population
growth and internal dissension have led to further village-building,
with the result that to-day there are some eleven villages with a
total population of over 3,000.

Despite their geographical position Hopi culture is in no
sense marginal. Their nearest Pueblo neighbours, the Zuni, are some
200 miles to the south-east, while the Navaho, recent comers to the
Hopi region, now completely surround them. Because the Spaniards
did not return in any force after the Rebellion, the Hopi lack certain political and religious institutions imposed on other Pueblos,
though they have shared in the material benefits which the Spanish
brought. [6]

Each major village is politically independent--the Hopi have acted together only on occasions when their welfare has been seriously threatened or under Government pressure. Their unity resides in their common language and culture: with the exception of the village of Hano[7] there are only slight dialectic differences from mesa to mesa and the social and cultural patterns encompass the entire tribe.

A preliminary examination reveals that each village is divided into a series of matrilineal, totemically named clans, which are linked or grouped into nameless but exogamous phratries. Each clan is composed of one or more matrilineal lineages, which, though nameless, are of great importance. The basic local organization is the extended family based on matrilocal residence and occupying the household of one or more rooms in common. In addition there are various associations, both societies and kiva groups, which are involved in the calendrical ceremonies.

The structure, social functions, and interrelationships of these groups can best be seen in the light of an analysis of the kinship system. For the Hopi the kinship system[8] is the most important element of their social structure; they have utilized it to define and determine social relations in most aspects of daily and ceremonial life.

The following chart (Fig. 1) illustrates the kinship system by means of a conventional genealogical diagram. The Hopi terminological system[9] is of the 'classificatory' type, with the father being classed with the father's brother and the mother with the mother's sister. But within each generation a wide variety of relatives is to be found. There are separate terms for grandfather and grandmother, but their siblings are classed in a variety of ways, some with the grandparents and others with the father, brother, or mother's brother. In the parental generation there are separate terms for the mother's brother and father's sister, but the former's wife is considered a 'female relative-in-law' whereas the latter's husband is classed with the grandfather. In ego's generation siblings are distinguished according to sex and age, except that a woman uses the same term for her younger siblings. Parallel cousins are treated as siblings, whereas cross-cousins are differentiated, the children of the father's sister being called 'father' and 'father's sister', while the children of the mother's brother are 'children' (male speaking) or 'grandchildren' (female speaking). In the children's and grandchildren's generations further apparently anomalous usages appear. It is obvious that the kinship system is not organized on any principle of 'generation' and the descent pattern from the father's

94

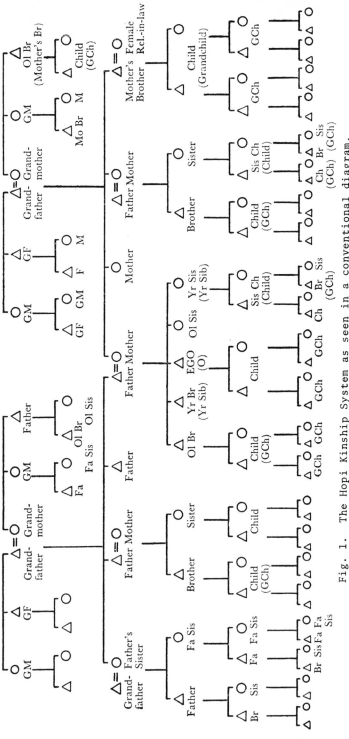

Fig. 1. The Hopi Kinship System as seen in a conventional diagram.
Ego = male. Where terms for female differ they are indicated in parentheses.

sister overrides generation, in a significant way. By utilizing this
pattern of descent and arranging relatives in terms of a 'lineage
diagram', the nature of the Hopi kinship structure becomes apparent:
the native grouping is on a 'vertical' or 'lineage', rather than on
a 'horizontal' or 'generation' basis.

Figs. 2-5 outline the central core of the Hopi kinship structure. Since descent is matrilineal the position of a male in the
lineage structure is different conceptually from that of a female.
Within the lineage both differentiate relatives according to generation and, to a more limited extent, sex and age. A male is in a
'peripheral' position with regard to the lineage; he tends to classify the mother's mother's brother with the older brother; his sister's children are within the lineage but his own children are outside. A female is in the direct line of descent and her children are
in the lineage, however, and she normally classifies the mother's
mother's brother with the mother's brother. With regard to persons
marrying into the lineage it tends to be considered as a unit by both
men and women. All women marrying men of the lineage, regardless of
generation, are classed as 'female relatives-in-law'; all men marrying women of ego's generation and below are classed together as 'male
relatives-in-law'. Children of men of the lineage are classed as
'children' (male speaking) or 'grandchildren' (female speaking).

The father's matrilineal lineage, which becomes related
through the marriage of ego's parents, is treated somewhat differently. In this lineage all the women are 'father's sisters' (or
grandmothers) and all the men are 'fathers', regardless of generation
or age. Further, any man marrying a woman of the father's lineage
is a 'grandfather' and all wives of the 'fathers' are 'mothers'; any
child of the men of the lineage is a 'brother' or 'sister'. These
terms are used by both males and females.

In the mother's father's matrilineal lineage, which is related to ego's lineage through the marriage of the mother's parents, we
find a parallel situation. All the women of this lineage are 'grandmothers' and all the men are 'grandfathers'; their spouses are likewise 'grandfather' or 'grandmother'. The father's father's matrilineal lineage, on the other hand, is not socially recognized, though
the father's father is called 'grandfather' and his siblings are
'grandparents'.

The Hopi thus divide consanguineal relatives in terms of
three lineages: the mother's (ego's), father's, and mother's father's
matrilineal lineages. In ego's own lineage we find a considerable
differentiation of relatives, but with reference to individuals mar-

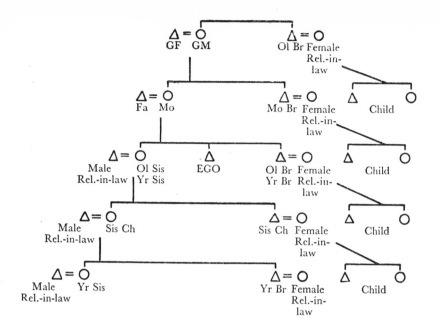

Fig. 2.   The mother's matrilineal lineage.
Ego = male.

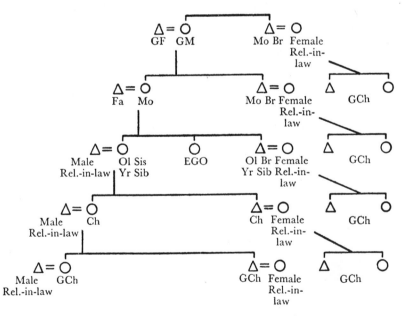

Fig. 3.   The mother's matrilineal lineage.
Ego = female.

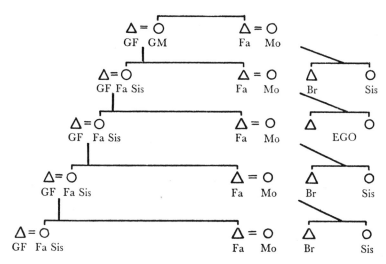

Fig. 4.   The father's matrilineal lineage.
Ego = male or female.

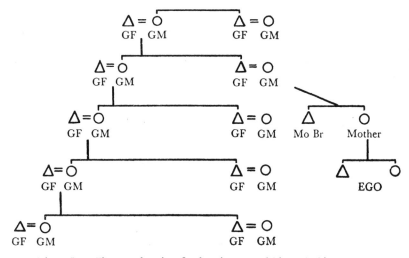

Fig. 5.   The mother's father's matrilineal lineage.
Ego = male or female.

rying into the lineage we note that they are classed together in terminological usage. Generation distinctions are important only within one's own lineage; with reference to outsiders related by marriage the lineage is conceived as a unit. For a male ego there is some tendency to organize male lineage relationships in terms of alternate generations, but this tendency is not standardized in social usage at present. The father's and mother's father's lineages, on the other hand, are treated as units, both with regard to their members and with reference to persons marrying into the lineage. The lineage diagrams suggest that the father's and mother's lineages are related to ego's in conceptually similar ways; each is attached through marriage of a man to a woman of the lineage, either mother or mother's mother. The father's father's lineage, on the other hand, is a whole lineage farther removed, and is not recognized by the Hopi, though the father's father's sister's descendants are just as close genealogically as the mother's father's sister's children. In terms of these lineage patterns the anomalous patterns of the conventional genealogical charts and the differences in terminology between males and females are explicable and intelligible.

We have noted that these three lineages form the central core or nucleus of the kinship system and give the basic differentiation of relatives. They are not limited to the five generations diagrammed--in Hopi theory they are timeless, stretching back to the Emergence and continuing into the future. They also serve as units for the extension of the kinship structure, by which a Hopi becomes related, in one way or another, to almost everybody in his village, to many people in other villages, and even to members of other tribes.

The primary extension of kinship is to the clan. A person is considered to be related to everybody in his own clan, regardless of whether the clan consists of one lineage or several, and to the members of his father's and mother's father's clans. While a Hopi distinguishes between 'own relatives' and 'clan relatives', in Hopi theory a clan is composed of genealogically related individuals even though connexions between component lineages cannot be traced at present.[10]

Kinship is further extended to all members of the associated or linked clans which make up the Hopi phratry,[11] so that a person is related to his own, his father's, and his mother's father's phratries. The phratry groupings, in Hopi theory, consist of clans which met or shared in some experience during the period of 'clan wanderings' which preceded the final settlement in the Hopi region; as such they are 'partners' rather than genealogically related clans, and the extension of kinship is on a more strictly social basis. Since the same or similar clans and clan groupings exist in other Hopi villages, a Hopi at birth has a large number of relatives to whom he can trace no genealogical connexion, but who are socially recognized. Of these the relatives of his own and his father's clan and phratry are most important.

This is only the beginning of the social extension of kinship, however. A 'ceremonial father' is chosen by his parents outside of the circle of clan relatives to act as sponsor in various societies and groups, and the novice becomes related to his clan and phratry group. A doctor who cures an individual of serious illness may 'adopt' the latter into his clan and phratry. Kinship terms applicable to the father's clan are used in these cases.

Marriage results in the acquisition of an additional set of relatives, since a man should marry outside of his own, his father's, and his mother's father's clans and phratries, in theory at least. For his affinal relatives a man employs the same kinship terms which his wife uses for her household and lineage, and the wife similarly uses the terms her husband uses for his relatives. These relationships are felt as extending to the spouse's clan, but such extensions are not important. This terminological usage is non-reciprocal since the spouses are called 'male relative-in-law' and 'female relative-in-law', in return, a usage which is explicable in terms of the marriage situation and the obligations involved.

There are further extensions of kinship on a symbolic basis. The village chief is considered as a 'father' and is so addressed on ritual occasions. Priests may be referred to as 'fathers'; kinship terms are used on occasions of ritual smoking and initiations. There is an extension of kinship to the world of nature. The sun is called 'father', the earth and corn are 'mother', the spider is 'grandmother' to all the Hopi. The plant or animal species which serve as clan names are frequently called 'father', 'mother', or 'mother's brother' by the clanspeople. Where similar clan names are used by other tribes, a relationship is felt.

These extensions of kinship, largely on the basis of the clan as the unit, result in any individual's having a large number of relatives. In certain cases there may be several ways of tracing relationship. Titiev has worked out the approximate order of closeness as follows: (1) immediate family, (2) mother's sisters and children, (3) others of household, (4) own clan, (5) father's household, (6) own phratry, (7) father's clan and phratry, (8) 'ceremonial father's' clan and phratry, and (9) 'doctor father's' clan and phratry. He points out that this order is confirmed by the incest regulations, marriage being forbidden within the first six groups, theoretically forbidden but tolerated within the seventh, and allowed within the last two.[12]

We have now outlined the formal kinship structure as it is reflected in terminological usage and have indicated the main mechanisms for extension. Of equal importance, for our purposes, is the domestic or household group into which a Hopi is born and in which he receives his primary orientation. The basic family unit is an extended family based on matrilineal descent and matrilocal residence. This group, which may consist of a woman and her husband, married daughters and their husbands, unmarried sons, and children of the daughters, normally occupies a set of adjoining rooms which it uses in common, and may be conveniently designated a 'household'. Even where increased numbers, conflicts between sisters, and modern conditions have led to further division, the conceptual unity of the household group remains.

The central core or axis of the household is composed of a line of women--a segment of a lineage. All the members of the segment, male and female, are born in the household and consider it their home, but only the women normally reside there after marriage. The men of the lineage leave at marriage to reside in the households of their wives, returning to their natal home on various ritual and ceremonial occasions, or in case of separation or divorce, which is frequent. Into the household in turn come other men through marriage, who take over the economic support of the household but have little to do with its ritual activities. If their marriages continue they gradually move from the status of relatives-in-law to that of fathers and grandfathers.

Thus the households, which from one point of view are merely a series of elementary families held together in the female line, achieve a more significant structure. We may view them as lines of women looking alternately to their brothers and to their husbands. On ritual occasions when men return to their natal household, the household group becomes a lineage, or a lineage segment; on ordinary occasions the household is composed of the same women plus their husbands and children. The household revolves about a central and continuing core of women; the men are peripheral with divided residences and loyalties.

There is no native term for the household nor is it considered an independent unit by the Hopi, since they think in terms of the clan. But the household is important in many contexts. In terms of the lineage diagrams we can see it overlapping the lineage groupings, uniting consanguineal and affinal kin in a domestic group. A Hopi born into such a household finds there representatives of practically all his important kin, and here he receives his basic orientation with regard to kinship, which serves as a pattern for later extension and elaboration. If his mother's sisters should live in separate households, their homes are equally his. Of great importance also is the father's natal household, the women of which play a special role in ego's life, as well as the households of other father's sisters, whether clan or ceremonial. Here are found other relatives who complete the kinship outline, except for the experience of marriage. A Hopi is thus linked to a set of households which parallel the lineages and clans to which he is related, but which provide a somewhat different and more concrete orientation. The interrelations between these two kinds of organizations provide one key to Hopi social structure and function.

SOCIAL RELATIONS AND USAGES

Having outlined the basic classification of relatives and the structural forms involved we might now briefly examine the social relations which make up the structure and the social usages in which they are embodied and maintained. The basic relationships are those of the elementary family, but because of conditions of descent and residence certain other relationships of a more distant order come to have great importance among the Hopi. Since space does not permit a detailed treatment the reader may be referred to other sources for further information on the behaviour patterns between relatives.[13]

The relation of a father to his child is of a different order from the relation of a woman to her children. A child belongs to the mother's lineage and clan but is a 'child' of the father's clan; although both are recognized as kin the two parental groups are rather sharply differentiated in attitudes and behaviour, as well as residence. The father's obligations to his sons are primarily economic: he is mainly responsible for preparing them to make a living, and his position is something like that of an older comrade and teacher. There is affection but little in the way of punishment, and while a boy respects his father he does not ordinarily fear him. The Hopi normally make little distinction between the father and the father's brothers, although behaviour towards more distant 'fathers' may be attenuated. Those fathers who assist their sons are in turn assisted and supported in later life; where 'fathers' are younger than their 'sons' the pattern of behaviour may be reversed.

The mother-daughter relationship, in contrast, is an exceedingly close one, based on clan ties, common activities, and lifelong residence together. The mother is responsible for both the economic and ritual training of her daughters. A daughter's behaviour is reciprocally one of respect and obedience, and in most cases affection as well. The position of the mother's sister is practically identical with that of the mother, particularly when she resides in the same household.

Whereas the relations of a father to his daughter are limited in scope, the relations of a mother to her son are almost as close as to her daughter. Even after marriage he frequently seeks her advice. She plays an important role in the selection of his 'ceremonial father' and in the marriage ceremonies. Her home is always his home; here he keeps his personal property, here he brings guests, and here he returns in case of divorce.

The bond between husband and wife varies with time and circumstances but is seldom close, since their primary loyalties are to their own lineages. In Hopi theory the best lands are owned by clans and divided among the households, the women owning the houses and the crops. Husbands farm their wives' lands and contribute otherwise to the support of the household. Though marriage is monogamous, separation is easy and there is a high rate of divorce in all of the villages.[14] Where conflicts or crises arise the husband may be treated as an outsider by the household, in which case he usually returns to his own household until reconciliation or remarriage. The serious social consequences of easy separation are mitigated by the extended family structure of the household, since the wife and small children can fall back on the larger family for economic support.

The sibling bond is a very strong one in Hopi society, being based on common blood and residence, and on mutual aid. The strongest and most permanent tie is that between two sisters, next is the relationship between brothers. Brothers frequently co-operate in economic and ritual activities throughout life, despite their living in different households. While two brothers may marry two sisters, or marry into the same clan, this is not a definite rule. The sororate and the levirate are not practised.

The relationship of sisters to one another, and to their mother, is the foundation of the Hopi household group. This relationship, based on the closest ties of blood, residence, and occupation, lasts from birth to death. Their children are brought up and cared for together; they co-operate in all the household tasks. Though quarrels occur, sisters generally manage to get along together.

The brother-sister bond, though close, is modified by the prevailing division of labour and the rules of residence. There are no restrictions or avoidances in their behaviour. A brother helps support his sister's household when necessary; together they may co-operate in ceremonial activities or in 'ceremonial parenthood'. An older brother has much in common with a younger brother but less with a younger sister; an older sister, on the other hand, engages equally in the task of taking care of her younger brothers and sisters.[15] The bond between them is the basis for a portion of their relationships to each other's children, as well. With regard to marriage, however, there is little or no tendency to brother-sister exchange between households.

A mother's brother has important relations with his sister's children. As male head of his sister's lineage and household his position is one of authority and control; he is the chief disciplinarian and is both respected and obeyed. The mother's brother has primary responsibility for transmitting the ritual heritage of the lineage or clan; he usually selects the most capable nephew as his successor and trains him in the duties of whatever ceremonial position he may control. The nephew usually respects or fears his mother's brother, but may gradually develop an affection for him as he grows older.

The mother's mother's brother is likewise an important relative. While alive he is the ritual head of the household and may act as a teacher, but he seldom actively punishes his sister's daughter's children, leaving that task to his sister's son. The Hopi frequently class the mother's mother's brother with the older brother, rather than with the disciplining mother's brother.

The grandparent-grandchild relation is more varied but in general is one of affection and attachment. By reason of residence a mother's father is usually closer to his grandson, often instructing him in Hopi lore and activities. The father's father has a similar relationship, but being in a different household, has normally fewer opportunities. This grandfather enters into a joking relationship with his grandson, and may pour water on him or roll him in the snow. The father's sister's husband enters into a special joking relationship centered in the father's sister.

Grandmothers likewise treat their grandchildren with kindness and affection, though the mother's mother occupies a dominant position in the household and as such must be respected and obeyed. The father's mother is closer to her grandchildren and shows them more affection. As a woman of the father's lineage, she shares with the father's sisters an important joking relationship with her grandson. The grandparent-grandchild relationship is widely extended and includes relatives in several conceptual categories; the Hopi have ignored these differences and classed them together despite differences in behaviour.

The relationship of a father's sister to her brother's children is one of the most interesting and important in Hopi life. At all life crises and on all ceremonial occasions the father's sisters play an important role. With the brother's son there is a very close relationship, with strong sexual overtones.[16] At the time of the boy's marriage, the father's sisters may 'find fault' with the bride, and all the women of the father's household and clan may descend on the boy's household and daub his female relatives with mud, as a means of showing how much they care for him.

This expression of jealousy takes a more direct form in the joking between a boy, his father's sisters, and their husbands. The latter, as 'grandfathers', may have rolled the boy in the snow on occasion. They may dispute over who can take care of the father's sister the better, and in some instances, at least, there are threats of castration on the part of the father's sister's husband.[17] A girl, on the other hand, will tease her mother's brother as to his relations with his father's sisters.

The father's sister's daughters, when unmarried, are not teased in this fashion; they choose their favourite mother's brother's sons as partners in Butterfly and other social dances. More distant father's sisters are also regarded with affection and may become sexual partners. The father's sister should probably be considered as a 'little grandmother'; her husband is called 'grandfather' and her brother's children are 'grandchildren'. The special term serves to segregate the women of the father's household and clan from the general group of genealogical grandparents.

The relations with relatives by marriage take a somewhat different and non-reciprocal form. Men marrying into a household share in the task of supporting it, and are judged on the basis of performance. If they get along well, there is a tendency for the wife's brothers to call them 'brother' rather than 'male relative-in-law'. Later, they become 'fathers' to the generation below. Two men married to women of the same household call one another 'partners'; they have similar tasks to perform in maintaining it.

The relations with 'female relatives-in-law' are somewhat different, though also non-reciprocal. Women marrying any men of the lineage are called by the term, 'female relative-in-law'; in return they use the husband's terms for his household and clan. These 'female relatives-in-law' do not form a localized group but have important duties whenever a woman of the husband's clan is being married, and on other occasions.

The primary obligations of 'relatives-in-law' are to the household and lineage with which they are immediately associated, but these are frequently extended to the clan. The return obligations amount to relatively little beyond the marriage itself, nor is there any extension to the relatives of these in-laws. On a household or lineage basis, however, there is a better balance. The husband's household loses an economic worker but gains a 'female relative-in-law'; correlatively the wife's household gains economic support and furnishes a worker for marriage and other activities. On a village-wide basis households gain 'male relatives-in-law' and lose brothers, men being shifted around from household to household.

This summary of basic relationships and patterns of behaviour makes it possible to characterize further the kinship structure of the Hopi. That structure is remarkably uniform from village to village, and has reached a high degree of consistency in the interrelations of its parts. The structural pattern gives further evidence of the importance of lineage and household groupings. The primary superordinate relationships, involving authority and control, are not organized on the basis of the elementary family or the parental generation, but are confined to ego's own lineage and concentrated largely in the mother's generation. The line of women maintains authority over the activities of the household, but the primary authority and punishing power is concentrated in the mother's brother. The father and his sisters, on the other hand, are in quite a different relationship, despite their similarity in generation. Correlated with these superordinate relationships is the primary reponsibility for transmitting the ritual and social heritage of the lineage and clan, the heritage of highest value in Hopi eyes.

Within the same lineage and generation are found the basic co-operative relationships--those characteristic between siblings. In Hopi theory one should always be able to depend on one's brothers and sisters for aid and support. The relationship between two sisters is perhaps the most fundamental, being the closest and most permanent in Hopi thinking. Brothers maintain close co-operation also, despite responsibilities in marriage. Brothers and sisters, on the other hand, have somewhat different but complementary duties towards the household and lineage, and their relations are in large measure expressed in their duties towards each other's children. Age differences between siblings are of no great moment: knowledge is considered of greater value than age, generally speaking.

The sibling relationship is perhaps the most widely extended of any Hopi kinship relation. The position of the mother's sister as a second 'mother', often indistinguishable from the biological mother in Hopi thought, is a reflection of this relationship. Occasionally the mother's mother's mother is classed as an 'older sister', parallel with the classing of her brother as an 'older brother'. More significant is the extension of sibling relationships to all the members of one's clan and phratry who are of the same age or generation, and to all the children of men of the father's clan and phratry, including the clans and phratries of the 'ceremonial' and 'doctor fathers', regardless of age. These extensions make available a vast number of potential sibling relationships and provide a lateral integration between a number of separate lineages and clans.

The relations of a man to his father's lineage and household are of a different order. Here are more affectionate relations, involving economic and ceremonial obligations without superordination or direct co-operation. The father's sister-brother's son relation is the most elaborated, involving affection and esteem tinged with sexual behavior,[18] along with ceremonial obligations which are repaid by salt-gathering trips and hunting activities. The father's relation to his children involves his economic activities on behalf of the household, activities which are reciprocated in later life by the son. These relationships are extended to all the men and women of the father's clan and phratry, and later to the 'ceremonial' and 'doctor father's' clans and phratries.

The grandparent-grandchild relationship is largely one of affection and comradeship without any particular obligations or exercise of authority, except for the mother's mother. This relationship is rather widely extended, both on a clan basis and to any very old person, suggesting that the Hopi look upon this relationship as a generalized one.

The relations between spouses are non-reciprocal, tenuous, and brittle, in contrast to the enduring relations between relatives by blood. Men marrying into a lineage and household offer economic support in exchange for sexual privileges and children; this relationship gradually becomes more co-operative as the husband acquires a greater stake in his wife's household. The wife, in turn, has certain obligations to her husband's lineage and clan.

This brief analysis of structural relationships in Hopi kinship illustrates the importance of the lineage in organizing and integrating the basic relationships within the group. Within the lineage associated with one's own household are the primary superordinate and co-operative relationships, which are basic to the transmission of the social heritage and the operations of daily life. Related to these are the affinal relationships, which help to maintain the household and lineage. The other related lineages and households share in a relation characterized by affection and interest, and involving many obligations which are later repaid, but with little or no superordination or direct co-operation.

Within the overlapping structures of the household and lineage the primary bonds and loyalties, in Hopi thinking, should lie with the lineage relatives; affines are not tolerated if they interfere with the integrity of the lineage. This is particularly true of women, who make up the core of both the lineage and household. Men, on the other hand, play a role in two households, their own and their wife's. Their major interests are normally much wider, going beyond these groups to the clan and associational structures, in which they play an important and significant role, in contrast to their position in the household.

Space does not permit the presentation of the details of the life cycle, in which the activities of lineage and household relatives may be seen during the period from birth to death.[19] Throughout this period we see the continuing importance of the mother's and father's lineages and households, with the addition of the 'ceremonial father's' lineage. On all ritual occasions the father's sisters, whether own or ceremonial, play an important role in relation to ego and his lineage, and their efforts are repaid by the latter. The exchanges consequent upon initiations of various kinds furnish a goodly portion of the economic exchanges in Hopi society; from each lineage and household there is a constant inflow and outgo of food, clothing, and other wealth.

SOME GENERAL PRINCIPLES

The kinship system may now be seen in larger perspective. The kinship system classifies relatives into groups on the one hand, and regulates their social behaviour on the other. Towards each class of kindred there is a definite relationship, expressed in terms of duties, obligations, and privileges, which serves to order social life with a minimum of conflict. Within each class of relatives there are degrees of 'closeness', and normally the intensity of the relationship varies with this social closeness.

The closest and most important set of relatives makes up the

lineage group; within this group occur both the most varied obligations and ties and the greatest differentiation in terminology. The
relation to the father's lineage and household is likewise important
but socially simpler--the terminology is also less complex. This
relationship serves as a pattern for the various ceremonial relationships which are possible in Hopi society. The relationship with the
mother's father's lineage is still simpler in both behaviour and terminology. The extensions of kinship on the basis of marriage follow
the pattern of one's own lineage and household.

While the elementary bilateral family can be isolated, the
matrilineal lineage serves to organize these family relatives in a
definite way, linking them together in a structure and giving them a
continuity they lack by themselves. Such families stretch back into
the past and prospectively forward into the future. The kinship system reflects this 'vertical' organization; even the 'life structure'
of the individual shows parallel features of organization.

The basic reciprocity in Hopi kinship terminology is reflected in the reciprocal behaviour patterns between most pairs of relatives. When the relationships are non-reciprocal, so also is the
terminology. Only in the case of such genealogically distant relatives as 'grandparents' have the Hopi classed together relatives with
somewhat different positions.

With regard to the kinship system it may be said that there
is a rather precise correlation between the present terminology and
the present social behaviour of relatives. There is little reason
to interpret the kinship system in terms of previous social conditions, nor is it desirable or necessary to restrict the analysis to
linguistic and psychological factors. When our knowledge of Hopi
history is increased, however, it will be indispensable in analysing
the shifts from Basin Shoshoni types of social structure to those of
the modern Hopi.[20]

We may now examine the extent to which the principles outlined by Professor Radcliffe-Brown in 'The Study of Kinship Systems'
are exemplified in the Hopi kinship system. We have noted that the
Hopi system is 'classificatory' in that lineal relatives are grouped
with collateral relatives, and that kinship covers a wide range. He
points out that in such systems 'the distinction between lineal and
collateral relatives is clearly recognized and is of great importance
in social life, but it is in certain respects subordinated to another
structural principle, which can be spoken of as the principle of the
solidarity of the sibling group'.[21] The importance of the bond between brothers and sisters in the Hopi social structure has already

been noted. It finds expression in the equation of the father with
the father's brother, and of the mother with the mother's sister, in
the various extensions of kinship, and in the household and lineage
activities. Interestingly enough it does not find expression here
in such institutions as the sororate or levirate, or in sororal polygyny or fraternal polyandry. In the light of the organization of
the Hopi household these customs would be inefficient or difficult
to carry out. Their absence does call into question the frequent
explanation of 'classificatory' terminologies as the direct result
of the levirate and sororate.

The principle of the 'distinction of generation', as noted
above, has only limited application. Within the lineage there is
superordination and authority, correlative with the responsibility
for transmitting the social and ritual heritage, but even here the
mother's mother's brother is frequently taken out of this role and
classed as a sibling. The grandparent-grandchild relation is one of
friendliness and general lack of authority; the Hopi have extended
this relationship rather widely and loosely, but on a lineage rather
than a generation basis.

The most important structural principle among the Hopi, however, is the principle which Professor Radcliffe-Brown has recently
referred to as the solidarity and unity of the lineage group. This
seems to be a composite principle, built up on the basis of unilateral descent and the equivalence of siblings. The main axis is the
mother-child relationship, particularly that of mother to daughter.
Correlated with this is the sibling relationship, particularly that
of two sisters.

We have already noted the expression of the solidarity of
the lineage as indicated in the internal relations between lineage
relatives, and in their treatment of outsiders connected by marriage.
The unity of the lineage group is noted particularly in the treatment
of the father's and mother's father's matrilineal lineages, and in
the organization of relatives by marriage. The central role of a
line of women in the lineage and household serves to tie together
these two basic institutions. The peripheral role of the father and
husband and his varying responsibilities for training and punishment
on the one hand, and economic support on the other, do not bind him
strongly to either institution; he finds his basic satisfactions in
the kiva dances and ceremonials in many cases.

The weakness of the husband-wife bond may be a structural
corollary of a strong lineage principle. Where primary loyalties
have developed to lineage and household it is difficult to develop

strong ties between spouses, particularly in the case of matrilocal residence and female ownership of house and land.[22] Wives usually side with their house or lineage mates in disputes involving their husbands; in crises even grandfathers may be treated as outsiders by the lineage group. Husbands often fail in the difficult adjustment to a new household; wives, who have little adjustment to make, easily fall back on the household in the case of separation or divorce.

Perhaps the most significant aspect of the Hopi lineage is its function of conserving and transmitting, not only the social and ritual heritage, but property rights, houses, and ceremonies as well, from one generation to the next. Professor Radcliffe-Brown has used the analogy of a corporation conserving an estate, and has pointed out the advantages of unilineal descent in achieving that goal.[23] Among the Hopi the women of a lineage or clan act as trustees with reference to land and houses, holding them in trust for the generations to come. Similarly they may own ceremonies and ritual paraphernalia, leadership being exercised by a mother's brother and passed to one of his sister's sons.

Explanations of kinship systems of the Hopi type have frequently been in terms of particular forms of marriage, specifically marriage with the mother's brother's widow. Such marriages, however, are not customary among the Hopi and in fact seldom occur. A more useful interpretation would seem to be in terms of the principles here sketched. The lineage principle has been shown to play a significant role in household and clan, in marriage, and in the conservation of Hopi values. The 'vertical' integration and continuity of Hopi society and culture is largely centred in the lineage. With regard to 'horizontal' or village-wide integration, the lineage groupings are tied together in a loose-knit way by the principle of the equivalence of siblings and by ceremonial and other bonds.

Hopi society, despite appearances, is not highly integrated. As it has no political superstructure, the clan and phratry groups tend to assert their position at the expense of the village. Hopi society has been held together by kinship ties, marriage bonds, and associational structures which cut across clan lines. Rituals and ceremonies are not highly centralized, being controlled by clans but performed by societies for the good of the village. In the past certain external pressures have also assisted in integrating the Hopi social system; observation of the present process of disintegration furnishes valuable insight into the nature of that integration.

Professor Radcliffe-Brown has said: 'All that a teacher can do is to assist the student in learning to understand and use the

scientific method. It is not his business to make disciples.'[24]
In the larger study of which this present paper is a small section,
I hope to show the relevance of certain of his concepts and prin-
ciples in the comparative study of social systems. Here I have tried
to show how one or two principles are exemplified in one group, the
Hopi. Taken with the other studies in this volume it may be a step
towards the natural science of society which has long been Professor
Radcliffe-Brown's major goal.

NOTES

[1]A. R. Radcliffe-Brown, 'On Social Structure', and 'The Study of
Kinship Systems', *Journal Royal Anthropological Institute*, lxx (1940),
lxxi (1941).

[2]See, in addition to his previously cited papers, 'The Social Organization of Australian Tribes', *Oceania*, v. i (1930-1).

[3]This study, "The Kinship System and Social Organization of the
Western Pueblos with Special Reference to the Hopi Indians', Ph.D.
Thesis, University of Chicago, 1933, was originally written as a doctoral thesis. Field work was carried out among the Hopi of Third
Mesa under the auspices of the Laboratory of Anthropology at Santa
Fe, New Mexico, during the summer of 1932; a research assistantship
provided by the Social Science Research Committee of the University
of Chicago made it possible, under Professor Radcliffe-Brown's direction, to become acquainted with comparable data for Pueblo and other
groups. The winter season of 1933-4 was spent among the Hopi, partly with Dr. Mischa Titiev, a co-worker of the summer of 1932, whose
monograph, 'Old Oraibi', *Papers, Peabody Museum of American Archaeology and Ethnology*, Harvard University, xxii (1944), has recently appeared. During the summer of 1940, my wife, Dorothy Eggan, and I began a study of social and cultural change among the Hopi villages
which is still in process, under the sponsorship of the Department
of Anthropology of the University of Chicago.

[4]See Titiev, op. cit., ch. vii, for a discussion of the relations
between Hopi ethnology and Pueblo archaeology. I have in preparation
an extended discussion of social and cultural change over a long period of time, utilizing the results of the archaeological excavations
at Awatovi under the direction of Dr. J. O. Brew and the studies of
Basin Shoshoni social organization made by Professor Julian Steward.

[5]For detailed discussions of the Hopi geographical environment
and their external adjustment, see C. D. Forde, 'Hopi Agriculture
and Land Ownership', *Journal Royal Anthropological Institute*, lxi
(1931); and J. T. Hack, 'The Changing Physical Environment of the
Hopi Indians of Arizona', *Papers, Peabody Museum of American Archaeology and Ethnology*, Harvard University, xxxv. 1 (1942).

[6]For a general account see E. C. Parsons, *Pueblo Indian Religion*,
Chicago: University of Chicago (1939).

[7]The village of Hano is composed of Tewa-speaking peoples from
the Rio Grande region who migrated westward and settled on First Mesa
after the Pueblo Rebellion in 1680. Their social organization has
been briefly but excellently described by B. Freire-Marreco, 'Tewa
Kinship Terms from the Pueblo of Hano, Arizona', *American Anthropologist*, N.S. xvi (1914), pp. 269-87. A comparison of her account
with those for the Tewa of the Rio Grande and with the present account will show the profound reorientation of Hano social structure;
for details see my forthcoming *Social Organization of the Western
Pueblos*.

[8]For a detailed presentation see Eggan, 'Kinship System'; Titiev, op. cit., has used the social organization as the basis for his masterly analysis of the whole round of Hopi culture.

[9]While English terms are used for convenience, these terms must be understood with reference to their Hopi applications and meanings, which latter are determined by the reciprocal behaviour involved. Terms used in a classificatory sense are usually enclosed in quotation marks.

[10]For reasons of kinship theory the analysis is here made from the standpoint of the lineage rather than of the clan. Titiev, op. cit., prefers an analysis in terms of the clan, but I believe the usefulness of the distinction can be demonstrated in comparative studies.

[11]E. C. Parsons, op. cit., for reasons which I cannot follow, prefers to call these groupings 'linked clans', but structurally they correspond to phratries despite their lack of a name. Compare Titiev's discussion of this problem, op. cit., ch. iv.

[12]Titiev, op. cit., pp. 13-14. The problem of cross-cousin marriage has been considered by Titiev, 'The Problem of Cross-Cousin Marriage among the Hopi', *American Anthropologist*, N.S. xl (1938).

[13]See Eggan, 'Kinship System'; Titiev, 'Old Oraibi', ch. ii; and L. W. Simmons (ed.), *Sun Chief*, New Haven: Yale University Press (1942), for details.

[14]Titiev, 'Old Oraibi', pp. 39-43, has a detailed discussion of divorce among the Hopi.

[15]This situation is consonant with the use of separate terms for 'younger brother' and 'younger sister' when a man is speaking, whereas a woman uses only one term 'younger sibling', for both.

[16]Compare Titiev's discussion of cross-cousin marriage noted above.

[17]See Simmons, op. cit., pp. 39-40 for examples.

[18]Dorothy Eggan, 'The General Problem of Hopi Adjustment', *American Anthropologist*, N.S. xlv (1943), pp. 357-73, has offered a possible psychological interpretation of this situation in terms of the Oedipus complex.

[19]See Eggan, 'Kinship System', and Titiev, 'Old Oraibi', for an account of the life cycle.

[20]Compare R. H. Lowie, 'Hopi Kinship', and 'Notes on Hopi Clans', *American Museum of Natural History, Anthropological Papers*, xxx, pts. 6 and 7 (1939); J. H. Steward, 'Ecological Aspects of Southwestern Society', *Anthropos*, xxxii. 1 and 2 (1937); and Titiev, 'Old Oraibi', ch. vii.

[21]A. R. Radcliffe-Brown, 'The Study of Kinship', p. 7.

[22]Under modern conditions in certain of the villages there is a shift to separate residences built and owned by the husband and to male ownership of land. Correlated with these features is a greater stability of marriage. Since the Government and missionaries have tried to bring about all of these 'improvements', it is now difficult to determine the nature of their interrelationships.

[23]A. R. Radcliffe-Brown, 'Patrilineal and Matrilineal Succession', *Iowa Law Review*, xx. 2 (1935).

[24]Id., 'On Social Structure', p. 1.

5

NORTHERN WOODLAND ETHNOLOGY

1967

The growth of our knowledge of Northern Woodland ethnology parallels
on a smaller scale the development of American anthropology as a whole.
For the purposes of the present survey I shall be concerned primarily
with the Algonkian-speaking populations north of the Great Lakes-St.
Lawrence region, although I will have something to say about their
linguistic relatives and neighbors to the south and west.

This northern region has had a long and interesting history,
dating from the voyages of Jacques Cartier in 1535, and has played
an important role in the development of our continent, but our scientific knowledge of its aboriginal peoples and their cultures is much
more recent. The central figure in our knowledge of the Northern
Woodlands is Frank G. Speck. Speck began his pioneer researches among
the Montagnais and Naskapi in 1908, and over the next two decades he
literally put them and their neighbors on the ethnographic map. By
1926 he was able to present a survey and interpretation of "Culture
Problems in Northeastern North America," which summed up what he had
learned and set the stage for further research.

Here he was primarily concerned with historical problems--
with the relations of the Northeastern Algonkians to their neighbors,
and with the origins of Northeastern culture patterns and their relations to the circumpolar culture complexes constructed by Birket-Smith
and Gudmund Hatt. Speck at this time saw the Northeast as "one of
the world's marginal culture zones, an archaic one, where human groups
have resided for a long time apart from cultural changes and innovations which have arisen elsewhere on the continent." (Speck, 1926,
p. 272) But he raised the question of whether the cultural simplicity of the area was pristine, or arrived at through cultural reduction;

Reproduced by permission of Temple University Publications,
Philadelphia, from *The Philadelphia Anthropological Society: Papers
Presented on its Golden Anniversary*, Jacob W. Gruber, editor (1967),
pp. 107-124.

and he touched on most of the problems which later were to be significant.

In the following two decades a number of Speck's students
and associates at the University of Pennsylvania, notably A. I.
Hallowell, D. S. Davidson, and Loren C. Eiseley, began field and li-
brary research on the Northern Woodlands, extending their activities
over a wider geographical area and a greater range of problems.
Joining them in this period were such scholars as Father John M.
Cooper and Regina Flannery of Catholic University; Julius Lips, W. D.
Strong, Diamond Jenness, Truman Michelson, W. J. Wintemberg, and Ruth
Landes, among others. Speck's early observations on "The Family
Hunting Band as the Basis of Algonkian Social Organization" (1915)
were tested and broadened, and the aboriginality of the family hunting territory system was debated. But of greater significance were
the new directions of research: a greater interest in problems of
ecology, a more sophisticated approach to social structure, a new
concern with processes of cultural change, a realization of the importance of archaeology and linguistics, and a growing awareness of
the role of the individual in social interaction and the significance
of personality structure for the understanding of the culture process.

Several of these new directions converge in the work of
Hallowell. Beginning with a survey of "Bear Ceremonialism in the
Northern Hemisphere" (1926), he concentrated his attention during
the decade of the 1930s on the Northern Ojibwa, or Salteaux, and spent
most of his summers systematically investigating a series of related
problems among the bands of the Lake Winnipeg-Berens River region.
Here he was able to study the ecology of the family hunting system
under neoaboriginal conditions, establish the significance of cross-
cousin marriage as a social system, and unravel the psychological
characteristics of the Northern Ojibwa with the aid of case studies
and projective tests.

This period culminated with the symposium on "Man in Northeastern North America" (Johnson, 1946), held at Andover in December
1941, but not published until after the war. This volume, which was
edited by Frederick Johnson and dedicated to Speck, is a landmark in
American anthropology. It not only summarizes (in 300 pages) what
had been accomplished in four decades of research, but outlines new
problems for the future. Douglas Byers' survey of the environment
of the Northeast is followed by five papers devoted to various aspects
of the archaeology of the region by W. C. McKern, James B. Griffin,
William A. Ritchie, Frederica de Laguna, and Albert C. Spaulding.
W. W. Howells surveys the physical types of the Northeast, and Carl

and Erminie Voegelin bring together the linguistic researches of Truman Michelson and Leonard Bloomfield. Hallowell discusses the psychological characteristics of the Northeastern Indians, and Margaret Fisher surveys the mythology of the region in relation to Algonkian mythology as a whole. The "descriptive survey" and "reconstructive interpretation" of the culture of the Northeastern Indians were prepared by Regina Flannery and John M. Cooper, respectively.

These discussions cast doubt on some of the earlier reconstructions of culture history in the Northern Woodlands. Father Cooper, in particular, critically reviews the hypotheses of his predecessors with regard to the origin and development of the Northeastern hunting culture and its accretions. He finds the evidence for the circumpolar "ice-hunting" and "snowshoe" stages insufficient, and proposes an ecologically conditioned "tiaga economy" in its place. He also considers the family hunting ground system as representing a more recent local development in the Northeast, though he still believes it antedates white contact.

In the meantime Speck had begun to penetrate further into the inner world of the Northeastern Indians, and in *Naskapi, the Savage Hunters of the Labrador Peninsula* (1935), he presented their conceptions of religion and cosmology. Here his linguistic skills and his ability to create close personal relationships with Indian friends were important ingredients in his success. By an analysis of native terms he was able to discover a systematic relationship between their view of the universe, their conception of man's relation to nature, and the proper conduct of man in society. Here a functional viewpoint is to the fore; though Speck is still concerned with distributions, these are subordinated to the understanding that can come from context.

The present writer became interested in the Northern Algonkians about this same time, in connection with an attempt to understand some puzzling features in the kinship systems of the Cheyenne, Arapaho, and Gros Ventre (Eggan, 1937). A few years earlier Hallowell had asked, "Was Cross-Cousin Marriage Formerly Practiced by the North-Central Algonkian?" (1928), on the basis of his study of kinship terms in early dictionaries. The question was answered in the affirmative by W. D. Strong, who had just returned from Northern Labrador where he found cross-cousin marriage in full operation among one of the bands of northern Naskapi (Strong, 1929). During the next few years the practice was reported by a number of investigators from several Northern Woodland groups. Hallowell's account of "Cross-Cousin Marriage in the Lake Winnipeg Area" (1937) outlined the char-

acteristics of the resulting social system, and proposed the hypothesis that variations in Northern Algonkian kinship systems are "intelligible as a result of acculturative processes and differences in
local conditions." (*ibid.*, p. 108) At about the same time Ruth
Landes was carrying out a series of studies of the Ojibwa of southern
Canada, and her comprehensive account of social organization on
the Rainy Lake reserve (Landes, 1937) provided some important differences. In the postwar period the application of Hallowell's working
hypothesis has proved remarkably productive in furthering our understanding of change in social systems.

In a region such as the Northern Woodlands, occupied by populations who depended primarily on hunting, fishing, and gathering for
their subsistence, the environmental characteristics are obviously
of great importance. In the early days of American anthropology, in
reaction to extreme conceptions of environmental determinism, the
environment was considered as an essentially neutral factor in cultural development. It sets limits but it was not a creative force.
Speck accepted this view, to begin with, but his early interest in
natural history, which led him to study the family hunting territory
system, soon took him beyond into the religious beliefs concerning
nature and the animal species. He also influenced several students
in these directions, notably D. S. Davidson, Loren C. Eiseley, and
A. I. Hallowell.

Davidson's detailed studies of the Grand Lake Victoria and
Tête de Boule bands (Davidson, 1926, 1928) showed important variations
in social organization which suggested environmental determinants.
These and other studies (Davidson, 1937) led to a greater concern for
the ecological characteristics of winter life, and to a consideration
of the significance of migratory and sedentary characteristics in the
game animals on which the Northern Woodland populations depended.
Speck and Eiseley accepted these considerations as valid in a paper
on the "Significance of Hunting Territory Systems of the Algonkian
in Social Theory" (1939), but were more concerned with the attack by
Diamond Jenness (1935) on the aboriginality of the family hunting
territory system.

One of my own students, Arch Cooper, investigated the "Ecological Aspects of the Family Hunting Territory System of the Northeastern Algonkians" (1942) in a Master's thesis, and suggested that the
variations could best be explained in ecological terms. He found
both a sociological and an ecological gradient from northeast to
southwest within the area, and developed a model to explain their interrelationships in terms of five factors: (1) the productivity of

the natural environment, (2) the definiteness of the local organization, (3) the degree of band cohesion, (4) the strength of patriliny, and (5) the relative frequency of elementary and extended family units. Hallowell (1949) also devoted attention to these problems, and has discussed "The Size of Algonkian Hunting Territories, A Function of Ecological Adjustment," utilizing his own field data from the Berens River region. Here he is relatively unconcerned with the question of the aboriginality of the system, but concentrates his attention on the specific conditions which control the variables of size and composition of the winter hunting groups, the size of the hunting tracts, and the rules governing their transfer.

The question of the aboriginality of the family hunting territory system of the Northeastern Algonkians has led to considerable controversy in the literature. Jenness, on the basis of his study of the Parry Island Ojibwa, had come to the conclusion that their system had developed since the advent of the fur trade, and that this conclusion might be applied to the Eastern Algonkians in general (1935, pp. 4-6). Julian Steward supported this position, on the basis of the intimate functional relationship of the family ownership system to the highly specialized economy introduced by the fur trade (1936, p. 339), and his own studies of the Athabascan-speaking Carrier of British Columbia. Since the documentary data in the *Jesuit Relations* could be interpreted either way, there was no adequate solution until Eleanor Leacock carried out field research among the Montagnais-Naskapi in 1950, centered on this specific problem. Her monograph on *The Montagnais "Hunting Territory" and the Fur Trade* (1954) clarifies the issues and comes to the conclusion that the family hunting territory is post-Columbian and definitely related to the fur trade in the area of southeastern Labrador. She also analyzes the dynamics of band and family composition in terms of modern acculturative forces--the fur trade, the trading post, and European settlement--and sees the same processes at work among other Arctic hunters. Her concluding sentences (p. 43) are worth quoting because they signalize a postwar point of view:

> "Acculturation" is now recognized as encompassing more than the final breakdown of Indian societies. . . . It is becoming increasingly evident that Indian tribal life as recorded in the nineteenth and even late eighteenth centuries reflected important changes which had already come about as a result of the Indians taking an active part in the worldwide growth of trade and commerce. . . . The present study has taken the position that the northern Algonkians are no exception. Their apparent primitivity is deceptive. In order to reconstruct their aboriginal culture, one cannot simply record their recent life and subtract those traits that are of obvious European origin. One must work from an understanding that fundamental socio-economic changes

have been taking place in some parts of their area for over three hundred years, one aspect of which is the development of the family hunting territory.

Hallowell has extended our knowledge in a different direction through his emphasis on the individual and his psychological characteristics. From his researches during the decade of the 1930s have come a remarkable series of papers which the Philadelphia Anthropological Society has recently published under the title *Culture and Experience* (1955). While his ultimate aim is to formulate the necessary and sufficient conditions that make human existence possible, he has also analyzed the characteristics of the Ojibwa world as it is conceptualized and experienced by the individual, and has tentatively formulated the psychological character structure of the Eastern Woodland Indians. Here he has built in part on the foundation furnished by Speck, but through his utilization of projective techniques and case histories he has been able to penetrate considerably further.

Hallowell's and Landes' studies of the Northern Ojibwa have stimulated a number of studies of the Southern Ojibwa or Chippewa in Minnesota and Wisconsin, who have had a somewhat different recent history and have been subject to a greater degree of reservation acculturation. Barnouw, in a study of *Acculturation and Personality among the Wisconsin Chippewa* (1950), emphasized the atomistic nature of their social structure and attempted to explain it in terms of a persistence of aboriginal patterns, reinforced by the partial maintenance of personality structure through child training and other procedures. This analysis, based on documentary data, field reports, and life history materials, has been supported by Ernestine Friedl (1956) and challenged by Bernard James (1961) and Harold Hickerson (1960). In his reply to the latter, Barnouw (1961) clarifies his position but continues to maintain his view that "social atomism" is an old Chippewa pattern.

In the light of Hallowell's accounts of the Northern Ojibwa, and R. W. Dunning's recent monograph (1959) on the same region, it is clear that Ruth Landes' characterization of Northern Ojibwa society as "atomistic" is not tenable in any terms but comparative ones. The further data provided by Hickerson in his recent monograph on *The Southwestern Chippewa, an Ethnohistorical Study* (1962) would seem to dispose of the concept of "social atomism," so far as the Southern Ojibwa are concerned. It is probable that the social isolation noted by Barnouw and others is a product of reservation life. Here Hallowell's observations on the Lac du Flambeau Ojibwa of Wisconsin (1955, Chapters 18 and 19) are pertinent. Comparing their personality struc-

tures as seen through the Rorschach data with those of the Berens
River and Lake Winnipeg region, he finds a continuity of basic psychological pattern, but emphasizes that important modifications in
their psychological structure have taken place.

> It is at Flambeau where we can see reflected in the Rorschach
> data an introversive personality structure being pushed to the
> limits of its functional adequacy. The whole trend is one that
> seems to be accelerating in a regressive direction. These peo-
> ple are being thrown back on their psychological heels, as it
> were. They are compelled to function with a great paucity of
> inner resources. There is a kind of frustration of maturity.
> [Hallowell, *ibid.*, pp. 351-52]

He goes on to point out that a large percentage of the subjects at
Flambeau fall into the "poorly adjusted" category and suggests that
there are factors at work which set barriers to the achievement of
personal adjustment, particularly the absence of any positive substitute for the aboriginal value system based on religious belief (*ibid.*,
p. 357). It seems probable that the Wisconsin Chippewa have arrived
at their present social and psychological condition largely through
deculturation under modern reservation conditions.

The present writer returned to the problem of cross-cousin
marriage in the postwar period and surveyed the new data available
from the Northern Algonkian groups in terms of Hallowell's hypothesis noted earlier (Eggan, 1955). It seems clear that cross-cousin
marriage had been the basis for the social structure of the northern
groups, and that a clan system had been added later among the Ojibwa.
The series of changes in kinship and marriage, which Strong documented for the Naskapi, were largely the result of mission influence on
the more southern bands, and it is highly probable that Catholic
teaching is responsible for the obsolescence of cross-cousin marriage
among the Montagnais nearer the St. Lawrence. But the series of
shifts among the Northern and Southern Ojibwa, and in the Plains
groups, must have a different explanation. Here the structural requirements of a wider integration incident to life in a more favorable environment, and constant warfare, have been significant factors
in the decline of cross-cousin marriage.

Harold Hickerson has made an important contribution to this
problem in his recent study of the Southwestern Chippewa (1962). He
traces these groups from their earlier residence at Sault Ste. Marie
to the south shore of Lake Superior (where they lived from 1679-1765),
and west into northern Minnesota and Wisconsin. Here they came into
continued conflict with the Eastern Dakota, or Sioux, and Hickerson
has documented the ecological basis of their warfare and its effects
upon social and cultural life. One important result of warfare was

that the village came to be the basic unit of social life, and the bands subordinate. For purposes of successful conflict against the larger Dakota villages, the Chippewa villages developed alliances and warrior organizations which were unknown in the north. Hickerson has found no reference to cross-cousin marriage for the Southwestern Chippewa in the historic period. He concludes that they "had long since dropped the practice of bilateral cross-cousin marriage, not through influences attributable to simple acculturative factors but for dynamic sociopolitical reasons." (*ibid.*, p. 86)

A study titled "Central Algonkian Social Organization" (1958) by Charles Callender clarifies and documents this situation from a different standpoint. In analyzing the kinship systems and social structures of the various Algonkian-speaking tribes south of the Great Lakes, Callender enlisted the aid of Charles Hockett (1964), who was able to reconstruct enough kinship terms to demonstrate the presence of cross-cousin marriage among the proto-Central Algonkian populations. Callender attributes the loss of cross-cousin marriage to such factors as larger populations incident to agriculture, corporate clan groups, complex village organization, and warfare.

At the other end of the Ojibwa continuum, Dunning (1959) has made the first detailed study of the structure and functioning of a band organization throughout its yearly cycle and in relation to the new influences from the outside world. The Pekangekum band, among whom he worked in 1954-1955, is the most isolated of the Berens River bands studied by Hallowell two decades earlier. Here we have a detailed account of the ecology and economy, the summer and winter groupings, and the patterns of marriage and kinship. Of particular importance are the changes since the war, where government subsidies have brought the small residential units in from the trap-lines and drawn them to the trading post. With the growth of population the band becomes more endogamous, and cross-cousin marriage begins to shift from close to more distant relatives.

A. L. Kroeber, some time ago (1939, p. 35), noted that the Ojibwa were among the least known of American tribes, despite the number of scholars who had studied them. It is clear from the above remarks that we now have most of the ingredients for a detailed and comparative account. The dissemination of the Ojibwa from a residence in the vicinity of Lakes Huron and Superior both northwest and southwest during the seventeenth and eighteenth centuries is well attested. The differences between the Berens River bands and the Minnesota and Wisconsin villages, let alone those of the Plains Ojibwa, indicate what can happen to society and culture within a relatively short time. The Northern Ojibwa (Salteaux) under neoaboriginal conditions reduced the size of their bands and spread their hunting-trapping units over wide but defined territories. Cross-cousin marriage shifted from a preferential to a prescriptive pattern, and the kinship terminology was modified accordingly. The totemic clan system was reduced in scope and significance, and the ritual system was simplified. Warfare was absent. The Southern Ojibwa, on the other hand, with greater economic resources, increased their population density, and the village and its institutions became the basic social unit. The winter hunting bands were subordinate to the village community, and the patrilineal clans may have developed additional ritual functions. The Midewiwin became a village or even intervillage institution. The narrow but intensive integration brought about by cross-cousin marriage was no longer adequate in the south, where loyalties and alliances were on a village level. And the century of continuous conflict with the Dakota over hunting grounds made survival depend upon matching the efficiency of the foe. If personality remained the same under these differences, it must be largely independent of society and culture.

The differences between the Northern and Southern Ojibwa can be clarified both by studying the intermediate groups along the border and by examining the neighboring Cree to the north and the Central Algonkians to the south. The Cree, in a severer environment, have most of the institutions of the Northern Ojibwa--except for the clan system. The Central Algonkian tribes have elaborated the clan and phratry system as corporate groups, and have developed village-wide leadership and institutions. There is no trace of cross-cousin marriage in the kinship system; the latter has shifted to an Omaha type consonant with the lineage organization and clan exogamy.

From the little knowledge we have of the Eastern and Southeastern Algonkian groups south of the St. Lawrence and along the eastern seaboard, it is probable that similar processes were at work. The Wabanaki, according to Speck (1926), showed radical changes in political life, social organization, and mythology as a result of contacts with the Iroquois and other groups to the south. A detailed comparison with the Southern Ojibwa might show many interesting parallels. The Southeastern Algonkians had a still more complex sociopolitical organization as a result of interaction with the Cherokee and other tribes of the Southeast, but we have few details of their organization and cultural life.

We have so far outlined some of the major developments in Northern Woodland ethnology, and it is time to say a few words about

future prospects. There are a number of recent developments which
will affect the future directions of research in the Northern Woodlands, as well as a number of problems which would repay intensive
research, now that we have more sophisticated conceptual tools and
greater resources.

In an earlier survey of "The Ethnological Cultures and their
Archeological Backgrounds" (Eggan, 1952) in the Eastern United States,
I emphasized the important role which archaeology was beginning to
play in the reconstruction of the culture history of that region.
George I. Quimby's recent account of *Indian Life in the Upper Great
Lakes, 11,000 B.C. to A.D. 1800* (1960) presents an outline of the
new knowledge gained from geology, paleontology, archaeology, paly-
nology, and radiocarbon dating, of the prehistory of this important
region. While the glaciers began their retreat about 11,000 B.C.,
the ice lasted north of the Superior basin until about 4500 B.C.,
according to Quimby, which effectively prevented the establishment
of plants and animals, as well as human populations, until a later
period. Since Hudson Bay is assumed to be the last continental center of glaciation, it is probable that the Labrador peninsula was
covered for an even longer period.

These data suggest that Speck's view of the Northeast as a
refuge area for "archaic" populations retaining earlier culture patterns is no longer tenable, even with the modifications suggested by
Father Cooper. But there is evidence of the northward spread of early man as the ice retreated or melted, and as vegetation and animals
took its place. Quimby identifies and dates a series of archaeological assemblages in the Great Lakes region, beginning with Paleo-
Indian hunters, Archaic Boreal Indians, the Old Copper culture, and
Early, Middle, and Late Woodland groups, some of the latter being
ancestral to historic tribes.

In the Northeast the archaeological sequences are not yet
clear. Here the Eskimo Dorset culture has a number of elements which
resemble Indian types, but the age of its earliest manifestations is
not known. I have not been able to keep abreast of archaeological
research in New England and the Maritime Provinces, though these are
obviously of great potential importance.

The utilization of historical sources and documentary data
has long been an important research technique with regard to the Eastern Woodlands generally. John M. Swanton in the Southeast and Speck
and his students in the East and Northeast have made masterly use of
these materials to delineate aboriginal and early historic culture
patterns. But in recent years there has been an increasing tendency

to utilize such materials for studies of social and cultural change. An important early study along these lines is F. M. Keesing's monograph, *The Menomini Indians of Wisconsin* (1939), which he subtitled "A Study of Three Centuries of Cultural Contact and Change." Vernon Kinietz' *The Indians of the Western Great Lakes, 1615-1760* (1940) presents the ethnographic data available in the documentary sources on five tribal groups, but without further interpretation.

The establishment of the National Archives and the passage of the Indian Claims Act have led to renewed research in the postwar period on specific questions but have also resulted in a number of important by-products. The rapprochement which is taking place between historians and ethnologists is one important event, signalized by the formation of the American Indian Ethnohistoric Conference and the publication of the journal *Ethnohistory*. Another is the establishment of archival collections on the Indian populations of particular regions, such as the archives of the Great Lakes-Ohio Valley Research Project at Indiana University. From such collections it is now possible to write an almost year-by-year account of many Indian groups, as well as to clarify and extend our knowledge of particular problems. Harold Hickerson's ethnohistorical account of the Southwestern Chippewa (1962) and Anthony Wallace's "Political Organization and Land Tenure among Northeastern Indians, 1600-1830" (1957), are examples of what we may expect in the immediate future. In the longer run we can look forward to a more sophisticated history of the American Indian, in which the cultural component will have adequate representation.

The potentialities of linguistics for the unraveling of ethnological problems has not as yet been systematically applied to the Northern Woodland regions. Through the pioneer researches of Bloomfield and Michelson we have considerable information on the Central Algonkian languages, but their subgroupings and relations to Western and Eastern branches are not yet clear. Here lexicostatistics should be of assistance in clarifying relationships and subgroupings. That Cree-Montagnais-Naskapi are dialects of one language, and Ojibwa-Ottawa-Salteaux-Algonkian another, from the standpoint of the linguist, has not been sufficiently taken into account in ethnological comparisons and interpretations. Nor have the possibilities of reconstruction of cultural traits through linguistic comparison been carried very far.

At the other extreme, Mary Haas' recent demonstration (1958) that the Algonkian and Gulf language stocks are genetically related presents us with new perspectives. When coupled with earlier sugges-

tions by Sapir and others, they suggest an ultimate genetic unity
for most of the languages in Eastern North America, omitting the Eskimo and Athabascans. This linguistic unity may make Kroeber's classification of the Eastern and Northern Woodlands as variants of a
single major culture area more intelligible, and may give us greater
control over the interpretation of the archaeological record.

The time now seems ripe, also, for anthropologists to return
to some of the classic problems of the Northern Woodlands with sharp-
er concepts and better controls. Totemism is one such classic problem, and the term "totem" itself is an Ojibwa word. While American
anthropologists, notably A. A. Goldenweiser, attempted to analyze
totemism out of existence, it is still very much alive. Even though
the Central Algonkian varieties may not be of classical type, they
are still highly relevant to the problems of man's relation to nature. Speck's characterization of hunting as a "sacred" activity
suggests one important approach.

Another series of problems lies in the field of religion.
The Midewiwin ritual, for example, is now ready for intensive study,
both in terms of its historical development and in comparison with
similar rituals elsewhere in the region. It has long been asserted
to be post-Columbian, but the evidence has not yet been assembled in
detail. The so-called *windigo* or *witiiko* psychosis, found mainly
among the Cree and Northern Ojibwa, is now under study by psychia-
trists with interesting results (i.e., Parker, 1960). But they have
analyzed the problem primarily from the standpoint of the victim,
largely ignoring the belief patterns of the society. Dunning (1959,
opposite p. 83) was able to get drawings of the *windigo* cannibal
spirit from eleven- and twelve-year-old boys, but no older person
would draw or discuss this spirit. Such "repression," if it is repression, should warrant investigation, along with the role these
beliefs may play in Northern Woodland groups. Their absence from Eskimo and Northern Athabascan society is intriguing in this connection.

Last, but by no means least, we come to the study of modern
Indian communities in their own terms. Acculturation studies are
relatively recent in American anthropology, but a number are already
under way in the Northern Woodlands, or recently completed. We have
noted the pioneer study of the Menomini by Keesing published just
before the war. This formed the basis for a more sophisticated study
of the processes in Menomini acculturation by George and Louise Spindler, who divided the Menomini into five acculturative categories
and studied the sociocultural and psychological aspects of change
among both men and women (G. Spindler, 1955; L. Spindler, 1962).

Sydney Slotkin's study of Menomini Peyotism (1952) in terms of its social and cultural role in reservation life, is also important in this connection.

A broader and longer term study is the "Algonkian project" of the Ethnology Section of the National Museum of Canada under the direction of Tom McFeat. Much of the early support for ethnological research in the Northeast originally came from museums, including the University Museum in Philadelphia, but after 1930 museums had limited resources for research and devoted much of their attention to displays and housekeeping. During the last few years, however, there are signs of a renaissance, led by ethnologists such as William Fenton, Donald Collier, John C. Ewers, and others. It is quite fitting, therefore, to find that Tom McFeat is proposing to utilize the resources of the National Museum for a systematic and long-term study-- or restudy--of the various Algonkian groups in the Northeast, beginning with the Montagnais-Naskapi and the Micmac and Malecite, and extending to the Cree and Ojibwa. McFeat has given us a preliminary survey of the proposals in "Museum Ethnology and the Algonkian Project" (1962).

The first objective of the study is to describe the stability and changes in group structure over the last hundred years, utilizing previous studies as a baseline. Here the ethnologists can often start with Speck's early data on band composition and territorial arrangements, and follow the changes down to the present. They distinguish two major types of groupings: "territorial" groups who are still hunters and trappers, and "reserve" groups who are usually employed for wages and who generally live on the government reserves.

For these groups they plan to investigate such questions as knowledge of the environment, space orientations, change in band structure, shifts in territorial arrangements, expressions of aggression, public opinion and values, problems of leadership, the character of the shifts from "territorial" to "reserve" groups, and relations with the White world. Some sixteen students and associates are currently at work on various phases of this project, so there should be a rapid accumulation of comparable data.

A comparison of this project with the original objectives of Frank Speck as he began his researches on the Montagnais some fifty years ago gives us an indication of how far anthropology has come in half a century. But it also reminds us of the continuity of anthropology, in that the data collected by these pioneers and the insights they had into Northern Woodland life are still valid and useful. They add a dimension to our data which we would not otherwise have,

and furnish a baseline against which to measure stability and change.
We can also see that anthropology progresses by asking new questions,
as well as on occasion returning to the old ones for a fresh look.

REFERENCES

Barnouw, Victor (1950). *Acculturation and Personality among the Wisconsin Chippewa*. American Anthropological Association, *Memoir* 72.

———— (1961). "Chippewa Social Atomism," *American Anthropologist*, 63, pp. 1006-1013.

Callender, Charles (1958). *Central Algonkian Social Organization*. Publications of the Milwaukee Public Museum, No. 7.

Cooper, Arch (1942). *Ecological Aspects of the Family Hunting Territory System of the Northeastern Algonkians*. Master's thesis, University of Chicago.

Davidson, D. S. (1926). "Family Hunting Territories of the Grand Lake Victoria Indians," *22nd International Congress of Americanists*, pp. 69-96.

———— (1928). "Notes on Tête de Boule Ethnology," *American Anthropologist*, 30, pp. 18-46.

———— (1937). "Snowshoes," American Philosophical Society, *Memoir* 6.

Dunning, R. W. (1959). *Social and Economic Change among the Northern Ojibwa* (Toronto, University of Toronto Press).

Eggan, Fred (1937). "The Cheyenne and Arapaho Kinship System," in Fred Eggan, ed., *Social Anthropology of North American Tribes*, (Chicago, University of Chicago Press, pp. 35-95.

———— (1952). "The Ethnological Cultures and their Archeological Backgrounds," in J. B. Griffin, ed., *Archeology of the Eastern United States* (Chicago, University of Chicago Press), pp. 35-45.

———— (1955). "Social Anthropology: Methods and Results," in Fred Eggan, ed., *Social Anthropology of North American Tribes*, rev. ed. (Chicago, University of Chicago Press), pp. 519-48.

Friedl, Ernestine (1956). "Persistence in Chippewa Culture and Personality," *American Anthropologist*, 58, pp. 814-25.

Griffin, J. B. (ed.) (1952). *Archeology of the Eastern United States* (Chicago, University of Chicago Press).

Haas, Mary (1958). "A New Linguistic Relationship in North America: Algonkian and Gulf Languages," *Southwestern Journal of Anthropology*, 14, pp. 231-64.

Hallowell, A. I. (1926). "Bear Ceremonialism in the Northern Hemisphere," *American Anthropologist*, 28, pp. 1-175.

———— (1928). "Was Cross-Cousin Marriage Formerly Practiced by the North-Central Algonkian?" *23rd International Congress of Americanists*, pp. 519-44.

———— (1937). "Cross-Cousin Marriage in the Lake Winnipeg Area," *Publications of the Philadelphia Anthropological Society*, 1, pp. 95-110.

———— (1949). "The Size of Algonkian Hunting Territories, A Function of Ecological Adjustment," *American Anthropologist*, 51, pp. 35-45.

———— (1955). *Culture and Experience* (Philadelphia, University of Pennsylvania Press).

Hickerson, Harold (1960). "The Feast of the Dead among the Seventeenth Century Algonkians of the Upper Great Lakes," *American Anthropologist*, 62, pp. 81-107.

————— (1962). *The Southwestern Chippewa, an Ethnohistorical Study*. American Anthropological Association, *Memoir* 92.

Hockett, Charles (1964). "The Proto-Central Algonkian Kinship System," in Ward H. Goodenough, ed., *Explorations in Cultural Anthropology* (New York, McGraw-Hill), pp. 239-57.

James, Bernard (1961). "Social-Psychological Dimensions of Ojibwa Acculturation," *American Anthropologist*, 63, pp. 721-46.

Jenness, Diamond (1935). *The Ojibwa of Parry Sound*. Anthropological Series 17, National Museum of Canada, *Bulletin* 78.

Johnson, Frederick (ed.) (1946). *Man in Northeastern North America*. Papers of the Robert S. Peabody Foundation for Archaeology, 3. Andover, Mass.

Keesing, F. M. (1939). *The Menomini Indians of Wisconsin*. American Philosophical Society, *Memoir* 10.

Kinietz, Vernon (1940). *The Indians of the Western Great Lakes, 1615-1760*. Occasional Contributions from the Museum of Anthropology of the University of Michigan, 10.

Kroeber, A. L. (1939). *Cultural and Natural Areas of Native North America*. University of California Publications in American Archaeology and Ethnology, 38.

Landes, Ruth (1937). *Ojibwa Sociology*. Columbia University Publications in Anthropology, 29.

Leacock, Eleanor (1954). *The Montagnais "Hunting Territory" and the Fur Trade*. American Anthropological Association, *Memoir* 78.

McFeat, Tom (1962). *Museum Ethnology and the Algonkian Project*. National Museum of Canada, Ottawa, *Anthropological Papers*, 2.

Parker, Seymour (1960). "The Wittiko Psychosis in the Context of Ojibwa Personality," *American Anthropologist*, 62, pp. 603-23.

Quimby, George I. (1960). *Indian Life in the Upper Great Lakes, 11,000 B.C. to A.D. 1800* (Chicago, University of Chicago Press).

Slotkin, Sydney (1952). *Menomini Peyotism*. American Philosophical Society, *Memoir* 74.

Speck, Frank G. (1915). "The Family Hunting Band as the Basis of Algonkian Social Organization," *American Anthropologist*, 17, pp. 289-305.

————— (1926). "Culture Problems in Northeastern North America," American Philosophical Society, *Proceedings*, 65, pp. 272-311.

————— (1935). *Naskapi, Savage Hunters of the Labrador Peninsula*. (Norman, Okla., University of Oklahoma Press).

Speck, Frank G., and Loren C. Eiseley (1939). "Significance of Hunting Territory Systems of the Algonkian in Social Theory," *American Anthropologist*, 41, pp. 269-80.

Spindler, George (1955). *Sociocultural and Psychological Processes in Menomini Acculturation*. University of California Publications in Culture and Society, 5.

Spindler, Louise (1962). *Menomini Women and Culture Change*. American Anthropological Association, *Memoir* 91.

Strong, W. D. (1929). "Cross-Cousin Marriage and the Culture of the Northeast Algonkian," *American Anthropologist*, 31, pp. 277-88.

Steward, Julian (1936). "The Economic and Social Basis of Primitive Bands," in R. H. Lowie, ed., *Essays in Anthropology Presented to A. L. Kroeber* (Berkeley, University of California Press), pp. 331-50.

Wallace, Anthony (1957). "Political Organization and Land Tenure among Northeastern Indians, 1600-1830," *Southwestern Journal of Anthropology*, 13, pp. 301-21.

6

CULTURE HISTORY DERIVED FROM THE STUDY OF LIVING PEOPLES

1936

I

In his introductory lecture, "The Subject Matter of Anthropology,"
Dr. Redfield has emphasized both the diversity of anthropology and
its unity. The unity of anthropology lies in its broad comparative
treatment of cultural phenomena, and in its primary concern with
primitive or preliterate groups; its diversity is apparent in the
logical character of its aims and in its subject matter. From this
diversity I wish to select certain aspects for more extended consideration: in regard to the logical character of anthropological products we shall be interested in the making of histories, in regard to
subject matter we shall be interested in the cultures of living peoples.

This selection of interests, involving the application of the
historical approach to the study of culture, is conventionally called
"ethnology." Traditionally, ethnology has been concerned with the
"History of Peoples" and has usually included racial and linguistic
history as well, but since these disciplines differ materially in
subject matter and techniques, the modern tendency has been to separate them. This separation, which is followed in the present series
of lectures, has been advantageous in many ways, but should not obscure their unity in terms of historical objectives, nor their contributions to an ultimate synthesis. An ethnologist working with a
tribe or region commonly uses historical information from all possible
sources.

Within the field of anthropology ethnology finds its closest
relations with prehistoric archaeology, which seeks to reconstruct
the history of past cultures. In the field of the social sciences

A lecture originally given before the Division of Social
Sciences, the University of Chicago, October 27, 1936.

the closest relationship is with history. Both the ethnologist and the historian deal with events in time and space and both attempt to organize cultural facts into integrated wholes, or "histories." The historian characteristically is concerned with the interpretation of documents, the ethnologist often is able to participate more directly in the flow of cultural activity. The resulting differences in techniques have obscured the fundamental similarity of approach.

While the majority of students of primitive peoples are interested in culture history, relatively few have been content with remaining exclusively historians. In addition to their interest in the history of cultures they have also been interested in making general statements about culture for one purpose or another. Dr. Redfield suggested the possibility of arranging anthropologists on a linear continuum with reference to their major interest, history or science, but for our purposes it will suffice to select those aspects of the work of various anthropologists which fall within the field of culture history.

In presenting the attempts of ethnologists to derive culture history from living peoples there are several possible approaches. We might outline the history of ethnology with particular reference to the contributions of various ethnologists, or, we might consider the various schools of ethnology in terms of their objectives and methods. Primarily, however, we are interested in the *kinds* of history attempted. We would like to know what ethnologists mean by the term "history," what kinds of historical products they produce, and the relation of these products to those of allied disciplines.

If historians were agreed as to what "history" is the task would be simpler, as there would be a standard by which to judge the views of ethnologists. From the standpoint of the historical products of ethnological research a rough division may be made between increments to an ultimate history and broad historical syntheses. The objective in both cases may be a history of mankind but the philosophy and procedure are quite different. In the first case the general history is carefully constructed from small bits, much like a mosaic is built up. When the pattern becomes apparent blank spaces may be filled in with some degree of confidence. In the case of historical syntheses, on the other hand, the pattern is largely formulated on the basis of certain assumptions or postulates and projected onto culture.

The numerous accounts of primitive peoples brought back by travelers and explorers furnished the raw material for the attempts at culture history made by early ethnologists. This material was "historical" in a wide sense, since it usually referred to events or customs occurring in a time-space context, but the historian had no techniques for dealing with it since the general cultural background was not known, texts were rarely available, and time perspective was not apparent. Students of primitive peoples thus became aware of the existence of individual cultures without having the materials to study them historically. They might have gone out and studied these cultures at first hand but that was to come much later. Instead they attempted to find a short-cut--a formula which would explain the historical development of all cultures.

The early ethnologies were simply compilations of all that was known of the various peoples of the world at the time, arranged to facilitate comparisons. These furnished material for the two great historical syntheses of the nineteenth century. The first great historical formula was the work of the so-called "classical evolutionists," Spencer, Morgan, Tylor, and others. Under the influence of the idea of "progress" they attempted a universal ordering of ethnographic data in terms of *time*. They assumed that cultural development everywhere followed definite laws--all cultures unfolded uniformly from the simple to the complex and culminated in the institutions of Western Europe. An individual culture was of interest merely as illustrating a point along the path of cultural progress; once this path was fully laid out all cultures could be allocated along it and the history of culture would be complete. The Polynesians, for example, were not studied with a view to working out the history of their movements and cultural development, but as examples of the most primitive form of family to be found.

The first great regional formulation of ethnographic data-- the first ordering in *space* on any large scale--was the work of Friedrich Ratzel. His geographical training led him to study the spatial distribution of cultural elements and peoples, and to emphasize the importance of the environment in cultural development.

These two great traditions dominated the last half of the nineteenth century and profoundly influenced all subsequent ethnological work. Each attempted to present a consistent picture of cultural development but so opposed were their fundamental assumptions that quite different "histories" resulted. The "evolutionists" stressed the uniform development of culture and explained cultural similarities as due to independent invention. Ratzel and his followers emphasized environment and the importance of diffusion and migration in bringing about cultural similarity, but because the "evolutionists" were largely concerned with institutions such as the family and religion, while Ratzel dealt more with material culture, the differences were not immediately apparent.

One way out of the dilemma was suggested by Franz Boas. Trained in Germany as a physical scientist and with first-hand knowledge of primitive peoples, he was among the first to show the speculative nature of the evolutionary assumptions and the limitations of the "comparative method" as practiced by the "evolutionists." If their assumptions were reversed so was the "history" which resulted. From the downfall of the "evolutionists" Boas salvaged their objective of "historical laws" but research and investigation were turned more and more in the direction sketched by Ratzel. The immediate results of his program were to be actual histories of the cultures of diverse peoples. Only from a study of these might conclusions be drawn as to the effects of environment and psychological conditions on culture and the relative importance of diffusion and independent invention.

This program formed the foundation for the "American historical school" of ethnology--from it the students of Boas received their objectives and methodology. In Europe, on the other hand, no such sharp break with the past occurred and ethnology took quite a different direction.

III

In any analysis of the kinds of history done by American ethnologists the outstanding characteristic is perhaps the variety of their conceptions of "history." In a recent discussion in the *American Anthropologist*, for example, Boas could not understand Kroeber's conception of history, so different was it from his own.

The work of Franz Boas covers a wide range and is rather difficult to characterize. His ethnological work has been largely confined to working out the historical development of social organization, secret societies, art forms, folktales and other aspects of culture in one region--the Northwest Coast. He feels that "to understand a phenomenon we have to know not only what it is but also how it comes into being." Descriptions of culture he does not consider to be "history"--they are raw materials out of which historical interpretations may be made through "archaeological, biological, linguistic and ethnographic comparisons." Except for his pioneer work on the Eskimo, he has not presented any integrated pictures of whole cultures, but rather historical hypotheses as to the interrelations of various aspects of culture and their movements within the areas concerned, or as to the ways in which culture patterns are built up into a unified whole. His methods are analytic--he breaks up culture into units which seem to have a history of their own and attempts to work out that history by the application of various techniques. Thus he deals with clans and totemism and art motifs and secret societies and myths, rather than with Tlingit or Nootka culture, or Northwest Coast culture. In his work Boas utilizes sound historical method-- the use of texts, respect for the uniqueness of phenomena, the necessity for cultural context, and caution in regard to generalizations. He recognizes that the history of primitive peoples of necessity involves reconstruction, since there are few or no records of earlier periods, but insists that this reconstruction be based on adequate data. Since historical reconstruction is partly dependent on a knowledge of the processes of cultural change, Boas has tended to short-circuit his historical presentations in an attempt to get at these processes by which reconstructions can be better made.

American ethnologists have spent considerable time and effort in working out techniques for historical reconstruction. Documentary evidence and archaeological remains often give clear insight into historical events, but are all too often lacking among primitive peoples. The ethnologist is usually faced with a set of cultural traits without any apparent time perspective. The distributions of these traits were first worked out and by analysis of the distributions, as well as by the interrelations of the traits themselves, a historical picture was gradually constructed. Spinden, for example, studied the distribution of maize agriculture in the New World and found that the center of the distribution was in Central America. Also agriculture was more complex in this region, both in regard to the methods used and the variety of plants grown. Furthermore, a wild ancestor of maize was found growing in the highlands of Mexico, which, together with the fact that evidence of maize is found in the early archaeological periods, led Spinden to assign the origin of maize agriculture to the Mexican highlands.

As such studies progressed a better conception of the processes of culture growth and change developed. Sapir, in bringing together the devices and techniques which had been developed up to 1916 for reading time perspective, was able to stress the processes of diffusion and borrowing, as against independent invention and convergence, as well as to emphasize the importance of the "culture-area."

The concept of the culture-area developed from the study of culture distributions. The cultures of North America, for example, were observed to fall into rough geographical groupings so that it was possible for Wissler to classify them as Plains culture, or Northwest Coast culture, or Eastern Woodlands culture, with a considerable degree of objectivity. But these descriptive areas had no historical depth--no one knew whether the Plains culture was older or younger than that of the Northwest Coast, or whether one part of the culture within an area was older than another.

Nelson's studies in the Southwest furnished an important clue. The principle that the more widely distributed species are usually the older had long been used in zoology; Nelson was able to show that the same thing was true of pottery types in the Southwest by means of archaeological methods.[1] Wissler attempted to apply this "age-area" principle to the culture-area. He had noted that the most typical and highly developed traits of a culture-area were usually near the center, whereas the tribes at the margins of the area usually had fewer of these typical traits, or in less developed form. Hence, he developed the hypothesis that culture traits usually originated in the center of an area and diffused in all directions to the margins. Using these assumptions he was able to view the culture-area dynamically--by studying the distribution of culture traits some insight into the history of the area might be obtained. Thus in the Plains culture-area the Sun Dance was a characteristic ceremony. By a comparative study of the Sun Dance in each of the tribes, Spier was able to show that the most complex form of the ceremony occurred in tribes occupying the central Plains whereas the marginal tribes had a very abbreviated ceremony in general. He therefore concluded that the ceremony probably originated in the central tribes and spread by diffusion to the marginal groups.

The distributional studies took two important directions. Boas had earlier (1912) sketched a brief "History of the American Race" based on the then imperfectly known distributions of cultural elements; as more information became available Wissler and Kroeber expanded this outline and attempted to reconstruct the history of aboriginal American culture in some detail. They found that Middle America possessed the highest aboriginal culture--furthermore, the distributions of such important activities as agriculture, pottery making, weaving, metal working, and highly developed political organization, were centered in this area. Here also were archaeological remains which indicated a long past. All this evidence indicated the probability that the primary cultural development had been in this

region and that traits had been diffused gradually to the north and
south. But the procedure was to treat each case on its merits. Certain developments were localized or had distributions indicating a
northern origin. Thus tailored clothing and the sinew-backed bow
gave evidence of Asiatic introduction. Others seemed to represent
local developments on the basis of ideas which had their origin in
Mexico, Yucatan, or Peru. Thus the history which was built up was
made up of a series of individual historical propositions, interpreted
according to assumptions which had a foundation in empirical observation and probability. Kroeber has further extended this type of reconstruction to the Old World, where he has shown that a similar development and dissemination of culture from a few focal centers such
as the Near East, India, and China has taken place.

The other important direction which distributional studies
took was towards the analysis of single cultures or culture-complexes
in order to determine their historical development. Thus Wissler
studied the Blackfoot analytically, tracing the distribution of each
trait of culture among the surrounding tribes. He found practically
nothing which was unique, and came to the conclusion that the Blackfoot had probably borrowed practically all of their culture traits.
Lowie, studying Plains Age-Societies, was able to come to tentative
conclusions as to their development by studying the relative distribution of various features. Thus he was able to show that the graded
societies were probably outgrowths of the ungraded societies, not
only because they appeared to be specializations of the latter, but
also because their distribution among the various Plains tribes was
much more limited.

One result of these distributional studies was that chronology
tended to become an end in itself. Some ethnologists were so occupied
with seeking time sequences that they did not pay much attention to
culture as such. The analysis of culture into traits and their subsequent comparative treatment often violated principles of historical
method by robbing them of their uniqueness and cultural context. The
normal procedure of historians of basing their analysis on chronology
was reversed--chronology here resulted from the analytic study. Generalizations which were formulated were used as tools for further
historical research. Another important result of these studies was
the conception of culture which gradually grew up. Culture came to
be viewed as a mere aggregation of traits brought together by the
historical accident of diffusion without any particular relations to
one another. Thus Lowie referred to "that planless hodge-podge, that
thing of shreds and patches called civilization," Wissler defined

tribal cultures by "enumeration" of their observable traits, and
Benedict pointed out that culture is built up of disparate elements
without any functional relationship.[2]

The historical products of these distributional studies were
often unsatisfactory, not only to historians but to ethnologists as
well. The historians often failed to recognize the products as "history"--they missed the preciseness of information, the personal emphasis, the textual controls, and an adequate chronology, and perhaps
underestimated the compensations in the form of broader outlines and
a non-ethnocentric world view. The ethnologists attempted to remedy
the methodological deficiencies in various ways, particularly by the
use of archaeological methods, or else turned to the study of other
aspects of culture.

With the American ethnologists who remained in the field of
culture-history one of the moot points has been the degree of probability required for historical reconstruction. Boas, aware that all
history of primitive peoples involves reconstruction, and interested
as well in historical processes, insists on a high degree of probability for acceptance. While he has suggested most of the techniques
which his students have applied to the study of distributions, he has
looked askance at their more extreme interpretations. Always he has
emphasized the multiplicity of factors which may influence cultural
development. Kroeber takes a wider view of history than does Boas
and is satisfied with a lesser degree of probability for his conclusions. Well aware of the difficulties of establishing chronology, he
takes the position that time sequences are only incidental to his-
tory--that its essential characteristic is the "endeavor to achieve
a conceptual integration of phenomena while preserving the quality
of the phenomena." The ethnologist and the historian have the same
type of job; the ethnologist merely has a harder one since he has
less to work with. For Kroeber, any descriptive synthesis of a culture is a "history"--thus he calls Boas' *Central Eskimo* a historical
study though Boas denies the term. The best example of the type of
history which Kroeber is interested in doing is found in his *Handbook
of the Indians of California*. In the Preface he states that "The
book is a history in that it tries to reconstruct and present the
scheme within which these people in ancient and more recent times
lived their lives." This synthesis represents the work of many years'
study and is based on hundreds of smaller historical studies by Kroeber and his associates. Its validity as "history" is determined not
only by the probability of the historical studies which serve as a
foundation but also by the degree of internal consistency achieved.

Radin, on the other hand, takes quite a different view of ethnological history. Of the various students of Boas, he is perhaps the closest to being an orthodox historian, though he has on occasion indulged in larger reconstructions. Radin emphasizes texts, persons, and specific events as the chief things of interest to the ethnologist. For him the main task of the culture historian is the description of a specific culture in a particular period, with as much of the past and as much of the contacts with other cultures as is necessary for full understanding. To this end he collects accounts of particular events and particular persons and submits his texts to historical examination. His monographs, such as the *Winnebago Tribe*, are largely collections of such texts analyzed and commented on by one who is thoroughly immersed in the language and culture of the people concerned.

On the margins of ethnology are various students whose work is partly historical and partly scientific, or who attempt to combine the two approaches in relation to special problems. The interest in general processes of culture growth exhibited by Boas is reflected in the work of many of his students. Spier, who has evidenced such an interest, has recently decided that historical reconstructions are misleading and unnecessary for studies of process, though not necessarily for culture history. Benedict, Mead, Fortune and others represent a newer trend in ethnology--a concern with the functioning of cultures as wholes. Kroeber considers the work of this group as "historical" in his sense of the term, but the objectives are more concerned with the general nature of culture. Recently students such as Lesser have attempted to combine the functional and historical approaches into one methodology. This approach views culture as made up of functionally interrelated elements, but stresses the fact that the dynamic character of culture results in a blurring of these relations at any one cross-section in time. Hence to fully see the nature of the functional relationships in any culture it is necessary to view them over a period of time. Such an approach is best applied to groups in rapid cultural change, such as the American Indians under white contacts, and may not be so necessary where cultures are more stable.

IV

Turning now to the kinds of history done by European ethnologists we find a somewhat different picture. There the reaction to "classical evolution" was less violent. Also there was no body of cultural material, comparable to that furnished by the American Indian, to stimulate the development of new techniques. Interest centered for the most part in wider historical syntheses which were often derived from hypotheses as to the nature of culture and culture growth. The resulting world histories have a simplicity and unity which is in contrast to the attempts of American ethnologists, but the methods used are ones which would be severely criticized by historians.

In England evolutionary theories dominated the field of anthropology and overshadowed the efforts of ethnologists to build up a culture-history. With few exceptions the ethnologists were largely amateurs, the professional anthropologists being more concerned with developing "laws" of evolution. When Haddon organized the famous expedition to the Torres Straits in 1898 he took along a group of psychologists, many of whom developed an interest in working out the history of culture. Haddon, who was a contemporary of Boas, had much the same interests. He was interested in working out historical relations in a limited region, or tracing the history of various culture complexes such as the outrigger canoe. He and Seligman have continued to work out the historical and geographical relations of peoples in Melanesia in much the same fashion as conservative American ethnologists would do. Rivers attacked the problem of Melanesian culture in a different way. Interested in cultural evolution he tried to work out the history of Melanesian society, first as exhibiting a development from the simple to the complex, and later in more historical terms. To begin with he saw the problem as one of internal development and attempted to isolate criteria for this development. As he was carrying out this analysis he came to the conclusion that the complexity of Melanesian society was not a matter of internal development but rather the result of contact with a higher immigrant culture. Then he attempted to isolate these two "cultures"-- the aboriginal and the immigrant, and study the effects of their contact. Here we have an interesting contrast in method--first the application of a hypothesis borrowed from biology or philosophy, and, second, the application of a hypothesis developed from actual investigation of culture in a given region. (That this latter hypothesis eventually proved too simple is beside the point.)

In recent years a wider historical synthesis has been developed by Elliot Smith and Perry. The conception of an "immigrant culture" is made specific and applied to the whole world. They assume that everything worthy of the name "culture" originated in Egypt and from there spread by migration of Egyptians to the rest of the world. Primitive culture is assumed to have been stagnant, men living like apes before the arrival of the Egyptians. The simplicity of this scheme is attractive to many non-anthropologists but it does not represent *history*--it is worked out prior to historical investigation and historical safeguards are not applied to its testing.

In Germany evolutionary theories had made little impression and ethnology tended to follow the directions indicated by Ratzel and the anthropogeographers. The interest in the distributions of cultural objects fitted in well with the emphasis on museums, and most of the ethnological work has been done in connection with these museums. The early work tended in the same direction as in America-- "culture complexes" were outlined for Africa and other regions and related to geographical areas. Graebner and his associates, however, soon developed this conception of "culture complexes," or *kulturkreise*, in a new direction. They thought of them in terms of time sequence--as blocks of culture which had developed successively and spread to various parts of the world. Historic cultures were mixtures of these original "complexes"; the problems of culture history were to be largely concerned with separating out the elements of particular cultures and assigning them to the appropriate strata. History was to be read in terms of the movements and interrelations of the *kulturkreise* involved.

This scheme had a basis in the observed similarities in culture between West Africa and Melanesia and in the analysis of long isolated cultures such as the Negrito and Australian, but the chronological relations of these "culture complexes," their origin, and their spread were largely postulated. Principles by which relative age of elements might be ascertained were set up, and objective criteria for cultural connection were established, but these could not remedy the unhistorical character of the procedure. Those things which a culture-historian would want to know as the end product of his research were here assumed as the beginning.

In recent years Pater Schmidt and his followers have done much to remodel the Graebnerian scheme. Whenever possible archaeological and linguistic evidence have been utilized and more attention has been paid to historical principles. But the assumptions of the original scheme are still largely accepted, the evolutionary stages set up are merely remodeled. As Kroeber points out, it still remains a scheme and not an empirically derived historical interpretation.

This brief sketch has not been fair to European ethnologists, since there are many ethnologists in Holland, Scandinavia, and other countries who have been doing the same kinds of historical investigation which we have outlined previously for American ethnologists. Thus Nordenskiöld has made careful studies of the distributions of culture traits in South America, Metraux has utilized documentary materials in the same region, and many German ethnologists have been interested in specific historical problems. But many European students of primitive cultures have tended to follow in the footsteps of their predecessors. They have attempted to derive their culture history from assumptions as to the nature of culture and culture change, by projecting these assumptions onto cultural materials. The necessity of empirically deriving these assumptions, or of demonstrating their validity, is not considered as a problem. The histories which result from the application of these assumptions consist of world or regional histories for the most part; histories of individual cultures or complexes are derived from the larger picture rather than being empirically worked out, and utilized to build it up.

V

Both in the approach to the history of primitive peoples and in the history achieved there is a significant difference between American ethnologists and many of their European colleagues. The student of ethnology, in attempting to evaluate the different kinds of history, is in something of a quandary. The various schools profess to follow historical method and authorities, but by applying their methods and assumptions, several different and contradictory "histories" may result.

The approach of the American ethnologists seems at present to give more consistent results. The culture history of the New World, as outlined by Wissler and Kroeber, is accepted in principle by practically all their colleagues, though they may argue about the probability of specific reconstructions or protest against too great an extension. Though the European schools accept *diffusion* as the main historical process, their postulates result in quite different "histories." Even within the same school different histories are often produced for the same region.

Fortunately, this situation is rapidly changing. Both in Europe and America there is a tendency to modify historical hypotheses and conclusions on the basis of new materials and information. Eventually there should result a history of culture which will have the adherence of a majority of students. The tendency toward a closer relationship between archaeology, ethnology, and history evidenced in contemporary anthropological research, and the utilization of information from all possible sources in working out ethnological problems, should contribute materially to that end.

Ethnology has already made important contributions to history, and should in the future make more. According to one historian, "anthropology has furnished the temporal and institutional perspective for history, and is in many ways the true background and threshold of history, [and] . . . has for the first time given a concrete and adequate basis for the conception of the unity of history."[3] As history becomes more concerned with the problems of cultural development, ethnology will play an increasingly important role as an auxiliary discipline.

While the relations of the various social sciences to one another has not been determined satisfactorily as yet, the concern of ethnology with the total cultures of all peoples and its objective approach to cultural phenomena should place it among the basic social sciences. To again quote the same historian, "The chronological sweep and methodological approach of anthropology, as well as its interest in the origins of every aspect of human culture, lead many to look upon it as the best of all introductions to social science and the study of man as a whole."[4]

NOTES

[1] He showed by archaeological excavations, that the more widely distributed pottery styles were the older. However, he pointed out that this conclusion only held for a limited area.

[2] It is only fair to note that these extreme conceptions of culture are no longer held by these ethnologists. Dr. Benedict in particular has almost completely reversed her position.

[3] H. E. Barnes. The New History and the Social Studies (New York, 1925), p. 305.

[4] Ibid., p. 275.

7

SOME PROBLEMS IN THE STUDY OF FOOD AND NUTRITION

(with Michel Pijoán)

1943

There has developed in recent years, as a result of an increased
knowledge of the significance of foods in body and health, a new opportunity for cooperation between students of culture and those concerned primarily with nutrition and disease. We have been aware that
there is some relation between *body economy and social economy*, but
in few cases has the anthropologist sufficient technical training to
study the effects of the diet of a people on their energy level, or
to diagnose accurately the results of deficiencies in iron, calcium,
or the various vitamins. The physician, on the other hand, seldom
has an interest in the cultural factors influencing diet, or if he
develops such interests, the time necessary to acquire knowledge and
information.

The production, distribution, and consumption of food is a
continuous process. Ordinarily the anthropologist does not concern
himself with what happens after food reaches the native's mouth, but
when we center our attention on food, the separation of the cultural
activities prior to--and accompanying--consumption from the physiological effects of consumption is not only artificial but makes any
scientific study of possible relationships between the two very difficult. In this age of specialization it would seem that collaboration between anthropologists and physicians interested in nutrition--
rather than additional training for either--is the better solution.

With the view to increasing the health and efficiency of our
human resources in this time of world crisis, Commissioner John Collier, in November, 1941, initiated a cooperative project for the
study of food habits and nutrition among the Spanish-American and

Reproduced by permission of the Inter-American Indian Institute from *America Indigena*, Vol. 3, No. 1, pp. 9-22, 1943.

Indian populations of New Mexico and Arizona, as a joint undertaking of the Office of Indian Affiars and the Department of Anthropology of the University of Chicago. In the Southwest the Indian and Spanish-American cultures still maintain themselves in vigorous, if modified, form but the pressure of increasing population on decreasingly available land, the erosion, silting, and flooding consequent upon overgrazing and forest cutting, and the rise of wage labor with dependence upon store-purchased goods, have resulted in serious problems of health, particularly from the standpoint of nutritional deficiencies.[1] It was felt that here, in cooperation with other federal and state agencies, an attempt might be made to so improve native standards of nutrition that general health and energy might, in turn, be improved.

Some account of our procedures may be of interest. The anthropologist (Eggan) in general charge of the project brought together a field staff consisting of Dr. Morris Siegel of Columbia University, Mr. James Watson and Mr. Antonio Goubaud, graduate students at the University of Chicago, and Dr. Solon T. Kimball and Miss Emma Reh of the Indian Service. We were asked to explore the ramifications of food throughout selected Spanish-American and Indian communities and to experiment with various techniques for gathering accurate and useful information. We were to be concerned particularly with the problem of ultimately modifiying food habits in the interests of better nutrition and health; hence we should emphasize the importance of studying changes and trends in food habits and of isolating the factors and processes involved in these changes. This latter emphasis is essential if we are to reach any conclusions as to the most *efficient* means of bringing about desired changes in nutrition, changes efficient with reference to economic factors such as cost and effort, and also with reference to necessary modifications of beliefs and customs.

The field group spent approximately one month in preliminary reading and discussion in order to acquire a common background and point of view, and to outline a common set of procedures so that it would be possible to compare our results.[2] We felt that by a careful comparison of variant adjustments to a similar environmental setting, particularly where we could control the cultural background, we might be able to bring about a selection of adjustments with reference to food which would be closer to modern nutritional standards. We prepared detailed outlines of the various aspects of culture which we believed would be relevant to "the study of food in all its ramifications". The outlines are rather extensive and we hope to publish them elsewhere, but the following brief memorandum prepared for the guidance of the field workers in using them may be of interest in illustrating our preliminary point of view.

The accompanying outlines represent some of the important axis with reference to the central problems of food and food habits. They are not questionnaires to be checked off but rather suggestions as to ways of organizing interview materials and of items which should be interviewed for. These outlines have differing degrees of weighting and relevance to our central problems. We want to become aware of all the data relevant to an "ideal study" centered around food and food habits but it is obvious that much of the environmental, social, and economic background can only be sampled in the present study. When available records or previous studies give information as to these aspects we should make use of them, and also indicate what additions or modifications would be useful, *for our purposes.*

With reference to our central concern with food and the cultural organizations surrounding foods, we need to secure detailed and direct materials. Here again we should emphasize the experimental character of our study--it may be more useful to try out and evaluate *several* techniques of securing data on various aspects of our problem than to secure superior data with a single technique. We should pay particular attention to failures--as well as successes--and attempt to find the reasons for each.

There are certain difficulties in connection with carrying out field research on preliterate or peasant peoples which do not occur to the same degree when nutritional studies are carried out in our own culture. We should pay particular attention to these difficulties and to the modifications in technique and interpretation which may be necessary.

Following are some brief notes on various aspects of our outline:

Land and Land Tenure: The problems of *land* and *land tenure* are difficult and touchy ones in most communities in contact with the government. The government surveys offer the best sources of data for our present studies; these should be used as the basis for interviewing as to *cultural factors involved*, changes in land holding, inheritance, etc.

Crops and Agricultural Practices: Closely associated with the above are the data relating to the use of the land. Not only do we want to know how the land is owned or held, how transmitted, acreage, location, character of the soil, and so on, but also the crops grown, the water supply, the native conceptions of soil and fertility, and the agricultural and farming practices. "It is as necessary to know the methods by which the people of a particular district produce their food, their economic motives, and the rules that govern the use of the land's resources, as it is to know the nature of the soil, its vegetation and fauna, or its general climatic conditions . . ." (A. I. Richards).

The agricultural techniques for preparation, planting, fertilizing, irrigating, weeding, and harvesting, the seasonal cycle for such activities, beliefs and ritual practices, the effects of drought, insects, etc., and the storage practices are obvious. We should get detailed information on all the crops--past and present--which they grow, with dates and conditions of introduction, where possible. We should get information on sources of seed, costs, relative importance and preference, growing season, how much produced, how preserved or stored, etc.

Domestic Animals: The number, kind, uses, and values of various domestic animals, the history of their introduction, the proportion they contribute to subsistence in sample family groups--the native knowledge as to care, selection, utilization--the question as to what are "good" animals (e.g., the Hopi and Navaho evaluation of goats over sheep in many cases), the prejudices and taboos, etc.

The uses to which domestic animals are put involves such things as transportation, dairy products (if any), food, feathers, wool (and blankets), rental and prestige factors. The character of governmental regulation, control and direction is important here, as elsewhere.

Wild Foods: Here the various ethnobotanies will be of considerable value--the ethnozoology is less well dealt with. The plants and animals, their contributions to the diet, past and present, their seasonal or other occurrences, the amounts available and gathered, the storage and preservation techniques, the native evaluations, their role in myth and ritual, and as "totemic" phenomena, are some of the important items.

Social and Economic Organizations: The character of the socio-economic structure, both in the recent past and at the present time, must be taken into consideration. Here a household census of the selected village or families should be instituted, gathering data on the people in the household, their kinship and marital relationships, the character of the household, the equipment, particularly of the kitchen, the relation of the household to farm lands, their trading habits, the round of agricultural and social activities, and the character of exchange of food and other goods.

The social division of labor, the socialization of the child
with reference to training for household activities, the cultural
emphasis on cooperation or competition, the obligations between households, would all be relevant.

The family or household income, the store surpluses, the native conceptions of ownership of house and crops, and food generally,
the obligations to hospitality, the social ratings (both of themselves
and of others), the duties of boys and girls, and the ages they begin,
are important.

Food Activities: The preparation and serving of food involves
such things as the character of kitchen facilities, knowledge of
storing and preservation, utilization of water, and condiments such
as salt, chili and even clay.

The cooking techniques, their origins and modifications, variations within the group, etc.--the recipes used (the native conception of *recipe* may be different from ours), and the traditional co-
operations involved, should be investigated.

The ordinary cookery *vs.* special cooking for feast days and
ceremonies, the ritual foods prepared for the gods, the taboos on
foods during ceremonies and the native explanations, are all of importance.

The character of food exchanges, the exchanges which actually
take place, the results accomplished in terms of social integration,
etc., should be considered.

Children's Diet: A detailed study of the development of food
habits in children is of great importance for an understanding of the
adult diet, and some students even feel that change in food habits
is only possible at an early level. The questions of infant feeding,
weaning, children's food preferences, the "proper" diet for children,
the degree of participation in adult eating activities, training in
food production and preparation, training in body habits, children's
illnesses and their actual or assumed relation to foods, are some of
the relevant topics.

Changes such as the use of canned milk or bottle feeding,
the use of citrus juices or cod-liver oil, the period at which solid
foods are given, the frequency of nursing, the degree to which children's games emphasize foods, are of importance.

Agencies of Change: Such agencies as the school, the mission,
the traders, the government and its various ramifications (farm agents,
irrigation experts, and home economists), tourists, the radio, government publications, etc., furnish actual or potential avenues of
change.

The significance of the trader, however, varies with the trading habits of the group, and with the personality of the trader as well. The role of the trader and other agencies, with particular reference to food habits, old and new should be an important part of our survey.[3]

In the meantime, the problems relating to nutrition and nutritional deficiencies were also considered by the group.[4] In addition to becoming acquainted with the "newer knowledge of nutrition",[5] which is now far enough advanced to furnish a reliable base for action, we tackled the difficult and controversial problems surrounding the diagnosis of nutritional deficiencies and their effects upon health. Here the physician (Dr. Pijoán) in charge of the nutritional and health aspects of the cooperative project provided the field group with an analysis of the nutritional and constitutional factors related to body economy and a detailed outline of the more specific physical findings in vitamin deficiency states. While the technical clinical observations, experiments, and analyses were to be carried out by the physician and his staff of assistants, we were interested in the extent to which field workers could be trained to make accurate diagnoses of nutritional deficiencies in children and adults.

The availability of a trained nutritionist (Miss Reh) made it possible to investigate the relations between qualitative and quantitative studies of diet, and to adapt the detailed procedures worked out by the Bureau of Home Economics of the Department of Agriculture in their studies of Family Food Consumption and Dietary Levels in various regions of the United States, to our purposes.

The physician (Dr. Pijoán) before joining our cooperative project had spent a year on an Indian reservation in Nevada where he became aware of the presence of a considerable degree of anemia, particularly among the children, a deficiency which was greatly aggravated by the altitude. To quote from his preliminary memorandum:

An example of body economy as it relates to social function was observed among the Shoshone Indians where, at an altitude of 5,800 feet, the dietary background high in carbohydrates, somewhat high in fat, low in protein, yielded individuals with a reduced hemoglobin content of the blood and an increased body mass due primarily to the storage of fat. Since it is well known that there is a relative decrease in the circulating blood volume in fat obesity, and since among these people the hemoglobin content was low, reduced oxygen capacity of the blood led to tissue anoxia. Upon exertion these individuals developed an oxygen debt. Lassitude was their main characteristic. Furthermore, resistance to disease decreased and various vicious circles took place wherein the recuperation factor was minimal. Chronic dental infections were prevalent as well as other chronic infections. In growing children it was noted that their ability in school and in exercise was inadequate. In certain controlled experiments this condition was corrected to a remarkable degree by proper nutrition. It is well to bear in mind that this experiment was conducted at an altitude of 5,800 feet where the oxygen content of the air was ten to fifteen percent less than at sea level. Hemoglobin is the oxygen carrier of the blood. An increase of hemoglobin content is essential body economy at a high altitude. The foregoing study among Shoshone school children indicates that there is a relationship between body economy and social function. It seems evident that in a nutritional survey some attention should be directed to the climate, the seasons, and to the geophysical environment of the inhabitants. Sources of water for irrigation, soil characteristics and seasonal temperature variations should be considered in evaluating a dietary condition of a community, since it is obvious that only certain foods can be grown during certain seasons. The wild and domestic animals which can be obtained from a locality should also be considered, as well as religious influences and other taboos. Clothing and housing are influenced by climate and may yield problems of hygiene, sanitation and food storage.

The formation of a habit pattern in diet is related significantly to the availability of food stuffs. This has been noted in a certain tribe where over a period of years it became increasingly easier for the Indian to produce or obtain certain carbohydrates almost to the exclusion of all other foods. There were many economic and sociological causes for this development. This diet composed primarily of these carbohydrates was markedly deficient in vitamins and animal proteins. Thus different diseases, i.e. scurvy, pellagra, beri-beri and rickets, and even constitutional characteristics are caused by a diet imposed by the geophysical and cultural environment.[7]

In discussing an adequate diet we must recognize many factors. First of all the body must assimilate proteins, fats, carbohydrates, minerals.[8] The proportion of these various substances plays a major role in sustaining body economy. When there is a deficiency in any of these, there are relative changes in tissue metabolism. Such a change in the physiological constitution of the individual alters his efficiency and may affect his function in society.

Of particular importance in the study of diet is the subject of vitamins. In many modern groups the trend in food patterns is toward a high carbohydrate diet to the virtual exclusion of vitamin-

and-mineral-containing fruits and vegetables. Due to diminishing availability of fish and game, or of domesticated animals and dairy products, and to the devitaminizing effects of preserving and cooking processes, previously existing well-balanced diets are often dislocated and a series of deficiency diseases result.

Deficiency in vitamin B1 manifests itself in the disease known as beri-beri. In children its onset is accompanied by diminished urinary secretion, constipation, and a somewhat increased rigidity of body resulting in extreme weakness and exhaustion, and frequently sudden death. Other symptoms are lack of appetite, shooting pains in the legs, slow and slightly irregular pulse, and muscular weakness in the legs which finally results in foot drop. While beri-beri is characteristically found in many Asiatic areas where polished rice forms the staple diet, it is not uncommon elsewhere as well. Yeast, wheat germ, whole cereals, nuts, legumes are rich in vitamin B1.

Deficiency in vitamin B2 (also called G or nicotinic acid) produces pellagra, which like beri-beri is non-contagious. This disease affects the skin, the gastro-intestinal tract, and the nervous system. The symptoms--which may exist collectively or independently-- include thick and somewhat rough and painful tongue, accompanied by gum infections and impairments of the mouth. Dry and scaly skin (sometimes rough and pigmented), first on the hands and forearms, and later on the face, neck, and feet may follow. The disease may be accompanied by itching and burning hands and feet, and intermittent attacks of profuse perspiration. Eventually a psychosis develops, characterized by vague, incoherent delirium, torpor, exaggerated reflexes, depression, loss of memory, and hallucinations. While pellagra is common in the southern United States, it is also found among various American Indian tribes in varying percentages. The best sources of vitamin B2 or G are liver, lean meats, milk, vegetables, fruits, eggs, whole cereals, yeast and wheat germ.

Vitamin C deficiencies result in the well-known disease of scurvy, which when present is further aggravated by sunlight. Symptoms are bleeding gums, failure to gain weight, a tendency to bruise easily (in some cases with hemorrhages in various parts of the body), painful joints, and a definitely lowered resistance to infection. In children there may be additionally weakness, depression, and even melancholia. Since the human body is incapable of synthesizing this vitamin, when the supply is depleted through infections or inadequate intake, it may take large amounts of vitamin C-containing foods to restore tissue saturation. From the standpoint of the laboratory the disease is easily diagnosable by chemical tests. Scurvy is found in

fairly high percentages among certain American Indian groups, particularly the Western Shoshone, where some 32% of the population is affected, and among the Papago where the incidence is also high. Fresh
vegetables and fruits--particularly citrous fruits--are high in vitamin C.

Deficiencies in vitamin D produce rickets at times when the
growth of the individual is rapid. Early symptoms are restlessness,
irritability, and head sweating. The head tends to become large and
somewhat square, the thorax deformed, and the abdomen protuberant
and "pot-bellied". The processes at the junction of the rib and the
cartilage in the anterior chest region may become enlarged. In adults
pelvic deformities resulting from rickets during childhood may lead
to difficulties in childbirth. The chief sources of vitamin D, in
addition to sunlight, are fish oils, egg yolk, and milk.

These deficiencies may occur singly or in various combinations. Of particular importance are the "threshold" or subclinical
vitamin deficiencies which are often overlooked, and which have a
chronic debilitating effect, resulting in early exhaustion and lowered resistance to infection, especially in the upper respiratory
zone.

Of particular importance in the treatment of vitamin deficiencies is the distinction between *maintenance* doses and *curative*
doses of vitamins. Where deficiencies are present through faulty
diet the standard daily amounts are insufficient to cure advanced
cases of vitamin deficiency. A much larger dose is required for
curing, but once that result is achieved, an individual may be kept
in good health by a maintenance intake.

The field work was carried out among the Papago, Navaho, and
Hopi Indians and in the Spanish-American villages of Cundiyo and
Cañon de Taos in the Rio Grande valley, from the middle of February
until the last of May, 1942. Previous studies[9] of these groups enabled us to achieve a more rapid orientation than would be usual and
to concentrate our attention more directly on food. Without this advantage the field season would normally need to be longer in order
to gain adequate understanding of the socio-economic aspects of diet
and to achieve the confidence and cooperation of the natives. In
areas where food habits are changing or where food has become a symbol of social status, it is very difficult to get accurate information as to foods eaten, and almost impossible to get quantitative
data on food consumption, without first gaining the complete confidence of the group being studied.

After the field studies were under way the phsyician (Dr.

Pijoán) made preliminary visits to each village or group being studied and carried out sample clinical observations and tests, particularly on the children. These examinations sensitized the field workers to the physical symptoms and signs of nutritional deficiencies, and at the same time made them aware of the difficulties involved in accurate diagnoses, particularly in incipient cases of deficiency. They served also to acquaint the physician with the character of the nutritional problems and to determine what more exact and objective tests and observations would be needed. At one or more later periods more extensive observations and measurements were carried out on both children and adults. These included milk balance studies of nursing mothers, determination of the iron content of mother's milk, studies of anemia in infants and children, the determination of the caloric, protein, calcium, and vitamin contents of the diet, and detailed studies of vitamin deficiencies by means of clinical observation and bio-chemical tests. In addition, native food plants for which no standard information as to nutritional content existed were gathered for nutritional analysis.

The results of our studies are now being assembled and it is hoped that they may be published in the near future.[10] Some preliminary conclusions may be of interest, however. In the study of food and nutrition the importance of collaboration between the anthropologist and the physician has, we believe, been clearly demonstrated. Each looks at the diet of a given people from a different, but complementary, point of view. If we are studying the effects of a particular diet with the view to proposing remedial measures where they may be necessary, both kinds of knowledge--the cultural and the nutritional--are essential. It is not enough to be able to point out that a particular diet has certain deficiencies. Only when we know the cultural habits and values organized around the food pattern can we begin intelligently to effect changes with a minimum of dislocation.

Collaboration between the anthropologist and the physician is important from another standpoint in that each affords a check upon the other's results. The diet of a group may diverge from generally accepted standards of nutrition but deficiencies must be established by clinical observation and tests before they are anything more than "probable". And since there may be other causes for many of the symptoms of nutritional deficiencies, the demonstration of a lack of corresponding food elements in the average diet affords an important control. Furthermore, if discrepancies between the two approaches *should* hold up under repeated checking in certain groups, it might well lead to a revision of our conception of *universal* nutritional

standards. We cannot be sure that racial and environmental factors
do not play a significant role in body economy without investigating
a wide range of races and cultures.[11]

When we have available a series of studies of peoples with
diverse diets, we will be able by comparison to isolate the effects
of various elements, and combinations of elements, in the diet. We
will also begin to understand the complex relationship between body
economy and social life. Linton has pointed out that the introduction of a new food may have produced far-reaching changes in population and culture in Middle America and the Southwestern United States.[12]
The reduction in social interaction consequent upon periodic malnu-
trition may have significant effects with regard to the development
of social institutions.[13] One important approach to our understanding of this relationship is through the study of food in all of its
ramifications.

Our studies of two Spanish-American villages show one (Cundiyo) with a rather adequate diet and a good health record, whereas the
other (Cañon) has a poor diet at present and a record of numerous nutritional disorders.[14] A few generations ago these two villages had
a similar economy and social life, and both were affected by the tremendous changes of the last few decades. But Cundiyo chose one way
of utilizing its limited resources and Cañon selected another. It
is too simple a solution to suggest that Cañon can cure its ills by
adopting the Cundiyo way of life. But when other Spanish-American
villages are studied and their solutions to the problems of food and
nutrition are available, it may be possible to select one or more
"ideal adjustments" within this Spanish-American culture type.

All investigation indicates that the changing of food habits
is a slow and difficult process. Dietary habits are strongly conditioned by childhood and daily experience, even where they are not
strongly integrated into social and religious life. A mere awareness
of nutritional inadequacy is not sufficient to bring about changes in
diet.[15] To change a single basic foodstuff may involve changes in
the whole field of production and distribution, and may bring about
far-reaching modifications in social and ritual life. Hence the long
term solution to nutritional deficiencies should not involve too rapid or radical changes, but should tend toward the adoption of desirable alternatives in the local culture pattern and environment. Entirely new foods should be introduced slowly and on an experimental
basis, and their effects on the total culture carefully studied and
evaluated.

In cultures where there has been a long period of stability

and relative isolation, the basic foodstuffs frequently become important social and ritual symbols. Among the Hopi and Navaho corn and beans are such foods. For the Hopi corn and beans are equally important in native thinking, and are involved in so many sacred and ceremonial contexts that any suggestion of modification is greeted with strong protest. Wild greens and meat, on the other hand, are classed together as "flavorings" and are considered far less important by the Indians.[16] To change Hopi habits with reference to corn would require the uprooting of practically their whole culture; to change their habits with reference to meats or vegetables would be relatively much simpler. In all cultures there are similar sacred and emotional attitudes toward certain foods, and a ramification of food into other aspects of culture. Only by a thorough knowledge of these social and cultural facts can we avoid costly mistakes and antagonism.

If we are concerned with immediate and practical problems with regard to food and nutrition, a clinical survey of a sample of the population by a trained physician would indicate which communities offer the most serious problems with regard to nutrition. These problems can then be ameliorated temporarily by curative dosages of vitamins and subsidization of the necessary energy foods and minerals. But a continuing satisfactory adjustment must be achieved within the cultural and environmental resources of the community and region. It should be easier to secure acceptance and adoption of familiar and tested solutions in the communities which have serious nutritional problems than to introduce new and untried solutions worked out in another culture and imposed without regard to whether or not they happen to fit the pattern of life within the community. Only by studying alternate adjustments to the problems of subsistence and by understanding the processes of cultural change can we apply our "newer knowledge of nutrition" efficiently and effectively.

NOTES

[1] For a detailed picture of this situation, see the forthcoming study *Man and Resources in the Middle Rio Grande Valley*, by Allan G. Harper, Andrew R. Cordova, and Kalervo Oberg.

[2] We found the studies by R. Firth, A. I. Richards, and others in *Africa* Vols. 7 (1934) and 9 (1936), and especially A. I. Richards, *Land, Labour and Diet in Northern Rhodesia* (Oxford, 1939) which is the best study of food available from the cultural standpoint, particularly useful for our orientation.

[3] From "Memorandum on Food Habits Outline", (typescript), prepared by Fred Eggan.

[4] In our preliminary study of these problems we were aided by the experience of Miss Louisa K. Eskridge, assistant supervisor of health education for the Indian Service, and by the preliminary reports of the Committee on Nutrition of the National Research Council.

[5]See especially E. V. McCollum, *Newer Knowledge of Nutrition*, 5th edit., 1939; and H. C. Sherman, *Chemistry of Food and Nutrition*, 1941.

[6]See, for example, Miscellaneous Publication N° 452, United States Department of Agriculture, 1941.

[7]From "Nutritional and Constitutional Factors as Related to Body Economy", (mimeographed) part I, by Dr. Michel Pijoán, M.D.

[8]The role of these factors in nutrition is well known and need not here be discussed in detail.

[9]We would like to thank Dr. Joseph Weckler and Mr. Donovan Senter for making available their unpublished materials on Cundiyo and Taos, respectively, and Dr. Florence Kluckhohn for allowing us to read her case histories of Spanish-American families. There is a voluminous literature available on the Indian groups.

[10]The onset of the war soon after the project was begun reduced its scope somewhat so that incomplete material is available for some groups, particularly the Navaho.

[11]There are suggestions in the literature that important differences do in fact exist.

[12]R. Linton, "Crops, Soils and Culture in America", in *The Maya and Their Neighbors* (New York, 1940), pp. 32-40.

[13]See, for example, the observations of A. I. Richards on the effects of the "hunger months" on the social life of an African tribe, in *Land, Labour and Diet in Northern Rhodesia* (Oxford, 1939), pp. 35-7.

[14]Morris Siegel and Marguerite King, *The Food Economy of Cundiyo, A Spanish-American Village in New Mexico*, Ms., 1942, and Antonio Goubaud and Michel Pijoán, M.D., *Food and Culture, a Nutritional Study of Cañon de Taos*, Ms., 1942.

[15]The campaign to get people to eat wholewheat bread failed almost completely, despite the knowledge of its greater nutritional value. Recent gains in this respect have come through enriching white flour with the vitamins and minerals which are removed in the milling process.

[16]See James Watson, *Hopi Foodways*, Ms., 1942.

8

THE ETHNOLOGICAL CULTURES AND THEIR ARCHEOLOGICAL BACKGROUNDS

1952

In almost all areas of the New World the traditional relationships
between the historic cultures and their archeological backgrounds
are in process of radical revision as the archeologists begin to reveal the full complexity of the past.[1] In this process of revision
the roles of the ethnologist and the archeologist have been shifting;
the integrating and synthesizing functions are more frequently assumed by the archeologist as his contributions to culture history
grow in significance. The ethnologist, in turn, has frequently shifted from the problems of culture history and its reconstruction to the
direct study of culture dynamics and the processes of cultural continuity and change or to the comparative study of social structures
and ritual. In the reconstruction and re-creation of the cultural
past it is essential that the new insights and new knowledge so gained
be fully utilized; the present paper offers some suggestions along
these lines.

In the eastern United States the relative uniformity of the
historic cultures long obscured their archeological diversity, and
the reconstructions of culture history for the area were correspondingly inadequate. Up to about 1930 the major anthropological activities in the region east of the Rockies were in connection with the
collection of ethnographical data and its ordering for specialized
ethnological interpretation. In this area there were, at the time
of first contact, some one hundred and fifty tribes divided into
eleven linguistic stocks (see map, Fig. 1).[2] The events concerned
with the conquest and settlement of the New World resulted in the
rapid extinction, coalition, acculturation, or removal of many of
these tribes, particularly along the eastern seaboard and the Gulf

---

Reproduced by permission of the University of Chicago Press,
Chicago, from *Archeology of the Eastern United States*, James B. Griffin, editor (1952), pp. 35-45.

Coast, so that our knowledge of their historic cultures will forever
be incomplete, despite the efforts of Speck and Swanton. In addition, the once heavily populated Ohio Valley was temporarily deserted,
or inhabited by shifting groups, in the early historic period. The
Plains tribes, on the other hand, retained their cultural integrity
almost up to the present century.

Concentration of ethnological investigation in the Plains
area was therefore natural. Under the auspices of the American Museum of Natural History and other institutions a considerable number
of Plains tribes were studied. On the basis of a series of distributional and comparative studies by our foremost ethnologists, Wissler formulated the Plains culture type and its variations, outlined
the chronological development of Plains culture, and developed a
theory of the relation of culture to environment which was designed
to explain the general form of the culture area.[3] There seemed little left to do in this area except to fill in the spaces.

No such organized effort took place in the Great Lakes-Gulf
regions in the period before 1930. Less than one-third of the still
extant groups had been studied systematically, and there were preliminary surveys only for the Southeast and the extreme Northeast.[4]
Many of the older monographs were incomplete or not oriented in terms
of modern problems. The degree of cultural diversity or unity east
of the Mississippi was not easily determined therefore, and the relationships with neighboring areas were correspondingly vague.

This situation was reflected in the classifications of the
eastern United States in terms of culture areas. Thus Wissler, without reference to historical relationships, classified the cultures
east of the Rockies into three culture areas: the Plains, Eastern
Woodlands, and Southeast, thereby allocating to this region one-
third of the areas he recognized north of Mexico.[5] In a notable revision made a decade later, Kroeber reduced the number of major areas
to six, each of which was "believed to represent a substantial unit
of historical development, or of a prevailing characteristic current
of culture."[6] Only one of these major areas was allotted to the region here under consideration:

> East of the Rockies there is not a single native culture of
> as high a degree of characterization as occurs west; nor, except
> in some regions near the minimum of subsistence potentiality,
> any as culturally uncharacterized as some of the western transi-
> tional cultures. In other words the Atlantic side of North Amer-
> ica is relatively uniform in its native culture. Its bent or di-
> rection is fundamentally similar everywhere. Once local subsis-
> tence adaptations and local culture imports are allowed for,
> there remains little in the way of local development; and, con-
> comitantly, no great degree of difference in culture intensifi-
> cation.[7]

Within his Eastern area (in itself a subdivision of his major Eastern and Northern area) Kroeber recognized some thirteen subdivisions or specialized types of culture (see map, Fig. 2). The division between his Eastern and Northern areas is placed at the line of the northern Great Lakes, in contrast to Wissler's trifold distinction centering on the mouth of the Missouri River; within the Eastern area pre-eminence is accorded the Southeast, but Kroeber found it difficult to organize his subdivisions in terms of their historical relations or cultural dependences.

During the same period (before 1930) archeology was making rather slow progress in the eastern United States. A considerable amount of work had been carried out in the mound area by Thomas,[8] Moore,[9] and others. The mound areas had been partly surveyed and mapped, and excavations had been carried out in the Southeast and Ohio areas. Holmes[10] had made a comprehensive study of the pottery of the eastern United States which gave some hint of the complexities of cultural development which lay beneath the surface. But the objectives of research were limited by museum needs and state boundaries, and the problems formulated were frequently narrow and inadequate. To dispel the mystery of the "Mound Builders" and to equate their finds with historic tribes were the dominant objectives.

In the Southeast and in portions of the Great Lakes region there appeared to be a close tie-up between the prehistoric and the historic cultures; only in Ohio and neighboring areas did there appear to be a sharp discontinuity. Archeological classifications on the pattern of culture areas were proposed by Holmes[11] and Wissler[12] which varied only slightly from one another and from the ethnological groupings. But Holmes warned archeologists that

> it is by no means assumed that the culture phenomena of any considerable area are uniform throughout. There may be much diversity, possibly great complexity of conditions. There may be a number of somewhat independent centers of development of nearly equal importance, or a single center may have spread its influence over a wide area. The mapping of the cultures will, in the end, take forms that cannot now be foreseen.[13]

The elaboration and documentation of this point of view was to take a long time, and the first steps were taken by the ethnologists. But with the decade of the thirties the center of gravity shifted to archeological research. The large-scale excavations of the depression period crowded a half-century of archeological research into a decade[14] and furnished a mass of material that is not yet completely digested. The prehistoric period was divided into some five cultural horizons, with complex interrelationships extending over an unknown but considerable time. Griffin, writing in 1941, summarized the results of the decade:

> Within the last ten years there has been an unusually large
> amount of activity in the region east of the Rockies and this
> has completely altered the general picture presented by Holmes,
> Wissler, and Shetrone. More material has been made available
> for study than in all the previous years of excavation, and it
> is natural that the interpretation of the history of the area
> has changed. We have experienced a shift in our conception of
> aboriginal culture in the Mississippi Valley. Formerly it was
> considered a province where there was no stratigraphy, where the
> archeological scheme was a static one, divided into culture areas.
> Now definite stratigraphic sequences are recognized throughout
> the area. If a culture area exists it includes almost the whole
> territory.[15]

The documentation of this revolution has already begun to
appear. Preliminary syntheses have been published covering most of
the region under consideration, and the studies to follow in this
volume will add considerably to our over-all knowledge. But it is
in a notable series of monographs by Griffin,[16] Lewis and Kneberg,[17]
Ritchie,[18] Strong,[19] Wedel,[20] Webb and Snow,[21] and others, that there
is found the best evidence for a new approach to the study of archeological cultures and their development. Here one finds an awareness
that prehistoric communities did not exist in a vacuum but were selectively adapted to certain features of the geographical and ecological environment and that the material remains may be interpreted in
terms of major cultural activities as well as classified and tabulat-
ed in terms of form. A classification of culture types, conditioned
on the comparison of detailed lists of traits, is well under way and
will, I believe, contribute to more precise historical inferences.
Documentary materials and historical methods are utilized in compe-
tent fashion. In short, the archeologists show evidence that they
are aware of their new responsibilities for making as complete an
interpretation of the archeological record as is possible.

The major source of assistance to the archeologists in carrying out their task of interpreting the past comes from the study of
living cultures. Here ethnology and linguistics are the traditional
disciplines, but we shall see that their newer sister, social anthropology, has much to offer as well.[22] The most obvious way of integrating archeological and historic cultures would be to work from
the historic period back into the past. Steward notes that "the direct historical approach is not only crucially important in ascertaining cultural sequences, but integrated with recent endeavors in
ethnology, it has a tremendous potential value to the more basic problems of anthropology."[23] For various reasons this approach was late
in application to the eastern United States, but it has already
achieved important results in specific areas. One problem has been

the difficulties and pitfalls of documentary research, even when documents are available. Furthermore, the direct historical approach frequently does not lead to deeper sequences; beyond the protohistoric or late prehistoric periods the trail is lost or becomes uncertain. At the historic end of the sequence the adding of a tribal name is without much significance unless there is information available as to the tribal culture which once prevailed. Despite these difficulties the potential values of ethno-historical research, combined with the direct historical approach to archeology, offer so much in the way of rewards that they should be strongly encouraged. But ethno-historical research is so specialized and time-consuming that its activities need to be coordinated and centralized.

Even where a direct tieup of archeological cultures and historic tribes is not possible, inferences from ethnology and linguistics can be extremely valuable. In Ohio the complex archeological situation resisted clarification for almost three decades. The initial confusion of Fort Ancient and Hopewell was replaced by a conception of their separate but contemporaneous existence. Kroeber,[24] in a review of Shetrone's[25] conclusions, criticized this view on *ethnological* grounds. He found it difficult to conceive of two such sharply differentiated cultures retaining their individuality under conditions of close contact over a considerable period of time, and suggested that the situation would make more sense, in terms of our knowledge of cultural behavior, if the two were separated in time. He further suggested that Fort Ancient might well be considered the later culture, despite its wider distribution.* The influence of these ethnologically oriented hypotheses was limited through delay in publication, but their general accuracy can be attested by comparing the conclusions reached by Griffin[26] on the basis of archeological data.

The various methods and techniques of achieving time perspective have been known for some time, but they have seldom been applied in any co-ordinated way in the area here under discussion. Sapir's[27] brilliant essay contains many insights and techniques, particularly in the field of culture and language, which will be extremely useful, particularly in connection with the archeological record. For the general validity of the broad reconstructions of culture history in various areas will depend in considerable measure on the coincidence of inferences arrived at independently from the data of ethnology, linguistics, and archeology.

[*As known at that time. F. E.]

It is in connection with these comparisons that the nature of classification in each field becomes of vital importance. The ethnologist, linguist, and archeologist each has a variety of classifications adapted to his immediate needs, but the broader problems require some co-ordination. The ethnologist uses the tribe as a convenient unit for cultural study; for larger groupings the trend is away from the "culture area" to the concept of "culture type,"[28] which emphasizes similarities in culture content rather than geographical grouping, and offers a basis for the determination of genetic relationships. For analytical studies of culture Linton[29] has pointed out the need for more objective classification of culture elements and has proposed a grouping in terms of item, trait, trait complex, and activity, which makes it possible to consider both form and function.

The classification of languages in terms of dialect, language, stock, and "superstock" represents a grouping based directly on genetic principles which is exceedingly useful in linguistics but which students of culture have made little use of because the language classifications frequently cut across cultural groupings. The less differentiated dialect groupings, however, frequently coincide with cultural divisions; the larger groupings, once more is learned about the rates of change in various language stocks, will offer a powerful tool for investigating the past.[30]

The nature of archeological knowledge in the eastern United States made it impossible to utilize immediately either the conventional ethnological and linguistic classifications, or the chronological classifications developed in the Southwestern archeological field. Early in the thirties the problem of archeological classification became acute, and a group of midwestern archeologists under the leadership of McKern developed the Midwestern Taxonomic Method to clarify the confusions resulting from the labeling of every assemblage as a "culture."[31] The basic concept is the "culture type," divorced from all temporal and geographical connotations. Through the comparisons of culture content five divisions are recognized, ranging from the *focus* made up of sites with a degree of correspondence suggestive of cultural identity, to the *base* which is characterized by fundamental traits relating to subsistence and organization. The task of linking these arbitrary culture types with ethnological and linguistic groupings is a difficult one but can be done in time. The broader problems of the relevance of the Midwestern Taxonomic Method for the problems of historical reconstruction have been raised[32] but will not be further considered here.

So far archeologists have not gone much beyond the reconstruction of the material aspects of prehistoric life. But recent developments in social anthropology hold out the possibility of reconstructing the social institutions of many prehistoric communities, without recourse to evolutionary or other formulas. For certain recent archeological cultures the direct historical method, once valid connections are established, offers an avenue by which late manifestations may be enlarged through inferences from ethnological horizons. For earlier cultures insights from the comparative study of social institutions will make it possible to determine with reasonable certainty the type of social organization prevailing and even to infer changes where the archeological data are adequate.

Social structures are mechanims to organize the members of a society to carry out various objectives in a relatively efficient manner. Comparative studies are beginning to show that there are a limited number of forms and that these are shaped by a combination of social and ecological factors. Steward's[33] pioneer study of the economic and social basis of primitive bands offers an excellent start in this direction. After noting the social and economic factors which make the "autonomous, land-owning socio-political group" greater than the elementary family in all known societies, he analyzes the functional and necessary relationships involved in the adjustment of various types of band organization. He shows that "the patrilineal band is most common because it is produced by recurring ecological and social factors which may be formulated into something akin to cultural law, and that the composite band occurs where there are special factors, which may be readily ascertained in each instance."[34] By a comparative study of existing band types Steward has determined the essential social and ecological factors in rather specific terms.[35] In a related paper he has applied his conclusions to the study of the development of Southwestern society.[36] His summary of the conditions of development is important enough to be quoted practically in its entirety:

> First, a low culture and/or unfavorable environment prevents dense population and precludes large population aggregates. It produces groups which, barring special contrary factors, are unilateral, localized, exogamous, and land owning. Descent is male or female largely according to the economic importance of man or woman in that culture.
>
> Second, increased food supply or other factors making for a denser population will produce either larger bands, occupying the same territory, more bands each occupying less territory, or multi-band villages.
>
> Third, large multi-band villages will be produced if tribal movements, war, or some other factor dislocates the unilateral

band, causing concentration, or if, in an increasing population, newly founded lineages fail to move away.

Fourth, it is not inevitable that these unilateral groups become clans, but they will do so if possession of a group name, common ceremonies, or other factors create solidarity and prevent the loss of recognition of kindred in succeeding generations. . . .

Fifth, in the course of these transformations political autonomy passes from the localized lineage to a wider group. . . .[37]

Here are conclusions which may be applied to the reconstruction of the *earliest* cultures in the eastern United States, as well as to later forms. Careful archeological research in favorable areas can reveal the level of population density at different periods, the size of the local groups and their concentration or dispersion, the arrangement of houses in the village and the outlines of household activity and division of labor, the subsistence patterns and ecological adjustment, the continuity or replacement of populations, and the outlines of ceremonial organization and practice.[38] From such data it should be possible to say a good deal about the social organizations of the Archaic and Early Woodland horizons of the eastern United States, as well as to trace the development of more complex institutions with the introduction of large-scale agriculture and town life. Such reconstructions need not remain mere guesses. By a more adequate analysis of historical social structures and their projections into the past through the direct historical approach it should be possible to check the conclusions reached through the application of social anthropology. Furthermore, if the hypothesis for the Asiatic origins of Woodland culture proposed by McKern[39] is verified, comparison with northern ethnological cultures may be relevant on the basis of Cooper's concept of marginal cultures.[40]

We have reviewed in the last few pages some of the ways in which the various disciplines of anthropology may contribute to the reconstruction and interpretation of cultural development. It will be useful now to turn to an examination of the present state of our knowledge in two or three areas of the eastern United States in order to see in what ways this knowledge may be applied.

We have noted above the differing perspectives on Plains culture and its classification developed by Wissler and Kroeber. From the vantage point of Late Plains institutions, and in the relative absence of archeological data, Wissler came to view Plains culture as static and essentially timeless. The introduction of the horse intensified these patterns; this intensification, reaching its peak in the eighteenth and nineteenth centuries, was responsible for reversing cultural values in the marginal areas and inhibiting the further development of sedentary life.[41] Kroeber, in a notable paper on "Native Culture in the Southwest,"[42] dissented from this interpretation on ethnological grounds. He viewed the High Plains as only sparsely inhabited for a long period. The basic culture was an Eastern Woodlands one along the margins of the Plains; as these people gradually moved out into the Plains, they divided their time between farming and bison-hunting. The introduction of the horse led to a florescence of the hunting life, and the focus of Plains culture shifted to the northern High Plains.

This historical hypothesis was confirmed in a striking manner by the archeological researches of Strong[43] and Wedel[44] in Nebraska, Kansas, and the Dakotas. In these regions they found that early hunting cultures were succeeded by semi-sedentary village-dwelling peoples who practiced both horticulture and bison-hunting; these in turn were succeeded by the protohistoric and historic tribes. The evidence further suggested several semi-sedentary prehistoric occupations, some of which had affiliations with protohistoric sites. By utilizing the direct historical approach, the historic Pawnee were linked with protohistoric sites on the Lower Loup River (Lower Loup Focus),[45] and the movement of the Cheyenne out onto the High Plains was confirmed.[46] In this view tribes such as the Pawnee were typical of the area in late prehistoric times, and the historic High Plains culture represented merely "a thin overlay associated with the acquisition of the horse."[47] Both Strong and Kroeber lean to the view that the uniformity of Plains culture is largely the result of historic factors rather than the result of environmental control.

But the High Plains area was not a cultural vacuum before the introduction of the horse. The early Spanish explorers of the southern Plains found two well-defined modes of life, a nomadic, buffalo-hunting, dog-transporting, and tipi-using one in the western portions, and a sedentary, village-dwelling, agricultural one in the east. In Coronado's time[48] the basic techniques for continuous life on the High Plains were well established, and the Folsom finds suggests a long occupancy of the region by bison-hunters. Granted that the groups were small before the introduction of the horse, and without the elaborations of ceremonial and societal life which came with greater wealth and leisure, the patterns of material life were still distinctive and formed the basic substratum for the historic cultures.

When first described most of the tribes of the northern High Plains had centered their culture around the horse, but this culture seems a logical development of the type of life described by Coronado.[49] If we examine the typical tribes of this area, however, there is good evidence that practically every group entered the High Plains in historic or protohistoric times,[50] the majority of them from the east and north. Whether the northern High Plains culture of historic times is primarily a development of earlier Plains patterns or an amalgam of modified northeastern and eastern traits is not yet clear; there is evidence that both processes were involved.[51] It is important to note for our purposes, however, that these diverse tribal cultures came to have a similar form, under the influence of environmental and historical factors.

Wissler attempted to work out the mechanisms involved in terms of a tendency for specialization to take place in the center of the ecological area and to diffuse to the margins.[52] The Plains area shows this central clustering of traits, and there is evidence that diffusion is an important process; but the historical evidence does not support the assumption of central origin and dissemination. The Cheyenne and Arapaho, generally considered the most typical High Plains tribes, entered the central Plains in relatively late times. Strong has shown that the Cheyenne, in particular, shifted from a sedentary, agricultural, village-dwelling group to a typical nomadic Plains tribe in the short period between 1750 and 1800.[53] They therefore borrowed or adapted practically their entire historic culture complex in very short order.

It is clear that Wissler's search for a dynamic factor in the ecological pattern led him to underestimate the importance of contact and migration in the Plains. If contact be given its proper weighting, the margins of culture areas, rather than their centers, may become the places where new developments take place. The increased mobility provided by the horse would make it possible for a marginal tribe moving to the center to assimilate and integrate a large number of new cultural ideas from all sides, thus building up a complex culture in a relatively short time. The application of such a hypothesis may give us a more adequate explanation for the development of at least some of the Plains culture patterns.

Such hypotheses are, however, inadequate to account for the uniformities observed in social structure. We have noted that there is a limited number of forms of social organization and that these are adjusted to social and ecological factors; furthermore, the patterns of kinship organization, like those of language, are not readily observable, and therefore difficult to borrow, even if consonant with the existing institutions. I have suggested elsewhere[54] that the basic features of Plains local organization and kinship represented adjustments to the conditions of Plains life. These conditions are both social and ecological, involving not only the need for protection against hostile raids but also the necessity for adjusting to the annual cycle of the buffalo. The uncertainties of Plains existence were great, compared with those of the village dwellers, and a flexible type of social structure was required.

Collier[55] has noted that the social organization of the Plains tribes took a series of forms: the camp circle, two types of large bands, the camp based on extended kinship, and the temporary hunting camp, each of which was adapted to the annual cycle of subsistence as well as to the social environment. It is important to note that tribes coming into the Plains with more complex formal social structures were in the process of giving them up in favor of the more flexible band and camp organization, and, conversely, the more simply organized Great Basin groups developed a more complex organization. To explain such uniformities in terms of borrowing is an oversimplification; the Crow, for example, in modifying their clan organization and kinship system in the direction of Plains patterns,[56] were adapting their own more complex organization to new requirements. They had not borrowed Plains social institutions outright in these cases but had modified their own in the direction of a more efficient adjustment to the exigencies of Plains life.

The events of the historic periods throw some light on the past; archeological evidence suggests a series of incursions by horticultural peoples from the east out into the Plains. In historic times very rapid readjustments were made by groups moving into the High Plains, and older patterns were obliterated or modified in a short period of time. In this process ecological factors are important, as well as historical factors; where these ecological factors are of long standing they can be utilized, as Steward suggests, in the analysis of social organization.

Our understanding of the High Plains will be greatly enhanced when more is known about the Prairie Areas along the eastern border. The recognition of this region as a distinct culture type, rather than as marginal to the High Plains, has the advantage of not subordinating culture type to geographical area to the extent that Wissler's formulation did. Within this area the great majority of the tribal groups speak Siouan languages, so that the ethnologist turns first to the classifications worked out by the linguists. Voegelin[57] has summarized our present knowledge of Siouan groupings in terms of four groups, two of which are relevant to the areas under discussion. In his Missouri River grouping he places Hidatsa and Crow, pointing out that they have differentiated more from each other than is generally recognized. Evidence that Chiwere and Dhegiha belong together has resulted in a new Mississippi Valley grouping, to which Mandan and Dakota are tentatively added. These conclusions are of considerable importance in view of the growing archeological evidence in this important region.

Kroeber's divisions of his Prairie Areas correspond rather closely with this new alignment: his Southern Prairie is composed entirely of Chiwere- and Dhegiha-speaking tribes, his Central Prairie is occupied by tribes speaking Dakota dialects, and his Northern Prairie area is occupied by the related Assiniboin- and intrusive Algonkian-speaking groups such as the Plains Cree and Plains Ojibwa. But while the Siouan-speaking tribes of this area have many cultural features in common, their basic social structures are quite different. Recent evidence on the Eastern Dakota[58] suggests a form of social organization and mode of life much closer to that of the Ojibwa than to that of the Southern Siouans; the Mandan and Hidatsa, on the other hand, shared common patterns.

Archeological research is beginning to document these similarities and differences and, indeed, in some cases has called them to attention. The Oneota Aspect comprises a series of foci, belonging in the Mississippi horizon, which have been tentatively identified with Chiwere-speaking tribes;[59] a further extension to Dhegiha-speaking groups is highly probable in terms of the close linguistic connections noted above and basic similarities in social organization and other aspects of culture. The archeological sites identified with Eastern Dakota groups, on the other hand, appear to belong in the Woodland horizon, along with the Menominee and other Algonkian-speaking groups.[60]

The linguistic distribution and the evidence of migration legends points to the possibility of an earlier homeland in the Ohio Valley. Thus Kroeber, in speaking of the decline in this area, suggests: "The legendary southwestward movement of the Dhegiha-Chiwere Siouans may have been part of one of the last phases of this period of evacuation and decay. It is tempting to think of the Mandan, Hidatsa, and Winnebago as similar emigrants; but it would be speculative to follow this idea out until a clearer picture of Mound Builder culture is available."[61] This hypothesis has received reinforcement by Voegelin's conclusion that Biloxi, Ofo, and Tutelo form an Ohio Valley Siouan group, with the implication that they dispersed from this region,[62] but the degree of linguistic and cultural differentiation among the Missouri River and Mississippi Valley groups suggests that such a series of movements, if ultimately demonstrated, took place over a fairly long period. The possible role of these Siouan-

speaking groups in the development of Mississippi cultures will be
briefly considered below.

A complex problem, the solution to which will throw considerable light on the development of culture types in the Prairie-Plains
areas, is that of the earth lodge complex. In the historic period
circular earth lodges were used by the Dhegiha-speaking Omaha, Osage,
Kansa, and possibly Ponca, the Chiwere-speaking Iowa and Oto, the
Mandan, Hidatsa, and Arikara of the Village Area, and the Pawnee of
the Middle Platte. This grouping not only cuts across Siouan linguistic divisions but includes Caddoan-speaking tribes as well.[63]
In the archeological horizons, while little or no trace of dwellings
has been found in connection with the earlier Woodland occupations of
of the Plains, the rectangular semisubterranean earth lodge is an
integral feature of the Upper Republican and Nebraska aspects of the
Mississippi horizon. The distribution of the earth lodge during this
period was much wider than in historic times;[64] the comparable distributions in the northern Plains are now in the process of being
worked out in connection with the Missouri Valley Survey.[65]

The situation in the central Plains suggests that the protohistoric and historic Pawnee structures developed out of Upper Republican forms. As Wedel notes:

> It is reasonable to believe that the historic circular Plains
> lodge evolved in the region out of the closely similar and clear-
> ly earlier rectangular structure. Architecturally, the earlier
> is if anything the more complicated of the two types, and it
> must have had a fairly long developmental background. Nothing
> so far found in the Plains suggests an incipient or formative
> stage, from which fact it might be inferred that the developed
> type was an importation.[66]

The historical relations between the earth-lodge complex of the central Plains and that of the Upper Missouri need to be clarified before the source of the complex can be adequately investigated. Wedel
has examined parallels from the Southeast and Southwest without arriving at any definite conclusions; in view of the extensions of earth-
lodge sites along the tributaries of the Upper Missouri and the historic occurrences of earth lodges in the Plateau, the Northwest must
also be thoroughly investigated.[67]

Despite the complexities of historical development all the
tribes of the Prairie Areas using earth lodges had a complex social
organization centering around the village, with a formal clan organization and kinship systems of a "lineage" type. The Dhegiha- and
Chiwere-speaking tribes of the Southern Prairie were organized in
terms of patrilineal clans grouped into exogamous moieties, with kinship systems of the Omaha subtype; the Mandan and Hidatsa of the Village Area were organized in terms of matrilineal clans and moieties,

with kinship systems of the Crow subtype.[68] The Pawnee and Arikara show certain specializations in village organizations, but accord with the village tribes in their emphasis on matrilineal descent.

The objective differences between these areas preclude direct borrowing of social institutions, but the parallel organization suggests the influence of some common factors. The increased density of population requisite for village life was made possible by the increased food supply resulting from combining maize agriculture with hunting and gathering. The utilization of fertile bottomlands along the Missouri and its tributaries made it possible for these villages to be both large and relatively permanent; the problems of integrating the population around common activities in connection with agriculture and hunting, with regard both to subsistence and to rituals, made the development of a segmentary clan organization highly probable.[69] Wherever it is essential to hold property in trust or to maintain rituals from generation to generation, unilateral organizations or "corporations" are far more efficient than bilateral ones.[70] The clan gives a greater degree of stability and permanence but has in turn a limited flexibility and adaptability to new situations.

The difference in descent pattern, from this point of view, is of less significance. Steward has suggested that descent is male or female, largely according to the economic importance of the sexes in the culture. In the village tribes the earth lodges were occupied by extended families based on matrilocal residence so that the women of a lodge represented a lineage group. These women co-operated in the activities connected with cultivating their fields and in various household tasks. Hunting and ceremonial activities were in the hands of the men and were organized largely on a clan or village basis. It is conceivable that the relatively greater importance of agriculture in the subsistence pattern and the greater efficiency of household co-operation were important factors in emphasizing the matrilineal line in residence, inheritance, and descent.

The patrilineally organized Southern Prairie groups offer a crucial case, but the details of local organization are not available. For the Omaha, however, Fortune[71] offers an important clue in a footnote. He notes that the earth lodge, which was inhabited during the agricultural periods, was organized in terms of matrilocal residence, whereas the tipis used during the hunting periods were organized on the basis of patrilocal residence. The women of the earth lodge co-operated in agricultural and household activities, despite the patrilineal organization of the society; for hunting activities tipi-mates and clansmen co-operated, with their wives taking care of the meat

and skins. With the reversal in values brought about by the horse
it is possible that hunting activities came to dominate to a greater
extent and brought about a greater emphasis on the patrilineal line.[72]
In this connection it is important to note that the moiety organization was expressed in the camp circle, where each clan had a specific
place, and not in the village, where matrilocal residence precluded
any spatial arrangement of the earth lodges in terms of moiety and
clan patterns. Matrilineally organized groups such as the Pawnee
and Crow apparently responded to such changes by shifting from a clan
toward a band type of organization and becoming more "bilateral" in
their kinship practices.

The above discussions may have some relevance to the Iroquois
problem so ably discussed in its various aspects by Fenton,[73] Griffin,[74] and others. Fenton has pointed out that "the major problem
in Iroquois culture history is that of explaining their intrusive
linguistic and cultural position."[75] Griffin has briefly characterized their cultural position as follows:

> The semisedentary villages of the Iroquois based on a maize
> economy certainly present a subsistence picture different from
> that of their Algonquian neighbors on the west, the north, and
> the northeast. The Iroquois agricultural-hunting economy includ-
> ed relatively permanent large villages, with a social structure
> highlighted bythe matrilineal household unit within the clan and
> by the possession of two moieties. The Iroquois tribal organi-
> zation was of a high order, and the conceptual framework of the
> "League" was a still further advance. Much of this sociopoliti-
> cal organization is at marked variance with the Algonquian tribes
> to the north and west and, to a somewhat less degree, with the
> bordering Algonquian groups to the east and south.[76]

Fenton notes the assumption that the Iroquois brought some basic patterns of their culture, such as village life based on maize agriculture and matrilineal clans, from a place where they were in contact
with an area of higher cultures, but states that the Iroquois did
not necessarily ever reside in the Southeast.[77]

There is a growing belief among students of the Iroquois
that they may have developed much of their distinctive mode of life
in the lower Great Lakes area. Flannery[78] has presented data which
indicate that the Iroquois have much in common with their neighbors
and that they have mutually influenced one another as well as having
been affected by influences from the south; Griffin[79] believes that
part of their culture is derived from the Hopewell horizon through
the Owasco and that the ancestors of the Iroquois may have been Hopewellian, or, as part of Point Peninsula, been in the Lower Great
Lakes region in Hopewellian times.

The distinctive and advanced character of Iroquois social
and political structure has been one of the major features, along

with maize agriculture and the associated ceremonial cycle, by which
they were linked to the Southeast. But it is quite possible for the
basic features of their social and political organization to have developed in the north. Given maize agriculture, which they may have
brought with them or received by diffusion, a greater concentration
of population would result. Greater emphasis on agriculture in a
favorable environment might well lead to the further organization of
women for agricultural co-operation and, ultimately, to the utilization of matrilineal principles for residence, inheritance, descent,
and succession. The tribal and intertribal organizations represent
devices designed to integrate larger groups for the purpose of protection, and were further elaborated under conditions of contact;
there is no adequate source from which they could have been borrowed.
In this connection it might be noted that the kinship systems are
"bilateral" and resemble those of neighboring areas to a much greater
extent than they do the "lineage" systems of the Southeast. If they
turn out to be originally based on cross-cousin marriage, their tie
with adjoining groups will be much more definite. There is no necessity, therefore, to postulate a southern origin for the Iroquois
on the basis of their social organization. While the linguistic and
cultural situation may point in that direction as their original
homeland, there is no need to assume that they arrived with their
full cultural equipment. Griffin[80] has suggested that the ancestors
of the Iroquois were probably in the north by A.D. 1200, which would
give them plenty of time to develop their complex institutions.

Turning now to the Southeast, we find an area where the potential values of ethno-historical research and the direct historical
approach are beginning to be realized on a large scale. Here the
archeologists can draw on Swanton's great researches;[81] the archeologists in turn can illuminate the course of cultural development underlying the historic tribes.[82]

Even where direct tieups of archeological cultures and historic tribes are not possible, influences from ethnology and linguistics may be extremely valuable. There is a general feeling that Mississippi cultures were brought into the Southeast by the ancestors
of the historic Muskogean-speaking tribes in late prehistoric times.[83]
Such an inference is based in part on the linguistic and cultural
situation at the time of first contact. While the linguistic differentiation between the major branches of Natchez-Muskogean is fairly
deep, the dialectic differentiation of the Muskogean group is much
less marked, and Haas's[84] revision of Swanton's classification indicates a center of gravity for the latter in the west-central portion

of the Southeast, with dialectic differentiation at the margins. More distantly related languages such as Natchez and Timucuan are found on the peripheries. The ethnological picture presents a similar pattern. The cultural distinctions between the Creek, Hitchiti, and Alabama were slight in comparison with their uniformities; Choctaw and Chickasaw varied somewhat from the Creek patterns but obviously belonged with them. The linguistic and cultural differentiations, therefore, are on approximately the same level and suggest either a recent expansion of these groups or the effects of the Creek Confederacy in the historic period.

The possibility of a relationship between Mississippi cultures and the later Creek-Choctaw-Chickasaw groups is made more probable by the identification of Mississippi archeological complexes in Tennessee,[85] Georgia,[86] and Mississippi,[87] with historic Muskogean-speaking tribes, with evidence of cultural discontinuity and replacement in most instances. The marginal areas, on the other hand, show cultural continuity at several points. In the Lower Mississippi region there is apparently an unbroken development from early Tchefuncte to historic Natchez; a similar continuity is apparent in the cultural developments in northwestern Florida and the Georgia coast. All of these marginal areas appear to derive from or share in a widespread Southeastern Woodland cultural horizon, and each was affected in varying degrees by Mississippi influences in its later stages.

The evidence from linguistics and archeology thus reinforces and makes more precise a hypothesis with regard to the dynamics of southeastern cultural development originally formulated by Swanton[88] on the basis of ethnological evidence alone. The conception of an indigenous Woodland culture into which Mississippi intrusions took place, with the forcing of the earlier populations to the margins, and the fusing of the two traditions and populations in varying degrees, offers a situation in which problems of culture process and culture change can be attacked on an archeological level and checked with ethnological data. A comparison of the marginal cultures holds out the possibility for reconstructing the earlier cultures in the area, as well as explaining the cultural similarities noted by Swanton[89] and Speck[90] between the Natchez, on the one hand, and the Eastern Siouans, Algonkians, and Cherokee, on the other.

The probability that languages more distantly related to Muskogean proper, such as Natchez and Timucuan, were early in the Southeast is strongly reinforced by the cultural continuity displayed by the marginal areas. In historic times tribes speaking Siouan, Yuchi, Iroquois, Caddoan, Tunican, and Algonkian were also marginal to the

Southeast proper. Sapir[91] has suggested that Siouan-Yuchi may form
an enlarged group comparable to Natchez-Muskogean and that Iroquois-
Caddoan makes up a similar group; these with Tunican, form the eastern portion of his proposed Hokan-Siouan "superstock." The genetic
relations of such a stock, if ultimately demonstrated, would take us
far into the past, but detailed studies of the proposed substocks
such as Siouan-Yuchi and Iroquois-Caddoan will be extremely useful
in working out the relative chronology of the archeological horizons
in relationship to linguistic differentiation. The possibility that
all the languages of an enlarged Southeast may be genetically related[92] further suggests that their differentiation may have taken place
largely within the area and that a considerable period of time may
be involved.

    That Muskogean-speaking peoples were bearers of Mississippi
cultures in the Southeast does not solve the problem of the origins
of Mississippi cultures but does give some useful hints. The Yuchi,
as noted above, have also been identified with this horizon in Tennessee; the Cherokee remains, on the other hand, appear to derive
from a different tradition. The general direction of the Mississippi
intrusion into the Southeast seems to have been from the northwest.
Griffin is inclined not to look for a single center but postulates,
instead, a gradual growth throughout the Mississippi Valley, in which
"various ideas and complexes developed in several centers the whole
to be welded into classic Middle Mississippi."[93] Within the area so
labeled on his maps,[94] there were, in early historic times, only
Siouan- and Algonkian-speaking tribes in addition to the groups already mentioned. The Algonkians of the Wisconsin and Illinois areas,
while ultimately derived from northern centers, had developed fairly
complex cultures comparable to those of their Siouan-speaking neighbors and show evidence of having been in the region for a considerable time. Only the Illinois and Shawnee were far enough south to
participate in the development of Mississippi cultures, however, and
the probability that Menominee ancestral culture belongs in the Woodland horizon suggests that the former have played a minor role. This
leaves the Mississippi Valley Siouan-speaking tribes, particularly
the Osage, Quapaw, Omaha, Ponca, and Kansa, as the most likely series
of tribes, in addition to the Muskogean groups, to be involved in the
development of Mississippi cultures. The place of the Caddoan area
in the development of Mississippi cultures depends on the evaluation
of the newly discovered role of Spiro as an intermediary for Middle
American influences and, of course, on its chronological relationships with Mississippi sites.[95]

In view of the evidence so far available I would look for the center of development for Mississippi cultures in the general Lower Missouri-Lower Ohio region, where we find some of the largest Mississippi sites: Cahokia, Kincaid, Angel and others. The establishment of tree-ring dates for one level at Kincaid[96] gives a basis for establishing correlations with other sites through trade materials and intrusive sherds and for estimating the period of development required. The assumed primacy of the Lower Mississippi in earlier archeological periods and the reputed position of the historic Natchez have led us to look gulfward too long. Kroeber[97] assigns to the Natchez a pre-eminent position in the Southeast, mainly on the basis of their class system and sun symbolism. But while the Natchez social structure was unique in its combination of class and exogamy, both class systems and exogamy were widespread in the Southeast.[98] Only among the Chitimacha is a true caste system reported, and here apparently only for the nobility.[99] The archeological evidence likewise does not support the assumption of a climax culture--in fact, the archeology of the contact period shows a relative decline.[100]

The central Mississippi region has been an important meeting place for diverse cultures, situated as it is on the borders of the Prairie, Ohio Valley, and Southeast areas, and at the confluence of the Missouri, Upper Mississippi, and Ohio rivers. We have pointed out above the importance of contacts in the development of culture,[101] and in this respect the region deserves important consideration. The direct historical approach and ethno-historical research may be able to verify, or disprove, the legendary history of the Mississippi Valley Siouan-speaking groups which brings them to their later homes from the Lower Ohio. The close relationship of the Dhegiha-speaking groups to the Chiwere, who have been identified with the Oneota Aspect, further suggests a relationship of these Siouan tribes with Mississippi cultures; their division into "Upstream" and "Downstream" peoples is suggestive of a former home on the Mississippi. Their possible connection with the Late Mississippi sites waits on further research but is, in my opinion, a useful working hypothesis.

The combination and coincidence of inferences from ethnology, linguistics, and archeology, then, promises to be very useful in unraveling the complex prehistory of the Southeast. Until the archeologists had progressed sufficiently to relate their materials to the ethnological horizons, such multidisciplinal approaches to cultural development were not possible. Griffin has noted that "this growing ability to assign definitely, or even tentatively, cultural blocks to known tribes is one of the most fortunate results of the recent

archeological activity in the Southeast."[102] With the tentative
identification of such sites as Moundville and Etowah as Creek, it
will be possible to expand greatly our knowledge of the protohistoric
and contact cultures by putting together the archeological and the
ethnological complexes.

But the problem of reconstructing cultures and cultural development in the periods preceding the Mississippi horizons is more
difficult. There is no continuity with historic cultures, except in
modified form at the margins, and our limited knowledge of Natchez,
Chitimacha, Timucua, and Cusabo will be a handicap in reconstruction.
But it may well be possible that we can utilize our greater knowledge
of Cherokee, Yuchi, and Caddo cultures in this connection, once their
role in Southeastern cultural development is better known.

In connection with such problems recent studies of social organization in the Southeast should prove useful.[103] The basic patterns of social structure in the historic Muskogean-speaking groups
are similar to those we have noted for the Iroquois and the village
tribes, and have developed, in my opinion, in response to similar
social and ecological factors. Studies with reference to the factors
bringing about social change in Southeastern tribes in historic
times[104] support this view and will be of great assistance in evaluating the possibilities of earlier changes. For the Mississippi
horizons we should be able ultimately to project back the historic
social patterns, at least in general terms. For earlier horizons
there is the possibility, mentioned above, of interpreting the archeological record along the lines suggested by Steward. Some of the
cave and shell-mound occupations, as well as the various occupations
described for Hiwassee Island,[105] suggest that sharp differences
from later forms will be found.

The great advances in archeological techniques and materials
in the eastern United States during the last fifteen years offer
both a challenge and a promise. The challenge involves nothing less
than the necessity of bringing the entire resources of our accumulat-
ed knowledge of man and his environment and culture to bear upon the
interpretation of the archeological record. The promise is that
through the co-operation of all the disciplines of anthropology this
task can be carried out. The increasing specialization within the
field of anthropology, as each discipline grows in complexity, makes
this task of co-operation more difficult, but it can be met in at
least two ways: by collaboration of groups of specialists on related
or common problems and by broader training for students in universities and museums. Dr. Cole saw this challenge and met it with a pro-

gram of training and research adequate to its needs; part of the promise is in this volume and in the work of his students and associates
who are already realizing a good portion of his goal of "making the
past live again."

NOTES

[1]See, e.g., Strong, 1943, and Martin, Quimby, and Collier, 1947.

[2]Our limited knowledge of many groups makes it impossible to indicate the exact number of tribes or dialect groups. Wissler, 1922,
Appendix, gives a convenient list. Cf. also the tribal maps in Kroeber, 1939, and Murdock, 1941.

[3]Wissler, 1920; 1926. See also Lowie, 1916, and Spier, 1921, and
the papers on which they are based.

[4]Speck, 1907a; 1926; and Swanton, 1928c. Some of the more important monographs for this period are those of Skinner (1913; 1915;
1921; 1925; 1927), Radin (1923), Speck (1907b; 1909), and Swanton
(1928a; 1928b; 1928d).

[5]Wissler, 1914; 1922.

[6]Kroeber, 1939, p. 20. It is one of the tragedies resulting from
the depression that this study, completed in 1931, was delayed so
long in publication. It represents a landmark in North American ethnology.

[7]Ibid., p. 60.

[8]Thomas, C., 1894.

[9]Moore, C. B., 1894-1918.

[10]Holmes, 1903.

[11]Holmes, 1914.

[12]Wissler, 1922.

[13]Holmes, 1914, p. 416.

[14]Setzler, 1943, p. 207.

[15]Griffin, J. B., 1946, pp. 39-40.

[16]Griffin, J. B., 1943.

[17]Lewis and Kneberg, 1946.

[18]Ritchie, 1944.

[19]Strong, 1935.

[20]Wedel, 1936.

[21]Webb and Snow, 1945.

[22]I have omitted discussion of physical anthropology in this connection since Neumann is making a basic contribution to this problem
in the preceding paper.

[23]Steward, J. H., 1942, p. 339.

[24]Kroeber, 1939, pp. 106-107.

[25]Shetrone, 1920; 1930.

[26]Griffin, J. B., 1943.

[27]Sapir, 1916.

[28]Cf. Linton, 1936, Chap. xxii, and Kroeber, 1939, p. 2.

[29]Linton, 1936, pp. 397-398.

[30]The limited number of linguists working in the eastern United States makes it imperative that anthropologists working in the area do something with the linguistic materials available. Such activities will result in more useful linguistic classifications. See, e.g., Voegelin, 1941; Voegelin, C. F. and E. W., 1946.

[31]See McKern, 1939, and Griffin, J. B., 1943, Appendix, for a discussion of the system.

[32]See Brew, 1946, pp. 44-66, and Jennings, 1947, for critical comments and appraisals.

[33]Steward, J. H., 1936.

[34]*Ibid.*, p. 331.

[35]*Ibid.*, pp. 343-345.

[36]Steward, J. H., 1937.   See also his important study of Great Basin sociopolitical groups (Steward, J. H., 1938).

[37]Steward, J. H., 1937, pp. 101-102.

[38]Recent excavations at Kincaid, the Angel site, in Kentucky, Tennessee, Alabama, Georgia, and other regions furnish evidence that such data are obtainable. For examples see Bennett, 1944;   Lewis and Kneberg, 1946; and others.

[39]McKern, 1937.

[40]Cooper, J. M., 1941.

[41]Kroeber, 1939, pp. 76 ff., presents a summary of interpretations of Plains culture. The following discussion is largely drawn from an independent analysis of "The Plains Area" which I presented at the annual meeting of the American Anthropological Association in December, 1939, in connection with a symposium on the present state of our knowledge of various fields.

[42]Kroeber, 1928.

[43]Strong, 1935; 1940.

[44]Wedel, 1938; 1940; 1947.

[45]Wedel, 1938.

[46]Strong, 1940.

[47]Strong, 1936, p. 362.

[48]See Winship, 1896.

[49]Winship (ed.), 1904, pp. 111-112 and 230, as quoted in Wissler, 1927, pp. 155-156.

[50]The Kiowa, who may be an exception, unfortunately moved into the southern Plains before they were studied.

[51]Archeological evidence will ultimately give us an outline of the sequence of events in this area.

[52]Wissler, 1926.

[53]Strong, 1940, p. 359.

[54]Eggan, 1937*b*, pp. 85, 88, 89 ff., especially. This analysis was made independently of Steward's studies noted above, and adds another series of cases.

[55]Collier, 1939. His forthcoming study of local groupings in the northern Plains will discuss these organizations in detail.

[56]Eggan, 1937*b*, p. 94; Collier, 1939.

[57]Voegelin, 1941, p. 249.

[58]Landes, n.d.; see also Wallis, 1947.

[59]See Griffin, J. B., 1937, and Wedel, 1940.

[60]Strong, 1940, pp. 358 ff., presents a summary of their historic movements.

[61]Kroeber, 1939, p. 91.

[62]Voegelin, 1941, p. 247. This is still a highly controversial question, since there is no good historical documentation for the Siouan groups in the Ohio Valley according to Griffin, and the area is marked as "Uninhabited in Early Historical Period" on the "Map of North American Indian Languages" by C. F. and E. W. Voegelin.

[63]Strong's (1940) evidence makes it possible to add the Algonkian-speaking Cheyenne to this list.

[64]Wedel, 1940, p. 328.

[65]Strong, 1940, gives a preliminary summary of the data and suggests that there may be differences between the central and northern Plains.

[66]Wedel, 1940, p. 321.

[67]The possible relation of the semisubterranean houses at the Fisher site to the Plains types should also be investigated in view of the affiliations of Fisher with Oneota.

[68]See Eggan, 1937b, p. 93, for a preliminary classification of these kinship systems.

[69]Cf. Steward's, J. H., (1937, pp. 101-102), conclusions quoted above.

[70]See Radcliffe-Brown, 1935, for an exposition of this point of view.

[71]Fortune, 1932, p. 24, note to chap. ii.

[72]The testing of this generalization obviously requires a much wider comparative survey than can be carried out here, but I hope to bring together the relevant evidence in the near future. The Ponca and Kansa emphasized hunting to a greater extent than the Omaha; the Osage and Quapaw apparently were more agricultural. An analysis of this series, if the data were available, would be of great importance.

[73]Fenton, 1940.

[74]Griffin, J. B., 1944.

[75]Fenton, 1940, p. 164.

[76]Griffin, J. B., 1944, p. 360.

[77]Fenton, 1940, p. 165.

[78]Flannery, 1939.

[79]Griffin, J. B., 1944, p. 372, and personal communication. See also the chapter by MacNeish in this volume.

[80]*Ibid.*, pp. 372-373. [This date would now be extended backward some 500 to 600 years.--Ed.]

[81]See Swanton, 1946, for a summary and bibliography.

[82]See Ford and Willey, 1941, and Griffin, J. B., 1946.

[83]I am indebted to Moreau Maxwell for many suggestions incorporated in the following discussion.

[84]Haas, 1941. Kroeber (1939, pp. 65-67) had criticized Swanton's (1922) groupings on the basis of dialect distribution.

[85]Lewis and Kneberg, 1946, chap. ii, equate the Hiwassee Island Focus with Muskogean peoples and the Dallas and Mouse Creek foci with the Creek and Yuchi, respectively.

[86]See Jennings, 1939; Kelly, 1938; and Willey, 1939, for the probable relations of Lamar and Ocmulgee Fields cultures to the protohistoric and historic Creeks.

[87]Jennings, 1941; 1944, discusses the relationships between Mississippi cultures and the historic Choctaw and Chickasaw.

[88]See Swanton, 1928c; 1946.

[89]Swanton, 1928c; 1935.

[90]Speck, 1920.

[91]Sapir, 1929.

[92]Except, of course, the Algonkian-speaking Shawnee who entered the area in historic times.

[93]Griffin, J. B., 1946, p. 75.

[94]*Ibid.*, Fig. 7, p. 76.

[95]If Krieger's (1947, p. 148) views as to the age of the Spiro materials hold up, it may be an important factor.

[96]See Bell's paper in this volume and the forthcoming Kincaid report.

[97]Kroeber, 1939, pp. 62 ff.

[98]Several writers have pointed out that the system, as described by the French, is unstable; Kroeber, himself, finds "something of the quality of a remnant" about it.

[99]Swanton, 1946, p. 661.

[100]Personal communication from George I. Quimby, Jr. This conclusion is based largely on ceramics, and he recognizes that it is not conclusive.

[101]See Dixon, 1928, for an exposition of this point.

[102]Griffin, J. B., 1946, p. 80. J. Joe Bauxar has made a detailed study of the Yuchi which illustrates the value of a multidimensional approach.

[103]See, e.g., Eggan, 1937a; Gilbert, 1937; 1943; Haas, 1939; 1940; and Spoehr, 1941; 1942; 1944; 1947.

[104]See, especially, Spoehr, 1947.

[105]Lewis and Kneberg, 1946.

BIBLIOGRAPHY

[Bell, Robert E.
1952 "Dendrochronology in the Mississippi Valley." In *Archeology of Eastern United States* (James B. Griffin, ed.), pp. 345-51, Chicago.]

Bennett, John W.
1944 "Archaeological Horizons in the Southern Illinois Region." *American Antiquity*, Vol. 10, No. 1, pp. 12-22, Menasha.

Brew, John Otis
1946 *Archaeology of Alkali Ridge, Southeastern Utah.* Papers of the Peabody Museum of American Archaeology and Ethnology, Harvard University, Vol. 21, Cambridge.

Collier, Donald
1939 Field Notes on Local Groupings in the Northern Plains. Ms.

Cooper, John M.
1941 *Temporal Sequence and the Marginal Cultures*. The Catholic
University of America, Anthropological Series, No. 10, Washington.

Dixon, Roland B.
1928 *The Building of Cultures*. New York.

Eggan, Fred
1937a "Historical Changes in the Choctaw Kinship System." *American
Anthropologist*, Vol. 39, No. 1, pp. 34-52, Menasha.

1937b "The Cheyenne and Arapaho Kinship System." In *Social Anthropology of North American Tribes* (Fred Eggan, ed.), pp. 35-95,
Chicago.

1939 "The Plains Area." Typescript of paper presented at the annual meeting of the American Anthropological Association,
Chicago.

Fenton, William N.
1940 "Problems Arising from the Historic Northeastern Position of
the Iroquois." In *Essays in Historical Anthropology of North
America*, Smithsonian Miscellaneous Collections, Vol. 100,
pp. 159-251, Washington.

Flannery, Regina
1939 *An Analysis of Coastal Algonquian Culture*. The Catholic
University of America, Anthropological Series, No. 7, Washington.

Ford, James A., and Gordon R. Willey
1941 "An Interpretation of the Prehistory of the Eastern United
States." *American Anthropologist*, Vol. 43, No. 3, pp. 325-
363, Menasha.

Fortune, Reo
1932 *Omaha Secret Societies*. Columbia University Contributions
to Anthropology, Vol. 14, New York.

Gilbert, William H., Jr.
1937 "Eastern Cherokee Social Organization." In *Social Anthropology of North American Tribes* (Fred Eggan, ed.), pp. 285-338,
Chicago.

1943 "The Eastern Cherokees." *Anthropological Papers*, No. 23,
Bureau of American Ethnology, Bulletin 133, pp. 169-413,
Washington.

Griffin, James B.
1937 "The Archaeological Remains of the Chiwere Sioux." *American
Antiquity*, Vol. 2, No. 3, pp. 180-181, Menasha.

1943 *The Fort Ancient Aspect, Its Cultural and Chronological
Position in Mississippi Valley Archaeology*. Ann Arbor.

1944 "The Iroquois in American Prehistory." *Papers of the Michigan Academy of Science, Arts, and Letters*, Vol. 29, pp. 357-
374, Ann Arbor.

1946 "Cultural Change and Continuity in Eastern United States
Archaeology." In *Man in Northeastern North America* (Frederick
Johnson, ed.), Papers of the Robert S. Peabody Foundation for
Archeology, Vol. 3, pp. 37-95, Andover.

Haas, Mary R.
1939 "Natchez and Chitimacha Clans and Kinship Terminology." *American Anthropologist*, Vol. 41, No. 4, pp. 597-610, Menasha.

1940   "Creek Inter-town Relationships." *American Anthropologist*, Vol. 42, No. 3, pp. 479-489, Menasha.

1941   "The Classification of the Muskogean Languages." In *Language, Culture and Personality* (Leslie Spier, A. I. Hallowell, and Stanley S. Newman, eds.), pp. 41-56, Menasha.

Holmes, William H.
1903   "Aboriginal Pottery of the Eastern United States." *Twentieth Annual Report, Bureau of American Ethnology, 1898-1899*, pp. 1-201, Washington.

1914   "Areas of American Culture Characterization Tentatively Outlined as an Aid   the Study of Antiquities." *American Anthropologist*, Vol. 16, No. 3, pp. 413-446, Lancaster.

Jennings, Jesse D.
1939   "Recent Excavations at the Lamar Site, Ocmulgee National Monument, Macon, Georgia." *Proceedings of the Society for Georgia Archaeology*, Vol. 2, No. 2, pp. 45-55.

1941   "Chickasaw and Earlier Indian Cultures of Northeast Mississippi." *The Journal of Mississippi History*, Vol. 3, No. 3, pp. 155-226.

1944   "The Archaeological Survey of the Natchez Trace." *American Antiquity*, Vol. 9, No. 4, pp. 408-414, Menasha.

1947   Review of *Hiwasse Island* by T. M. N. Lewis and Madeline Kneberg. *American Antiquity*, Vol. 12, No. 3, pp. 191-193, Menasha.

Kelly, A. R.
1938   "A Preliminary Report on Archeological Exploration at Macon, Georgia." *Anthropological Papers*, No. 1, *Bureau of American Ethnology*, Bulletin 119, pp. 1-68, Washington.

Krieger, Alex D.
1947   "The Eastward Extension of Puebloan Datings Toward Cultures of the Mississippi Valley." *American Antiquity*, Vol. 12, No. 3, pp. 141-148, Menasha.

Kroeber, Alfred L.
1928   *Native Cultures of the Southwest*. University of California Publications in American Archaeology and Ethnology, Vol. 23, No. 9, Berkeley.

1939   *Cultural and Natural Areas of Native North America*. University of California Publications in American Archaeology and Ethnology, Vol. 38, Berkeley.

Landes, Ruth
n.d.   "The Santee or the Eastern Dakota." Manuscript based on field notes.

Lewis, T. M. N., and Madeline Kneberg
1946   *Hiwassee Island: An Archaeological Account of Four Tennessee Indian Peoples*. Knoxville.

Linton, Ralph
1936   *The Study of Man*. New York.

Lowie, Robert H.
1916   *Plains Indian Age-Societies: Historical and Comparative Summary*. Anthropological Papers of the American Museum of Natural History, Vol. 11, Pt. 13, New York.

McKern, W. C.
1937   "An Hypothesis for the Asiatic Origin of the Woodland Pattern." *American Antiquity*, Vol. 3, No. 2, pp. 138-143, Menasha.

1939   "The Midwestern Taxonomic Method as an Aid to Archaeological
       Culture Study." *American Antiquity*, Vol. 4, No. 4, pp. 301-
       313, Menasha.

[MacNeish, Richard S.
  1952 "The Archeology of the Northeastern United States." In *Ar-
       cheology of Eastern United States* (James B. Griffin, ed.),
       pp. 46-58, Chicago.]

Martin, Paul S., George I. Quimby, Jr., and Donald Collier
  1947 *Indians before Columbus; Twenty Thousand Years of North Amer-
       ican History*. Chicago.

Moore, Clarence B.
  1894*a* "Certain Sand Mounds of the St. John's River, Florida."
         Journal of the Academy of Natural Sciences of Philadelphia,
         second series, Vol. 10, Pt. 1, pp. 5-103.

  1894*b* "Certain Sand Mounds of the St. John's River, Florida."
         Journal of the Academy of Natural Sciences of Philadelphia,
         second series, Vol. 10, Pt. 2, pp. 129-246.

  1894*c* "Certain Shell Heaps of the St. John's River, Florida, Hither-
         to Unexplored." Pt. 5. *American Naturalist*, Vol. 28, pp. 15-
         26, Philadelphia.

  1896*a* "Certain River Mounds of Duval County, Florida." *Journal of
         the Academy of Natural Sciences of Philadelphia*, second series,
         Vol. 10, Pt. 4, pp. 448-502.

  1896*b* "Two Mounds on Murphy Island." *Journal of the Academy of
         Natural Sciences of Philadelphia*, second series, Vol. 10,
         Pt. 4, pp. 503-516.

  1896*c* "Certain Sand Mounds of the Ocklawaha River." *Journal of the
         Academy of Natural Sciences of Philadelphia*, second series,
         Vol. 10, Pt. 4, pp. 517-543.

  1897   "Certain Aboriginal Mounds of the Georgia Coast." *Journal
         of the Academy of Natural Sciences of Philadelphia*, second
         series, Vol. 11, Pt. 1, pp. 4-138.

  1898*a* "Certain Aboriginal Mounds of the Coast of South Carolina."
         Journal of the Academy of Natural Sciences of Philadelphia,
         second series, Vol. 11, Pt. 2, pp. 146-166.

  1898*b* "Certain Aboriginal Mounds of the Savannah River." *Journal
         of the Academy of Natural Sciences of Philadelphia*, second
         series, Vol. 11, Pt. 2, pp. 167-172.

  1899   "Certain Aboriginal Remains of the Alabama River." *Journal
         of the Academy of Natural Sciences of Philadelphia*, second
         series, Vol. 11, Pt. 3, pp. 289-347.

  1900   "Certain Antiquities of the Florida West-Coast." *Journal of
         the Academy of Natural Sciences of Philadelphia*, second
         series, Vol. 11, Pt. 3, pp. 350-394.

  1901   "Certain Aboriginal Remains of the Northwest Florida Coast,
         Pt. 1." *Journal of the Academy of Natural Sciences of Phila-
         delphia*, second series, Vol. 11, Pt. 4, pp. 419-497.

  1902   "Certain Aboriginal Remains of the Northwest Florida Coast,
         Pt. 2." *Journal of the Academy of Natural Sciences of Phila-
         delphia*, second series, Vol. 12, Pt. 2, pp. 125-335.

  1903*a* "Certain Aboriginal Mounds of the Florida Central West-Coast."
         Journal of the Academy of Natural Sciences of Philadelphia,
         second series, Vol. 12, Pt. 3, pp. 361-438.

1903*b* "Certain Aboriginal Remains of the Apalachicola River." *Journal of the Academy of Natural Sciences of Philadelphia*, second series, Vol. 12, Pt. 3, pp. 440-492.

1904 "Aboriginal Urn Burial in the United States." *American Anthropologist*, Vol. 6, No. 5, pp. 660-669, Lancaster.

1905*a* "Certain Aboriginal Remains of the Black Warrior River." *Journal of the Academy of Natural Sciences of Philadelphia*, second series, Vol. 13, Pt. 2, pp. 125-244.

1905*b* "Certain Aboriginal Remains of the Lower Tombigee River." *Journal of the Academy of Natural Sciences of Philadelphia*, second series, Vol. 13, Pt. 2, pp. 245-278.

1905*c* "Certain Aboriginal Remains of Mobile Bay and Mississippi Sound." *Journal of the Academy of Natural Sciences of Philadelphia*, second series, Vol. 13, Pt. 2, pp. 279-297.

1905*d* "Miscellaneous Investigations in Florida." *Journal of the Academy of Natural Sciences of Philadelphia*, second series, Vol. 13, Pt. 2, pp. 298-325.

1907*a* "Moundville Revisited." *Journal of the Academy of Natural Sciences of Philadelphia*, second series, Vol. 13, Pt. 3, pp. 337-405.

1907*b* "Crystal River Revisited." *Journal of the Academy of Natural Sciences of Philadelphia*, second series, Vol. 13, Pt. 3, pp. 406-425.

1907*c* "Mounds of the Lower Chattahoochee and Lower Flint Rivers." *Journal of the Academy of Natural Sciences of Philadelphia*, second series, Vol. 13, Pt. 3, pp. 426-456.

1908 "Certain Mounds of Arkansas and Mississippi." *Journal of the Academy of Natural Sciences of Philadelphia*, second series, Vol. 13, Pt. 4, pp. 481-600.

1909 "Antiquities of the Ouachita Valley." *Journal of the Academy of Natural Sciences of Philadelphia*, second series, Vol. 14, Pt. 1, pp. 6-170.

1910 "Antiquities of the St. Francis, White, and Black Rivers, Arkansas." *Journal of the Academy of Natural Sciences of Philadelphia*, second series, Vol. 14, Pt. 2, pp. 254-362.

1911 "Some Aboriginal Sites on Mississippi River." *Journal of the Academy of Natural Sciences of Philadelphia*, second series, Vol. 14, Pt. 3, pp. 366-476.

1912 "Some Aboriginal Sites on Red River." *Journal of the Academy of Natural Sciences of Philadelphia*, second series, Vol. 14, Pt. 4, pp. 482-640.

1915. "Aboriginal Sites on Tennessee River." *Journal of the Academy of Natural Sciences of Philadelphia*, second series, Vol. 16, Pt. 3, pp. 431-487.

1916*a* "Additional Investigation on Green River, Kentucky." *Journal of the Academy of Natural Sciences of Philadelphia*, second series, Vol. 16, Pt. 3, pp. 431-487.

1916*b* "Additional Investigation on Mississippi River." *Journal of the Academy of Natural Sciences of Philadelphia*, second series, Vol. 16, Pt. 3, pp. 492-508.

1918 "The Northwestern Florida Coast Revisited." *Journal of the Academy of Natural Sciences of Philadelphia*, second series, Vol. 16, Pt. 4, pp. 514-577.

Murdock, George P.
1941 *Ethnographic Bibliography of North America.* Yale Anthropo-
      logical Series, Vol. 1, New Haven.

[Neumann, Georg K.
1952 "Archeology and Race in the American Indian." In *Archeology
      of Eastern United States* (James B. Griffin, ed.), pp. 13-34,
      Chicago.]

Radcliffe-Brown, Arthur R.
1935 "Patrilineal and Matrilineal Succession." *Iowa Law Review*,
      Vol. 20, No. 2.

Radin, Paul
1923 "The Winnebago Tribe." *Thirty-seventh Annual Report, Bureau
      of American Ethnology, 1915-1916*, pp. 35-550, Washington.

Ritchie, William A.
1944 *The Pre-Iroquoian Occupations of New York State.* Rochester
      Museum of Arts and Sciences, Memoir No. 1.

Sapir, Edward
1916 *Time Perspective in Aboriginal American Culture.* Canada
      Department of Mines, Geological Survey, Memoir 90, Anthro-
      pological Series, No. 13, Ottawa.

1929 "Central and North American Indian Languages." *Encyclopedia
      Britannica*, Vol. 5, 14th edition, pp. 138-141, Chicago.

Setzler, Frank M.
1943 "Archaeological Explorations in the United States, 1930-1942."
      Acta Americana, Vol. 1, No. 2, pp. 206-220.

Shetrone, Henry C.
1920 "The Culture Problem in Ohio Archaeology." *American Anthro-
      pologist*, Vol. 22, No. 2, pp. 144-172, Lancaster.

1930 *The Mound Builders.* New York.

Skinner, Alanson B.
1913 *Social Life and Ceremonial Bundles of the Menomini Indians.*
      Anthropological Papers of the American Museum of Natural
      History, Vol. 13, Pt. 1, New York.

1915 *Associations and Ceremonies of the Menomini Indians.* Anthro-
      pological Papers of the American Museum of Natural History,
      Vol. 13, Pt. 2, New York.

1921 "Material Culture of the Menomini." *Indian Notes and Mono-
      graphs*, Miscellaneous No. 20, Museum of the American Indian,
      Heye Foundation, New York.

1925 *Observations on the Ethnology of the Sauk Indians.* Bulletin
      of the Public Museum of the City of Milwaukee, Vol. 5.

1927 *The Mascoutens or Prairie Potawatomie Indians.* Part III:
      Mythology and Folklore. Bulletin of the Public Museum of
      the City of Milwaukee, Vol. 6, No. 3.

Speck, Frank G.
1907a "Some Outlines of Aboriginal Culture in the Southeastern
      States." *American Anthropologist*, Vol. 9, No. 2, pp. 287-
      295, Lancaster.

1907b *The Creek Indians of Taskigi Town.* American Anthropological
      Association Memoir, Vol. 2, No. 2, Lancaster.

1909 *Ethnology of the Yuchi Indians.* Anthropological Publications,
      University Museum, University of Pennsylvania, Vol. 1, No. 1,
      Philadelphia.

1920   *Decorative Art and Basketry of the Cherokee.* Bulletin of the Public Museum of the City of Milwaukee, Vol. 2, No. 2.

1926   "Culture Problems in Northeastern North America." *Proceedings of the American Philosophical Society*, Vol. 65, No. 4, pp. 272-311, Philadelphia.

Spier, Leslie
1921   *The Sun Dance of the Plains Indians: Its Development and Diffusion.* Anthropological Papers of the American Museum of Natural History, Vol. 16, Pt. 7, New York.

Spoehr, Alexander
1941   *Camp, Clan, and Kin among the Cow Creek Seminole of Florida.* Field Museum of Natural History, Anthropological Series, Vol. 33, No. 1, Chicago.

1942   *Kinship System of the Seminole.* Field Museum of Natural History, Anthropological Series, Vol. 33, No. 2, Chicago.

1944   *The Florida Seminole Camp.* Field Museum of Natural History, Anthropological Series, Vol. 33, No. 3, Chicago.

1947   *Changing Kinship Systems.* Field Museum of Natural History, Anthropological Series, Vol. 33, No. 4, Chicago.

Steward, Julian H.
1936   "The Economic and Social Basis of Primitive Bands." In *Essays in Anthropology Presented to A. L. Kroeber* (Robert H. Lowie, ed.), pp. 331-350, Berkeley.

1937   "Ecological Aspects of Southwestern Society." *Anthropos*, Vol. 32, Nos. 1-2, pp. 87-104, St. Gabriel Mödling bei Wien.

1938   *Basin-Plateau Aboriginal Sociopolitical Groups.* Bureau of American Ethnology, Bulletin 120, Washington.

1942   "The Direct Historical Approach to Archeology." *American Antiquity*, Vol. 7, No. 4, pp. 337-343, Menasha.

Strong, W. Duncan
1935   *An Introduction to Nebraska Archeology.* Smithsonian Miscellaneous Collections, Vol. 93, No. 10, Washington.

1936   "Anthropological Theory and Archaeological Fact." In *Essays in Anthropology Presented to A. L. Kroeber* (Robert H. Lowie, ed.), pp. 359-370, Berkeley.

1940   "From History to Prehistory in the Northern Great Plains." In *Essays in Historical Anthropology of North America*, Smithsonian Miscellaneous Collections, Vol. 100, pp. 353-394, Washington.

1943   *Cross Sections of New World Prehistory.* Smithsonian Miscellaneous Collections, Vol. 104, No. 2, Washington.

Swanton, John R.
1922   *Early History of the Creek Indians and Their Neighbors.* Bureau of American Ethnology, Bulletin 73, Washington.

1928a "Social Organization and Social Usages of the Indians of the Creek Confederacy." *Forty-second Annual Report, Bureau of American Ethnology, 1924-1925*, pp. 23-472, Washington.

1928b "Religious Beliefs and Medical Practices of the Creek Indians." *Forty-second Annual Report, Bureau of American Ethnology, 1924-2925*, pp. 473-672, Washington.

1928c "Aboriginal Culture of the Southeast." *Forty-second Annual Report, Bureau of American Ethnology, 1924-1925*, pp. 673-726, Washington.

1928d "Social and Religious Beliefs and Usages of the Chickasaw
       Indians." *Forty-fourth Annual Report, Bureau of American
       Ethnology, 1926-1927*, pp. 169-273, Washington.

1935 "Notes on the Cultural Provinces of the Southeast." *American
       Anthropologist*, Vol. 37, No. 3, pp. 373-385, Menasha.

1946 *The Indians of the Southeastern United States.* Bureau of
       American Ethnology, Bulletin 137, Washington.

Thomas, Cyrus
1894 "Report on the Mound Explorations of the Bureau of American
       Ethnology." *Twelfth Annual Report, Bureau of American Eth-
       nology, 1890-1891*, pp. 3-730, Washington.

Voegelin, Carl F.
1941 "Internal Relationships of Siouan Languages." *American
       Anthropologist*, Vol. 43, No. 2, pp. 246-249, Menasha.

Voegelin, Carl F., and Erminie W. Voegelin
1946 "Linguistic Considerations of Northeastern North America."
       In *Man in Northeastern North America* (Frederick Johnson, ed.),
       Papers of the Robert S. Peabody Foundation for Archaeology,
       Vol. 3, pp. 179-194, Andover.

Wallis, Wilson D.
1947 *The Canadian Dakota.* Anthropological Papers of the American
       Museum of Natural History, Vol. 41, Pt. 1, New York.

Webb, William S., and Charles E. Snow
1945 *The Adena People.* The University of Kentucky Reports in
       Anthropology and Archaeology, Vol. 6, Lexington.

Wedel, Waldo R.
1936 *An Introduction to Pawnee Archeology.* Bureau of American
       Ethnology, Bulletin 112, Washington.

1938 *The Direct-Historical Approach in Pawnee Archeology.* Smith-
       sonian Miscellaneous Collections, Vol. 97, No. 7, Washington.

1940 "Culture Sequence in the Central Great Plains." In *Essays in
       Historical Anthropology of North America*, Smithsonian Miscel-
       laneous Collections, Vol. 100, pp. 291-352, Washington.

1947 "Culture Chronology in the Central Great Plains." *American
       Antiquity*, Vol. 12, No. 3, pp. 148-156, Menasha.

Willey, Gordon R.
1939 "Ceramic Stratigraphy in a Georgia Village Site." *American
       Antiquity*, Vol. 5, No. 2, pp. 140-147, Menasha.

Winship, George P.
1896 "The Coronado Expedition, 1540-1542." *Fourteenth Annual
       Report, Bureau of American Ethnology, 1892-1893*, Pt. 1,
       pp. 329-613, Washington.

Winship, George P., editor
1904 *The Journey of Coronado, 1540-1542. . . . As Told by Himself
       and His Followers.* New York.

Wissler, Clark
1914 "Material Cultures of the North American Indians." *American
       Anthropologist*, Vol. 16, No. 3, pp. 447-505, Lancaster.

1920 *North American Indians of the Plains.* American Museum of
       Natural History, Handbook Series No. 1, second edition, New
       York.

1922 *The American Indian.* Second edition, New York.

1926 *The Relation of Nature to Man in Aboriginal America.* New York.

1927 *North American Indians of the Plains.* American Museum of Nat-
       ural History, Handbook Series No. 1, third edition, New York.

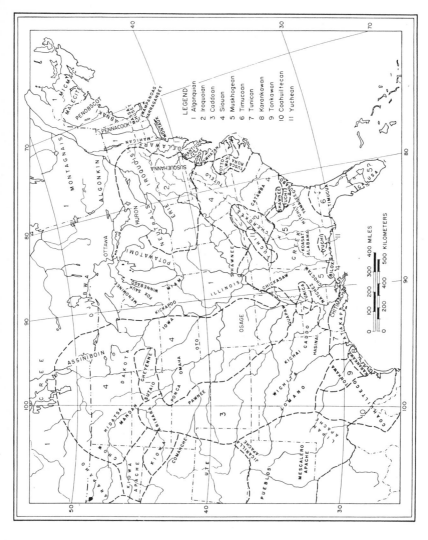

Fig. 1.--Tribes and linguistic stocks in the eastern United States *ca.* A.D. 1700 (after Swanton)

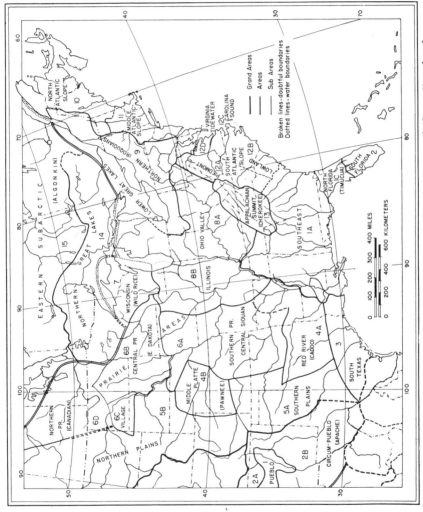

Fig. 2.--Culture areas in the eastern United States (after Kroeber)

9

SOCIAL ANTHROPOLOGY AND THE METHOD

OF CONTROLLED COMPARISON*

1954

I

The contemporary student of anthropology is in a difficult position in attempting to achieve a sound orientation in our rapidly changing and developing discipline. Nowhere is this more true than in the general field of cultural anthropology, where there is an apparent schism between those who call themselves ethnologists and the newer group of social anthropologists. Ethnology, which has had its major development in the United States, has been concerned primarily with culture history and culture process; social anthropology, on the other hand, is primarily a product of British anthropology and has emphasized social structure and function as its major concepts. These differences in emphasis and interest have led to considerable misunderstanding on both sides. As one who has had a foot in both camps for some two decades I may perhaps be permitted some observations on this situation, along with some suggestions as to a common meeting-ground.[1]

Since World War II rapid changes have taken place in all branches of anthropology. Genetics and the experimental method, plus a host of new fossil finds from Africa, are revolutionizing physical anthropology; archeology, with the aid of radiocarbon dating and other new techniques, is beginning to achieve a world-wide chronology and is turning to cultural anthropology for further insight into cultural development; linguistics, with structural methods well established, is returning anew to historical problems and re-examining the relations of language and culture. But ethnology, one of whose tasks it

---

*Presidential paper, 1953, American Anthropological Association.

Reproduced by permission of the American Anthropological Association from the *American Anthropologist* 56:743-763, 1954.

is to synthesize and interpret the conclusions reached by its sister disciplines, is lagging behind.

It is not clear how long anthropology can remain partly a biological science, partly a humanity, and partly a social science. As we shift from the descriptive, data-gathering phases of anthropology to analysis, interpretation and theory, it is inevitable that realignments will come about. My predecessors in the presidency during the postwar period have sketched some of these new developments and realignments as they have seen them.[2] It is highly probable that the forces for fusion will prevail over the tendencies to fission in the near future, so far as the United States is concerned; in England the forces are more nearly balanced, and the outcome is more uncertain.[3] In the long run we may or may not follow the patterns set by other disciplines.

Turning to the field of cultural anthropology, one of the important developments of the last few years has been the series of articles and books defining, denouncing, or defending "social anthropology." Murdock, in the most outspoken attack, notes that: "For a decade or more, anthropologists in other countries have privately expressed an increasingly ambivalent attitude toward recent trends in British anthropology--a curious blend of respect and dissatisfaction" (1951:465). His analysis of the strengths and weaknesses of British social anthropology, as revealed in current productions, and his diagnosis of the social anthropologists as primarily "sociologists" have led to replies and counterreplies.

At the International Symposium on Anthropology sponsored by the Wenner-Gren Foundation a special session was devoted to "Cultural/ Social Anthropology," in which various scholars presented the usages current in their respective countries. Tax's (Tax and others 1953: 225) summary of the consensus is to the effect that we ought to "use the words 'cultural' and 'social' anthropology interchangeably and forget about the question of terminology"; but Kroeber in his "Concluding Review" (1953:357-76) returns to the problem of society and culture and finds distinctions. If these distinctions were merely a question of factional dispute or of alternate terms for similar activities, we could agree, with Lowie (1953:527-28), on some neutral term such as "ethnography"--or allow time to make the decision in terms of relative popularity.

But the distinctions being made are not merely a matter of British and American rivalry or of terminology, and it is essential that we realize that there is a problem and that it is an important one. After accepting contemporary British social anthropologists as "true ethnographers" interested in the realities of culture, Lowie (1953:531) goes on to unequivocally reject Fortes' contention that "social structure is not an aspect of culture but the entire culture of a given people handled in a special frame of theory" (Fortes 1953a: 21). However, many British social anthropologists would go even further than Fortes! In general they make a clear distinction between the concepts of *society* and *culture* and think of social anthropology as concerned primarily with the former. Murdock's (1951:471) startling conclusion that the Britishers are sociologists was anticipated by Radcliffe-Brown (1931a) and recently reaffirmed by Evans-Pritchard: "I must emphasize that, theoretically at any rate, social anthropology is the study of all human societies. . . . Social anthropology can therefore be regarded as a branch of sociological studies, that branch which chiefly devotes itself to primitive societies" (1951:10-11). In contrast, the current Americanist opinion subsumes social structure as one aspect of culture, following Tylor (Lowie 1953:531), or separates the two but gives primacy to the concept of culture.

Before we read our British brethren out of the anthropological party, however, it might be wise to see whether we may not have taken too narrow a view of cultural anthropology. Lowie, who, along with many American anthropologists, takes his cultural text from Tylor, defines the aim of ethnography as "the *complete* description of all cultural phenomena everywhere and at all periods" (1953:528, italics Lowie's). It may be both possible and useful to view the "capabilities and habits acquired by man *as a member of society*" under the heading of social structure, despite the fact that Lowie finds it inconceivable. We might wait for the remainder of Fortes' materials on the Tallensi before rendering a verdict. And if we look more closely at Tylor's famous definition it seems clear that anthropology should be concerned with *both* society and culture, as they are interrelated and reflected in human behavior. We need a complete description and interpretation of both social and cultural phenomena, not to mention those concerned with the individual, if we are going to think in global terms. I would agree with Hallowell that society, culture, and personality may "be conceptually differentiated for specialized types of analysis and study. On the other hand, it is being more clearly recognized than heretofore that society, culture and personality cannot be postulated as completely independent variables" (1953:600). We can wait until we know more about each of these concepts before we rank them as superior and inferior.

More important, we cannot afford to ignore the contributions of the British social anthropologists to both theory and description.

In the last thirty years they have been developing a new approach to the study of man in society, which is currently producing significant results. It is no accident that many of the best monographs of the postwar period have come out of the small group of British social anthropologists. Reviewing *African Systems of Kinship and Marriage*, Murdock states (1951:465) that "the ethnographic contributions to the volume reveal without exception a very high level of professional competence in field research and in the analysis of social structural data, equalled only by the work of the very best men in other countries." What some of these contributions are has been recently pointed out by Firth (1951*a*, *b*), Evans-Pritchard (1951), and Fortes (1953*a*, *b*), among others. While Fortes recognizes that they lack the wide and adventurous sweep of American anthropology, "the loss in diversity is amply balanced by the gains we have derived from concentration on a limited set of problems" (1953*a*:17). Most American anthropologists are inclined to attribute the relative excellence of these contributions to good field techniques or perhaps to superior literary abilities, considering the British theoretical approach as rather barren and lifeless. But this seems to me to be a mistake. The structural point of view makes possible a superior organization and interpretation of the cultural data, and good monographs may well be related to this point of view. If we are to meet this competition (particularly in view of Firth's [1951*a*] account of their new directions) we need to do more than label our British colleagues as "comparative sociologists" or invoke the magical figures of Tylor and Franz Boas.

If I may venture a prescription based on my own experience, we need to adopt the structural-functional approach of British social anthropology and integrate it with our traditional American interest in culture process and history. For the weaknesses of British social anthropology are in precisely those aspects where we are strong, and if we can develop a way of relating the two approaches we can perhaps save ethnology from the destiny to which Kroeber has assigned it—"to a premature fate or a senescent death as one may see it" (1953: 366). I feel encouraged in this attempt because I have a genuine interest in both culture and social structure and because Murdock believes I have succeeded "in fusing functional analysis with an interest in history and an awareness of process in a highly productive creative synthesis" (1951:469).

In contrast to most of my contemporaries I arrived at this synthesis without too many conflicts. My early anthropological education was in the Boas tradition as interpreted by Cole, Sapir, and

Spier--with additions from Redfield. But before the mold had hardened too far I came under the influence also of Radcliffe-Brown. The early thirties was a period of intense excitement among graduate students at Chicago, enhanced by debates between Linton and Radcliffe-Brown and heated arguments about functionalism. Redfield's (1937) account gives something of the flavor of this period, as well as a brief characterization of Radcliffe-Brown's contributions to anthropology. And Linton's *Study of Man* (1936) shows definite evidence of the impact of the structural and functional points of view on his thinking: culture and society are clearly differentiated, though they are mutually dependent, and concepts such as social system, status and role, integration and function are intermixed with the more usual cultural categories. But *The Study of Man*, while widely admired, was little imitated by Linton's colleagues--though it has had important effects on social science as a whole and on some of his students.

Once we were in the field, however, some of us discovered that the alternatives about which we had been arguing were in reality complementary. We found that the structural approach gave a new dimension to the flat perspectives of American ethnography and allowed us to ask new kinds of questions. Functionalism gave us meaningful answers to some questions and enabled us again to see cultures as wholes. But we also maintained an interest in cultural regions and a concern for culture process and cultural development. The resulting data were utilized for a variety of purposes. Some students prepared "descriptive integrations" which approximated to that complex reality which is history. Others were attracted to the formulation of general propositions as to society or culture. I, myself, began by working in limited areas on problems of kinship and social structure, utilizing comparison as a major technique and attempting to see changes over time. When Radcliffe-Brown went to Oxford in 1937 we put together some of these studies under the ambitious title, *Social Anthropology of North American Tribes*.

The distinction between society and culture, far from complicating the procedures of analysis and comparison, has actually facilitated them. Generalization requires repeatable units which can be identified, and social structures, which tend to have a limited number of forms, readily lend themselves to classification and comparison. Cultural data, on the other hand, tend to fall into patterns of varying types which are more easily traced through time and space. Social structures and cultural patterns may vary independently of one another, but both have their locus in the behavior of individuals in

social groups. Depending on our problems one or the other may be
central in our analysis, and we may utilize one or another of the
basic methods of investigation--history or science. I would agree
with Kroeber (1935:569) that these latter need differentiation, "precisely because we shall presumably penetrate further in the end by
two approaches than by one," but I see no reason why we should not
use the two approaches together when possible.

The crucial problem with regard to generalization, whether
broad or limited, is the method of comparison which is used. In the
United States, for reasons which I will mention later on, the comparative method has long been in disrepute and was supplanted by what
Boas called the "historical method." In England, on the other hand,
the comparative method has had a more continuous utilization. Nadel
(1951:222-55) discusses the techniques and limitations of the comparative method and the nature of the results which may be obtained
from its application. As Radcliffe-Brown has stated: "It is only
by the use of the comparative method that we can arrive at general
explanations. The alternative is to confine ourselves to particular-
istic explanations similar to those of the historian. The two kinds
of explanation are both legitimate and do not conflict; but both are
needed for the understanding of societies and their institutions"
(1952a:113-14).

The particular adaptation of the comparative method to social
anthropology which Radcliffe-Brown has made is well illustrated in
The Huxley Memorial Lecture for 1951, where he begins with exogamous
moiety divisions in Australia and shows that the Australian phenomena
are instances of certain widespread general tendencies in human societies. For him the task of social anthropology is to "formulate and
validate statements about the conditions of existence of social systems . . . and the regularities that are observable in social change"
(1951:22). This systematic comparison of a world-wide variety of
instances, while an ultimate objective of social anthropology, is
rather difficult to carry out in terms of our present limited knowledge of social systems. We can make some general observations about
institutions such as the family; and the war between the sexes in
aboriginal Australia has some interesting parallels with the world
of Thurber. But I am not sure, to give one example, that the "Yin-
Yang philosophy of ancient China is the systematic elaboration of the
principle that can be used to define the social structure of moieties
in Australian tribes" (1951:21), though Radcliffe-Brown's analysis
and wide experience give it a certain plausibility.

My own preference is for the utilization of the comparative

method on a smaller scale and with as much control over the frame of
comparison as it is possible to secure. It has seemed natural to
utilize regions of relatively homogeneous culture or to work within
social or cultural types, and to further control the ecology and the
historical factors so far as it is possible to do so. Radcliffe-
Brown has done this with great skill in *The Social Organization of
Australian Tribes* (1931*b*). After comparing the Australian moiety
structures and finding their common denominators, I would prefer to
make a comparison with the results of a similar study of moiety structures and associated practices of the Indians of Southern California,
who approximate rather closely the Australian sociocultural situation.
The results of this comparison could then be matched against comparable studies of Northwest Coast and other similar moiety systems,
and the similarities and differences systematically examined by the
method of concomitant variation. I think we would end up, perhaps,
with Radcliffe-Brown's relationship of "opposition," or the unity of
opposites, but we would have much more, as well, in the form of a
clearer understanding of each type or subtype and of the nature of
the mechanisms by which they are maintained or changed. While I
share Radcliffe-Brown's vision of an ultimate science of society, I
think that we first have to cultivate more intensively what Merton
(1949:5) has called the middle range of theory. I suggest the method
of controlled comparison as a convenient instrument for its exploration, utilizing covariation and correlation, and avoiding too great
a degree of abstraction.

Before examining the ramifications and possible results of
such exploration it may be useful to glance at selected aspects of
the history of anthropology to see how certain of the present differences between American and British anthropologists have come about.
We are somewhere in the middle of one of Kroeber's "configurations
of culture growth," and it is important to see which patterns are
still viable and which are close to exhaustion.

II

The early developments in American cultural anthropology have been
delineated by Lowie (1937) and parallel in many respects those which
were occurring in England. In addition to Morgan, Bandelier, Cushing,
J. O. Dorsey, Alice Fletcher, and others were among the pioneers
whose work is today largely forgotten in the United States. For with
the advent of Franz Boas a major break was made with the past, resulting not so much from his program for cultural anthropology as in
its selective implementation. Boas in "The Limitations of the Com-

parative Method" (1896) outlined a program which included two major
tasks. The first task involved detailed studies of individual tribes
in their cultural and regional context as a means to the reconstruction of the histories of tribal cultures and regions. A second task
concerned the comparisons of these tribal histories, with the ultimate objective of formulating general laws of cultural growth, which
were psychological in character (1940:278-79). This second task,
which Boas thought of as the more important of the two, was never to
be fully implemented by his students.

Boas formulated this program in connection with a destructive
criticism of the comparative method as then practiced in England and
America. After stating as a principle of method that uniformity of
processes was essential for comparability, he goes on to say: "If
anthropology desires to establish the laws governing the growth of
culture it must not confine itself to comparing the results of growth
alone, but whenever such is feasible, it must compare the processes
of growth, and these can be discovered by means of studies of the
cultures of small geographical areas" (1940:280). He then compares
this "historical method" with the "comparative method," which he
states has been remarkably barren of results, and predicts that it
will not become fruitful until we make our comparisons "on the broader and sounder basis which I ventured to outline." The requirement
that only those phenomena can be compared which are derived psychologically or historically from common causes, valuable as it may have
been at that time, has had the effect of predisposing most of Boas'
students against the comparative method--except in linguistics where
genetic relationships could be assumed--and hence against any generalizations which require comparison. And the processes which Boas
sought in a study of art and mythology on the Northwest Coast proved
more difficult to isolate than was anticipated. Kroeber notes that
though Boas was "able to show a multiplicity of processes in culture,
he was not able--it was impossible in his day and perhaps is still--
to formulate these into a systematic theory" (1953:368).

In the "Formative Period"[4] of American ethnology, from 1900
to 1915, these were minor considerations. There were the vanishing
Indian cultures to study, and it was natural for the students of Boas
to concentrate on the first portion of his program. They wrote theses,
for the most part, on specific problems, or to test various theories
which had been advanced to explain art, or myth, or ritual, generally
with negative results. This clearing of the intellectual air was
essential, but it also led to excesses, as in Goldenweiser's famous
study of totemism (1910). It also resulted in the ignoring of earlier

anthropologists and even contemporaries. Alice Fletcher's *The Hako: A Pawnee Ceremony* (1904) excellently describes and interprets a ritual but was never used as a model.

The major attention of the early Boas students was devoted to the task of ordering their growing data on the American Indian in tribal and regional context. During this and the following periods many important monographs and studies were published, which formed a solid base for future work. The climax of this fact-gathering revolution was reached with the culture-area concept as crystallized by Wissler (1914, 1922), and in the studies by Boas on the art, mythology, and social organization of the Northwest Coast.

The period which followed, from 1915 to 1930, was a "Florescent Period" in American ethnology. The culture area provided a framework for the analysis and interpretation of the cultural data in terms of history and process. Sapir opened the period with his famous *Time Perspective* (1916), which began: "Cultural anthropology is more and more rapidly getting to realize itself as a strictly historical science. Its data cannot be understood, either in themselves or in their relation to one another, except as the end-points of specific sequences of events reaching back into the remote past." Wissler, Lowie, Kroeber, Spier, Benedict, and many others provided a notable series of regional studies utilizing distributional analyses of cultural traits for chronological inferences--and for the study of culture process. Wissler developed the "law of diffusion" and then turned his attention to the dynamic factors underlying the culture area itself. In *The Relation of Nature to Man in Aboriginal America* (1926) he thought that he had found them in the relationship of the culture center to the underlying ecology. The great museums dominated this period, and American anthropology shared in the general prosperity and optimism which followed the first World War.

One result of these distributional studies was that chronology tended to become an end in itself, and some ethnologists became so preoccupied with seeking time sequences that they did not pay much attention to culture as such. The analysis of culture into traits or elements and their subsequent treatment often violated principles of historical method by robbing them of their context. The normal procedure of historians of basing their analysis on chronology was here reversed--the chronology resulted from the analytic study. The generalizations as to process which were formulated were used as shortcuts to further historical research.

Another important result of these studies was the conception of culture which gradually developed. Culture came to be viewed as

a mere aggregation of traits brought together by the accidents of
diffusion. Here is Benedict's conclusion to her doctoral disserta-
tion: "It is, so far as we can see, an ultimate fact of human nature
that man builds up his culture out of disparate elements, combining
and recombining them; and until we have abandoned the superstition
that the result is an organism functionally interrelated, we shall
be unable to see our cultural life objectively, or to control its
manifestations" (1923:84-85).

The revolt against this mechanical and atomistic conception
of culture came both from without and from within. Dixon (1928) criticized both Wissler's procedures and his conceptions of the processes
of culture growth, as well as his formulation of the dynamics of the
culture area. Spier (1929:222) renounced historical reconstruction
as misleading and unnecessary for understanding the nature of the
processes of culture growth, advocating in its place a consideration
of the actual conditions under which cultural growth takes place.
Benedict was soon engaged in the study of cultural patterns and configurations, and her *Patterns of Culture* (1934) represents a complete
reversal of her earlier position--here superstition has become reality.

During this period there was little interest in social structure as such, even though Kroeber, Lowie, and Parsons all studied
Pueblo life at first hand. The shadows of Morgan, McLennan, Spencer,
and Maine still loomed over them, and sociological interpretations
were generally rejected in favor of psychological or linguistic ones.
Lowie, however, began to develop a moderate functional position and
sociological orientation with regard to social organization, perhaps
best exemplified in his article on "Relationship Terms" (1929).

The "Expansionist Period" which followed, 1930-1940, was a
time of troubles and of transition for American ethnology. The old
gods were no longer omniscient--and there was an invasion of foreign
gods from overseas. The depression brought the great museums to
their knees and temporarily ended their activities in ethnological
research; the center of gravity shifted more and more to the universities, as the social sciences grappled with the new social problems.
This was a period of considerable expansion for cultural anthropology, much of it in terms of joint departments with sociology. Archeology also experienced a remarkable expansion during the decade,
partly as a by-product of its ability to utilize large quantities of
WPA labor. The chronological framework that resulted, based on stratigraphy and other techniques, further emphasized the inadequacy of
the reconstructions made from distributional analyses alone.

In the meantime *Argonauts* and *The Andaman Islanders* had been published but had made relatively little impression on American scholars. Malinowski's field methods were admired, and his functional conception of culture struck some responsive chords; as for Radcliffe-Brown, his "ethnological appendix" was utilized but his interpretations of Andamanese customs and beliefs were largely ignored. Soon afterwards, however, Malinowski began developing social anthropology in England on the basis of the functional method and new techniques of field research. Brief visits by Malinowski to the United States, including a summer session at the University of California, plus the work of his early students in Oceania and Africa, led to a considerable increase in his influence, but during the 1930's he was largely preoccupied with developing a program of research for Africa.

In 1931 Radcliffe-Brown, who had been first in South Africa and then in Australia, brought to this country "a method for the study of society, well defined and different enough from what prevailed here to require American anthropologists to reconsider the whole matter of method, to scrutinize their objectives, and to attend to new problems and new ways of looking at problems. He stirred us up and accelerated intellectual variation among us" (Redfield 1937:vii).

As a result of these and other forces American ethnologists began to shift their interests in a variety of directions. Kroeber re-examined the relationship between cultural and natural areas in a more productive way and formulated the concept of culture climax to replace Wissler's culture center. He also explored the problem of culture elements more thoroughly, in the course of which he organized the Culture Element Survey; at the other end of the cultural spectrum he wrote *Configurations of Culture Growth* (1944). Herskovits, who had earlier applied the culture-area concept to Africa, developed a dynamic approach to the study of culture (1950) which has had important results. Redfield, in the meantime, was beginning the series of studies which resulted in *The Folk Culture of Yucatan* (1941)--a new and important approach to the study of social and cultural change.

During this period, also, Steward was beginning his ecological studies of Great Basin tribes, Warner was applying social anthropological concepts and methods to the study of modern American communities, and Sapir was shifting his interests in the direction of psychiatry. Linton, with his perception of new and important trends, had put them together with the old, but his interests also shifted in the direction of personality and culture. Acculturation became a respectable subject with the Redfield, Linton, and Herskovits' "Memorandum on the Study of Acculturation" (1936), and applied anthropology

secured a foothold in the Indian Service and in a few other government agencies.

These developments, which gave variety and color to American
ethnology, also tended to leave a vacuum in the center of the field.
We will never know for sure what might have developed out of this
interesting decade if World War II had not come along.

The "Contemporary Period"--the decade since the war--is difficult to characterize. In part there has been a continuation of
prewar trends, in part a carry-over of wartime interests, and in part
an interest in new problems resulting from the war and its aftermath.
There is a growing interest in complex cultures or civilizations,
such as China, Japan, India, and Africa, both at the village level
and at the level of national culture and national character, and new
methods and techniques are in process for their study and comparison.

One postwar development of particular interest in connection
with this paper has been the gradual but definite acceptance in many
quarters in this country of social anthropology as a separable but
related discipline. Of even greater potential significance, perhaps,
is the growing alliance between social psychology, sociology, and
social anthropology as the core groups of the so-called "behavioral
sciences," a relationship also reflected in the Institute of Human
Relations at Yale and in the Department of Social Relations at Harvard, as well as elsewhere.

Perhaps most important of all the postwar developments for
the future of anthropology has been the very great increase in the
interchange of both students and faculty between English and American
institutions, including field stations in Africa. The Fulbright program, the Area Research Fellowships of the Social Science Research
Council, the International Symposium on Anthropology of the Wenner-
Gren Foundation, and the activities of the Carnegie, Rockefeller, and
Ford Foundations have all contributed to this increased exchange. I
am convinced that such face-to-face contacts in seminar and field
represent the most effective way for amalgamation of techniques and
ideas to take place. The testimony of students back from London or
Africa is to the general effect that our training is superior in
ethnography and in problems of culture history but is inferior in
social anthropology: kinship, social structure, political organization, law, and so on. There are exceptions, of course, but we would
like the exceptions to be the rule.

For the details of the complementary developments in England we are
indebted to Evans-Pritchard's account in *Social Anthropology* (1951)
and to Fortes' inaugural lecture entitled *Social Anthropology at Cambridge Since 1900* (1953c). There are differences in emphasis between
the Oxford and Cambridge versions, but in general the developments
are clear.

In England cultural anthropology got off to a fine start
through the efforts of Tylor, Maine, McLennan and other pioneers of
the 1860's and 1870's, but their attempts to construct universal
stages of development ultimately fell afoul of the facts. The nineteenth-century anthropologists in England were "armchair" anthropologists; it wasn't until Haddon, a zoologist by training, organized
the famous Torres Straits expedition of 1898-1900 and converted an
assorted group of psychologists and other scientists into ethnologists that field work began. But from this group came the leaders
of early twentieth-century British anthropology: Haddon, Rivers, and
Seligman. According to Evans-Pritchard, "This expedition marked a
turning point in the history of social anthropology in Great Britain.
From this time two important and interconnected developments began
to take place: anthropology became more and more a whole-time professional study, and some field experience came to be regarded as an
essential part of the training of its students" (1951:73).

During the next decade a gradual separation of ethnology and
social anthropology took place, culminating, according to Radcliffe-
Brown (1952b:276), in an agreement to use "ethnography" for descriptive accounts of nonliterate peoples, "ethnology" for historical reconstructions, and "social anthropology" for the comparative study of
the institutions of primitive societies. The institutional division
of labor also took a different organization which has led to different views as to how anthropology should be constituted.

Sir James Frazer dominated social anthropology in the early
decades of this century, and the conceptions of evolution and progress held sway long after they had given way in American anthropology.
But Fortes notes that, while anthropologists had a magnificent field
of inquiry, the subject had no intrinsic unity: "At the stage of
development it had reached in 1920, anthropology, both in this country
and elsewhere, was a bundle-subject, its data gathered, so to speak,
from the same forest but otherwise heterogeneous and tied together
only by the evolutionary theory" (1953c:14).

Ethnology flourished for a period under Haddon, Rivers, and
Seligman, but with the advent of Malinowski and Radcliffe-Brown "so-

cial anthropology has emerged as the basic discipline concerned with custom and social organization in the simpler societies" (Fortes 1953*c*:16). From their predecessors the latter received their tradition of field research and the principle of the intensive study of limited areas--a principle that Malinowski carried to its logical conclusion.

Beginning in 1924 Malinowski began to train a small but brilliant group of social anthropologists from all parts of the Commonwealth in the field techniques and functional theory that he had developed from his Trobriand experience, but his approach proved inadequate for the complex problems encountered in Africa. This deficiency was remedied in part by the advent of Radcliffe-Brown, who returned to the newly organized Institute of Social Anthropology at Oxford in 1937 and proceeded to give British social anthropology its major current directions. Evans-Pritchard discusses this period with the authority of a participant, and I refer you to his *Social Anthropology* for the details--and for a summary of what a social anthropologist does.

The postwar developments in England have been largely a continuation of prewar developments together with a considerable expansion stimulated by government support of both social anthropological and applied research. Unlike the situation in the United States there is no large established group of sociologists in England, and social anthropology has in part filled the gap. Major theoretical differences as to the nature of social anthropology as a science or as a humanity are developing, but these differences are subordinate to a large area of agreement as to basic problems, methods, and points of view. Just as the American ethnologists of the 1920's had a common language and a common set of problems, so do the British social anthropologists today.

One important key to the understanding of British social anthropology resides in their conception of social structure. The contributions in this field with regard to Africa have been summarized by Fortes in "The Structure of Unilineal Descent Groups" (1953*a*). Here he points out that the guiding ideas in the analysis of African lineage organization have come mainly from Radcliffe-Brown's formulation of the structural principles found in all kinship systems, and goes on to state that he is not alone "in regarding them as among the most important generalizations as yet reached in the study of social structure" (p. 25). For Fortes the social structure is the foundation of the whole social life of any continuing society.

Not only have the British social anthropologists produced an outstanding series of monographs in recent years but they have organized their training programs in the universities and institutes to insure that the flow will continue. In the early stages of training there is a more concentrated program in social anthropology in the major British universities, though the knowledge demanded of other fields is less, and linguistics is generally conspicuous by its absence. Only the top students are given grants for field research. As Evans-Pritchard (1951:76-77) sketches the ideal situation, the student usually spends at least two years in his first field study, including learning to speak the language of the group under observation. Another five years is allotted to publishing the results, or longer if he has teaching duties. A study of a second society is desirable, to avoid the dangers of thinking in terms of a single society, but this can usually be carried out in a shorter period.

Granted that this is the ideal procedure, it still offers a standard against which to compare our American practices. My impression is that our very best graduate students are approximating this standard, but our Ph.D. programs in general require considerably less in terms of field research and specific preparation. We tend to think of the doctorate as an earlier stage in the development of a scholar and not a capstone to an established career.

This proposed program, however, has important implications for social anthropology itself. If each anthropologist follows the Malinowskian tradition of specializing in one, or two, or three societies and spends his lifetime in writing about them, what happens to comparative studies? Evans-Pritchard recognizes this problem: "It is a matter of plain experience that it [the comparative study] is a formidable task which cannot be undertaken by a man who is under the obligation to publish the results of the two or three field studies he has made, since this will take him the rest of his life to complete if he has heavy teaching and administrative duties as well" (1951:89).

In place of the comparative method he proposes the "experimental method," in which preliminary conclusions are formulated and then tested by the same or other social anthropologists on different societies, thus gradually developing broader and more adequate hypotheses. The old comparative method, he says, has been largely abandoned because it seldom gave answers to the questions asked (1951:90).

This concentration on intensive studies of one or two selected societies has its own limitations. The hypotheses advanced on such a basis can often be modified in terms of studies easily available for comparison. Thus Schneider (1953:582-84) points out that

some of Evans-Pritchard's generalizations about the Nuer could well
have been tested against the Zulu data. The degree to which comparison may sharpen hypotheses is well illustrated by Nadel's study of
"Witchcraft in Four African Societies" (1952). There is a further
reason for this lack of interest in comparative studies on the part
of Evans-Pritchard in that he thinks of social anthropology as "belonging to the humanities rather than to the natural sciences" (1951:
60) and conceives of his task as essentially a historical one of
"descriptive integration." His colleagues are currently disagree-
ing with him (Forde 1950; Fortes 1953*c*).

Schapera (1953) has recently reviewed a number of studies
utilizing some variation of the comparative method and finds most of
them deficient in one respect or another. The comparative approach
he advocates involves making an intensive study of a given region and
carefully comparing the forms taken among the people of the area by
the particular social phenomena which are under scrutiny, so as to
classify them into types. These types can then be compared with those
of neighboring regions. "Social anthropology would benefit considerably, and have more right to claim that its methods are adequate, if
in the near future far more attention were devoted to intensive regional comparisons" (p. 360).

One difficulty in the way of any systematic and intensive
comparison of African data is being remedied by the Ethnographic Survey under the direction of Daryll Forde. The absence of any interest
in linguistics is a major criticism of a group who advocate learning
a language to carry out researches in social structure but who ignore
the structure in the languages which they learn. Lévi-Strauss (1951)
has pointed out some of the problems in these two fields, and it is
difficult to see why they are neglected.

Ultimately the British anthropologists will discover that
time perspective is also important and will encourage archeology and
historical research. The potentialities of Greenberg's recent genetic classification of African languages, and the subgrouping of Bantu
languages through shared correspondences and lexico-statistical techniques, are just beginning to be appreciated. And for those who demand documents there are the Arab records and historical collections
such as the Portuguese records for Delagoa Bay. That the same tribes
speaking the same languages are still in this region after four hundred years suggests that there is considerable historical material
which needs to be utilized. For our best insights into the nature of
society and culture come from seeing social structures and culture
patterns over time. Here is where we can distinguish the accidental

from the general, evaluate more clearly the factors and forces operating in a given situation, and describe the processes involved in
general terms. Not to take advantage of the possibilities of studying social and cultural change under such relatively controlled conditions is to do only half the job that needs to be done.

IV

These brief and inadequate surveys indicate that cultural anthropology has had quite a different development in the United States and
England and suggest some of the reasons for these differences. They
also suggest that the differences may be growing less. In the United
States ethnology began with a rejection of Morgan and his interest
in the development of social systems, and an acceptance of Tylor and
his conception of culture. Tylor's views by-and-large still prevail,
though since the 1920's there have been many alternative definitions
of culture as anthropologists attempted to get a more *rounded* view
of their subject. In England, as Kroeber and Kluckhohn (1952) have
pointed out, there has been more resistance to the term "culture";
on the other hand, Morgan is hailed as an important forerunner, particularly for his researches on kinship. Prophets are seldom honored
in their own country.

Both Kroeber (1953) and Redfield (1953) have recently reviewed
the role of anthropology in relation to the social sciences and to
the humanities and have emphasized the virtues of a varied attack on
the problems that face us all. With Redfield, I believe we should
continue to encourage variety among anthropologists. But I am here
particularly concerned with cultural anthropology, and I am disturbed
by Kroeber's attitude toward ethnology: "Now how about ethnology?"
he writes in his Concluding Review of Anthropology Today, "I am about
ready to abandon this baby to the wolves." He goes on to detail some
of the reasons why ethnology appears to be vanishing: the decrease
in primitives, the failure to make classifications and comparisons,
and the tendencies to leap directly into large-scale speculations
(1953:366-67). His solution is to merge ethnology with culture history and, when that is soundly established, to extricate the processes
at work and "generalize the story of culture into its causal factors."
This is a return to the original Boas program.

My own suggested solution is an alternate one. While there
are few "primitives" in our own back yard, there are the new frontiers
of Africa, India, Southeast Asia, Indonesia, and Melanesia to exploit.
Here is still a complete range in terms of cultural complexity and
degree of culture contact. Africa alone is a much more challenging

"laboratory" in many respects than is the American Indian. And for those who like their cultures untouched there is interior New Guinea.

The failure to make adequate classifications and comparisons can in part be remedied by borrowing the methods and techniques of the social anthropologists or by going in the directions pioneered by Murdock (1949). Social structure gives us a preliminary basis for classification in the middle range while universals are sought for. Steward's "sociocultural types" are another step in the directions we want to go.

The tendency to leap directly into large-scale speculations is growing less and will be further controlled as we gradually build a foundation of well-supported hypotheses. Speculations are like mutations in some respects--most of them are worthless but every now and then one advances our development tremendously. We need to keep them for this reason, if for no other.

If we can salvage cultural anthropology in the United States, I do not worry too much about the "anthropological bundle" falling apart in the near future. As a result of the closer co-operation among the subdisciplines of anthropology in this country new bridges are continually being built between them, and joint problems, and even new subfields, are constantly being generated. So long as our interaction remains more intensive than our relations with other disciplines, anthropology will hold together.

One thing we can do is to return to the basic problems American ethnologists were tackling in the 1920's and 1930's, with new methods and points of view and a greater range of concepts. I have elsewhere (1952:35-45) discussed the potential contributions that such a combined approach could achieve, and for the Western Pueblos I have tried to give a specific example (1950). But in terms of present possibilities, not one single region in North America has had adequate treatment. Nor are the possibilities of field research in North America exhausted. The Cheyenne, for example, are still performing the Sun Dance pretty much as it was in Dorsey's day. But despite all the studies of the Sun Dance we still do not have an adequate account giving us the meaning and significance of the rituals for the participants and for the tribe. One such account would enable us to revalue the whole literature of the Sun Dance.

The Plains area is now ripe for a new integration which should be more satisfying than the older ones. In addition to Wissler's and Kroeber's formulations, we now have an outline of cultural development firmly anchored in stratigraphy and radiocarbon dates, and a considerable amount of documentary history as well as a series of monographs on special topics. By centering our attention on social structure, we can see the interrelations of subsistence and ecology, on the one hand, and political and ritual activities, on the other. For those interested in process we can ask: Why did tribal groups coming into the Plains from surrounding regions, with radically different social structure, tend to develop a similar type? The answer is not simply diffusion (Eggan 1937*a*). Once this new formulation of the Plains is made, new problems will arise which will require a more complex apparatus to solve.

Another type of comparative study which has great potentialities is represented by the investigation of the Southern Athabascan-speaking peoples in the Plains and the Southwest. Here the same or similar groups have differentiated in terms of ecology, contacts, and internal development. Preliminary studies by Kluckhohn, Opler, Hoijer, Goodwin, and others suggest the possibilities of a detailed comparative attack on the problems of cultural development in this relatively controlled situation. Bellah's (1952) recent study of Southern Athabascan kinship systems, utilizing Parsons' structural-functional categories, shows some of the possibilities in this region.

In the Southwest I have attempted to work within a single structural type in a highly integrated subcultural area and to utilize the archeological and historical records, which are here reasonably complete, to delimit and interpret the variations which are found (1950). Clyde Kluckhohn looks at the Southwest from a broader standpoint and with a different but related problem: "One of the main rewards of intensive study of a culture area such as the Southwest is that such study eventually frees investigators to raise genuinely scientific questions--problems of process. Once the influence of various cultures upon others in the same area and the effects of a common environment (and its variant forms) have been reasonably well ascertained, one can then operate to a first approximation under an 'all other things being equal' hypothesis and intensively examine the question: Why are these cultures and these modal personality types still different--in spite of similar environmental stimuli and pressures and access over long periods to the influence of generalized area culture or cultures? We are ready now, I believe, for such studies--but no one is yet attempting them seriously" (1954:693).

The Ramah Project, directed by Kluckhohn, has been planned so as to furnish a continuous record of a series of Navaho from childhood to maturity and of the changes in their culture as well. This project is in its second decade, and a variety of participants have produced an impressive group of papers. So far Kluckhohn's major monograph has concerned *Navaho Witchcraft* (1944), which he has interpreted in both psychological and structural terms and which breaks much new ground. A newer project in the same region involves the comparison of the value systems of five groups: Navaho, Zuni, Mormon, Spanish-American, and Texan, but the results are not yet available.

Comparative studies can also be done on a very small scale. The few thousand Hopi are divided into nearly a dozen villages, each of which differs in significant ways from its neighbors in terms of origins, conservatism, contacts, independence, degree of acculturation, and specific sociocultural patterns. And on First Mesa the Hano or Hopi Tewa, who came from the Rio Grande around A.D. 1700, still maintain their linguistic and cultural independence despite biological assimilation and minority status--and apparently differ significantly in personality traits as well. Dozier's (1951) preliminary account of this interesting situation suggests how valuable this comparison may eventually be.

How much can be learned about the processes of social and cultural change by comparative field research in a controlled situation is illustrated by Alex Spoehr's researches in the Southeast. Here some preliminary investigations by the writer (1937b) had led to tentative conclusions as to the nature of changes in kinship systems of the Creek, Choctaw, Chickasaw, and other tribes of the region after they were removed to reservations in Oklahoma. Spoehr (1947) not only demonstrated these changes in detail but has analyzed the historical factors responsible and isolated the resulting processes.

Here Redfield's (1941) comparative study of four Yucatecan communities in terms of progressive changes in their organization, individualization, and secularization as one moves from the tribal hinterland through village and town to the city of Merida should also be mentioned. The significance of its contributions to comparative method has been largely overlooked in the controversies over the nature of the "folk society" and the usefulness of ideal types.

We can also begin to study particular social types wherever they occur. Murdock's *Social Structure* (1949) demonstrates that similar social structures and kinship systems are frequently found in various parts of the world. We can compare matrilineal social systems, or Omaha kinship systems, in different regions of the world without restricting ourselves to the specific requirements originally laid down by Boas. Thus Audrey Richards' (1950) comparison of matrilineal organizations in Central Africa will gain in significance when set against the Northwest Coast data. When variant forms of matri-

lineal or patrilineal social systems are compared from the standpoint
of structure and function, we will have a clearer idea of the essential features of such systems and the reasons for special variants.
The results for matrilineal systems promise to give quite a different
picture than Lowie originally drew of the "Matrilineal Complex" (1919),
and they will help us to see more clearly the structural significance
of cultural patterns such as avunculocal residence and cross-cousin
marriage.

These and other studies will enable us ultimately to present
a comprehensive account of the various types of social structure to
be found in the regions of the world and to see the nature of their
correlates and the factors involved in social and cultural change.
It is clear that new methods and techniques will need to be developed
for the evaluation of change over time; quantitative data will be
essential to establish rates of change which may even be expressed in
statistical terms.

I have suggested that there may be some virtues in combining
the sound anthropological concepts of structure and function with
the ethnological concepts of process and history. If we can do this
in a satisfactory manner we can save the "ethnological baby" from the
fate to which Kroeber has consigned it--what we call the infant when
it has matured is a relatively minor matter. In suggesting some of
the ways in which comparative studies can be made more useful I have
avoided questions of definition and ultimate objectives. This is
only one of the many ways in which our science can advance, and we
have the personnel and range of interests to cultivate them all.

After this paper was substantially completed the volume of
papers in honor of Wilson D. Wallis entitled *Method and Perspective
in Anthropology* (Spencer 1954) became available. Much of what Herskovits says with regard to "Some Problems of Method in Ethnography" is
relevant to points made above, particularly his emphasis on the historical approach and the comparative study of documented change (1954:
19) as well as on the importance of repeated analyses of the same
phenomena. And Ackerknecht's scholarly survey of "The Comparative
Method in Anthropology" emphasizes the importance of the comparative
method for cultural anthropology: "One of the great advantages of
the comparative method will be that in a field where the controlled
experiment is impossible it provides at least some kind of control."
He sees signs of a renaissance: "In whatever form the comparative
method may reappear, it will express the growing desire and need in
cultural anthropology to find regularities and common denominators
behind the apparent diversity and uniqueness of cultural phenomena"
(p. 125).

Kroeber, in commenting on the papers in this volume, subscribes "wholeheartedly to Ackerknecht's position. My one criticism is that he doesn't go far enough. He sees the comparative method as something that must and will be revived. I would say that it has never gone out; it has only changed its tactic" (1954:273). He goes on to point out that all science ultimately seeks knowledge of process, but that this must be preceded by "description of the properties of the form and substance of the phenomena, their ordering or classification upon analysis of their structure, and the tracing of their changes or events" (pp. 273-74). These are the essential points that I have tried to make with reference to cultural anthropology.

On both sides of the Atlantic there is an increasing willingness to listen to one another and a growing conviction that the varied approaches are complementary rather than competitive. We can agree, I think, with Radcliffe-Brown: "It will be only in an integrated and organized study in which historical studies and sociological studies are combined that we shall be able to reach a real understanding of the development of human society, and this we do not yet have" (1951:22). It seems to me that it is high time we made a start-- and indeed it is well under way.

In time we may be able to simplify and further order our conceptual schemes in terms of direct observations on human behavior. Sapir, in perhaps a moment of insight, once defined culture "as a systematic series of illusions enjoyed by people." But culture, like the "ether" of the nineteenth-century physicists, plays an essential role today and will do so for a considerable time to come. The distant future is more difficult to predict--I think it was Whitehead who remarked that the last thing to be discovered in any science is what the science is really about!

NOTES

[1] The publication of this paper has been delayed through no fault of the editors. The opportunity to attend the Eighth Pacific Science Congress in Manila in November, 1953, plus the competition afforded by the Apache Crown Dancers at our Tucson meetings made it easy to follow the precedent, begun the year before by President Bennett, of not reading a presidential address. I have written this paper rather informally, however, and have attempted to give a somewhat personal interpretation of social and cultural anthropology as practiced in the United States and in Great Britain. I have addressed myself primarily to my American colleagues, since there are a number of recent addresses directed toward British anthropologists; and I have omitted many important contributions from here and abroad through reasons of space and competence. Several friends have been kind enough to make suggestions for improvement, notably Edward Bruner, David Schneider, and Milton Singer. I would also like to thank the editors for their forbearance.

[2]See, particularly, Benedict (1948), Hallowell (1950), Beals (1951), Howells (1952), and Bennett (1953).

[3]With regard to the general problem of the integration of anthropological studies Daryll Forde, in his recent presidential address (1951) to the Royal Anthropological Institute, emphasized the importance of this integration and suggested the concept of ecology as a possible common point of reference for all the varied fields of anthropology.

[4]For the limited purposes of this paper I have utilized the terms which Bennett applied to the Andean area in his presidential paper of last year, though I am sure better terms can be found.

[5]The term "social anthropology" has been used by American anthropologists in the past: both Wissler and Radin wrote textbooks under that title, but these involved no new points of view. Chapple and Coon's *Principles of Anthropology* (1942) did present a new point of view, even dispensing with the concept of culture, but has not been widely accepted in the United States.

REFERENCES CITED

Ackerknecht, Erwin H.
  1954 On the comparative method in anthropology. *In:* Method and Perspective in Anthropology, ed. R. F. Spencer. Minneapolis.

Beals, Ralph
  1951 Urbanism, urbanization, and acculturation. American Anthropologist 53:1-10.

Bellah, R. N.
  1952 Apache kinship systems. Cambridge, Harvard University Press.

Benedict, Ruth
  1923 The concept of the guardian spirit in North America. Memoirs of the American Anthropological Association No. 29.

  1934 Patterns of culture. Boston and New York, Houghton Mifflin Co.

  1948 Anthropology and the humanities. American Anthropologist 50: 585-93.

Bennett, Wendell C.
  1953 Area archeology. American Anthropologist 55:5-16.

Boas, Franz
  1896 The limitations of the comparative method in anthropology. Science, n.s. 4:901-8.

  1927 Primitive art. Instittutet for Sammenlignende Kulturforskning, Series B, No. VIII. Oslo.

  1940 Race, language and culture. New York, The Macmillan Co.

Chapple, Eliot and Carleton Coon
  1942 Principles of anthropology. New York, Henry Holt.

Dixon, R. B.
  1928 The building of cultures. New York, Scribners.

Dozier, Edward P.
  1951 Resistance to acculturation and assimilation in an Indian pueblo. American Anthropologist 53:56-66.

Eggan, Fred
  1937a The Cheyenne and Arapaho kinship system. *In:* Social Anthropology of North American Tribes, ed. Fred Eggan. Chicago, University of Chicago Press.

1937*b* Historical changes in the Choctaw kinship system. American Anthropologist 39:34-52.

1950 Social organization of the Western Pueblos. Chicago, University of Chicago Press.

1952 The ethnological cultures and their archeological backgrounds. *In:* Archeology of the Eastern United States, ed. J. B. Griffin. Chicago, University of Chicago Press.

Eggan, Fred (ed.)
1937 Social anthropology of North American tribes. Chicago, University of Chicago Press.

Evans-Pritchard, E. E.
1951 Social anthropology. London, Cohen & West Ltd.

Firth, Raymond
1951*a* Contemporary British social anthropology. American Anthropologist 53:474-89.

1951*b* Elements of social organization. London, Watts and Co.

Fletcher, Alice
1904 The Hako: a Pawnee ceremony. 22nd Annual Report, Bureau of American Ethnology. Washington, D. C.

Forde, Daryll
1947 The anthropological approach in social science. Presidential Address, Section H, British Association for the Advancement of Science. London.

1950 Anthropology, science and history. Man, 254.

1951 The integration of anthropological studies. Journal of the Royal Anthropological Institute 78:1-10.

Fortes, Meyer
1953*a* The structure of unilineal descent groups. American Anthropologist 55:17-41.

1953*b* Analysis and description in social anthropology. Presidential Address, Section H, British Association for the Advancement of Science. London.

1953*c* Social anthropology at Cambridge since 1900, an inaugural lecture. Cambridge University Press.

Goldenweiser, A. A.
1910 Totemism: an analytic study. Journal of American folklore 23:1-115.

Hallowell, A. Irving
1950 Personality, structure, and the evolution of man. American Anthropologist 52:159-73.

1953 Culture, personality and society. *In:* Anthropology Today, by Alfred L. Kroeber and others, pp. 597-620. Chicago, University of Chicago Press.

Herskovits, Melville J.
1950 Man and his works, the science of cultural anthropology. New York, A. A. Knopf.

1954 Some problems of method in ethnography. *In:* Method and Perspective in Anthropology, ed. R. F. Spencer. Minneapolis.

Howells, W. W.
1952 The study of anthropology. American Anthropologist 54:1-7.

Kluckhohn, Clyde
1944 Navaho witchcraft. Papers of the Peabody Museum of Harvard University XXII, No. 2.

1949 The Ramah project. Papers of the Peabody Museum of Harvard
      University XL, No. 1.

1954 Southwestern studies of culture and personality. American
      Anthropologist 56:685-97.

Kroeber, Alfred L.
1935 History and science in anthropology. American Anthropologist
      37:539-69.

1939 Cultural and natural areas of native North America. Berkeley,
      University of California Press.

1944 Configurations of culture growth. Berkeley and Los Angeles,
      University of California Press.

1953 Introduction (pp. 1-4) and Concluding Review (pp. 357-76).
      In: An Appraisal of Anthropology Today, ed. Sol Tax and
      others. Chicago, University of Chicago Press.

1954 Critical summary and commentary. *In:* Method and Perspective
      in Anthropology, ed. R. F. Spencer. Minneapolis.

Kroeber, Alfred L. and Clyde Kluckhohn
1952 Culture, a critical review of concepts and definitions.
      Papers of the Peabody Museum of Harvard University XLVII,
      No. 1.

Kroeber, Alfred L. and others
1953 Anthropology today, an encyclopedic inventory. Chicago, Uni-
      versity of Chicago Press.

Lévi-Strauss, Claude
1951 Language and the analysis of social laws. American Anthro-
      pologist 53:155-63.

Linton, Ralph
1936 The study of man. New York, D. Appleton-Century Co.

Lowie, Robert H.
1919 The matrilineal complex. University of California Publica-
      tions in American Archaeology and Ethnology XVI:29-45.

1929 Relationship terms. Encyclopedia Britannica, 14th ed.

1937 The history of ethnological theory. New York, Farrar & Rine-
      hart, Inc.

1953 Ethnography, cultural and social anthropology. American An-
      thropologist 55:527-34.

Malinowski, B.
1922 Argonauts of the western Pacific. London, Routledge.

Merton, R. K.
1949 Social theory and social structure. Glencoe, The Free Press.

Murdock, George Peter
1949 Social structure. New York, The Macmillan Co.

1951 British social anthropology. American Anthropologist 53:465-
      73.

Nadel, S. F.
1951 The foundations of social anthropology. Glencoe, The Free
      Press.

1952 Witchcraft in four African societies: an essay in comparison.
      American Anthropologist 54:18-29.

Radcliffe-Brown, A. R.
1931a The present position of anthropological studies. Presiden-
      tial Address, Section H, British Association for the Advance-
      ment of Science. London.

1931*b* The social organization of Australian tribes. Oceania Monographs, No. 1.

1933 The Andaman Islanders. Reprinted with additions. Cambridge. (1st ed., 1922.)

1951 The comparative method in social anthropology. Huxley Memorial Lecture. London.

1952*a* Structure and function in primitive society, essays and addresses. London, Cohen and West Ltd.

1952*b* Historical note on British social anthropology. American Anthropologist 54:275-77.

Radcliffe-Brown, A. R. and Daryll Forde (eds.)
1950 African systems of kinship and marriage. London, Oxford University Press.

Redfield, Robert
1937 Introduction to: Social Anthropology of North American Tribes, ed. Fred Eggan. Chicago, University of Chicago Press.

1941 The folk culture of Yucatan. Chicago, University of Chicago Press.

1953 Relations of anthropology to the social sciences and to the humanities. *In:* Anthropology Today, by Alfred L. Kroeber and others, pp. 728-38. Chicago, University of Chicago Press.

Redfield, Robert, Ralph Linton and Melville J. Herskovits
1936 Memorandum on the study of acculturation. American Anthropologist 38:149-52.

Richards, Audrey I.
1950 Some types of family structure amongst the Central Bantu. *In:* African Systems of Kinship and Marriage, ed. A. R. Radcliffe-Brown and Daryll Forde. London, Oxford University Press.

Sapir, Edward
1916 Time perspective in aboriginal American culture: a study in method. Canada, Department of Mines, Geological Survey, Memoir 90, Anth. Ser. 13. Ottawa.

Schapera, I.
1953 Some comments on comparative method in social anthropology. American Anthropologist 55:353-62.

Schneider, D.
1953 Review of: Kinship and Marriage among the Nuer, by E. E. Evans-Pritchard. American Anthropologist 55:582-84.

Spencer, R. F. (ed.)
1954 Method and perspective in anthropology, papers in honor of Wilson D. Wallis. Minneapolis, University of Minnesota Press.

Spier, Leslie
1929 Problems arising from the cultural position of the Havasupai. American Anthropologist 31:213-22.

Spoehr, Alexander
1947 Changing kinship systems. Anthropological Series, Chicago Natural History Museum, Vol. 33, No. 4.

Tax, Sol and others (ed.)
1953 An appraisal of anthropology today. Chicago, University of Chicago Press.

Wissler, Clark
1914 Material cultures of the North American Indian. American Anthropologist 16:501 ff.

1922 The American Indian. 2nd ed. New York, Oxford University Press.

1926 The relation of nature to man in aboriginal America. New York, Oxford University Press.

10

SOCIAL ANTHROPOLOGY AND THE EDUCATIONAL SYSTEM

1957

Anthropology and education, in theory, should have reasonably close
working relations, since both are concerned with the transmission of
the social heritage from one generation to the next and with the
processes by which that transmission is achieved. But educators in
the middle of these processes are occupied by the task of keeping
the operations going, particularly in this period of changing models,
and have little time or opportunity to step outside their educational
institutions and see them as a system in the society as a whole. And
anthropologists, with some notable exceptions, are reluctant students
of our own society and culture. Where they are interested in education, they have been more concerned with studying the educative processes in simpler situations in which the society can be comprehended
as a whole. When they look at our own educational system, they may
have perspective, but they lack familiarity with its details and problems, except as they may teach in a university or college or have
children in the local school system.

On the periodic occasions when educators and anthropologists
meet in conference on common problems, these differences are clearly
demonstrated. There is much agreement at a relatively high level of
abstraction, but such conferences seldom get down to concrete cases,
nor do they formulate and carry through any joint research projects.
The recent Stanford Conference on Education and Anthropology did an
excellent job with regard to outlining the problem areas in education
to which anthropology might contribute and in presenting the thinking
of some of our best anthropologists as to how that contribution might
be made. Both the educators and the anthropologists present agreed
that they had learned a great deal from the interaction. But more
significant long-term results are likely to come from the few anthro-

Reproduced by permission of the University of Chicago Press,
Chicago, from *The School Review*, Autumn 1957, pp. 247-59.

pologists who are working actively in departments of education or who hold joint appointments in both fields.

My task in this symposium is both easier and more difficult than that of most of my colleagues in the social sciences. The economics, or the politics, or the history, or the psychology of education has a familiar ring to most people--and particularly to those concerned with the educational system itself. The "anthropology of education," on the other hand, brings little response from either the layman or the educator. A principal faced with practical problems never thinks of consulting an anthropologist. A generation hence, however, anthropologists may be as common in school systems as psychologists are at present. For the terms "social" and "cultural" are appearing in the vocabulary of professional educators with increasing frequency, and these are the major concepts with which the social anthropologist is concerned.

Social anthropology itself is only one discipline in the complex of anthropology, but it is the one of greatest potential interest to educators. Anthropology started with the objective of studying the whole of man--man as a biological organism, as a social being, and as a creator and carrier of culture--and of seeing these aspects in relation to one another. Inevitably anthropology has divided into specialties, but it has attempted with considerable success to maintain this overall view. Physical anthropologists, who are particularly concerned with the origins and evolution of man, the formation of races, and the biological basis for behavior, have often used the school as a convenient laboratory for the study of physical growth and its correlations with other indices of development. Maria Montessori's applications of physical anthropology to pedagogy are well known in the history of education, but the major contribution of physical anthropology has been an indirect one--the destruction of the myth of racial superiority.

Cultural anthropology developed out of an interest in man's social institutions and traditional ways of life. Columbus and Magellan opened up a new world to the scholar, and the ordering, analysis, and interpretation of the cultures of the non-Western world gradually became the province of the cultural anthropologist. At first the emphasis was evolutionary or historical, in keeping with the intellectual climate of the nineteenth century. More recently there has been a shift in the direction of comparative and generalizing interests, and the gradual differentiation of social anthropology as a separate subdiscipline. And social anthropologists, in turn, have begun to study our own modern civilization with a fresh eye and by the use of methods and concepts developed in connection with smaller non-literate societies.

Unlike their more specialized social-science colleagues, social anthropologists approaching an American community attempt to see it as a whole. They may first dissect out the various social institutions and trace their ramifications, but their main job is to put the pieces together in a meaningful relationship. And the social anthropologist adds one priceless ingredient which has come from his broad, comparative study of all kinds of peoples--the concept of culture. All of us work and live continuously in a world of specialized habits which we have learned in the family, in school, or elsewhere. These we are normally unaware of, just as we are unaware of the order, or grammar, of the language we speak. Only by studying another and radically different society, with different customs and ways of life, can we return to our own society and see our specialized habits in new perspective. The anthropologist is our closest equivalent to the man from Mars.

If you, as teacher or administrator, were able to spend a year observing the educational system of an American Indian, or African, or Southeast Asian group, you would find superficial similarities and puzzling differences. If you visited the Hopi Indians on their reservation, for example, you might be delighted with the order and decorum in the classroom, but you would miss the energy and competitiveness of many American schools. And when the local teacher told you that a girl receiving an A on her report card might burst into tears at being so singled out, you might be interested enough to follow the children home to the villages on top of the mesas.

You have seen pictures of these pueblo villages, each inhabited by several hundred Indians who wrest a difficult living from the semi-desert plateaus of northern Arizona. As you penetrate beneath the surface, you find that most things are "backward"--or are done quite differently from the way we are accustomed to do them. And yet the Hopi Indians have resided on and around these mesas since about 500 A.D. and have managed to transmit the bulk of their social heritage from generation to generation right down to the present day.

The social organization is radically different from ours. Each household has an old grandmother and her daughters and their children, with husbands who live with them and cultivate their fields but whose loyalties and obligations are mainly to their sisters' households. The father is a comrade to his children and teaches his sons economic pursuits, but the major teacher is the mother's brother, the head of the clan, and it is he who is called on in case punishment is needed.

Hopi education begins in the extended family and clan and continues through adolescence in the ritual societies concerned with impersonating the gods for community welfare and the necessary rain. This is an intensive and long-continuing education, often in an emotionally charged atmosphere, and it has enabled the Hopi Indians to maintain their culture in the face of tremendous pressures for change. The values of conformity have been emphasized, along with passive resistance; co-operation is a virtue and competition a threat to the security of all. Social control is in terms of public opinion; there are no Hopi policemen in the secular sense, though "bogeymen" katcinas and witches are a supernatural threat and a powerful force for conformity to traditional behavior.

The observer who had achieved this much familiarity with Hopi society and culture would have a greater appreciation of the difficulties involved in integrating American-style schools with Hopi community life and of turning out graduates who can easily make their way in the competitive American society. When he returns to his own school system, he is also likely to "see" things which earlier he was not so aware of: the role of the family and neighborhood in the educational process, the relations between teacher and student, and particularly the relations between student and student. And many behavioral characteristics of school children which were formerly taken for granted as "natural" will be seen to be cultural.

If our teacher or administrator had enough time, he or she might apply for a Fulbright award and spend another year among the Igorots of the Mountain Province in the Philippines, where the pagan mountaineers still live in grass-thatched wooden houses and cultivate rice in terraced valleys and sweet potatoes in gardens around the houses or in hillside clearings. Here the family organization is much like our own in structure and function. On closer inspection, the villages in some regions are found to be organized in wards, and for each ward of 25-50 households there is a central stone platform with an adjoining low hut in which the old men sleep.

Each of these ward centers is an independent unit for certain purposes, but they co-operate to carry out the group activities and ceremonials which insure community welfare and continuity. Each center is a political center, where the old men decide disputes and enforce the customary law. Each center is also a religious center, since the ceremonies are either held at one or another or are celebrated simultaneously at each. The platforms are likewise social lounging places for the males of the ward. And last, but not least, the ward centers are schools. Boys at the age of six or seven leave

their homes and frequent the centers, returning to their homes for
meals and other activities but sleeping in the ward huts with the old
men. The older boys supervise the younger group and teach them their
tasks. The old men, in turn, teach the boys the history and rituals
of the ward and village and allow them to learn the prayers by assist-
ing and observing. Here there is a pure age hierarchy--the oldest
man is in charge of the group until he dies or is disabled, when the
next oldest takes his place.

Of interest, also, are the patterns of courtship and marriage.
Girls likewise leave their natal households after the day's tasks are
finished and repair to a girls' sleeping house or to the house of a
widow. Here in the evening come groups of adolescent boys to sing
and banter and engage in courtship activities. Once a girl accepts
a boy, he is allowed to sleep in the girls' house. When the couple
decide to marry, ceremonies in which the respective households take
part are first held, and then ceremonies involving the ward and the
whole community. At these latter ceremonies the couple are given a
house and their inheritance of rice fields and other wealth and are
treated as full adults--a practice which may be one factor in the
unusual degree of self-reliance and initiative which is found among
these people. If children are born, the alliance between the families
is cemented and divorce seldom takes place. In contrast to the sexual
freedom of the courtship period, adultery after marriage is a very
serious crime and is punished by ostracism and supernatural sanctions.

Here, our observer would find, the public schools and the
mission schools have an easier task than among the Hopi, in certain
respects at least. The children are used to leaving home at an early
age, and a dormitory in a mission school has many of the attractions
of the ward center. But there are certain unsolved problems: What
happens to the rituals which are essential to community welfare and
integration when the old men die? What will happen to the whole complex of marriage and land inheritance when marriage with strangers
begins to take place? And who will look after the old people and
scratch their feet to put them to sleep?

Our observer can leave these questions to be worked out by
others, but, as he returns to his own community school, he may note
some additional features that formerly escaped his attention and may
perhaps think more seriously about some of the problems of adolescence. He may, for example, be more aware of the significance of
"age grading" and the educational influence of peer groups. The
rivalries and competition of classes may be seen to have some social
functions. He may decide to investigate further the extra-curriculum

activities to see who participates and in what roles and how participation is related to school and neighborhood. He may also begin to
think about the relation of his school to the larger community and
may consider the question whether he and the school should be agents
in maintaining the traditional values or leaders in adapting to the
new values that are emerging in our society. Before he left for the
visit to the Hopi and to the Philippine mountains, he had few doubts,
but now he is not so sure. Are there some alternatives which may fit
the future needs of our society and the emotional requirements of
well-developed personality better than our present ambivalent attitudes toward courtship and early marriage? Have those adolescent
cliques he sees ranging the halls and the highways already developed
new alternatives?

Our observer may also become somewhat dissatisfied with the
contents of the educational journals. Discussions of the problems of
increased numbers of students, of the shortage of teachers, of the
securing of financial support, and the innumerable surveys don't sig-
nify as much as they should. In fact, the problems they pose are
not scientific problems at all--no matter how practical or important
the reports sound or how much money was spent in carrying out the
surveys.

At this point our educator may wish he had never heard of
anthropology nor left our safe shores, either mentally or physically.
For not only do his initial questions remain unanswered, but a whole
host of unfamiliar and more difficult questions have been raised by
his brief excursion to exotic lands. He can either retreat or go on.

If he chooses to go on, he has already acquired some assets.
He has learned to look at institutions as having an organization and
a function, and as being parts of a larger whole. He has seen that,
by looking at the relations of one institution to the others in society, he can begin to understand the one institution better. He has
learned to see similarities and differences by comparing instances.
He has become aware of the concept of culture and has learned that
he, like every other human being, participates in a culture. He has
become less ethnocentric. He now begins to look for that ideal study
of the school system in a community which will make everything clear
and will answer all, or most, of his new questions. As he ransacks
the literature in search of these studies, he gradually comes to the
realization that there aren't any, at least not any of the type that
he would like to find. For there are only a few social anthropologists to exploit all the social experiments that collections of human
beings have been making since men arrived on earth, and the non-lit-

erate world offers a much greater range of social and cultural phenomena than does our own. And the few social anthropologists concerned with American society have generally concentrated on its larger
dimensions and organization. If the educator wants more detailed
understanding of the educational system from the standpoint sketched
here, he has to become his own social anthropologist. If he does so,
he will find that there are many useful by-products in addition to
the major objectives. But we should warn him at this point that, after he has made a social anthropological study of a school system in
a typical community, he will have developed further questions which
seem more important and which require still further researches.

Social anthropologists have made some studies of communities
in various parts of the United States. From these and the more extensive studies of sociologists, we are familiar with the social
structure of typical communities in various regions. The educator interested in beginning a study of the educational enterprise in his
own community can gain some understanding of the overall patterns
from these studies. From the anthropologically oriented accounts he
will get a greater emphasis on informal organizations and more attention to cultural detail, along with a methodological emphasis on participant observation, extensive interviewing, and "just listening."

It is not particularly important where the educator starts
in his attempt to unravel the educational system. He will be interested in everything--the minutes of the board meetings and who has
influence with the board; the ideas of teachers, and what they talk
about in the restrooms and at informal gatherings; the behavior of
children in school and out; the material used in courses and the reactions to it; and many more things. Of course not all of his observations will be of equal importance, but all are relevant to some of
the systems of organization and patterns of behavior that make up a
school.

We have devices available for continuous experimental observation, tape recorders and photographic equipment, and these can often
be utilized to provide raw materials for analysis and interpretation.
The recordings and films need to be supplemented by interviews with
teachers and with students, and with members of the community and the
parents as well. The factions which form in many American communities
on the issue of traditional versus newer methods of education should
be studied rather than condemned, for they are often valuable keys
to an understanding of community-school relationships.

Education, we will remember, is concerned with the *transmission* of the social heritage from generation to generation and there-

fore is a conservative institution. Hence school boards are generally chosen from the traditionally minded. Teachers, on the other hand, are usually interested in newer ideas and procedures; the more so, the younger they are. The administrators are in the middle, forced to make some compromise with the two extremes. How policy decisions are made in such cases is frequently not shown in the minutes of board meetings but can be discovered nevertheless.

Teachers are perhaps more predictable, having passed through a series of uniform tasks designed to train them to present specific materials in a standard way. Even so, there is much to be learned about teachers: their basic attitudes toward their work, their conception of children, the informal leadership which exists in the group, their role in the parent-teachers' association and other organizations, and, last but not least, their status in the community. If there are several schools in the community, it may be possible to find how they are ranked by teachers and why; in large cities this can be done by noting the requests for transfers.

The heart of the school is the teacher-student relation. What goes on in the classroom day by day and hour by hour is essential to our understanding of the educational process. Here we need the kind of patient and detailed observations that Gesell has made of children of various ages, *plus* an interpretation of the interactive behavior by a variety of social scientists. Studies under way on recorded interviews demonstrate that linguistic behavior and body motion are relevant in unexpected ways. Sociometric observations and content analysis are familiar tools, and small-group techniques offer important hypotheses on leadership and learning situations.

As yet, little material from classroom activities has been analyzed in such form. From preliminary studies of recorded protocols, however, it is clear that there are a number of *unintended* aspects of the learning process which may conflict with desired goals, as well as a great deal of activity which is largely irrelevant. For those who would modify or *re*-form the curriculum, the recording and the analyzing of a year's program in a single school would be more helpful than the study of any number of books.

Perhaps the greatest modification of the educational system will come from the study of the pupils themselves. We have tested and examined them in the school situation, but we have seldom studied their subculture. We know more about the organization and behavior of "Street Corner Society" than we do about the social and cultural life of children in a community school. This cultural and social life is transmitted from one generation of school children to the next and does not continue into adult life. It includes attitudes toward adults and toward schooling that contribute greatly to inefficient education. In exaggerated form it enters into the "teen-age" behavior reported in our daily press, but its day-by-day character is, in the long run, more effective in bringing about inefficient education. It isn't easy to study children (adults stick out like a sore thumb), but Mead and others have developed successful methods which might be adapted to this problem. And we must remember that many of the attitudes and behavior patterns that complicate the educative process are developed in the home before the child comes to school. Until we are aware of these in detail, we cannot develop procedures for their modification or elimination.

Some of the consequences which might follow if educators were seriously to study their own school systems and communities, both from within and from an outside vantage point, have been indicated above. In particular, the educator would have a conception of the community different from that which he has held before. He would see it, in part, as a complex organization of people and skills that have developed in order to get certain tasks accomplished for the welfare of all. He would also see the school system in a new light--as an institution penetrating into almost every aspect of community life, and mutually influencing, and being influenced by, every major institution in the society.

The administrator might have less certainty as to "right" and "wrong" procedures and policies and might be more willing to experiment with the curriculum and with new methods and techniques. Much of our school society and culture is traditional and wrapped in a long enough history to give it a semisacred quality which has kept it from being disturbed. This acquisition of authority is, of course, what always happens to social institutions, but the fact should be so recognized. By being aware of alternative possibilities and being willing to consider them without prejudgment, the administrator should be able to make effective changes. Even some of the procedures that "primitive" people have developed may come to have merit.

The major role which an educator with such an enlarged viewpoint might play would concern our larger society. We have competing systems of values, and the arguments reverberate throughout our social institutions. In the schools one example is the problem of equal treatment of all children (as befits the theory that all are born equal) versus the special consideration of ability (as related to our specialized and ranked adult society). Our society has now reached the point where perhaps half of the positions in business and industry are open to competition and merit, and the other half are filled on the basis of kinship and family influence, with a shift in the direction of competition on the basis of ability. Currently, also, we are in the midst of an organized effort to reorient our school system in the direction of producing more scientists and engineers--activities which require both selection for abilities and specialized training. Because of these pressures, let alone the competition from Russia, we may confidently predict that our educational system is not going to look the same a dozen years hence.

If the educator still wants help at this stage from the anthropologists, he may find them evincing greater interest, primarily in terms of the vast amount of materials that will be available on the education process. For the anthropologist is, and has long been, interested in the processes of culture-building and of social and cultural change. Except for the end products, these processes are difficult to study in the field with limited time and few facilities. But these same processes take place in every classroom every day, under conditions which can be reasonably well controlled. Not only the anthropologist, but also the social psychologist, the sociologist, and every student of human behavior, will be interested in the data and results which will be available.

As the educator begins to assimilate and correlate the variant conclusions from the multitudinous studies, he will find himself getting farther and farther away from the simple procedures that go on in the classroom and will long for the good old days when all he had to do was to supervise a stable, ongoing curriculum--or so it seemed. At this point he may resign and take a position in the educational system of some underdeveloped country that has not gone beyond the teaching process, or he may become an anthropologist and escape to that last refuge--the highlands of New Guinea.

BIBLIOGRAPHY

1. Dorothy Eggan, "Instruction and Affect in Hopi Cultural Continuity," *Southwestern Journal of Anthropology*, XII (Winter, 1956), 347-70.
   The educational process in the Hopi setting, with enough bibliography for further explanation. (The Igorot material is from my field notes and is not yet published. I am also indebted to John and Carlotta Connelly for observations on Hopi education.)

2. Solon T. Kimball, "Social Science Research and Higher Education." A memorandum prepared for the Social Science Research Council, October, 1956. (For preliminary discussion but not for quotation).
   I have learned much from Dr. Kimball's excellent memorandum, which I hope will soon be available in published form. It deals primarily with college and graduate education but has relevance for the whole educational system.

3. George D. Spindler (editor), *Education and Anthropology.*
Stanford, California: Stanford University Press, 1955.
An outstanding summary of what anthropology might contribute to
the field of education. Jules Henry's article (section vii) contains some protocols on classroom observations which are both interesting and illuminating. The bibliography lists the more important publications available.

4. George D. Spindler, "Education in a Transforming American
Culture," *Harvard Educational Review*, XXV (Summer, 1955), 145-56.
An analysis of the problems that educators face in a changing
society, plus some observations on the make-up of the "ideal
American boy."

11

LEWIS H. MORGAN IN KINSHIP PERSPECTIVE[1]

1960

I

One hundred years ago Lewis H. Morgan discovered that the Algonkian-speaking Ojibwa on the southern shores of Lake Superior had a pattern of grouping relatives similar to that he had earlier recorded among the linguistically unrelated Iroquois Indians of New York state. This discovery stirred his scientific imagination and led him to initiate and carry through a monumental comparative study of kinship systems, which was to have far-reaching and unexpected results. The steps by which he reached his conclusions as to the nature of kinship systems, and their relevance to the history of the American Indians and to the evolution of human society, were first presented in detail in *Systems of Consanguinity and Affinity of the Human Family* (1871), and later developed as a theory of cultural evolution in *Ancient Society* (1877). With these evolutionary conceptions we are not here concerned. They have been reviewed by Bernhard J. Stern (1931), Robert H. Lowie (1936; 1937:54-67), and Leslie A. White (1948), among many others; and White has recently completed a major study of the evolution of culture based in part on Morgan's ideas. We believe, however, that Morgan's discoveries in the field of kinship, as presented in *Systems*, have not received the consideration which they deserve.

Anthropologists generally have been uniform in their praise of *Systems*, in contrast to their reactions to *Ancient Society*. Leslie A. White, who considers *Systems* to be "one of the most significant anthropological treatises ever written," notes that it has been called "monumental" by Haddon and Radcliffe-Brown, a "towering monument" by Lowie, and "perhaps the most original and brilliant single achievement

Reproduced by permission of the Thomas Y. Crowell Company, New York, from *Essays in the Science of Culture; In Honor of Leslie A. White*, G. Dole and R. Carneiro, editors (1960), pp. 179-201.

in the history of anthropology" by Murdock (White 1957:257, with references). Sol Tax says that *Systems* "rounded out the subject matter of the science of social organization," and "is a contribution that ranks with any in ethnology" (1955:458). And Evans-Pritchard lists *Systems* as one of the "books which we regard as our early theoretical classics" (1951:27).

But despite this high praise few anthropologists or their students read *Systems*. One reason may well be its "monumental" character; indeed Rivers noted that "the very extent of the material he [Morgan] collected has probably done much to obstruct the recognition of the importance of his work" (1914:5). Franz Boas in his pioneer monograph on *The Central Eskimo* (1888) not only did not collect kinship terms but for some reason did not utilize those published by Morgan a decade earlier from the same region. With Boas' later (1896) attack on the comparative method, it was understandable that his students should neglect Morgan, and many of them did, although Kroeber, Lowie, and Spier were notable exceptions. But perhaps the major reason for the neglect of *Systems* is that many students find kinship exceedingly dull. Not until they have collected and interpreted kinship data themselves do they begin to appreciate the magnitude of the task which Morgan accomplished.

II

Morgan was not the first to "discover" kinship systems. According to Tax (1955:445), that honor belongs in modern times to Lafitau, a French Jesuit missionary who described the Iroquois and Huron classifications of consanguineal kindred as early as 1724. Morgan was unaware of Lafitau's researches when he collected the materials later published in *The League of the Ho-dé-no-sau-nee, or Iroquois* (1954), but he presents essentially the same information and adds a brief list of kinship terms in the Seneca language. White has recently published a portion of Morgan's Journal, written in 1859, which presents the circumstances under which he was led to undertake the researches on kinship. In it Morgan notes that "when I first came upon this peculiar system of consanguinity, which was as early as the year 1846 among the Seneca Iroquois, I did not as much as surmise that it extended beyond this Indian family, and much less that it might have important ethnological uses. In other words, I supposed it was a system of their own invention" (White 1957:260).

This was the year that Morgan, as a result of his assistance in the litigation against the Ogden Land Company, was made a member of the Seneca Hawk clan, a circumstance which greatly facilitated his researches on the structure and principles of the league. According to Stern (1931:18) Morgan never actually lived among the Iroquois for any extended period. But he did recognize the social importance of kinship and that the terminology formed a clear and definite system: "These relationships, so novel and original, did not exist in theory, but were actual, and of constant recognition and lay at the foundation of their political as well as their social organization" (Morgan 1954, I:82). He also tried to understand the bilateral, bifurcate-merging kinship system by reference to the matrilineal clan system, though he somewhat confused clan and family: "each tribe [clan] being in the nature of a family, the ties of relationship which bind its individual members together are indispensable" (1954, I:74).

For the next several years Morgan devoted himself to his business interests, and "Indian affairs were laid entirely aside." But in the summer of 1858, while at Marquette on Lake Superior, he met some Ojibwa and obtained their kinship terminology:

> To my surprise somewhat, and not a little to my delight, I found their system was substantially the same as that of the Iroquois; thus, by including a second stock language, extending very greatly the area of its distribution. From this time I began to be sensible of the important uses which such a primary institution as this must have in its bearing upon the question of the genetic connection of the American Indian not only, but also upon the still more important question of their Asiatic origin (in White 1957:263).

With this discovery interest in kinship became a principal preoccupation for the next decade. Morgan's basic assumption was that both the Seneca and Ojibwa terminologies "were derived from a common source since it was not supposable that two peoples, speaking dialects of stock-languages as widely separated as the Algonkin and Iroquois, could simultaneously have invented the same system, or derived it by borrowing one from the other" (1871:3).

This assumption, while it simplified Morgan's analysis, also limited his conclusions. By dismissing the alternatives of independent invention and borrowing before testing them against the full data, Morgan lost an important opportunity to contribute to ethnological method. And as Tax (1955:457) has pointed out, he was beginning to use a circular argument, namely, "that kinship terms can be used to reconstruct history because they remain constant, we know they remain constant because they are widespread among people who once were one and who have otherwise changed, and we know they were once one because the kinship systems are the same."

Morgan notes in his Journal the discovery of the same kinship system among the Dakota, and his resolve to pursue the inquiry into kinship in systematic fashion. His first task was to prepare a sched-

ule containing almost every known relationship, which he tested on
the Seneca and then sent to missionaries and Indian agents on the
various reservations, and to a selected number in other countries.
The results were disappointing but enough answers were received to
encourage Morgan to visit reservations in Kansas and Nebraska and to
collect the necessary data himself. Here he collected twelve schedules, all of which were similar; and from French traders he was able
to learn of the existence of the same system among most of the Plains
tribes.

On his return from the field he received a letter from an
American missionary among the Tamil in India which presented their
system of relationship. To Morgan's astonishment it was practically
identical with that of the Seneca and he believed "that we had now
been able to put our hands upon decisive evidence of the Asiatic origin of the American Indian race" (White 1957:267). He was thus led
to extend his inquiry to Asia, Australia, Africa, and to the islands
of the Pacific, which he did with the aid of the Department of State
and the Smithsonian Institution, while continuing his own field work
in both Canada and the United States.

Tax (1955:456-63) has sketched the steps by which Morgan set
out to solve the historical problems that he had posed. The American
Indian systems he had collected or received from correspondents largely conformed to a single broad type he called "classificatory," since
in these systems certain lineal and collateral relatives were classed
together, in contrast to Semitic and Celtic nomenclatures which were
"descriptive" in character. This broad uniformity of kinship helped
convince Morgan that kinship systems were exceedingly stable. When
many of the Asian systems were found to be similar to those of the
American Indian, Morgan felt he had demonstrated the origin of the
American Indian in Asia and their dispersal from a common source.

But with the schedules from the Pacific there were some surprises. The Hawaiian terminological system was "classificatory" to
a much higher degree than were the American Indian systems. The
Hawaiians normally made no terminological distinctions between relatives of the same generation, those of the first ascending generation
being "parents," those of ego's generation being "siblings," and
those of the first descending generation being "children," with sex
being indicated where necessary by the addition of the terms for male
or female. The American Indian systems Morgan was familiar with generally equated the father and the father's brother, and the mother
and the mother's sister, but had separate terms for the mother's
brother and the father's sister, and for their offspring.

Morgan set out to account for these differences. He had early identified the Iroquois--and most American Indian systems--with a society organized on the basis of clans, in contrast to the European systems which he believed were related to the development of property as an institution. He now set out to find a social system which would fit the Hawaiian pattern of terminology: he found an answer in some notes appended by the Hon. Lorin Andrews, one of the judges of the Hawaiian supreme court: "The relationship of *pinalua* is rather amphibious (*sic*). It arose from the fact that two or more brothers with their wives, or two or more sisters with their husbands, were inclined to possess each other in common. . . ." To which the Rev. Artemus Bishop added: "This confusion of relationships is the result of the ancient custom among relatives of the living together of husbands and wives in common" (Morgan 1871:457). With this apparently authoritative information Morgan concluded that "the Hawaiian custom affords a probable solution of the Hawaiian system of relationship" (1871:457), since the kinship terms were the logical results of such a pattern of marriage.

Morgan assumed that kinship systems arose in connection with social systems, but changed so slowly that they might survive changes in social conditions and thus reflect earlier conditions of society. He had rejected the possibility that the same kinship system could arise independently in separate areas. Since the Malayan (Hawaiian) system could be explained on the basis of a "communal family" and the Ganowanian (American Indian) could develop from the Malayan by the addition of clans, the basis was laid for the development of a series of evolutionary stages, starting from an assumed promiscuity and ending with monogamy. It is this sequence, with its elaborations, which Morgan thought was the crowning achievement of his kinship studies, and which bore the brunt of criticism during the next decades. As White points out (1948:142-43), the theory of family evolution seemed plausible in the light of the evidence available to Morgan, but "the consensus is that Morgan's theory is untenable." And Tax (1955:463) notes that "the assumptions Morgan made, such as that of dependence of kinship terms on social structure and the lag of terminology in social change, are historically more important than the exact sequence of evolution that he set up."

Morgan went on to write *Ancient Society* (1877), based on *Systems* but with a broader conception of cultural evolution as a product of successive inventions permitting increasing control over the sources of subsistence. The debates that ensued involved attacks upon the validity of Morgan's terminologies as evidence: McLennan claimed that

"the classificatory system is a system of mutual salutations merely"
(1886:273), since he found no evidence in Morgan's work as to any
rights or duties related to the terms in the classificatory system;
and this criticism was "convincing enough to delay the study of kinship for thirty years" (Tax 1955:464), until Rivers and others revived it by producing the missing evidence.

But if the raw materials on kinship in *Systems* are still of
"inestimable value" we might return to these data and see what Morgan
missed by pursuing the problems of the ultimate origins of the American Indian and the evolution of human society, rather than the more
immediate implications of the data he had assembled. For Morgan the
terminological systems were a means to other ends--he was not apparently interested in the concrete, behavioral aspects of kinship as a
social system and therefore failed to make certain of the discoveries
that lay within his grasp.

III

When Morgan began his comparative investigations of American Indian
kinship systems, he quite naturally took the Seneca as his model.
But in the interim since the publication of the *League of the Iroquois*
in 1851, his conceptions of kinship had advanced considerably. When
he recorded the Seneca system in December, 1858, he did so with a
greatly augmented schedule which approximated a genealogical chart
and covered both consanguineal and affinal terms, ranging as far as
the fourth collateral line on both sides of ego. This huge schedule,
with its more than 200 entries, was unwieldy and difficult to use,
but Morgan wanted to cover every possibility. Not until Rivers' invention of the "genealogical method" (1900:74-82) as a result of his
researches on the Torres Straits expedition was a better technique
developed for recording kinship and other sociological data.

During the years 1859-62, Morgan personally recorded some 56
terminological systems, mainly on Indian reservations in the United
States and Canada, and from visitors to Washington, D.C. and New York,
as well. During this period of intensive field research, perhaps the
first to be devoted to the solution of specific anthropological problems, Morgan made a number of important discoveries about kinship,
as well as about other aspects of social organization such as clans.
In the first place, he noted the universality of the use of terms of
relationship: "I have put the question direct to native Indians of
more than fifty different nations, in most cases at their villages
and encampments, and the affirmation of this usage has been the same
in every instance" (1871:132). Correlated with this usage he found

a general reluctance to use or mention personal names, a custom which
he believed to contribute to the maintenance of the kinship system.

Yet with all his field experience in collecting terminologies,
Morgan's conception of the kinship system was deficient. Despite his
long contact with the Iroquois and his adoption by the Hawk clan of
the Seneca tribe, Morgan missed an essential aspect of the kinship
system--the day-to-day behavior patterns between relatives. He realized that kinship relations were real, and basic to the political
and social organization, but he never probed deep enough to lay this
foundation bare. If he had gone below the clan level to the world
of actual kinship behavior, he would have discovered that particular
relatives had rights and obligations beyond inheritance and succession. Had he translated the speeches at his adoption, detailing the
rights and duties of relatives, he could have understood better the
relations between terminology and behavior, between household and
lineage, and between lineage and clan. The history of social organization might then have taken a different course, as Rivers has
pointed out (1914:17). Yet, where his real interests were involved,
as in political matters, he did probe the relations between form and
practice. He says, with regard to the title of sachem, "how far
these titles were hereditary in that part of the family of the sachem
who were of the same tribe [clan] with himself, becomes the true question to consider" (Morgan 1954, I:83). That he answered the question
inadequately, so that it waited until Goldenweiser for a partial solution, is another matter.

Hence, despite his innovations in collecting terminological
data by schedules, and in the native language, Morgan was severely
handicapped at the very start of his comparative studies. He was
not conditioned by his Iroquois experience to inquire into social
behavior and marriage practices among the Indian tribes that he studied, and thus to find a major part of the modern answer to the question: why the "classificatory" system? Nor were conditions on the
newly established reservations ideal for field work. White agents,
and even missionaries of long experience, often had great difficulty
in interpreting, so that Morgan came to prefer Indian informants who
knew a little English, where such could be found. He also discovered
that women were the best informants on kinship: "It was not always
possible to complete a schedule without consulting the matrons of the
tribe" (1871:136).

Morgan was aware that kinship terminology is systematic, even
though not simple. The American Indian system, he said, "is so diversified with specializations and so complicated in its classifications

as to require careful study in order to understand its structure and principles" (1871:132). It is on this point that Morgan's comparative method was deficient: while he was concerned with the *similarities* that made the kinship systems "classificatory," he was not concerned to the same degree with the differences that he noted--differences that in modern perspective give us kinship systems, such as the "Crow" and "Omaha," which are based on different principles of classification, in part, at least. And as the Seneca model gradually hardened into the American Indian System, he increasingly ignored minor variations as possible indicators of change.

Morgan recognized the great importance of linguistics, and especially the significance of cognates and other linguistic features, for determining genetic relationships between tribes, and the linguistic classifications he used for the eastern United States were not very different from those later established by Powell. But Morgan, with his growing conviction that the American Indians were one in race and origin, thought there was evidence in the kinship terminologies for an ultimate linguistic unity as well. He believed that kinship terminology was more stable than other aspects of vocabulary, and thus would reflect earlier relationships more clearly.

Morgan began his examination of the American Indian systems by using the Iroquois, specifically the Seneca, as a standard for comparison. In his early account of Seneca kinship in *The League of the Iroquois*, he analyzed Seneca terminology in detail, relating the kinship grouping to clan membership (1954, I:81), and noting the merging of collateral with lineal kin. He was also impressed with the Iroquois rules of exogamy in which marriage was forbidden with consanguineal kin. In the more detailed account of Seneca kinship given in *Systems*, Morgan utilizes a series of diagrams to present the system as a whole from the standpoint of both male and female egos. But these diagrams, while they fit the logical and analytical purposes he had in mind, are borrowed from Roman models and fail to present the Iroquois system in adequate fashion. Morgan was puzzled by the Seneca use of "cousin" terms between the children of a brother and a sister, in contrast to the sibling terms used between the children of two brothers or two sisters. He thought the use of cross-cousin terminology to be a later development designed "to remove an irregularity which amounted to a blemish" (1871:158), the irregularity apparently being a logical one. The relationship of a mother's brother to his sister's son, on the other hand, Morgan believed to be a function of the mother's brother's position of authority in the matrilineal clan. This position Morgan thought to be widespread among American Indian tribes, whether matrilineal or patrilineal, although originally derived from the matrilineal system.

In exemplary fashion Morgan next compares the terminological system of the Seneca with those of their close linguistic relatives, the Cayuga, Onondaga, Oneida, and Mohawk. He finds they agree with the Seneca in both pattern and classification and vocabulary, with one important exception: they classify the father's sister with the mother instead of as an "aunt," and she in turn calls her brother's children "son" and "daughter." This deviation he finds difficult to explain in terms of long association and intermarriage of the Iroquois tribes, particularly as the Tuscarora and Wyandot follow the Seneca practice and use a cognate term for "aunt." "It is one thing to borrow a term of relationship and substitute it in the place of a domestic term of equivalent import, but quite a different undertaking to change an established relationship and invent a new term for its designation" (1871:165).

With regard to the classification of the father's sister, the Iroquois were divided rather evenly. We can see now in the light of Lafitau's earlier researches that Morgan made the correct choice in selecting the Seneca pattern as the standard. But in the light of his interpretation of the Malayan (or Hawaiian) system as an earlier stage in the development of systems of kinship terminology, the classification of the father's sister as "mother" by the Iroquois would have to be interpreted as a survival, and thus place the Iroquois on a lower level of American Indian development rather than with the "highest rank." If Morgan had seriously investigated this important variation, he might have discovered that it was an initial step in the modification of the kinship system under white acculturation or changed conditions, and that comparable shifts were underway in the Southeastern tribes at the same period. For when Morgan studied the Iroquois in the nineteenth century they had been under white pressures for over 250 years.

But for Morgan, the most remarkable fact with reference to this system was that "it is identical with the system now prevailing amongst the Tamil, Telegu, and Canarese peoples of South India. . . . The discrepancies between them are actually less, aside from the vocables, than between the Seneca and the Cayuga" (1871:166). This last statement might well have caused Morgan to pause and reconsider his basic assumptions, both as to change and origins. In particular, it should have led him to reexamine his negative answer to the question of "whether in any portion of uncivilized society, as now organized, there are at present operating causes adequate to the production and therefore to the constant reproduction of this remarkable system of relationship" (1871:474). For while Morgan did an excellent technical job of comparison, controlling it with linguistic and other checks, he had ruled out the alternate working hypotheses of independent invention or borrowing which were actually the keys to the interpretation of many of the parallels which he found.

IV

The next major grouping that Morgan discusses is composed of the Siouan-speaking tribes of the Prairie and Plains regions. This group, including the Dakota, the Central Siouans, and the Village Tribes of the Upper Missouri, shows a number of important variations in social organization and kinship which Morgan noted without appreciating their implications. The Dakota groups--Santee, Teton, and Yankton-- plus the closely related Assiniboin had expanded westward from the Minnesota region in historic times. Morgan recorded the terminologies of eleven out of thirteen named bands and found them identical in pattern and cognate in vocabulary. Comparing the Yankton with the Seneca kinship system he found them identical in "ten indicative features," and in minute agreement throughout, including the affinal patterns. Morgan further noted that "the terms of relationship are the same words, in nearly every instance, under dialectic change. This shows that the terms have come down to each nation as a part of the common language; and that the system, also, was derived by each from the common source of the language" (1871:175).

Though Morgan is here anticipating part of Sapir's (1929) famous classification, his determination of cognates by inspection is premature; it is clear from later research that the Seneca and Yankton systems have not descended unchanged from a common prototype though certain terms may ultimately prove to be cognate. The reduction of the comparison to ten "indicative relationships," restricted for the most part to close consanguineal kin, made it easier to ignore variations and resulted in the overlooking of important clues. Thus, if Morgan had examined his Dakota schedules more carefully he would have discovered that the "cousin" terms were derived from the terms for "siblings-in-law," and he might have been led to a more careful investigation of the affinal system and rules of marriage. Nor does Morgan concern himself with the possible significance of the lack of clans among the Dakota. He was already impressed with the enduring nature of the kinship system: "We shall be led step-by- step to the final inference that this system of relationship originated in the primitive ages of mankind, and that it had been propagated like language with the streams of the blood" (1871:176).

The Central Siouans of the Missouri region formed a reasonably compact grouping and Morgan was aware that they were derived
from the same source as the Dakota dialects. He also found their
systems of consanguinity and affinity to be one and the same. They
agree with the Dakota in the ten indicative features of the "classificatory" system, but with regard to cross-cousins Morgan discovered
a striking difference. The mother's brothers' children, instead of
being called "cousin," are classed as "mother's brother" and "mother,"
and this pattern descends in the male line indefinitely; correlatively
the children of the father's sister are "nephew" and "niece," or "son"
and "daughter."

Morgan carefully checked this strange terminological usage
on a number of reservations and found it uniform. If he had not been
so strongly attached to the Iroquois system as the model for a clan-
organized society, the correlation of the "line of uncles" with the
mother's patrilineal clan might well have been noted and the "Omaha"
pattern of kinship defined. For these Central Siouan systems, together with the cognate Winnebago, provided much better evidence of
clan orientation in their kinship systems than did the Iroquois and
Dakota, as Lowie (1917:152-54) long ago pointed out. Morgan's own
explanation was that "a mother's brother and his lineal male descendants are thus placed in a superior relationship over her children
with the authority the avunculine relationship implies in Indian society" (1871:179), but if he had inquired of his Central Siouan informants as to the actual role played by the mother's brother in
these patrilineal societies he would have found it quite different.

Morgan's schedules for the Village Tribes of the Upper Missouri region, the Mandan and Hidatsa, with the related Crow of the
Plains, were incomplete, but he found sufficient evidence to establish their general relationship to the "classificatory" system.
Morgan was unable to establish the terms for cross-cousins among the
Mandan, but recorded the father's sister as "aunt," male speaking,
but "mother" with a female ego. The Hidatsa classed the father's
sister as a "grandmother," and the mother's brother as an "older
brother," whereas the closely related Crow called the father's sister
"mother." Both the Crow and Hidatsa were recorded as classifying the
father's sister's children with the father and mother but the further
extensions of this pattern were not noted. Morgan states that this
form of classification will appear among the Gulf and Prairie tribes,
but as we shall see below, it appeared in a form which prevented Morgan from realizing the nature of the parallelism, and discovering
the "Crow" type of matrilineal kinship. The partial parallels with

the Iroquois in the classification of the father's sister with the
mother apparently escaped Morgan's attention.

The Gulf Nations, the Choctaw, Chickasaw, Creek and Cherokee,
were well-known and important tribes already removed to reservations
in Oklahoma. Early in 1859 Morgan had received detailed schedules
on the Choctaw from Edwards, Copeland, and Byington, veteran missionaries who spoke the language and knew the Choctaw well, and he later
received additional schedules for the remaining tribes from other
missionaries. Here the descendants of the father's sister were "father" and "father's sister," for a male speaker, and "father" and
"grandmother" for a female speaker. But the father's sister's *son's*
son is also recorded as "father," this relationship term continuing
in the *male* line. "The analogue of this is found in the infinite
series of uncles among the Missouri nations, applied to the lineal
descendants of my mother's brother" (1871:191).

I have elsewhere (1937) discussed the Choctaw and other southeastern kinship systems and have attempted to put them in historical
and acculturational perspective. It seems clear from the researches
of Spoehr (1947) and others that the Choctaw and other Southeastern
tribes formerly had kinship systems of a "Crow" type, with the line
of fathers and father's sisters descending through the *female* line,
but that they were in the process of changing the pattern of descent
when recorded for Morgan. He was thus prevented from discovering
the "Crow" type of matrilineal kinship among these tribes and in per-
ceiving its similarity to those of the Mandan and Hidatsa, as well
as possibly discovering the correct analogy between these systems
and those of the Central Siouans--that they are both related to the
pattern of unilineal descent. But Morgan might well have engaged in
a more adequate comparison of the Iroquois and the southeastern
tribes, since the parallels in social organization and political
structure were detailed and extensive. But by this time the other
goal loomed larger: "If identity of system proves unity of origin,
all of the Indian nations thus far named are of one blood" (1871:193).

Morgan was concerned to some extent with the "deviations from
uniformity" which he found in comparing the various American Indian
systems, principally those with regard to uncle and aunt, nephew and
niece, and cross-cousins. He compared the various Siouan-speaking
tribes in an attempt to determine which pattern of cross-cousin nomenclature was the oldest. Since there is no doubt that the pattern
found among the Iroquois and Dakota "is the most perfect form,"
Morgan (1871:193) concludes that the Omaha and Crow-Choctaw types
are the older, and of these the latter is the most ancient. "A crit-

ical examination of all the forms of the system of relationship will show that its development is under the control of principles within itself; and that the direction of the change when attempted, was predetermined by the elements of the system."

The Prairie Nations, the term Morgan employs for the Pawnee and Arikara, were little known and Morgan was not able to collect a full schedule of terms. He was impressed by the extension of kinship terms up and down four generations from ego, and he recorded the classing of the father's sister with the mother, and her children as father and mother. This pattern is recognized as descending in the *female* line, which Morgan considered a variant from the Choctaw form. Hence, the "Crow" pattern of terminology was never clearly recognized, even though here clearly defined.

Morgan concludes his discussion up to this point with the statement: "The constancy and uniformity with which the fundamental characteristics of the system have maintained themselves appear to furnish abundant evidence of the unity of origin of these nations, and to afford a sufficient basis for their classification together as a family of nations" (1871:199).

V

Morgan next turned his attention to the great Algonkian family which occupied the territory around the Great Lakes, with outliers in the Plains and down the Atlantic coast. The Ojibwa system, it will be remembered, started Morgan on his comparative study, and it became the standard for the Great Lakes tribes, such as the Ottawa, Potawatami, and Cree. The similarity between the Ojibwa and Iroquois-Dakota systems he finds so great as "to excite astonishment." Except for the use of step-relationship terms for father's brother and mother's sister, and for their children, among the Ojibwa and other Great Lakes tribes, Morgan considered the consanguineal and affinal terminologies to be essentially the same as those of the Iroquois and Dakota. But these differences are crucial in terms of Morgan's conception of "classificatory" systems; he prejudges the issue in part by the use of "step-father" and "step-mother" as translations of terms not at all obviously related linguistically to the terms for father and mother. And in a footnote he suggests: "I think, if re-examined, it will be found that my mother's sister is my mother, and my father's brother my father, *Ego* a female, and that my sister's son, *Ego* a female, is my daughter" (1871:204, footnote 1; ["daughter" is an error, should be "son"]).

Here, also, as in the Dakota case, the terms for cross-cousin are clearly derived from those for siblings-in-law; and, further, the terms for father's sister and mother's brother are similar to, or identical with, the terms for parents-in-law. If Morgan had inquired into the marriage practices of the Ojibwa and their neighbors he would almost certainly have discovered the custom of cross-cousin marriage, which was still extensively practiced among the Canadian Ojibwa and Cree when Hallowell studied them (1937), though perhaps already given up south of the border. The discovery of a close relationship between cross-cousin marriage and kinship terminology, which had to wait for Rivers (1914), might have diverted Morgan from his dependence on the past to explain the details of the "classificatory" system; at the least it would have suggested some possible differences in origin of the Ojibwa as compared with the Iroquois.

The Ojibwa, Ottawa, and Potawatami all possessed patrilineal, exogamous clans, but the Cree, with cognate terminology for the most part, were clanless. The Central Algonkian tribes, inhabiting the prairies and parklands of what are now Wisconsin, Illinois, Indiana, and Michigan all had kinship systems of the same basic pattern as those of the Central Siouans, and specifically a classification of cross-cousins in which the mother's brother's children were "mother's brother" and "mother," and correlatively the father's sister's children were "nephew" and "niece," or "son" and "daughter," depending on the sex of ego. The Central Algonkian tribes likewise classified the father's brother with the father and the mother's sister with the mother, thus confirming Morgan in his view that the step-relationships of the Ojibwa were "simply a refinement upon an original system" (1871:205). He also noted the parallel differences between the various systems for classifying cousins among both the Siouans and Algonkians: he interpreted this not in terms of diffusion or as the result of similar causes, but as evidence for a similar pattern of change in a predetermined direction (1871:211-12).

To this group Morgan adds the Cheyenne, whose system of terminology is "classificatory" though the terms for cousins were not obtained. Morgan suggested that they probably followed the Omaha pattern, but later research (Eggan 1955a) indicates that the Cheyenne classified cross-cousins with siblings, along with a majority of other Plains tribes. Morgan believed that sibling terms were originally used for cross-cousins, in accordance with life in the "communal family," but that with the advent of clan organization separate cross-cousin terms were developed. Presumably Morgan would have placed the clanless Cheyenne as intermediate between the Malayan and Ganowanian systems, but this is not certain. When Morgan later notes the use of sibling terms for cross-cousins among the Gros Ventre, he merely says: "This last classification is not in accordance with the principles of the system" (1871:227).

Examining the terms of relationship among the Algonkian nations thus far considered, Morgan observed that they "are, for the most part, the same original words under dialectical changes. From this fact the inference arises that the terms, as well as the system, have come down to each from a common source; thus ascending to the time when all of these nations were represented by a single nation, and their dialects by a single language" (1871:217). That the Central Algonkian languages are genetically related is well known from Bloomfield's work. Recently Charles Hockett (n.d.) has reconstructed proto-Central Algonkian kinship terms and finds clear evidence of a system based upon cross-cousin marriage. Driver and Massey (1957: 437) report a recent unpublished reconstruction of proto-Siouan kinship terminology by Hubert Mathews which suggests that an Omaha type of structure was basic to Siouan kinship. If these reconstructions are valid, the Central Algonkians and the Central Siouans, instead of representing parallel developments, would be convergent, with diffusion and interaction possibly playing an important role.

Morgan goes on to examine the Eastern Algonkians, where he finds a considerable number of variants on the basic "classificatory" system which are ascribed in part to disintegration and in part to error; and the Blackfoot, Blood, and Piegan, whose partially recorded systems resemble those of the Great Lakes. The twenty-four Algonkian tribes Morgan surveys are considered to be identical in major features to the "classificatory" system. He also notes that: "There is a not less striking identity in the classification of marriage relatives, amongst the widely separated Algonkian nations, which it would have been interesting to trace had it been necessary to strengthen, from this source, the principal argument for unity of origin. The marriage relationships, standing alone, would have been sufficient to demonstrate this question" (1871:228). As we have seen above, attention to the marriage system in terms of behavior, and the relations of affinal to consanguineal terminology, would have been even more useful.

In succeeding sections Morgan analyzed the more fragmentary data secured on the Athabaskan-speaking peoples, the tribes of the Columbia River region, the Shoshoni and Ute, scattered Pueblos, and the Eskimo, and found greater divergences than among the kinship systems so far considered. The tribes of the Columbia River region, in particular, which Morgan believed to be the source of dissemination of the American Indian stocks, showed considerable diversity, both in language and in kinship. The Spokane, for example, one of the Salish-speaking tribes, was found to have a different terminological system for males and females, and in addition made some discriminations not provided for even by Morgan's elaborate schedules. But all of these groups in one way or another were judged worthy of admission to the "classificatory" system, with the sole exception of the Eskimo which in "the greater and most important fundamental characteristics of this system . . . is wanting" (1871:277). Morgan wasn't quite willing to place the Eskimo among the "descriptive" systems, even though it tended strongly in that direction, so he classed it somewhat reluctantly with the Ganowanian, Turanian, and Malayan systems.

VI

From Morgan's standpoint his great discovery with regard to kinship was the classificatory system of relationship. Rivers gives him full credit:

> I do not know of any discovery in the whole range of science which can be more certainly put to the credit of one man than that of the classificatory system of relationship by Lewis Morgan. By this I mean, not merely was he the first to point out clearly the existence of this mode of denoting relationship, but it was he who collected the vast mass of material by which the essential characters of the system were demonstrated, and it was he who was the first to recognize the great theoretical importance of his new discovery (1914:4-5).

Rivers goes on to point out that Morgan was largely to blame for the rejection of the importance of this discovery by his critics, since

> He was not content to demonstrate, as he might to some extent have done from his own material, the close connection between the terminology of the classificatory system and forms of social organization. There can be little doubt that he recognized this connection, but he was not content to demonstrate the dependence of the terminology of relationship upon social forms, the existence of which was already known, or which were capable of demonstration with the material at his disposal. He passed over all these early stages of the argument and proceeded directly to refer the origin of the terminology to forms of social organization which were not known to exist anywhere on the earth and of which there was no direct evidence in the past (1914:5-6).

Rivers' own contributions to the rehabilitation of Morgan's views, including the demonstration of the close connection between kinship terminology and certain forms of marriage, and the conception of systems of relationship as a key to the history of social institutions, is well known. I have elsewhere (1955b:519-51) discussed the significance of Rivers' contributions when applied to the social organization of the Algonkian-speaking peoples of Northeastern North America where cross-cousin marriage is an important social institution. But of still greater importance has been the recognition that the kinship usages of a people constitute a social system composed of *both* terminology and social behavior, of which marriage is only one aspect.

The basic reason why Morgan failed to make the most from the materials on kinship that he collected would seem to be that he was not primarily interested in understanding kinship systems as such, but rather in using them as means to other ends. His frames for comparison were adequate, and he utilized linguistic and other controls, but as the "evidence" for the ultimate unity of the American Indians and their derivation from Asia seemed more and more definite, the rigor of the comparison became more relaxed. We have noted that alternate explanations to derivation from a common source, such as independent invention or borrowing, were ruled out in advance, and when Morgan returned to them it was not to test them against the data but to emphasize the correctness of the original assumptions. In the light of our present knowledge of kinship systems, we tend to emphasize the influence of common factors in bringing about similar social systems. Similarly, the assumption of the stability of the terminological system over long periods, and in the face of linguistic change, was never seriously examined, although the Iroquois tribes offered an important example of possible change in the classifications of the father's sister, and the classifications of cross-cousins in other linguistic stocks offered clear evidence of variation over relatively short periods. In recent years cross-cousin terminology has formed the basis for both Spier's (1925) and Murdock's (1949) classifications of kinship systems, and offers an index to the social structure as well. Today we might well reverse Morgan's assumption and consider the terminological patterns as relatively sensitive indicators of social change. Spoehr's (1947) study of changes in Southeastern tribes under acculturation makes this conclusion clear, and it is supported by my own (1937; 1950; 1955a) researches in the Southeast, Plains, and Pueblo regions.

If Morgan had been more concerned about the possible alternate explanations of kinship patterns and their stability, and if he had investigated the variations which he found with the same enthusiasm that he did the similarities, he would have been in a position to contribute a great deal more to the theoretical study of kinship than he in fact did. And the comparative method might have been salvaged and restored to usefulness rather than being abandoned by American ethnologists after Boas' (1896) attack.

From a larger perspective, Lowie has wondered what Morgan's scheme

> might have been like if chance has first thrown him among the clanless Paiute, the wealth-craving Yurok, the pedigree-mad Polynesians, or the monarchial Baganda. Proceeding from the Seneca and encountering for hundreds of miles nothing but broadly comparable social structures, Morgan prematurely generalized what primitive society was like, even though on an apparently wide inductive basis. And when he had once formulated the generalization, he could dismiss contradictory evidence from the Columbia River tribes with the cheap auxiliary hypothesis that their clan organization had fallen into decay (1936:174).

It is true that Morgan believed that of the nations north of Mexico "the Iroquois deservedly hold the highest rank," and his view of kinship was forever complicated by the fact that the Iroquois system of terminology, with its balanced bilateral character, did not rest conformably on a matrilineal clan system, as he supposed. Hence he was not able to isolate types within or outside the classificatory system, nor to see the correlation of unilineal clans with "Omaha" and "Crow" systems. The task of understanding the Iroquois social system and its development still faces anthropologists, and Morgan's critics have added little to our basic knowledge. However, Merlin Myers' forthcoming structural-functional analysis, based on recent field work in Canada, should dispel some of the mystery, and Harry Basehart's historical study, when published, will contribute further to our understanding.

But Morgan cannot be held responsible for the fact that so many of the tribes he studied at first-hand happened to have broadly similar social systems. He expended considerable effort to reach as many tribes as were accessible to study in the 1860's; he could not know that Northern and Eastern North America would turn out to be a single major culture area (in, for example, Kroeber's [1939] classification), in contrast to the much greater differentiation in Western North America. Lowie's strictures with regard to premature generalization are more relevant. Morgan's major generalization with regard to the "classificatory" system was made early and defended at every turn, despite mounting evidence that it was not universal. Even the Ojibwa terminology which began the comparison did not fit the main "indicative features" of the "classificatory" system.

Leslie A. White has evaluated Morgan's contribution to kinship as follows:

> Although Morgan failed to see that kinship in human society is primarily and essentially a social phenomenon and only secondarily and incidentally a biological matter, he did discover and appreciate the fact that relationship terms are sociological devices employed in the regulation of social life. A relationship term is the designation of an individual or class of individuals that

is socially significant. Every society of human beings is divided into social classes or groups, which, with reference to any
individual in the society, are designated with kinship terms such
as "uncle," "sister," "mother-in-law," etc. One's behavior toward
one's fellows varies, depending upon the category of relationship
in which the person stands. Since the categories are labelled
with kinship terms, a close functional relationship obtains
between kinship nomenclature and social organization and behavior.
These are the views and postulates upon which a modern school of
social anthropology bases much of its work. They were discovered,
elucidated and established by Morgan many decades ago (1948:144).

With much of White's evaluation we can readily agree. Morgan clearly
recognized the social importance of kinship and was aware that the
terminology formed a definite system. With regard to the functional
relationships obtaining between kinship nomenclature and social organization behavior, Morgan recognized such relationships macroscopically,
but was little concerned with them at the level of the individual
tribe. The Malayan (Hawaiian) system he related to particular forms
of marriage, and the Ganowanian, or American Indian system he correlated with clans. Only rarely, as in the case of the mother's brother, does he attempt to relate particular terminology to special status or behavior. Modern social anthropology is built in part on Morgan's discoveries, but much of its progress has been in the directions
which Morgan neglected--the detailed structural and functional analysis of individual tribes and communities.

In modern perspective certain of Morgan's assumptions and
discoveries with regard to kinship require modification. Kinship
terminology is no longer considered to be the stable institution Morgan envisaged, enduring over centuries and furnishing evidence of
genetic relations no longer apparent otherwise. The unity or diversity of the American Indians as a race, and their ultimate derivation
from Asia, rest today on other evidence than kinship terminologies.
The evolutionary stages of family development are no longer tenable.
Even the "classificatory" system, now that the dust of controversy
has settled, has less significance than Morgan envisaged, although
it is still an important theoretical concept (cf. Radcliffe-Brown
1941).

But even so it is remarkable how close to the truth he actually came. He grasped the essential principles and considered the
possible explanations. That he rejected the explanations that modern
social anthropology accepts was in some measure due to the intellectual fashions of the time. And there is much else that remains. The
insights that Morgan achieved through saturation in kinship for a
decade are scattered throughout *Systems*, waiting to be utilized. And
above all there are the raw data that he collected on kinship termin-

ologies which become increasingly valuable as we learn more about
kinship systems. It may well be that Morgan himself is the best
evaluator of his contributions to the study of kinship. After summarizing what he has done, in the Introduction to *Systems*, he says:
"The tables, however, are the main results of this investigation.
In their importance and value they reach far beyond any present use
of their contents which the writer may be able to indicate. If they
can be perfected, and the systems of the unrepresented nations be
supplied, their value would be greatly increased" (1871:8). Of his
methods of comparison he was properly modest:

> If these tables prove sufficient to demonstrate the utility of
> systems of relationship in the prosecution of ethnological inves-
> tigations, one of the main objects of this work will be accom-
> plished. The number of nations represented is too small to ex-
> hibit all the special capacities of this instrumentality. The
> more thoroughly the system is explored in the different nations
> of the same family of speech, especially where the form is clas-
> sificatory, the more ample and decisive the evidence will become
> which bears upon the question of their genetic classification
> (1871:809).

In his emphasis upon *systems* of relationship and their controlled comparison Morgan is much closer to modern scholarship than
were many of his critics. After a long interval of neglect Morgan's
Systems of Consanguinity and Affinity of the Human Family is coming
into its own and the data in the tables are being expanded by the
addition of new tribes and deepened by the collecting of contemporary materials from the same tribes. There is even talk of reprinting
Systems. And on the basis of his pioneer insights into kinship new
methods of investigation have developed which do in fact carry us
far beyond the stage which Morgan had achieved. He predicted this
eventuality and would be puzzled by the length of time it has taken
us to get this far beyond him.

NOTES

[1] I am indebted to a Ford Foundation Faculty Grant for providing
assistance in the preparation of this paper; and to the Center for
Advanced Study in the Behavioral Sciences, Stanford, California, for
various facilities. I would like to thank my colleagues at the Center, particularly Raymond Firth, Meyer Fortes, and Clifford Geertz,
and the editors of this volume for their comments and suggestions,
and Mrs. Isabel S. Caro for editorial assistance and advice.

BIBLIOGRAPHY

Boas, Franz
    1888 "The Central Eskimo." *Annual Report of the Bureau of [Amer-
        ican] Ethnology*, 6(1884-85):399-669.

1896   "The Limitations of the Comparative Method of Anthropology."
        Science, 4:901-908.

Driver, Harold E. and William C. Massey
  1957 "Comparative Studies of North American Indians." *Transactions
        of the American Philosophical Society*, 47:165-456.

Eggan, Fred
  1937 "Historical Changes in the Choctaw Kinship System." *American
        Anthropologist*, 39:34-52.

  1950 *Social Organization of the Western Pueblos*. Chicago, The
        University of Chicago Press.

  1955a "The Cheyenne and Arapaho Kinship System." In *Social Anthro-
        pology of North American Tribes*, revised edition, ed. by Fred
        Eggan, pp. 35-95. Chicago, The University of Chicago Press.

  1955b "Social Anthropology: Methods and Results." In *Social An-
        thropology of North American Tribes*, revised edition, ed. by
        Fred Eggan, pp. 485-551. Chicago, The University of Chicago
        Press.

Evans-Pritchard, E. E.
  1951 *Social Anthropology*. London, Cohen & West.

Hallowell, A. Irving
  1937 "Cross-Cousin Marriage in the Lake Winnipeg Area." *Twenty-
        fifth Anniversary Studies*, ed. by D. S. Davidson. *Publica-
        tions of the Philadelphia Anthropological Society*, 1:95-110.

Hockett, Charles
  n.d. "A Reconstruction of the Proto-Central Algonquian Kinship
        System." Unpublished manuscript.

Kroeber, A. L.
  1939 "Cultural and Natural Areas of Native North America." *Uni-
        versity of California Publications in American Archaeology
        and Ethnology*, 38.

Lowie, Robert H.
  1917 *Culture and Ethnology*. New York, Boni & Liveright.

  1936 "Lewis H. Morgan in Historical Perspective." In *Essays in
        Anthropology Presented to A. L. Kroeber in Celebration of
        his 60th Birthday*, pp. 169-181. Berkeley, University of
        California Press.

  1937 *The History of Ethnological Theory*. New York, Farrar &
        Rinehart.

McLennan, J. F.
  1886 *Studies in Ancient History*. 2nd edition. London, Macmillan
        and Co.

Morgan, Lewis H.
  1954 *League of the Ho-dé-no-sau-nee or Iroquois*. Reprinted by
        Human Relations Area Files, New Haven, 2 vols. (From edition
        of H. M. Lloyd, 1901, based on 1851 edition.)

  1871 "Systems of Consanguinity and Affinity of the Human Family."
        Smithsonian Contributions to Knowledge, 17.

  1877 *Ancient Society*. New York, Henry Holt & Co.

Murdock, George P.
  1949 *Social Structure*. New York, The Macmillan Company.

Radcliffe-Brown, A. R.
  1941 "The Study of Kinship Systems." *Journal of the Royal Anthro-
        pological Institute*, 71:1-18.

1950 "Introduction." In *African Systems of Kinship and Marriage*, ed. by A. R. Radcliffe-Brown and Daryll Forde, pp. 1-85. London, Oxford University Press.

Rivers, W. H. R.
1900 "A Genealogical Method of Collecting Social and Vital Statistics." *Journal of the Royal Anthropological Institute*, 30: 71-82.

1914 *Kinship and Social Organization*. London, Constable & Co., Ltd.

Sapir, Edward
1929 "Central and North American Languages." *Encyclopaedia Britannica*, 14th edition, 5:138-141.

Spier, Leslie
1925 "The Distribution of Kinship Systems in North America." *University of Washington Publications in Anthropology*, 1:71-88.

Spoehr, Alexander
1947 "Changing Kinship Systems." *Field Museum of Natural History, Publications, Anthropological Series*, 33:151-235.

Stern, Bernhard J.
1931 *Lewis H. Morgan, Social Evolutionist*. Chicago, The University of Chicago Press.

Tax, Sol
1955 "From Lafitau to Radcliffe-Brown." In *Social Anthropology of North American Tribes*, revised edition, ed. by Fred Eggan, pp. 445-481. Chicago, The University of Chicago Press.

White, Leslie A.
1948 "Lewis H. Morgan: Pioneer in the Theory of Social Evolution." In *An Introduction to the History of Sociology*, ed. by H. E. Barnes, pp. 138-154. Chicago, The University of Chicago Press.

1957 "How Morgan Came to Write Systems of Consanguinity and Affinity." *Papers of the Michigan Academy of Science, Arts, and Letters*, 42:257-268.

12

CULTURAL DRIFT AND SOCIAL CHANGE

1963

*Culture is stable, yet culture is also dynamic, and manifests
continuous and constant change.*
Melville J. Herskovits

In his dynamic conception of culture presented in *Man and His Works*
(1948), Melville J. Herskovits has utilized cultural drift and historic accident as the major processes by which change comes about.
"Together," he says, "they act to give a culture at a given moment
in its history the forms it manifests, and endow it with the sanctions that give these forms meaning and permit them to function in
the lives of the people" (1948:581). For Herskovits cultural drift
represents the cumulative effect of small variations whose day-by-
day effect is scarcely noticeable, but whose continuation results in
long range directional changes in both the character and form of social life. He contrasts this slow accumulation with the more dramatic and abrupt changes resulting from cultural innovations or external factors, and notes that no adequate study of culture can neglect
either process:

> The complexity of culture is such that both may be operative,
> in different aspects of culture, at the same time; in which case
> we may have an explanation for the abrupt shifts in cultural fo-
> cus that present so puzzling a phenomenon (1948:581).

The concept of cultural drift was first coined some forty
years ago by Edward Sapir as an analogue to his more famous concept
of linguistic drift, but Sapir made only casual use of it and until
recent years it has received little attention. According to Sapir
(1921:253) "The drift of culture, another way of saying history, is
a complex series of changes in society's selected inventory--addi-

Reproduced by permission of the University of Chicago Press
from *Current Anthropology* 4:347-55, 1963.
This was one of a series of papers in honor of, and in memorial to, Melville J. Herskovits.

tions, losses, changes of emphasis and relation;" and he thought of the drift of language and culture as essentially unrelated processes.

Some years ago the present writer, in "Some Aspects of Cultural Change in the Northern Philippines" (1941), found that as one went from the interior down to the coast--from Ifugao through Bontok, Tinguian and Ilocano--there is a regular series of changes in social, political, economic and religious institutions, a series which has a definite direction. To define these changes he adapted the concept of cultural drift from Sapir and noted that an awareness of this drift is essential to a proper understanding of the changes he was studying in Tinguian culture.

> Changes, which on the surface seemed to be the results of Spanish or American contacts, turned out on closer inspection to be native cultural changes. Resistance to change, on the one hand, or rapid acceptance, on the other, seemed explicable in many cases in terms of this "drift" (Eggan 1941:13).

This paper was originally presented at a Symposium on Acculturation, and in his introductory comments to the published papers, Herskovits notes (1941:3) that "'cultural drift' may indeed--in more cases than has been realized--account for changes which superficial analyses of an acculturative situation might hold to be due to the circumstances of contact alone."

More recently in an examination of "Some Social Institutions in the Mountain Province" (1954) the writer has argued for the view that the large compact towns, the ward organization, the ceremonial platforms with associated council and sleeping houses for men and boys, and the girls' dormitories for courtship and trial mating, were not brought into the central Mountain Province of Northern Luzon by migration but developed *in situ* in relatively recent times as specializations on a more generalized and wider base. Part of the evidence on which this hypothesis has been based is presented in "The Sagada Igorots of Northern Luzon" (1960), where some of the problems "facing" Sagada social structure are examined in greater detail. Here the writer returns to the concept of cultural drift and points out that recent studies make it possible to compare the Mountain Province groups in greater detail and with better historical perspective.

> Ultimately we need to see the development of Mountain Province institutions and practices as a whole. When this has been done, the processual and historical components represented by the concept of cultural drift will be clarified, and we can see the directions of social and ceremonial development, and the factors affecting them, in clearer perspective (Eggan 1960:50).

David F. Aberle has further illuminated the concept of cultural drift in the course of his important paper on "The Influence of Linguistics on Early Culture and Personality Theory" (1960). Here he shows the importance of the linguistic model in the development of Americanist studies of culture, and in particular, those of Edward Sapir and Ruth Benedict. Aberle notes the parallels in the two areas-- languages and cultures each change through "drift," and the changes have both direction and consistency. Aberle goes on to point out that, while Sapir considers the drifts of language and culture as non-comparable and unrelated processes, "he is not rejecting the analogy of drift as such, but the idea that the drift of a particular language is related in any causal or functional way to the drift of the culture associated with the speakers of that language" (1960:10-11).

In a different context, G. P. Murdock has been concerned with the processes involved in the evolution of social organization. In *Social Structure* (1949:198-199) he notes that:

> The phenomenon of linguistic drift exhibits numerous close parallels to the evolution of social organization, e.g., limitation in the possibilities of change, a strain toward consistency, shifts from one to another relatively stable equilibrium, compensatory internal readjustments, resistance to any influence from diffusion that is not in accord with the drift, and noteworthy lack of correlation with accompanying cultural norms in technology, economy, property or government.

He goes on to advance the conclusion that social organization is a semi-independent system comparable to language, but not quite so "closed," since it can be shown to change in response to external events in identifiable ways.

A. L. Kroeber seems not to have made much use of the concept of cultural drift in his earlier writing, though he notes, in *Configurations of Culture Growth*, that his use of "secondary parallelism" corresponds to Sapir's "drift" in related languages (1944:449, footnote 2). And in his *Anthropology* (1948) he talks about "prevalent directions of drift" only with reference to diffusion from culture centers to their margins (1948:423). But in his later study, with Clyde Kluckhohn, of *Culture: A Critical Review of Concepts and Definitions*, the two authors discuss cultures as systems, and note that:

> All systems appear to acquire certain properties that characterize the system *qua* system rather than the sum of isolable elements. Among these properties is that of directionality or "drift." There is a momentum quality to cultural systems. The performance of a culturally patterned activity appears to carry with it implications for its own change which is by no means altogether random. Forms in general, as D'Arcy Thompson has shown, have momentum qualities. The existence of "drift" in one aspect of culture (linguistics) has been fairly well established. There is probably "cultural drift" in general. There may even be in some sense "cultural orthogenesis" within particular limited scopes; that is, the direction of at least some culture change is more predetermined by earlier forms of the culture than caused by environmental press and individual variability (1952:189).

Here the influence of Herskovits is apparent while the phrasing suggests that the statement is primarily the contribution of Kluckhohn.

It is clear from this brief survey that the concept of cultural drift has considerable relevance, both for cultural theory and in terms of increased understanding of the processes involved in social and cultural change. According to Herskovits:

> The concept of *cultural drift* follows logically from the idea of culture as the consensus of the variables in the beliefs and modes of behavior of a people. As we have seen, the presence of deviations from norms of concept and conduct, most of them so small as to go largely unrecognized, is important in giving to a culture an inner dynamic that, in the long run, results in alterations that may be of the most profound character. These variants, however, do not all have the same dynamic significance. They tend to be random variations, in the sense that they represent all kinds of departures from all sorts of norms. They are dynamically significant only when they begin to accumulate, and thus give direction to cultural change (1948:581-2).

The directional significance of cultural drift has relevance to some of the larger problems with which anthropologists are concerned, and notably those of cultural evolution. As Herskovits notes, the theory of cultural evolution was based initially on the steady and regular introduction of new elements. "As a result, human civilization was envisaged as a kind of stream, moving down the ages with an irresistable force, that following the contours of history, would eventually reach its ordained end" (1948:580).

Sapir uses a parallel metaphor for linguistic drift, not for language as a whole but for the linguistic stock.

> Language is not merely something that is spread out in space, as it were--a series of reflections in individual minds of one and the same timeless picture. Language moves down time in a current of its own making. It has a drift. If there were no breaking up of a language into dialects, if each language continued as a firm, self-contained unity, it would still be constantly moving away from any assignable norm, developing new features unceasingly and gradually transforming itself into a language so different from its starting point as to be in effect a new language (1921:160-61).

But Sapir, though he refers to language as "a mountainous and anonymous work of unconscious generations," finds the source of the drift in the "unconscious selection on the part of its speakers of the individual variations which are cumulative in some special direction" (1921:166). As such he sees the changes which take place in a language as historical rather than evolutionary. But as Aberle points out he makes no attempt to show *why* linguistic drift takes a particular direction. It is interesting that in language, where the drift is most easily perceived, the causes are more difficult to isolate. But other aspects of culture may be more amenable to such study, once

consistent directions of change have been worked out. This seems to
be particularly true of social organization where a number of recent
studies have illustrated regularities of change, and where the factors involved are more accessible to observation.

Recent developments in the field of biological evolution may
also be relevant in this connection. In addition to progressive adaptation to new conditions through natural selection, and the effects
of mutation and hybridization, one other evolutionary mechanism has
been isolated--the variance due to random genetic drift. Random genetic drift, sometimes called the Sewall Wright effect after its dis-
coverer, is "drift" of a somewhat different sort than the phenomena
found in language and culture, but certain of the parallels are in-
structive. In the first place, it depends for its operation on the
isolation of the breeding population, and isolation is one important
factor in both dialect formation and cultural variation. Genetic
drift also increases in importance as the size of the population is
reduced. Restriction in size of the breeding population increases
the variance of the distribution of gene frequencies, and this variance is compounded in successive generations. Hence it is possible
for small populations not only to lose particular genes but to change
their genetic composition rather considerably in a relatively short
time. It is possible that linguistic and cultural change may be more
rapid in small isolated groups, as well, though as yet we have no
good studies.

In the case of random genetic drift we know more about the
mechanisms involved but the directions of drift and their significance
is less clear. Here the accidents of selection seem to play an important part. In the evolution of actual populations, all four of
the main evolutionary mechanisms are probably in operation at the
same time. As Boyd points out:

> The relative importance of each for the future of the group
> will depend partly upon the size of the population, and partly
> upon accident. The interaction of the various evolutionary forces
> is an interesting and important subject. . . . In very large pop-
> ulations genetic drift has less importance and very small selec-
> tive advantages and disadvantages will eventually have their ef-
> fect (1950:158).

In a different connection Charles Erasmus (1950:384-85) has
pointed out the significance of the principle of limited possibilities in regard to both culture and biology, and has called attention
to the similarities between George Simpson's view of evolution and
the concept of cultural drift in that both imply limiting conditions
and both are evolutionary--though neither is unilinear. And E. Z.
Vogt (1960:21) has called attention to the relative significance of

long and short run changes, the latter being frequently cyclical
whereas the former may be cumulative in a particular direction.

Gerald D. Berreman, in a study of cultural variation in the
Himalaya hills (1960) has utilized the concept of cultural drift as
a means to a clearer understanding of the origin and maintenance of
cultural differences. He uses "cultural drift" as a concept parallel
to Sapir's linguistic drift and analogous to genetic drift, and defines it as "the process of divergent or differential cultural change."
He further suggests (1960:788) that "cultural change, like genetic
evolution, comes about as a result of *variation, selection,* and *transmission* while drift or divergent change requires the additional condition of *isolation*." While he is primarily concerned with the relevance of drift for the conception of culture areas, he is well aware
of its significance for the study of cultural change.

With regard to the question of the direction of cultural
drift, Herskovits has made some further suggestions.

> The concept of drift, the piling up of minor variations that
> are in accord with pre-existing tendencies, must be considered
> as associated with the idea of cultural focus. We have advanced
> the idea that because there is a lively interest in the focal as-
> pect of a culture, change is more likely to occur in the insti-
> tutions lying here than in those found in other of its aspects.
> Granting that change is not haphazard, but directional, then the
> increased range of variation in the focal aspect of a culture
> would not only continuously tend to produce a wider range of var-
> iants in line with the direction in which institutions were mov-
> ing, but would also make for more decided change than in other
> aspects (1948:584).

These various statements relating to the concept of cultural
drift show both a growing consensus and an awareness as to the importance of this concept. They also illustrate the stimulation that
anthropologists have derived from Herskovits' detailed treatment of
cultural drift in *Man and His Works*. There is not space to summarize his chapter on "Cultural Drift and Historic Accident" with regard to the problems of cultural variation, nor is this necessary
for present purposes. These two concepts, he says:

> . . . bring us one step further in attaining an understanding of
> how cultures develop, especially as this concerns the selective
> nature of change. If we recognize the importance of differential
> variation in providing a basis both for change and selection,
> then drift is to be regarded as the expression of the process
> whereby some variants come to be of more importance than others
> to a particular people at a given time (1948:593).

With these introductory remarks we might now shift our attention to the Mountain Province of Northern Luzon to see what extent
the problems and processes noted above may be illuminated by sociocultural data from a series of contiguous groups in a relatively isolated region.

The Mountain Province of Northern Luzon contains some eight major ethnic groups (see fig. 1) with a total population of around 250,000 and an average density of 50 persons per square mile. In broad perspective it might be considered a culture area, but there are important differences in agriculture, settlement patterns, and social institutions which cut across geographical lines and dialect groupings. The basic unit is the village or group of related villages; as one goes from one local group to another, changes occur in both dialect and custom, without any sharp linguistic breaks. There are no "tribes" in the ordinary sense, and the larger ethnolinguistic units recognized by the ethnologist have little basis in native society (cf. the Keesings 1934).

Some years ago, in viewing the Mountain Province from the vantage point of the Tinguian on the western slopes of the Cordillera Central, the writer pointed out (1941:12ff.) that certain of the variations in Mountain Province social institutions were not haphazard but had a definite direction. Thus as one proceeds from the Ifugao in the east to the Ilocano in the west, village organization becomes more complex, kinship terminology shifts from a Hawaiian to an approximation of the European or "Eskimo" system, with a gradual narrowing of the range of effective kinship and an increasing differentiation of relatives; territorial ties increase in strength relative to kinship bonds; and political centralization and class differentiation increase. Along with these changes occur corresponding variations in marriage customs, parental control, and preferential marriage, as well as possibly related shifts in religious beliefs and prestige activities.

At that time relatively little was known about the Kankanay, Bontok, and Kalinga peoples, who occupy the central areas of the Mountain Province, but studies published since the war by Keesing, Barton, and the present writer, among others, have partially filled this gap. In addition, Edward Dozier has recently completed a field study of the Northern Kalinga and has kindly allowed me to utilize his notes and unpublished manuscripts (1960, 1961). These data enable us to examine the sequence of changes which takes place as one goes from the Northern Kalinga to the Southern Kalinga, and on via Bontok to the Northern Kankanay as represented by Sagada. For the Kalinga we have some historical perspective, in that the Northern Kalinga institutions are also found among the closely related Southern Kalinga, though modified by the introduction of wet rice terrace agriculture from the south which has greatly increased population density. Dozier's observations on the Southern Kalinga, a generation after Bar-

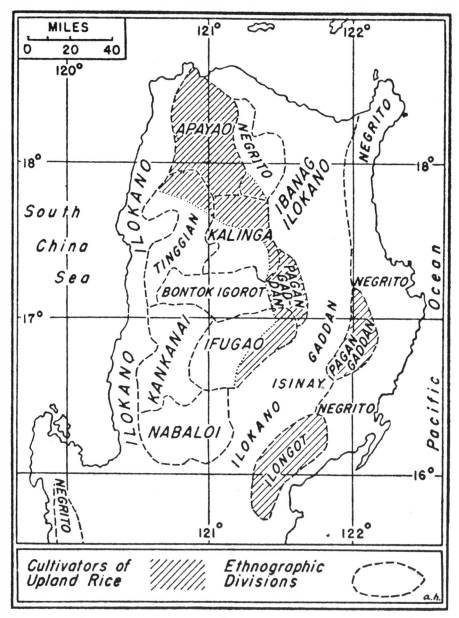

Fig. 1.--Ethnographic map of northern Luzon. (After Barton, *Philippine Pagans* [London, 1938].) Lubuagan is in Southern Kalinga and Sagada is in the Northern Kankanai region.

ton's earlier studies, give us a further stage in the process of
change.

The comparison of the Kalinga variations with the social institutions of the Bontok and Sagada villages is not so well controlled,
but the basic institutions are clearly similar and the more elaborate
ward organization, with its public institutions, is almost certainly
built upon a common foundation.

The Northern Kalinga are shifting dry rice cultivators who
live in small hamlets organized into endogamous "regions." Each region considers itself to be a group of kinsmen and treats outsiders
as potential enemies, though they may speak a common dialect and participate in similar cultural activities. Within the region each sibling group is the center of a kinship circle, or personal kindred,
which extends laterally to the third cousins on both sides and includes spouses, as well. This kinship circle represents the ultimate
range of kinship obligation; it is also the theoretical exogamic unit
through marriage with third cousins and beyond is freely condoned.

Within the region all are kinsmen, even though some are beyond the range of effective obligation. Hence the region can be
viewed in terms of sets of overlapping kinship circles, and the members of a region conceptualize it as a kinship unit. From the standpoint of an outsider the members are a group of kinsmen and any one
may be killed to satisfy vengeance.

The major interaction with neighboring regions in the past
centered around warfare and feuding, except for trading relations and
more recently peace pacts. Along with trading relationships there
was a system of concubinage, and prominent men frequently had mis-
tresses in one or more communities. But intermarriage was relatively
rare, and generally with refugees from neighboring regions.

The regions in the north are relatively small in size, averaging from 500-700 in population and containing 10-12 hamlets in some
150 square miles of territory. All observers have remarked on the
great variety of physical types among the Kalinga, in contrast to
their neighbors, and have generally explained the variation in terms
of migrations, or the introduction of prisoners in Spanish times.
But these small endogamous units should be ideal for the study of increased variance due to random genetic drift. There is also a great
deal of phonetic variation in the Kalinga regions in comparison with
their neighbors. But the dialects are mutually intelligible over
the whole Kalinga region, evidence that their differentiation is not
of great age.

The political organization is relatively simple. Authority

was generally in the hands of leading warriors, called *maengal*, in
the Spanish period. With the decline of feuding, influential headmen,
the *lakay*, have come to the fore, and are responsible for adjusting
disputes within the region. They usually act as pact-holders in the
peace pacts that have spread rapidly during the American period, as
well.

The Southern Kalinga, studied by Barton (1949), likewise are
organized in endogamous regions. But here there has been a major
cultural transformation through the introduction of irrigated rice
agriculture in terraced fields. This introduction came via the Bontok peoples to the south in the last few generations, and is still
spreading to the north. It has had a dramatic effect upon population density and community size, and this has affected other aspects
of Kalinga culture, as well.

These latter changes were going on before the war, when Barton was there, but he had no base line against which to measure them.
The Lubuagan region, which he studied in some detail, covered an area
of about 15 square miles and contained about 2,400 people in 15 hamlets. In addition, an endogamous colony (Uma) of some 850 population
resided over the mountain to the west.

Barton interpreted the Southern Kalinga situation as one of
incipient statehood based on the greater importance of the territorial ties and the bonds which it engendered. He saw the peace pacts,
the rights of citizenship, and the rise of the *pangats*, or political
leaders, as evidence for a greater territorial emphasis. Coming from
the Ifugao, who make little use of the territorial ties, Barton saw
the Kalinga, by comparison, as politically organized. But Dozier
finds that kinship is still the basic bond within the region.

In Ifugao the kinship circles are structurally identical to
those of the Kalinga, except for the latter's recognition of spouses
as relatives, but are scattered over several neighboring regions.
Barton warn us that the terms: "home region," "feuding region," and
"war region" are conceptual units and not territorial ones. Among
the Kalinga the coalescence of kinship circles within a territorial
unit makes it easy to generalize this relationship and utilize the
region as a convenient reference point, particularly from the outside.
But peace pacts provide the test. Particular kinship circles may remain outside the regional peace pact if they feel that vengeance has
not been sufficiently satisfied.

The effects of population increase among the Southern Kalinga,
which were beginning to be apparent in Barton's time, were much more
developed in 1959-1960 when Dozier was there. The population had

greatly increased and in Lubuagan certain hamlets were contiguous
with the larger center. The effective size of the kinship circle,
already reduced before the war by the omission of the descendants of
third cousins (who are an integral part of the Northern Kalinga kinship circle), is now further reduced to the range of second cousins,
a reduction in the number of recognized relatives by almost half.
Feuds within the region, relatively unknown in the north, were beginning to be common in Barton's day, and have increased in intensity
in the postwar period. With a larger population there is less overlapping of kinship circles and hence greater opportunities for feuds
to develop. The mutual relatives, with conflicting loyalties and in
jeopardy to both sides, were anxious for peace. The rise of the
pangats, the kinship leaders who serve as go-betweens in the settling
of disputes, is related to this increased feuding. Their role as
pact-holders in the peace pacts with neighboring regions is political,
however, even though their authority ultimately rests on their own
prowess, supported by their kinship groups.

Within the Kalinga community, whether north or south, the
elementary family is dominant and makes up the household, sometimes
with the addition of one or two parents or other relatives of the
couple. The average size of the household is larger in the north,
according to Dozier, but the increased population in the Lubuagan
region has raised the average size in the last generation, apparently
because of the overcrowding. Economic activities are usually shared
by relatives in two or more households. In both areas there is a
tendency for daughters to remain close to their parents. This matrilocal residence is stronger in Lubuagan where the wife's relatives
have the obligation to construct a new house for the married couple.
In the north both sets of relatives share in this obligation.

The role of the new rice technology in the changes noted
above presents an important problem. In both areas dry rice farming
by slash and burn techniques continues (cf. Scott 1958), and the major work units in both the north and the south remain the cooperating
extended households. But the introduction of wet rice technology,
with irrigation and terracing, and the possibility of growing two
crops a year, has raised the population ceiling tremendously. In
neither the north nor the south is there any clear evidence for bilateral descent groups with corporate control of property. Rather
the initiative in constructing terraces seems everywhere to come from
the family or individual. In the south neighbors and relatives may
pool their labor to build and maintain irrigation ditches, and water
rights are controlled by customary procedures. In the Lubuagan re-

gion there are "supervisors" for the three major areas of irrigated
rice fields who are responsible for allocating water rights, setting
the times for planting, and harvest, and settling disputes over land.
These positions are inherited in certain families, which Dozier thinks
may be descent groups, but their duties have lapsed with the extension of modern governmental operations.

The new rice technology has increased the average wealth and
also greatly increased the wealth differentials. Arranged marriages
are utilized in Kalinga society, not only for purposes of family alliance, but to preserve and enhance inherited wealth, both in rice
lands and heirlooms. It is probable that the wealthier families in
the south tend to arrange marriages with closer kin--more marriages
with second cousins may occur than in the north, though this is not
yet demonstrable. The class situation in the south, however, is
better developed. The *kadangyan* "aristocrats" and the *pangats* com-
mand more wealth and assert more privileges than do the *maengal* and
lakay of the north.

The new technology has also stabilized the settlement pattern. In the north, hamlets have to move periodically and may expand or decline without much concern or difficulty. In the south the
hamlets are stabilized and have expanded greatly. That this expansion is due to population increase rather than immigration is clearly
indicated by the genealogies collected by Dozier. With the great
increase in population, the older social institutions which operated
reasonably effectively in the north are now partly dysfunctional in
the south. Lubuagan region is no longer a kinship unit in actuality,
but is composed of a large number of kinship circles, with not enough
overlapping to maintain the feeling of kinship unity. The shift to
a sub-regional basis, or to territorial units, is one possibility
but such changes apparently take considerable time. The temporary
solution in the south has been to reduce the effectiveness of kinship
to the range of second cousins, to make parents keep their daughters
nearby to a greater extent, and to increase the number of *pangats* who
act as mediators of the increased number of local disputes. Correlatively the relations with outside regions have been facilitated by
the extension of the peace pact system and trade; and modern conditions are affecting regional isolation and bringing about increased
interaction and intermarriage.

Part of this process can be seen at work in the colonies
which have been mentioned above. Barton noted some half dozen endogamous colonies, representing an expansion of a region's population
into contiguous areas. Uma, a colony of Lubuagan, was originally

cultivated intermittently by dry farming, but eventually irrigated fields were made and it developed a permanent population. In 1941 it had only one peace pact of its own; by 1960 it had become politically independent of Lubuagan, though it still continued intermarriage with the parental region. Uma now has its own satellite hamlets, however, and the next step would be complete independence. In the north, where population is also currently increasing, the surplus population often has to migrate to the margins of the Kalinga region, formerly kept relatively empty by warfare and malaria but now habitable with modern sanitation. These communities likewise maintain ties with the parental regions, but are in the process of developing their own peace pacts and independence.

In the central Mountain Province the Bontok communities, and the Northern Kankanay, as well, have taken an additional step and have shifted, in part, to a territorial basis. Bontok and Northern Kankanay communities share the same basic institutions and are fairly closely related linguistically, as well. Here the earlier subsistence patterns were based on root crops--taro and yams, and later sweet potatoes, or camotes. But wet rice agriculture had an earlier beginning in this region than in Kalinga, though perhaps no more than a century or two.

Kalinga expansion into the Mountain Province is almost certainly from the north and east, up the Chico and Saltan rivers and their tributaries. Bontok and Northern Kankanay expansion is clearly from the south and west. The border region between Bontok communities and the southern-most Kalinga communities is not as yet well known, beyond an early study by Daniel Folkmar, as yet unpublished, but it is clear that cultural influences have spread both ways, though especially to the Kalinga.

The social institutions in Bontok and Sagada, therefore, are not directly comparable to those of Kalinga, except in a more general way. Both are built on a similar pattern of bilateral kinship, but nowhere in the south is there the development of endogamous regions. Rather here, marriage has been utilized to knit neighboring communities together in a loose network.

In the Bontok area the shift to wet rice agriculture resulted in a rapid increase in population and the development of large concentrated settlements. From such population centers as Bontok itself, satellite communities such as Samoki and Barlig have developed as independent communities. In these Bontok communities the village is differentiated into geographical wards adjacent to one another but each with a separate set of institutions, including a ceremonial and political center, with an informal council of old men, a men's and boys' sleeping shed used also for visitors, and a girls' dormitory used for courtship purposes. There is no overall political structure, and peace pacts were characteristically made by each ward on behalf of the whole community. The community participates, however, in a common ceremonial cycle, and certain ritual activities are performed by persons whose position is inherited in certain families (see Keesing 1949).

This cultural complex apparently spread to the Northern Kankanay, who are relatively close linguistic neighbors, some two or three centuries ago. In such a community as Sagada we can trace in outline the expansion of population and the development of the ward organization. Here, formerly separate communities have also joined into larger ones, though the fusion is not as yet complete (Eggan 1960).

At an earlier stage these Kankanay communities were partially organized in terms of bilateral descent groups, with corporate rights in hill farms and pine forests. But these descent groups became obsolescent with population expansion and survive only marginally among the Northern Kankanay, and possibly among the Bontok.

The development of a ward or territorial organization has affected the kinship structure. The writer has argued (1960:30-31) that with the increase in population in Sagada and neighboring communities the bilateral descent groups became less efficient in carrying out community needs. Likewise, the kinship circles were affected, both by the earlier cessation of warfare and feuding in late Spanish times, and by the greater overlapping consequent upon population increase and the resulting difficulties in settling disputes between different kinship groups.

One result has been, as in the southern Kalinga, to reduce the effective range of the kinship circle to second cousins, and to allow marriage beyond this limit. But the correlative shift to a ward organization has further weakened kinship obligations through establishing a competing solidarity. The ward organization presents a discrete group whose membership at any one time is clearly defined, despite the differing kinship circles of its component members. Each ward has an informal council of old men who settle problems within the ward, and in joint sessions mediate inter-ward conflicts. Village solidarity is aided by the joint performance of communal rituals and other activities under the leadership of the old men, or of particular priests who inherit their positions in family lines.

In this area peace pacts are recent and rare, though they are

found in the Bontok area. Instead, marriage between communities is
the major means to a wider integration. In contrast to the endogamous Kalinga, some ten percent of Sagada marriages are with neighboring communities.

Sagada and its neighbors, if the Sagada situation is typical,
thus started out with small groups of kindred who, under conditions
of relative isolation and adequate space, could act as corporate
groups in terms of bilateral descent. The early Kalinga, building
on a similar kinship base, utilized endogamy and regional boundaries
to give them an equivalent corporate base. Population expansion, resulting from the new rice technology, brought similar problems to
both. The solutions to these problems were in part convergent, and
in part parallel. With increased density and size of population, the
Southern Kalinga regions lost their unitary character and became more
diversified in terms of the component kinship groups. In Sagada the
bilateral descent groups and the personal kindreds likewise lost much
of their reason for existence. In both areas there has been a rise
in the number and character of internal disputes and a decrease in
external dangers. The concomitant rise of a class of mediators and
the decline of war leaders is found in both areas. The further shift
to territorial ward units apparently took place first in the Bontok
region, and has not as yet crossed the border of Southern Kalinga,
though certain components of the ward complex have spread to Tinglayen and other Southern Kalinga towns. And the ward organization
has not spread to all of the Kankanay-speaking communities, but only
to the Northern portion, where the population is densest.

Within the kinship systems themselves, the most significant
shift has been in the reduction of the range, and in the strength of
the obligations to kinsmen. Under aboriginal conditions, where one's
life literally depended on one's kin, great efforts were made to
maintain a large circle of loyal kinsmen. The attitudes toward kin
described by Barton's informants in *Philippine Pagans* (1938) were
probably once characteristic of the whole Mountain Province, and, indeed, of Philippine society generally. Under modern conditions there
is a tendency to reduce the effective range and strength of kinship
ties and obligations, except where politics has become important.
In the lowland areas the kinship framework still remains but the obligations are now selectively implemented.

The form of the kinship systems in Kalinga, Bontok, and Sagada is generally similar. There are specific terms for parental siblings, and cousins are differentiated from siblings, as among ourselves. At first glance these seem quite different from the Hawaiian

type found among the Ifugao, with its extension of parental terms
and its use of sibling terms for cousins. But Ifugao can make use
of special terms for clarity of reference, and in Sagada and Kalinga
parental terms are extended to uncles and aunts and sibling terms to
cousins in direct address. One specific difference between Northern
and Southern Kalinga is that the latter has only a single term for
parental siblings, whereas the former makes the normal sex distinction in reference.

There are also important differences in the patterns of courtship and marriage, though marriage is everywhere an alliance of kin
groups. In Kalinga marriages are characteristically arranged by the
parents concerned and usually involve the union of distant cousins.
Where inherited property is of concern, the arrangements may be between second cousins, thus compounding the property within the kinship group. In Bontok and Northern Kankanay towns the young men and
girls generally arrange their own marriages through courtship in the
girls' dormitories. But wealthy families attempt to arrange marriages to conserve property, though such engagements may be later
broken. In Southern Kalinga the Bontok pattern of sleeping practices
has been partly introduced though without the sexual freedom, except
where couples are already parentally engaged.

This summary survey of the changes in social institutions
from north to south in the central Mountain Province, while differing
in detail, parallels in a general way the series earlier described
(Eggan 1941) for the Ifugao-Bontok-Tinguian-Ilocano. Thus, in both
instances, there is a general increase in size and complexity of village organization; an increase in territorial ties relative to kinship bonds; and an increase in political centralization and class
differentiation. And while the basic form of the kinship system remains the same in the central Mountain Province, there is a narrowing
of range from north to south, as well as a shift from endogamous regions to the utilization of marriage for alliance. Parental control
of marriage, however, is stronger in the north where property considerations are not so important, though it is also found to some extent
in the south. Custom in the Mountain Province favors residence of
the newly married couple near the wife's parents, but this varies
with local circumstances rather than being a general rule.

In the east-west sequence all of the ethno-linguistic groups
concerned are wet rice cultivators with roughly equivalent densities
of population; in the north-south sequence there is a major shift in
the Kalinga from dry rice "shifting cultivation" to permanent fields
based on irrigation and terracing. Here introduced technology has

brought about a different ecological adjustment and has greatly raised the population ceiling. While the advent of American control has modified the situation to a considerable extent, we can still see the general effects of the increased population pressure on social institutions.

Our two series thus complement one another, as well as add new factors or components, in terms of our ultimate understanding of Mountain Province institutions and practices. Here we have limited our perspective to certain social institutions, and have omitted consideration of marginal groups, such as the Isneg, or Apayao, and the Nabaloy. But we have presented enough data to illustrate the regularity of change under relatively controlled conditions, and the relevance of the concept of cultural drift.

Returning now to the concept of cultural drift in the light of the Mountain Province materials, we can see certain features of social change in clearer perspective. Herskovits, in summarizing the writer's earlier formulation in "Some Aspects of Culture Change in the Northern Philippines," concluded his statement (1948:588) as follows:

> Here we are presented with an interaction between established drift and outer compulsions, which means an additional factor has to be taken into account. This factor is one we have called historical accident. Therefore it is well for us, at this point, to turn to a consideration of the nature and significance of this concept. With an analysis in hand, we may then assess the manner in which accidental happenings act to reinforce or counteract the drifts already present in the cultures where they occur.

By "historic accident" Herskovits refers to the abrupt innovations that arise within a culture, or result from contact with other peoples, and thus modify the expected sequence of events. Drift influences what is to be taken into a culture, whether developed within or introduced from without, and offers an explanation for the reinterpretation of new elements in terms of established patterns (1948:593-94).

It is clear that random variation about a norm will not change the norm, except by disintegrating it. It is selection of some sort that is responsible for directional changes. And, as Aberle (1960:6) notes, "selection in cultures is not simply a reduction in random behavior, that on the contrary it has other important adaptive functions in addition to making face-to-face relationships intelligible."

But unlike language, and perhaps other aspects of culture, social change is not continuous. As Murdock has suggested, social systems shift from one to another relatively stable equilibrium.

Otherwise the expectancies of face-to-face relationships break down. To take one example, the recognition of the kinship circle as extending to the range of third cousin among the Kalinga does not mean that every individual treats his third cousins precisely alike. Aspiring leaders will cultivate their kinsmen on all possible occasions, whereas a poor man may have difficulty in implementing his relationship with his first cousins.

Where theory and practice differ, we can suspect directional change. Thus Barton notes that for the Southern Kalinga before the war the kinship group theoretically includes the third cousins, but in practice the tendency is toward a narrowed group.

> Collective responsibility for an offense reaches to the third cousins, although it is considered in bad taste to kill a man's third cousins for his offense. Active support and backing to a kinsman involved in controversy hardly reaches beyond second cousins. Forebearance in case of tort hardly reaches the third cousins and is pretty thin when it reaches the second. Distribution of the proceeds from the sale of fields and valuable heirlooms includes the more influential of the second cousins only when the sale is large. Weregilds ought always, theoretically, to include the third cousins but . . . often they do not receive them (1949:82).

One might ask: "Where is the norm?" Here there seems to be only a series of sliding scales. But with greater historical perspective we can see that among the Northern Kalinga theory and practice coincide to a greater extent. Further, a generation later Dozier finds a new norm among the Southern Kalinga established at the level of second cousins. In this perspective Barton's statement tells us much more than that practice does not correspond with theory. It gives us some insight into the cultural focus of the society and its hierarchy of values. In the north the activities centering around feuds and vengeance are paramount; in Southern Kalinga these have become secondary to wealth and prestige.

The factors responsible for this shift are both external and internal. The introduction of new techniques of agriculture from the south and the relative peace imposed by American occupation both were important, but in different ways. Despite the apparent advantages of wet rice agriculture it was taken over relatively slowly in the Mountain Province, and the process is still going on. But once underway a whole series of other changes were in prospect. Some of these are direct outgrowths but many of them are the indirect results of changes in population density and distribution. Social relationships which worked well with small dispersed populations may become obstacles to continuing social life when population density is increased.

The partial shift from kinship to territorial ties, which Maine emphasized as so important for the development of the state, is here seen in different perspective. The utilization of a ward organization in Bontok and Sagada does not have the revolutionary implications that Maine envisaged. It is one of the very few alternatives open to a kinship based society when population is increased and opportunities for wider social integration are available.

Not all societies necessarily change their social structure under new conditions, at least immediately. The Ifugao, in this respect are the most interesting and puzzling case. They early developed wet rice agriculture, as their extensive terrace system and elaborate irrigation practices amply testify. But despite increasing population density they continued to dwell in small, scattered hamlets and to organize their social life almost entirely on the basis of kinship. Territorial bonds were little developed and political organization was at a minimum. But they have had to develop an elaborate system of customary law to settle disputes between the kinship groups. Here adaptation took the form of shoring up the system rather than modifying it in accord with new values. As Hoebel (1949:3) has pointed out, the Ifugao system "shows up nicely the limitations in a legal order that depends primarily upon the kinship group for its operation."

The above observations also suggest that the direction of change with regard to social institutions may well be sought in terms of adaptation. We can look at a society both in terms of its adaptation to the environment and in terms of its internal adaptation. Internal adaptation results in the mutual adjustment of the interests of various groups making up the society, and unless the groups can cooperate to an adequate extent the society must change or disintegrate.

Cultural drift may thus differ to a considerable extent from linguistic drift in that the factors responsible are more amenable to observation and control. This is particularly true of social institutions, and social change may need to be treated separately from changes in cultural patterns for these purposes.

If our analysis is correct, historic accidents, the abrupt innovations from within or without, may only slowly affect the culture through modifying the small day-by-day changes in new directions. Dramatic as are the long term effects of wet rice technology on Mountain Province society and culture, the transformation moved slowly and often indirectly, affecting the system of production and distribution, modifying the power system, changing loyalties and obligations, and introducing new values. In this process there is a shift from one equilibrium to another, but it is a dynamic equilibrium destined for further change. The strain towards consistency is there but the development of new tensions may keep it from being realized in any complete way.

Whether shifts in cultural focus are cause or result, they play an important role in showing the directions of change and facilitating the reinterpretation of old culture patterns. One basic shift in the Mountain Province in the last century has been from the prestige surrounding success in warfare to the prestige attendant upon the possession of wealth. The former was an achieved position based in large measure on personal qualities of bravery, strength, and leadership; the latter tends to be based on inherited wealth and position, in larger measure, though personal qualities are still important. An awareness of this shift is of considerable importance in assessing the various sociocultural constellations in the Mountain Province.

Whether cultural drift is history or evolution is a question that has not been answered, as yet. Sapir considered the drifts of language and culture to be historical, whereas Murdock talks about the "evolution" of social organization in analogous terms. The recent distinction made by Sahlins and Service (1960) between specific evolution and general evolution may be relevant. Specific evolution "creates diversity through adaptive modification," and for culture, "the historic development of particular cultural forms is specific evolution" (1960:12-13,43). But it is not yet clear that these particular developments add up to "the succession of culture through stages of overall progress" which is general evolution.

In these brief remarks we hope we have added some illumination to the concept of cultural drift which Melville Herskovits has rescued from the neglect into which it had fallen and forged into an instrument for the study of cultural change. The considerable number of anthropologists who have found the concept of "drift" useful during the last decade testifies to its relevance for these problems, and we believe we have shown that it is particularly relevant to change in social institutions. In our studies of social and cultural change we are gradually shifting from an emphasis on external factors to a concern for inner dynamics and adaptive processes. To adequately utilize the concept of cultural drift we need historical perspective so that trends can be defined and controlled. And once we have such historical perspective we have the possibility of defining more clearly the role of the individual in social and cultural change. If our analysis is correct the concept of cultural drift may be even more important than Herskovits realized, though he clearly saw its significance for an understanding of the fundamental assumptions and problems of anthropology as a science.

REFERENCES CITED

Aberle, D. F. 1960. "The Influence of Linguistics on Early Culture and Personality Theory," in *Essays in the Science of Culture in Honor of Leslie A. White*. Edited by G. Doyle and R. Carneiro. New York.

Barton, R. F. 1938. *Philippine Pagans*. London.

————. 1949. *The Kalinga, Their Institutions and Custom Law*. Chicago.

Boyd, W. C. 1950. *Genetics and the Races of Man*. Boston.

Berreman, G. D. 1960. Cultural Variability and Drift in the Himalayan Hills. *American Anthropologist* 62, No. 5:774-94.

Dozier, E. P. 1960. M.S. The Kalinga of the Upper Saltan and Mabaca River Valleys.

————. 1961 "Land Use and Social Organization Among the Non-Christian Tribes of Northwestern Luzon." Paper presented at the Annual Meeting of the American Anthropological Association, Philadelphia, November, 1961.

Eggan, F. 1941. Some Aspects of Culture Change in the Northern Philippines. *American Anthropologist* 43, No. 1:11-18.

————. 1954. Some Social Institutions in the Mountain Province and Their Significance for Historical and Comparative Studies. *Journal of East Asiatic Studies* III, No. 3:329-35.

————. 1960. "The Sagada Igorots of Northern Luzon," in Social Structure in Southeast Asia. Edited by G. P. Murdock. *Viking Fund Publications in Anthropology*, No. 29. New York.

Erasmus, C. J. 1950. Patolli, Pachisi, and the Limitation of Possibilities. *Southwestern Journal of Anthropology* 6, No. 4:369-81.

Folkmar, D. M.S. *Tinglayen*. H. O. Beyer Collection. n.d. Manila.

Herskovits, M. J. 1941. Some Comments on the Study of Cultural Contact. *American Anthropologist* 43, No. 1:1-10.

————. 1948. *Man and His Works, The Science of Cultural Anthropology*. New York.

Hoebel, E. A. 1949. "Introduction" to R. F. Barton, *The Kalinga, Their Institutions and Custom Law*. Chicago.

Keesing, F. M. 1949. Some Notes on Bontok Social Organization, Northern Philippines. *American Anthropologist* 51, No. 4:578-601.

Keesing, F. M. and M. Keesing. 1934. *Taming Philippine Headhunters*. London.

Kroeber, A. L. 1944. *Configurations of Culture Growth*. Berkeley.

————. 1948. *Anthropology*. New York.

Kroeber, A. L. and C. Kluckhohn. 1952. Culture, A Critical Review of Concepts and Definitions. *Papers of the Peabody Museum of American Archaeology and Ethnology, Harvard University*, Vol. XLVII, No. 1. Cambridge.

Murdock, G. P. 1949. *Social Structure*. New York.

Sahlins, M. and E. Service. (Eds.) 1960. *Evolution and Culture*. Ann Arbor.

Sapir, E. 1921. *Language*. New York.

Scott, W. H. 1958. A Preliminary Report on Upland Rice in Northern Luzon. *Southwestern Journal of Anthropology* 14, No. 1:87-105.

Vogt, E. Z. 1960. On the Concepts of Structure and Process in Cultural Anthropology. *American Anthropologist* 62, No. 1:18-33.

Wright, S. 1929. The Evolution of Dominance. *The American Naturalist* 63:556-61.

13

ALLIANCE AND DESCENT IN A WESTERN PUEBLO SOCIETY

1964

Julian Steward has made a number of important contributions to the study of Pueblo society, most notably in his "Ecological Aspects of Southwestern Society" (1937), where he first proposed a model for the development of clans from a band organization, under the influence of changing social and ecological conditions; and in his *Basin-Plateau Aboriginal Sociopolitical Groups* (1938), where he describes the ecological factors which underlay the development of western Pueblo society. I have elsewhere (1950:126-30) utilized these contributions for a preliminary discussion of western Pueblo social structure and its probable development. Here I would like to examine the Hopi model for their own society more closely and see the relevance of alliance and descent theory for an understanding of its characteristics and its development over time.

In historical perspective, Radcliffe-Brown combined certain aspects of both descent and alliance theory in his now classic work on *The Social Organization of Australian Tribes* (1931), but in his Introduction to *African Systems of Kinship and Marriage* (1950) he emphasized the significance of unilineal descent for our understanding of social structures. At about the same time Lévi-Strauss was developing the basis for alliance theory in his great work on preferential systems of marriage (1949), which has stimulated the researches of Homans and Schneider, Needham, Leach, Dumont, and many others. While alliance theory has developed primarily from the study of societies with prescriptive marriage systems, it is highly probable that it may have a wider relevance.

Edmund Leach, in his recent study of Pul Eliya, a Sinhalese village which lacks formal unilineal descent groups, has proposed a further formulation:

Reproduced by permission of Aldine Publishing Company, Chicago, from *Process and Pattern in Culture*, Robert A. Manners, editor (1964), pp. 175-84.

> It will be found that in the Sinhalese village of Pul Eliya it
> is locality rather than descent which forms the basis of corpo-
> rate grouping. . . . The concepts of descent and affinity are
> expressions of property relations which endure through time.
> Marriage unifies; inheritance separates; property endures. A
> particular descent system simply reflects the total process of
> property succession as effected by the total pattern of inheri-
> tance and marriage (1961:7, 11).

From this standpoint kinship systems have no reality except in relation to land and property, and economic activities and relationships
are 'prior' to kinship relations. Leach stresses the role of the
natural environment: "It is the inflexibility of topography--of
water and land and climate--which most of all determines what people
shall do" (1961:9).

The western Pueblos--Hopi, Hano, Zuni, Acoma and Laguna--all
live in a semi-desert environment where rainfall is uncertain and
arable land limited. All conceive of their societies as in a "steady
state," unfolding according to preordained pattern, and continuing
in a "timeless" existence. All are organized in terms of matrilineal
descent and matrilocal residence, with kinship systems of the classical Crow type. But in these intricately ordered societies the
choice of a marriage partner is apparently left to chance, beyond the
restrictions of clan and phratry exogamy. Further, the marriage bond
is easily broken, and divorce may occur on the initiative of either
partner.

In Basin society Steward (1938:241ff.) has described a great
variety of types of preferential marriage which can be seen as attempts to achieve integration beyond the basic family group: sister
exchange, sororal polygyny, fraternal "polyandry," and, in certain
areas, cross-cousin marriage and a unique modified form, pseudo cross-
cousin marriage, which Steward was the first to describe. He notes
that marriage was an economic alliance in a very real sense, and that
"multiple interfamily marriages are a simple device for strengthening
and the sororate and levirate for continuing an alliance between two
families, but there is no obvious reason why cross-cousin or pseudo
cross-cousin marriage should have developed in some localities but
not in others" (1938:245).

None of these forms of preferential marriage are found among
the western Pueblos who are strictly monogamous. We are interested
in the conditions under which preferential marriage develops and
whether in non-prescriptive systems marriage creates enduring alliances between descent groups. Are the principles of alliance and
descent in complementary opposition and have we failed to understand
such systems by not taking an adequate view of affinity? I shall try

to answer some of these questions with particular reference to the Hopi Indians. Here I am indebted to the researches of my colleagues, Mischa Titiev and Edward Kennard, and to the as yet unpublished studies of John Connelly on Second Mesa in the post World War II period.

The Hopi Indians have resided in a number of villages on the southern edge of Black Mesa in northeastern Arizona for well over a thousand years. Despite an agricultural technology, limited rainfall and other factors kept the population ceiling at around 2500 persons until the 1930's. The villages are distributed on three mesas, to take advantage of small springs and limited areas suitable for growing corn, beans and squash, plus the grazing of sheep introduced by the Spaniards.

Time after time during their history, the Hopi have faced the threat of extinction or dispersal through periodic drought or epidemic disease. During the latter half of their history nomadic enemies entered the region, and later the Spaniards established missions for a 50-year period. With the Pueblo Rebellion of 1680 the Tewa and other refugees fled to the Hopi country, some remaining to become the Hopi Tewa of First Mesa, recently studied in detail by Edward Dozier (1954).

During this long period the Hopi never created a political community, nor developed the use of force to any great extent. Rather they relied on dispersal of their villages, constructed in part for defense, and on a reputation for superior supernatural assistance to ward off their enemies. Within their small communities they developed an elaborate socio-ceremonial structure tied to the clan system, on the one hand, and to the control of the most valuable agricultural land. The Hopi way, embodied in tradition, was maintained by an elaborate system of training and indoctrination, culminating in important initiation rituals; and by the diffuse sanctions of public opinion. Crises involving the possibilities of major change were handled through the development of factions which might lead to village splitting and new village units.

The Hopi model for their society centers around a traditional "mother" village, a "colony" village, and a "guard" or protector village, and this pattern is repeated in smaller compass on both First and Second Mesas. On Third Mesa, Oraibi stood in apparent exception. But Oraibi had reached unmanageable size in the late 19th century and had already established a colony at Moencopi. Titiev (1944) has excellently described the process of splitting which led to the establishment of Hotevilla in 1906, and later to other villages. But under less acculturative pressures Hotevilla might well have conformed more closely to the Hopi model as a "guard" village--the population which seceded from Oraibi was largely composed of traditionalists who wished to maintain the Hopi system and were willing to resist the American government to achieve that end.

Within Hopi society there is a strong tendency to village endogamy, so far as the major villages are concerned. Intermarriage between mesas has played a relatively minor role in Hopi socio-cultural integration, so far as our evidence goes. Within each mesa there is more intermarriage, particularly with the colony villages. On First Mesa there are now no pure blooded Tewas, though the Hopi-Tewa have retained their social identity and language through a strict observance of matrilocal residence, as Dozier has indicated.

Within the village marriage plays a more significant role. In Hopi theory each major village is composed of matrilineal clans whose position in the village is determined by the order of arrival and the ceremonial possessions which they brought with them. Each major clan has a named clan house, usually on the plaza or in a central location, in which its ceremonial possessions are kept. Associated with the clan house are the clan lands traditionally assigned to the clan, from which it gets its major support.

At the head of the prestige hierarchy is the Bear Clan, the members of which arrived first in the Hopi region and made a compact with Masau'u, the god of life and death, in which he gave the Hopi agricultural land and crops in exchange for the carrying out of the proper rituals. Later comers received portions of this estate in exchange for the performance of the ceremonies they brought for the production of rain. The last groups often possessed no rituals and offered their services as guards. Their position was marginal and often they were not assigned clan lands.

Here is a structural situation in which prescriptive marriage patterns might well be utilized to stabilize and maintain the clan prestige hierarchy. In the Shoshonean region to the north there is evidence for a variety of preferential marriage practices, including sister-exchange and various forms of cross-cousin marriage; and Titiev (1938) has suggested that the behavioral patterns among the Hopi between a man and the women of the father's matrilineal clan may be related to an earlier pattern of cross-cousin marriage. Yet, as we have noted, there is no apparent regulation of marriage beyond clan and phratry exogamy.

Though the Hopi phrase their social structure in terms of clans, we can see it in operation more clearly at the household and lineage level. Within a village the average population for a clan is around 30-40 persons, though the range may be from one to over 100 persons. Such a group is often divided into one or more lineages, and where large, a lineage may be further divided into segments. One lineage or lineage segment is the "prime" lineage (following John Connelly's terminology) and occupies the clan house. Closely related lineage segments occupy "supporting" and "reserve" households, aiding the prime lineage in carrying out its duties and being supported from its resources in land. At this level the threat of lineage extinction through the lack of childbearing females is relatively frequent and supporting lineages of groups so afflicted move into the clan house and take over its ceremonial and other activities.

More distant lineages, even of the same clan, have a marginal position and in times of crisis are expendable. In case of drought all resources are concentrated for the preservation of the central clan core, and other clansmen are forced to migrate or starve. As conditions improve the clan may slowly grow in population through natural increase and from returning or other migrants.

The whole clan in a particular village occasionally becomes extinct through failure to produce childbearing women. In such cases a related clan from the same phratry may move into its clan house and position and gradually fill its place. When these possibilities are exhausted efforts will be made to re-seed the clan by securing a clanswoman from another village. In the last analysis any woman-- even a Navaho--can re-establish a clan household and maintain its activities in the absence of better claimants.

In Hopi theory a clan never "dies"--its members continue its activites in the underworld. But in practice there is fairly rapid change, even in the short period for which we have good records. The pre-eminent Bear Clan died out on First Mesa over a century ago, and attempts to re-seed the clan have so far failed. The Hopi do not employ genealogical controls to any great extent, which facilitates substitution and continuity at the expense of unilineal descent. But this is a fiction which is essential to maintain unilineal descent systems in small scale societies anywhere.

The Hopi household is composed conceptually of a line of women who look to their husbands for economic support and to their brothers for ritual support. Men circulate in Hopi society. They join their wives' households first as husbands and later as fathers. Here they have few rights and ideally play a passive role, giving advice if asked but not interfering in household-lineage matters. They retain their ties in their natal household, however, where they are responsible for discipline and the proper performance of ritual roles.

The tension between these contrasting roles is one of the reasons for a high divorce rate.

The roles within the household are mirrored in the larger society of the village. The village chief, interestingly, is a "father" rather than an "uncle"--he is ideally detached but sympathetic and deeply interested and concerned with the welfare of all his "children." The oldest woman of the clan is the clan "mother," and her brother normally is the male head of the clan. Correlatively, the oldest Bear clan woman is normally the village "mother."

Marriage establishes a number of important ties between the households and clans concerned. The first marriage, in particular, requires a considerable amount of reciprocal exchange of food and clothing between the households concerned since the marriage garments are essential for entrance to the afterworld. From the standpoint of the women of a household they lose economic services when a brother marries but they gain a "female relative-in-law," in the person of his wife, who is extremely important. "You have to earn your mïwi," Hopi women will say. They will assist one another on all the numerous occasions when corn meal has to be ground or piki made. And when children are born they are rivals for their affection.

A man married into a household brings economic support. He is called "male relative-in-law," to begin with, and assists in the cultivation of the fields belonging to his wife's lineage and household. Here he may cooperate with his wife's father to a greater extent than with his wife's brothers, particularly if they are married. His wife, in turn, is a "female relative-in-law" to his sister's household.

The household ties brought about by marriage are of more enduring importance to women. Women are responsible for the storage and preparation of food, and the houses belong to them. Without a household to support him, a man cannot carry out his ceremonial duties in Hopi society. The women of a given household lose brothers and gain husbands. They also gain "sisters-in-law" to aid them and they themselves become "sisters-in-law" to their brothers' wives' households. Any particular woman gains a husband and gives her periodic labor service in exchange. From the standpoint of the society the "sisters-in-law" circulate in the opposite direction from that of husbands, but the circuits are not fixed.

Men, on the other hand, leave a familiar household where they often have close ties with their mothers and sisters to enter an alien household where they are on trial--with only sexual privileges as compensation. In this situation separation is frequent and remarriage to another partner is easy. When children are born a man's status improves. While his child belongs to his wife's descent group, it is also a "child" of his clan and his clanswomen take a special interest in his son on all ritual occasions. He is a favorite partner for his "aunts" of equivalent age and his marriage elsewhere is greeted with strong expressions of jealousy.

A man married into a household and well established in their eyes is often permitted to assist in the rituals controlled by that household. On occasion he may even carry out major ceremonial duties, particularly if his son should be the designated heir but as yet too young. Such activities raise the status of his own clan and may facilitate the establishment of his sister's sons in more advantageous positions than they might normally be entitled to. Correlatively a "child" of a clan may be permitted to carry out ritual activities in the absence--or youth--of a clansman. Such privileges are expected to be transferred back to the controlling clan, and generally are, but occasionally the transfer is not carried out. In these and other ways changes in ceremonial alignment take place in the presence of the dogma of a traditionally established order.

The major interest of Hopi men is in the ceremonial system. A "ceremonial father" inducts a boy into the Katcina cult, and later into one of the four men's societies involved in Tribal Initiation ceremonies, as well as into any other ceremonies to which he happens to belong. Since the "ceremonial father" is normally not a relative the membership in these societies cuts across clan lines and represents a cross-section of the society. Since each ceremony is "owned" by a particular clan, which furnished the chief priest and maintains the ceremonial objects, and since various subordinate ceremonial roles are likewise owned, an individual's potential status is established more or less at birth. Marriage into key households and induction into the proper kiva ceremonial groups offer the major means of achieving a higher ceremonial position.

Competition between individuals for status positions is not supposed to occur, either within the household or in the ceremonial system. But competition between household groups and between kiva groups is rampant. Processions of women laden with trays piled high with cornmeal are currently increasing in some villages, leading to talk of a return to more standard exchanges. And kiva groups compete not only in putting on ceremonial events but in the unity of their thoughts and desires for rain and crops. There is a further competition between villages involving both ceremonial performance and hospitality.

In Hopi society the basic opposition is between men and women. The warp of Hopi society is made up of descent lines which are easily broken but which should be repaired at all costs. These descent lines are carried by women and have their locus in the clan households to which are attached land and sacred possessions. Men oscillate between these lines, cultivating their wives' fields and performing rituals for their sisters. But the major horizontal strands holding Hopi society together are made up of the ceremonial societies. These are principally male, though there are a few female society groups on similar patterns.

The Hopi model of their society is a simplified one. They recognize only clan groups terminologically, though they place them in nameless but exogamous phratries. They exercise little genealogical control over the clan, and the phratries are related only in terms of common traditional experiences in early times. But they implicitly recognize the different lineages and lineage segments within a named clan by their differential treatment of such groups. That they seek to restore a broken clan line, not by substituting a connection through males but by substituting a woman in the household, suggests that social realities are more important than genealogical purity, as well as that the Hopi model is more than a statistical resultant of individual choices.

Alliance as a basic principle is more difficult to evaluate. At the household and lineage segment level alliances are formed and maintained by the exchange of brothers for husbands and the exchange of female labor in connection with ritual events. These are balanced exchanges and of most significance to the women involved. From the standpoint of the households they are unstable alliances, subject to frequent change of marital partners. But on a larger scale the instability may be adaptive. Through establishing new marriage ties men may develop new opportunities for advancement in the social and ceremonial hierarchy. And there is growing evidence that this may be a directed rather than a random process in that desirable matches will be encouraged by the households concerned and undesirable ones discouraged.

We noted earlier that the Hopi never developed a political society, a point well made by Titiev. Instead the Hopis have developed a theocratic organization, based on a ritual hierarchy, that frequently has to struggle with political problems. These problems are generally dealt with in terms of *ad hoc* factions which explore the alternatives in terms of traditional teaching and the realities of the situation.

The task of the village chief and his advisors is to keep the factions within bounds. Here his basic control over land and the ceremonial system can be utilized to reward loyal supporters and to weaken dissidents. At Oraibi a weak Bear Clan was unable to control the factional pressures that developed where a greatly enlarged population on an inadequate land and water base was caught in new acculturative pressures. At Shongopovi the same factional situation was successfully handled by a strong Bear Clan. At such times major changes in the prestige hierarchy may take place in a relatively short period.

Alliances between clans are continually developing out of common ceremonial activities or in terms of control of kiva groups. Where there is a persuasive leader such alliances may form the basis for factions, and if continued over a long enough period are frequently strengthened by intermarriage. Conversely, spouses in different factions may be encouraged to separate. This is possibly the reason for the very high divorce rate Titiev found for Old Oraibi and the fact that when the split came households went or remained as units.

In Hopi society alliance through preferential marriage and exchange was not utilized to perpetuate the status hierarchy as formulated in Hopi theory. Rather marriage was utilized as a mechanism to take advantage of weaknesses in the system and to raise the ritual position of one's own household and clan. This might have dangerous consequences since such shifts often involved the manipulation of power to which one did not have the traditional right, and such power might punish as well as serve.

It may well be that survival in the Hopi situation required a more flexible system than one of "perpetual alliance." The relative lack of marriage between major villages which had a common clan-phratry grid and a common ceremonial system is further evidence that the alliance principle was subordinate to descent. Further, the kinship system offers little evidence of affinal extension. Only the individuals married into the lineage and clan were classed as affinals and they in turn used consanguineal terminology for their affines on the model of their spouse's usage--or employed teknonymy.

I think it is clear that while alliance theory may well have a wider relevance it is not an adequate substitute for descent theory in the case of the Hopi. On the other hand, the attempt to apply it to the Hopi situation has given additional insights into the different roles of men and women in Hopi society and a better understanding of the significance of marriage as a means to mobility in a theoretically rigid society.

Nor do I think the Hopi data support Leach's emphasis on locality rather than descent as the basis for corporate grouping, though land and water resources are certainly important to the Hopi. The aphorism, "marriage unifies; inheritance separates; property endures," tells us little about the Hopi system. Economic activities may well be "prior" to kinship relations, but the statement that the kinship systems have no reality except in relation to land and property does not make sense in terms of their universality.

The Hopi model for their society differs in important respects from that of the western Shoshoni but there are also certain ways in which they are similar. Both were geared to survival in an uncertain environment and to achieve that end they were prepared to save the core groups at the expense of marginal ones. With a more concentrated water supply and the presence of maize agriculture, the Hopi were able to greatly expand their population and to organize it in terms of corporate descent groups. In this process marriage shifted from its preferential character to a regulation by clan and phratry exogamy, but its significance for alliance is still apparent though not formally organized. The task of tracing this development through the archaeological and ethnographic record is well underway, but it is possible only because of the foundations established by Julian Steward.

BIBLIOGRAPHY

Connelly, John
   1956   "Clan-Lineage Relations in a Pueblo Village Phratry." Unpublished M.A. thesis, University of Chicago.

Dozier, Edward
   1954   "The Hopi-Tewa of Arizona," *University of California Publications in American Archaeology and Ethnology* 44:259-376. Berkeley and Los Angeles.

Eggan, Fred
   1950   *Social Organization of the Western Pueblos*. Chicago: University of Chicago Press.

Leach, Edmund
   1961   *Pul Eliya, a Village in Ceylon: A Study in Land Tenure and Kinship*. New York: Cambridge University Press.

Lévi-Strauss, Claude
   1949   *Les Structures élémentaires de la parenté*. Paris: Presses Universitaires.

Radcliffe-Brown, A. R.
   1931   "The Social Organization of Australian Tribes," *Oceania Monographs*, No. 1. London: Macmillan and Co.

   1950   "Introduction" to *African Systems of Kinship and Marriage*, A. R. Radcliffe-Brown and Daryll Forde (eds.), London: Oxford University Press.

Steward, Julian H.
 1937 "Ecological Aspects of Southwestern Society," *Anthropos* 32: 87-104.

 1938 *Basin-Plateau Aboriginal Sociopolitical Groups.* *Bureau of American Ethnology.* *Bulletin 120:* Washington, D.C.: Smithsonian Institution.

Titiev, Mischa
 1938 "The Problem of Cross-Cousin Marriage among the Hopi," *American Anthropologist* 40:105-11.

 1944 *Old Oraibi.* *Papers of the Peabody Museum of American Archaeology and Ethnology* 22:1. Cambridge.

14

LEWIS H. MORGAN AND THE FUTURE OF THE AMERICAN INDIAN*

1965

I

Lewis H. Morgan was one of the nineteenth century's foremost social
scientists. He has been credited with creating the science of anthropology, and was a major exponent of social evolution on a world-wide
scale. Scholars as diverse as Charles Darwin, Francis Parkman, Henry
Adams, and Karl Marx have praised his work, and in his later years
he received most of the honors that American science could bestow:
membership in the American Academy of Arts and Sciences, election to
the National Academy of Sciences, and president of the American Association for the Advancement of Science. For some reason, Morgan was
never honored with membership in the American Philosphical Society,
perhaps because his "reference group" was Boston and Cambridge, or
possibly because of his espousal of social evolution.

Morgan holds an important position in intellectual history
as the first American social scientist who could hold his own with
European scholars. As Carl Resek says in his recent biography, *Lewis
Henry Morgan: American Scholar*, "no other American in his own time
or since has looked on human society in quite the manner that Morgan
did, and few have wandered down the paths of scholarship that he
charted."[1] But in the controversies over social and cultural evolution around the turn of the century, Morgan's ideas were largely dis-
credited and the anthropological baby was thrown out with the evolutionary bathwater. In recent decades there has been a revival of

*This paper is adapted from one of a series of lectures given
at the University of Rochester in the spring of 1964 under the general title of "Lewis H. Morgan and the American Indian." I am indebted to the University of Rochester for appointing me Morgan Lec-
turer for that year, and for arranging for the publication of the
lectures in the near future.

Reproduced by permission of the American Philosophical Society
from the *Proceedings of the American Philosophical Society*, Vol. 109,
No. 5, pp. 272-276.

interest in Morgan's conceptions of evolution, largely as a result of the efforts of Leslie A. White.

Today I want to speak of Morgan, not as a social evolutionist, but as a pioneer student of the American Indian. The roots of modern anthropology are both broader and deeper than Morgan, but we shall see that his contributions were both important and useful. He was the founder of the scientific study of kinship, which is basic to modern social anthropology. His objective methods for the collection and comparison of kinship terminologies, the results of which were published in *Systems of Consanguinity and Affinity of the Human Family*,[2] are still valid. He prepared the first modern ethnographic account of an Indian tribe--the famous *League of the Iroquois*[3]--in which he attempted to describe Indian life in its own terms and not in terms of our Western culture. He was the first anthropologist to organize systematic field research to solve definite scientific problems. And he had important ideas on the problems faced by the American Indians and how they might be solved. We shall find him a better prophet than many of his contemporaries.

II

Lewis H. Morgan became an ethnologist almost by accident. He was born in 1818 in the old Iroquois territory of the "finger lakes," and his early interest in Indians was a romantic one. But a chance encounter with a young Seneca, Ely S. Parker, in an Albany bookstore gave him an entrée to Iroquois life and traditional history. The Iroquois in the 1840's in New York State were restricted to a few small reservations, which they were attempting to hold against the encroachments of the Ogden Land Company and other speculators. Ely S. Parker had been selected by the chiefs to go to school and become familiar with the ways of the white world so that he could help them protect their lands. He later had a distinguished career as aide-de-camp to General Grant, and also served as Commissioner of Indian Affairs for a brief period.

Morgan's initial interest in the Iroquois lay in developing a constitution for a new secret society (The Grand Order of the Iroquois) which was to be modeled after the Iroquois Confederation, but he soon became interested in the nature of Iroquois society, and in helping the Indians in the immediate problems they faced. With Parker's assistance, and utilizing his own legal training, he began to investigate systematically the nature of Iroquois society. His aid in the struggle against the Ogden Land Company resulted in his adoption by the Senecas, which further facilitated his studies. When

the *League of the Iroquois* was published in 1851, it presented the
first detailed account of a matrilineal descent system, as well as
of the operations of the confederacy. The Iroquois were divided into
clans based on descent through women, and each clan section lived together in a longhouse, the husbands moving in with their wives at
marriage. The women selected the chiefs from among their brothers
or mother's brothers, and the inheritance of property and position
was in the female line. The League or Confederacy was made up of
chiefs appointed from each tribe and met periodically to discuss the
affairs of the whole Iroquois nation.

But Morgan's pioneer study did much more. Along with an account of the old Iroquois ceremonies, it included a chapter on the
"new religion" of Handsome Lake, a Seneca sachem, who around the
year 1800 received a revelation from the Great Spirit which remodeled the ancient faith by incorporating new doctrines. Today the
Handsome Lake code is the "old religion" and we recognize it as an
example of "revitalization" movements which are instrumental in maintaining a society under stress. For those who violated the rules
there was a House of Torment, but for those who followed the injunc-
tions against drunkenness and other evils the Great Spirit provided
a heaven from which all whites were excluded. There was one exception: George Washington, "Destroyer of Villages," was allowed to
dwell just outside the gates. Handsome Lake was told:

> The man you see is the only pale-face who ever left the earth.
> He was kind to you, when in the settlement of the great difficul-
> ty between the Americans and the Great Crown, you were abandoned
> to the mercy of your enemies. . . . For this reason, he has been
> allowed to leave the earth. But he is never permitted to go
> into the presence of the Great Spirit.[4]

Here we can see some of the processes of cultural adjustment at work.

Morgan's interest in the American Indian was greatly enhanced
a few years later by his discovery that the Ojibwa Indians of Michigan, who spoke a different language, had the same pattern of grouping
relatives that he had earlier found among the Iroquois. He had become interested in the history of the American Indians and he saw
that their kinship systems might show evidence of their unity as a
group, and their ultimate derivation from Asia. The patterns of
grouping relatives, he thought, were highly stable and would persist
beyond the changes in language which obscured their genetic relationships.

With this hypothesis he set out to collect kinship terminologies from missionaries, traders, and Indian agents. The results not
being too satisfactory, he undertook four field trips up the Missouri
River in the summers of 1859-1862, visiting the newly established

reservations and mission stations in Kansas and Nebraska Territory and the upper Missouri region, all the way to the foot of the Rockies. Morgan's Journals of these expeditions have recently been published[5] and give a fascinating account of the frontier during this period. Here he collected comparative material on some nineteen Indian tribes. The kinship systems of all of these tribes belonged to what he called the "classificatory" system, in which the term for "father" was extended to his brothers, and the term for "mother" was extended to her sisters, in contrast to our own "descriptive" system. This "classificatory" system became the model for the American Indian, and when, later, a missionary reported a system which was almost identical to that of the Iroquois from the Tamils of Southern India, Morgan felt his hypothesis had been demonstrated. Columbus was right after all, he observed.

If Morgan had been able to visit the Indians beyond the Rockies, he would have been forced to modify his hypothesis, since he would have found a great variety of kinship systems which were quite different from those east of the Rocky Mountains. His hypothesis as to the origins of the American Indians in Asia was correct, but for the wrong reasons. Later research has shown that kinship systems are not stable over vast periods of time but are remarkably sensitive to changing conditions. Here Morgan's data are invaluable as a baseline from which to measure changes.

While Morgan was confirming, as he thought, his historical hypothesis, he received some kinship terminologies from Hawaii which startled and puzzled him. For these were far more "classificatory" than any of the American Indian systems, in that the terms for "father" and "mother" were extended to all relatives in their generation, and similarly for relatives in other generations. Accepting a suggestion from the Rev. Joshua McIlvaine that this might be the result of a system of primitive promiscuity,[6] for which there were some hints in classical writings, Morgan became a social evolutionist and went on to write *Ancient Society*,[7] which established his popular fame. The coincidence of certain of Morgan's ideas about the importance of property, derived from some ten years of litigation over land claims in Upper Michigan, with those of Marx and Engels, led to *Ancient Society's* becoming a socialist classic and a model for modern Soviet thinking on social evolution.

III

Morgan was vitally interested in the future of the American Indian, and--unlike many of his contemporaries--he believed the Indian had a future. Through his association with the Iroquois, he was one of the first scholars to see the problems of the Indians from their point of view, and to discuss the alternatives to extinction. During Morgan's lifetime tremendous changes took place as the frontier moved westward and reached the Pacific, and at the time of his death, in 1881, the Indian question seemed farther from solution than ever.

In his early work with the Iroquois he expressed the view that their only hope was in becoming agricultural and civilized, and ultimately citizens with the same privileges and obligations as whites. These objectives, he believed, could only be obtained through education and Christianity, and he saw the mission boarding school as the best instrument for this purpose. He advocated a system of public education for the Indians: "It is time," he said (in 1851), "that our Indian youth were regarded, in all respects, as a part of the children of the State, and brought under such a system of tutelage as that relation would impose."[8]

But when Morgan visited the Missouri region he found that the transition to civilization was a more difficult one than he had thought. He saw the venality of Indian agents at first hand, and he lost some of his faith in mission establishments as agents of civilization and education. With the transfer of the Indians from the War Department to the Department of Interior, the new Indian agents were political appointees rather than army officers, and soon made "Indian affairs" synonymous with graft and corruption. And while some mission schools excited his admiration, others seemed more interested in the annual government subsidy of $75 per child for board, room, and schooling.

On the frontier he also saw the problem of race mixture in new perspective. Some of the most intelligent Indians he met were of mixed blood and he notes in his Journal:

> I think an amalgamation with the Indians by the white race . . . is destined to take place, and that Kansas will be the theater of the first honest and regular experiment.[9]

He thought the whites would be toughened physically and benefited mentally, but the Kansas settlers did not wait to find out, but brought about a further removal of the Indians to Indian Territory as soon as possible.

As a result of his conversation with various Indian leaders, Morgan believed that the time was at hand to reverse the government policy toward the Indians:

> A convention of the most sensible men of the several nations has been proposed, [he wrote in 1859] and within a year or two we may witness such a convention. Great results would flow from it. Our people would be astonished at the amount of ability and

experience and wisdom these nations, broken and scattered as they are, could assemble. . . . Such a convention would be a new and great event in the history of the Indian.10

But such a convention had to wait almost exactly a hundred years.

Morgan's experiences on the frontier convinced him of the necessity for a different policy towards the Indians and he hoped that he might be appointed Commissioner of Indian Affairs. He was very likely the best qualified candidate in the country, but Lincoln's campaign manager had promised the position to an Indiana politician. When Grant was elected president, hope flared anew, but again he lost out. President Grant, however, did appoint his former aid and Morgan's protégé, Ely S. Parker, and Morgan had high expectations. But the scandals and corruption of the Grant regime forced Parker to resign, though he was personally blameless.

Morgan defended the Sioux Indians, after the defeat of General Custer, pointing out that Custer had experienced the precise fate that he had intended for the Indians. He also called attention to the continued absence of any systematic program for the administration of Indian affairs, and urged a separate department, with cabinet rank, to be put in the hands of some outstanding man. He had earlier suggested the creation of separate Indian territories, one for the eastern tribes and one for the Plains Indians, and he now returned to these proposals and suggested a "factory" system for the reservations and a "pastoral" system for the still wild tribes. The "factory" system was for more advanced tribes, and Morgan described an experiment among the Ojibwa near Sault Sainte Marie where a missionary had organized groups of Indians to make articles for the tourist trade, with great success. The Plains Indians could be taught to raise herds of cattle as a substitute for the recently vanished buffalo.[11] His new evolutionary theories were invoked to explain the failure of the Indians to progress more rapidly:

We wonder that our Indians cannot civilize, but how could they, any more than our own remote barbarous ancestors, jump ethnical periods? They have the skulls of barbarians and must grow toward civilization as all mankind has done who attained to it by progressive development.[12]

But in Mexico and Central America, and in the Andes, as well, civilization had been achieved by Indians related to those we have surveyed, and not different in race from Morgan's Iroquois. And Morgan's own observations on the Indian frontier challenged his new theories. In his final discussion of the "Indian Question" he came closer to the truth. In pointing out the failure of the governmental policy with regard to the 400,000 Indians still remaining in the United States in 1878, he laid down some guide lines for the future:

They and their posterity will live in our midst for centuries
to come, because Indian arts for the maintenance of life are far
more persistent and effective than we are disposed to credit.
The Indian tribes hold a more important position in relation to
us than their numbers would imply. It is for this reason that
they form no part of our social and political system, are not a
part of our people, and stand without the pale of the Government.
But as the aborigines of the country and its ancient proprietors,
they stand to us in a special relation. . . . We are responsible
for them before mankind if we do not perform our duty towards
them intelligently and as it becomes the superior race.[13]

IV

If Morgan could return today he would find the Indian problem still
with us and the attempted solutions not too different from his own
suggestions. There are now over 500,000 Indians in the United States,
and within their lifetime governmental policy has shifted from autoc-
racy to welfare; to John Collier's "new deal"; to the post-war policy
of termination of federal controls; and to the present emphasis on
the economic development of reservation resources. The current objectives are (1) maximum Indian economic self-sufficiency, (2) full
participation of Indians in American life, and (3) equal citizenship
privileges and responsibilities.[14]

But when the American Indian conference that Morgan had envisaged was finally convened in Chicago in June, 1961, their leaders
asked for the return of Indian lands and the protection of Indian
rights and privileges against the encroachments of both state and
federal governments. To quote from their "Declaration of Indian Purpose":

. . . In our day, each remaining acre is a promise that we
will still be here tomorrow. Were we paid a thousand times the
market value of our lost holdings, still the payment would not
suffice. Money never mothered the Indian people, as the land
has mothered them, nor have any people become more closely attached to the land, religiously and traditionally.[15]

Above all they asked for understanding in their struggle to hold to
identity and survival--"to regain in the America of the space age
some measure of the adjustment they enjoyed as the original posses-
sors of their native land."[16]

We noted above that Morgan attempted to view the Iroquois in
their own terms. As he looked at the Indian world he saw it from
the standpoint of the Iroquois. Thus he belabored William H. Prescott and Hubert H. Bancroft for accepting the views of the Spanish
chroniclers as to the "empire" of Montezuma--the Aztecs were, after
all, merely the Iroquois confederation writ large. But his interest
in "Ancient Society" gave him a new vision of the world:

Democracy in government, brotherhood in society, equality in rights and privileges, and universal education, foreshadow the next higher plane of society to which experience, intelligence and knowledge are steadily tending. It will be a revival, in a higher form, of the liberty, equality and fraternity of the ancient gentes.[17]

Read either in evolutionary terms, or in terms of mankind's struggle to achieve a satisfying life, it is a vision which has significance for the modern world. Morgan's Iroquois had it in one form and we are currently trying to attain it, not only for ourselves, but for all races and peoples.

NOTES

[1]C. Resek, *Lewis Henry Morgan: American Scholar* (Chicago, 1960), p. vii.

[2]*Smithsonian Contributions to Knowledge* 17 (Washington, D.C., 1871).

[3]*League of the Ho-de-no-sau-nee, or Iroquois* (Rochester, Sage & Brothers, 1851).

[4]*Ibid.*, p. 257. Washington's title, "Destroyer of Villages," is the name given to all presidents of the United States.

[5]*Lewis Henry Morgan: The Indian Journals, 1859-62*. Edited and with an introduction by Leslie A. White (Ann Arbor, University of Michigan Press, 1959).

[6]Resek, *Lewis Henry Morgan: American Scholar*, pp. 93-98.

[7]*Ancient Society, or Researches in the Lines of Human Progress from Savagery through Barbarism to Civilization* (New York, Henry Holt and Co., 1877).

[8]Morgan, *League of the Iroquois*, p. 453.

[9]Morgan, *Indian Journals*, p. 42.

[10]*Ibid.*, pp. 38, 39.

[11]Morgan, "The Hue and Cry against the Indians," *Nation*, 23 (July, 1876): pp. 40-41; "Factory Systems for Indian Reservations," *ibid.*, pp. 58-59.

[12]Morgan, "The Indian Question," *Nation* 27 (November, 1878): p. 332.

[13]*Ibid.*, p. 332.

[14]*Report to the Secretary of the Interior by the Task Force on Indian Affairs* (mimeographed, Washington, D.C., July 10, 1961), p. 8.

[15]*Declaration of Indian Purpose*. Proceedings of the American Indian Chicago Conference (Chicago, 1961), p. 16.

[16]*Ibid.*, p. 20.

[17]Morgan, *Ancient Society*, pp. 561-562.

FROM HISTORY TO MYTH: A HOPI EXAMPLE

1967

The relation between tradition and history has been the subject of endless controversy, not only in anthropology but in related disciplines as well. There has been much uncritical use of myth as history, but we are no longer as intransigent as Robert H. Lowie, who, almost a half century ago, stated categorically: "I cannot attach to oral traditions any historical value whatsoever under any conditions whatsoever" (Lowie, 1915, 598). Lowie's dictum was directed in part against Roland B. Dixon and John R. Swanton, whose "Primitive American History" (1914) utilized tradition, along with linguistic and documentary evidence, to reconstruct some aspects of American Indian history in a manner which today seems quite conservative.

Both Dixon and Swanton replied immediately (1915, 599-600), and a lively discussion ensued which led Lowie to return to the problem in his presidential address to the American Folk-Lore Society the following year. In his earlier paper he had stated: "We are not concerned with the abstract possibility of tradition preserving a knowledge of events; we want to know what historical conclusions may safely be drawn from given oral traditions in ethnological practice" (1915, 598). In his restatement of the problem he reiterates that he is not denying to oral traditions any value whatsoever, but he finds this value to be psychological and cultural rather than historical. For Lowie, the general conclusion is obvious: "Indian tradition is historically worthless, because the occurrences, possibly real, which it retains, are of no historical significance; and because it fails to record, or to record accurately, the most momentous happenings" (Lowie, 1917, 165).

Lowie is here arguing that Indian traditionalists are not

Reproduced by permission of Mouton & Co., The Hague, from *Studies in Southwestern Ethnolinguistics*, Dell Hymes and William E. Bittle, editors (1967), pp. 33-53.

scientific historians and have little historical sense. From this point of view, "The question whether they retain the memory of actual events, while interesting in itself, is of no moment for our present problem. The point is, not whether they recollect happenings, but whether they recollect the happenings that are historically significant" (Lowie, 1917, 167). Such claims, Lowie believed, must be established empirically and he found his own experience to be totally opposed. "Our historical problems", he concludes, "can only be solved by the objective methods of comparative ethnology, archaeology, linguistics, and physical anthropology" (1917, 167).

It is with the question of the extent to which the memory of actual events is retained in oral tradition that the present paper is primarily concerned. Today we are more willing than Lowie was in 1917 to settle for the "actual events"--if we can find some way of identifying them in the matrix of tradition and myth. We are also concerned with aboriginal theories of the universe and world view, not as garbled history but as philosophical constructions in their own right. Since Malinowski, we are familiar with the conception of myth as a charter for human institutions, and modern social anthropologists have documented the adjustment of myth and genealogy to existing social reality. But those who work with myth and tradition have continued to be intrigued by the possibilities of extracting genuine historical data from the "hodge podge of aboriginal lore."

From the standpoint of a general theory of the role of communication in society, the controversy has to do with the nature of the relationship between certain functions of language and certain modes of its use. In particular, to what extent and in what way is the "time binding" role of language constrained by dependence on a certain channel (oral) and a certain genre (myth)? Put somewhat more generally, what are the sociocultural conditions under which particular degrees and kinds of transmission through language will occur?

The Pueblo Southwest at first glance seems a prime area for the documentation of Lowie's extreme position. In the two decades before the turn of the century, large amounts of traditional materials had been gathered on Zuni and Hopi by such pioneers as Cushing and Stephen, and these data formed the basis for elaborate reconstructions of Pueblo society and its development. For the Hopi, these reconstructions were largely the work of J. Walter Fewkes, who took the clan legends as history and in "Tusayan Migration Traditions" (1901) and other works proceeded to account for Hopi society by the coming together of different clans from different directions. These attempts ultimately foundered, as I have shown elsewhere (Eggan, 1950), both because accounts from different villages were contradictory and because Fewkes did not understand the nature of a clan system. And at Zuni, A. L. Kroeber (1917) had been unable to find more than traces of the mytho-social organization that Cushing (1896) had recorded in the 1880's and he interpreted the directional phratry grouping given by Cushing as merely the reflection of the existing distribution of clan groups in the town. Hence, when Ruth Benedict presented her important study of "Zuni Mythology" (1935) she emphasized the psychological and cultural characteristics of myth and tradition rather than their historical aspects.

But the time now seems appropriate for a renewed attack upon the historical problem: how can we identify the actual events in myth and tradition and what historical conclusions may safely be drawn from given oral traditions? We have more data and better historical controls than were available to Lowie in 1915, and we should be more sophisticated in our handling of social and cultural data. What we would like to know, to begin with, is what a particular group does with significant events in terms of its cultural values, social structure, and world view. If we can discover this we may have a means of segregating history from myth.[1]

One approach to this problem is through a study of the process of myth-making. The Hopi Indians are still creating myths, and for some examples we are fortunate in having independent historical controls. The case we will present involves a group of Hopi Indians from First Mesa who went to Fort Defiance, Arizona, around the middle of the nineteenth century, to visit the new Indian Agency set up in the center of the Navaho country. They traveled under the leadership of the Walpi chief, and on their return they were attacked by the Navaho and several were killed.

We have two versions of these events, recorded some forty years later, by A. M. Stephen and published in his *Hopi Journal* (1936). One of these is a summary account and one is from a participant in the events. We also have a third version of these events, in semi-myth form, recorded by a Hopi Indian from a Second Mesa village and published in 1936. We can further date the time of the events by independent documentary sources as occurring between 1853-1856, a period just after the United States had secured possession of the territory of New Mexico.

Stephen's first version is presented under the date November 22, 1892, and is as follows:

Sometime before the Civil War a party of ten Hopi'tü went to

Fort Defiance to receive certain goods from the agent, of which prints seem to have been the most valuable. The ten were Ha'ni, Djasjini, To'chi, Taba'ko, Wiki (not the same Wiki, i.e. chief of the Antelope society), Masha'li (who was Antelope chief and also Town chief), Tavwu'pu, Lemo'a (a Navajo, but who had been given to the Walpi during a famine when he was a boy), Ma'kani, and the uncle of Hi'li. Returning with their gifts, they camped a few miles west from Pueblo Colorado and just before dawn were attacked by a band of Navajo, two or three of whom had firearms, and four of the Hopi were killed, viz., Wiki, Masha'li, Tavwu'pu and Lemo'a.

Ha'ni was badly wounded with arrows, but recovered. Djasjini lay close to the ground and, holding a saddle over his head, heard bullets and arrows pelting against it. A bullet cut his leg. To'chi ran for the villages and reached Sun spring at sunrise. He yelled as he approached and the people ran down to the spring, and there he told them of the disaster. The rest of the party reached the mesa late in the second day. The women sat in groups wailing on the house tops. Men sat huddled in their blankets, and no food was prepared or eaten. At that period neither women nor children ever went to the springs for water for fear of being killed or captured by the Navajo.

After this disaster a large band of Hopi went on a foray to the north and killed many Navajo and drove home a lot of sheep. (Stephen, 1936, 1002)

A. M. Stephen already knew Navaho when he began his studies of the Hopi Indians of First Mesa in 1882 and had unusual opportunities for observation, as his *Hopi Journal* attests. The brief account given above is interspersed between unrelated current happenings and is probably a summary of informal discussions. The Wuwutcim ceremony had just ended the previous week and this was a likely time for the retelling of difficulties with the Navaho. The four men's societies which cooperate in Wuwutcim were primarily responsible, along with the war society, for the protection of the villages, and it is possible that this account was related by Hani, who was in charge of Wuwutcim as chief of the Singer's society in 1892.

Relations between the Navaho and Hopi had long alternated between friendly trading and hostile raiding. But in the period following Mexican independence in 1821, the northern territories were left to shift for themselves, and Navaho raiding, both on the Rio Grande settlements of New Mexico and on the Pueblos, was intensified. During this period the Hopi were often engaged in defensive warfare or in retaliatory raids. With the advent of U.S. control, following the Treaty of Guadelupe-Hidalgo in 1848, the first task was to restrain the Navaho, and Fort Defiance was established in 1852 in the heart of their territory.

Some three weeks later Stephen recorded a longer version of these events from a participant, Djasjini, a Tewa from the adjoining village of Hano who was married into a chiefly family in Walpi. Under date of December 11, 1892, Stephen writes as follows:

Old Djasjini says this is good to his bowels to see me living
here in a chief's house. This is the good house of the old, not
the worthless innovations of dwellings such as in Sichomovi and
Tewa. Now I will receive the good influences, etc., etc.

When he was a boy the Navajo used to be very friendly. They
lived all round on the mesas and came to the villages, lots of
them, every day. They had not many horses then, nor had the
Hopi, and the Navajo used to bring wood to the villages on their
backs and carry up water from the springs to the houses, for
corn.

"I was fleet of foot then and was always going and, being so
much among the Navajo, I acquired their tongue. That is why I
can speak their tongue so well. I am getting very old now, my
ears are bad, and my teeth can no longer cut. How old am I?
Fifty, maybe a hundred years, I can not tell. When I was a boy
of so big (eight or ten years) there was a great comet in the
sky and at nights all the above was full of shooting stars--ah!
that was a very long time ago, maybe a hundred years, maybe more.

I remember very well when the Mexicans owned the River country. I had long been a full grown man before I saw an American.
The first Americans we ever saw did not come from the American
country (east), but from California, and they had many spying
instruments. (Ives' party.)

We knew that there were American soldiers at Fort Defiance,
and this party of Americans was trying to get there, and I went
with them to show them the way. We reached there in six days.
There were many soldiers there and much stores, but the chief
of the party I had guided said he could not get any of these for
me, but gave me a paper for forty dollars and said if I would
take that to Alavi'a (Santa Fé) I would get much silver money
and other American valuables. But the Navajo in that region were
bad and I knew better than to attempt to get there and back.
They gave me a great deal of bread and other things, and I set
out for home, arriving here with my load on the third day.

Many years after that the Navajo were foolish and fought
everybody, and a great host of American soldiers came to this
region. They were mounted and could not find sufficient water
at any suitable place for a camp. They had a Navajo with them
who spoke Spanish and the chief, communicating through him, inquired of us (Walpi) where was there any good camping place. I
took them to Boñsikya. At that time the Cañon was full of different kinds of trees, around the springs and water courses were
dense jungles of willows, wild olive, and rushes, and in the open
glade the grass was over knee high.

I led them over the mesa and across Tyelshsakad, and thence
down the bad trail where Eïpañï used to have his corn field
(about three quarters of a mile below the school) and in going
down one of their mules fell over the cliff and went bumping
from ledge to ledge to the bottom and lay there dead, and all the
the soldiers instead of sorrowing threw back their heads and
roared with laughter. They camped there, and when they were in
column they reached up to the springs where the school now is,
and their tents were in line for that distance. (This was Kit
Carson and the New Mexican volunteers in 1863).

One of the soldier chiefs wished to carry a paper to Fort
Defiance and he took a small party of soldiers, and I went with
them up the Cañon to show them the trail. This was in the evening and I camped with them near the little spring (opposite my

old house), and on the following morning before it was daylight down came great boulders, tree trunks and limbs, right in among us, and behold! there was a crowd of Navajo up on the edge of the Cañon pelting us with stones, while others continued to roll down boulders. The soldiers instantly began firing their guns at them, and for a truth that was a disagreeable spot, and I got away from it as soon as possible. I came back to where the main body of the soldiers were camped, and the chief gave me a bag of flour and a live sheep. Not such little flour bags as we see now, but a great one that I could scarcely lift, and I was sorely puzzled how to convey the flour and sheep home, so I camped with them till the next day when two Walpi chanced to come over with a burro.

Not long after this ten of us went to Fort Defiance, we heard of such a multitude of soldiers being there that we were fain to see. We had no other reason for going. (See p. 1002.)

Masha'lĭ was a good man. He was a chief, a great and good chief. He was uncle of Sa'miwi'ki.

The tents of the soldiers were stretched in two lines extending from Black Rock to the fort, and the wagon road passed between the line, for truth there was an immense number of soldiers. The chief told us that many of the soldiers were foolish and might harm us if we went near them after dark, so when one of them sounded a metal horn we were put in a room in the fort and the door was locked. But in the day time we were allowed to roam about anywhere, and we gathered up more shirts, breeches, and old shoes than we could carry, and the soldiers gave us knives and metal; our possessions were in great high heaps.

We had been there two or three days when some Navajo came quite close to the fort and we heard shouting between them and the soldiers, so we thought it is bad for us to be here and we have an ill road (a bad prospect) for our homeward journey, but we said, "Let us go!" We had three burros and these as well as ourselves were loaded down with clothing, flour, and other good things the soldiers gave us. We could only travel slowly and the first night we camped on the mountain among some hogans the soldiers had burned, but one of them was still habitable and we slept in it. The next night we slept at the little spring at the foothills east from Wuko ba'kabĭ, great reeds (Ganado). On the third evening we reached the foot of Red hill (about twelve miles west from Ganado) and as it was getting dark we came upon some corn fields in which some stalks were still standing here and there. There was a brush fence surrounding the fields, and Masha'lĭ said we may as well camp here. We saw a fire up on the foothill and two went to get a brand so that we might have a camp fire. When they returned they told us that the Navajo at whose fire they had been had told them there were four desperate bad Navajo camped up on the mesa and each of them had a band with him, and this man suggested that we should come to his hogan and sleep. But Masha'lĭ said, "It may be a ruse to trap us. We are just as well here." So we made a fire near the fence and lay down around it, our feet to the fire. In the early morning before day light the Navajo in great numbers came down upon us and we were awakened by showers of arrows and bullets. The four mentioned on p. 1002 were killed. Lesma (Ha'ni) was stuck full of arrows; a bullet went through my thigh, here, and another one through the edge of my hand, here. I set up the pack saddle and some things before my head, and how the bullets pattered upon my shelter! We couldn't lie there to let them kill all of us, so we got up and ran. It was dark, no moon, and we knew not where we ran, but we kept together , all except To'chi who wasn't hit.

We ran in a devious round about and helped along Lesma, sometimes carrying him, but we were all more or less wounded. To'chi ran to the villages, and we got in on the second day late in the afternoon. The Navajo got our burros and all the wealth the Americans had given us, and they killed our chief. We sent couriers with this intelligence to the Ko'honino, to the tribes dwelling beyond San Francisco Mountains, to the Apache, the Zuñi, the Ute, to everybody living around the Navajo, telling of their evil deed to us. We helped the American soldiers and we waylaid the Navajo wherever we found them, and we killed many of them. The Navajo were fools then. They are fools very often. The Hopi does not like to quarrel. He likes to sit at peace with his mantle wrapped round him this way, but he can fight and kill, and he did."

Djasjini can form no intelligent conception of the time that has passed since these affrays, but his memory of the occurrences is as vivid as if they had occurred last week. He remembers the colours and peculiarities of the Americans' horses and can enumerate every trifling article they gave him and describe his journey with Ives and among the soldiers with very minute detail, but when you ask him when was all this, he says indifferently, a long time ago, maybe a hundred years, who knows, it is not well to count the years, it makes us old. (Stephen, 1936, 1016-1019)

This account is highly interesting, particularly as to Navaho-Hopi relationships and for the early contacts with Americans. Djasjini mentions no motivation for the trip beyond curiosity, but it is probable that the Hopi had learned that the new Indian Agent for the Navaho was also responsible for them and had goods to distribute.

In other entries in Stephen's *Hopi Journal* we learn that Dodge was agent during the regime of Mashali, and that he helped straighten out some land troubles at Sichomovi, a suburb of Walpi-- perhaps at a later time than the events we are concerned with. And in an entry under date of February 22, 1893, Stephen reports that "Hani and other elders in Chief kiva say that forty years ago, when Elichi (Dodge) was agent at Fort Defiance, the Hopi got their first wool or cotton cards" (Stephen, 1936, 1181).

We find a brief description of Captain Henry Dodge in Ruth Underhill's *The Navajo* (1956). Captain Dodge had participated in Colonel Washington's expedition against the Navaho in 1849, where he was in charge of Pueblo scouts. He was appointed agent to the Navaho in 1853, and Ruth Underhill describes him as follows:

Captain Henry Dodge, who wore a red shirt with his cavalry trousers, was a veteran of the Rocky Mountain expedition and of the Santa Fé Trail. He had commanded a company of volunteers on the ill-fated expedition when Narbona was killed. . . . Dodge liked Indians and really planned to do something for the Navajos besides treaties. (Underhill, 1956, 103-104)

One of his first projects was the distribution of gifts brought by ox team from Santa Fé. If he had lived, the Navaho might have fared better, but unfortunately for both the Navaho and the Hopi, he was killed by marauding Apaches in 1856 while out hunting.

These data help us to repair Djasjini's chronology--always a weak point in Pueblo accounts--and to fix the date of the events we are interested in as occurring between 1853-1856. The guidance of the Ives party (in 1858) to Fort Defiance and the events connected with Kit Carson's (1863-64) campaign against the Navaho are in proper chronological order, though the time between them is exaggerated, but Djasjini places the Hopi expedition *after* Kit Carson's campaign rather than a decade earlier, where it belongs.

Hopi accounts of observed events, as Stephen notes, are remarkably accurate and detailed. *Hopi returning from a journey were expected to give their kiva and village mates a minute account of everything seen and done* before going about other business. The practice is still followed in conservative villages.

Mashali, whom Djasjini refers to as a good man and a "great and good chief," was a member of the Dove clan of the Snake phratry grouping. As such he was not entitled to be village chief--that position belonged to the Bear clan. But the Bear clan proper had apparently died out some time before 1850 and the Snake clan had managed to take over the village chieftancy in this crisis. The Spider clan--in the same phratry group as Bear--moved into the Bear clan house and took over the ceremonies and masks belonging to the Bear clan, but were apparently too weak to maintain control of the village chieftancy. In Stephen's time this group had become known as "Bear", though Fewkes discovered that Kotka, the Bear clan chief, "really belongs to the Kokyan (Spider) clan of the Bear phratry" (1901, 604, fn. 2).

In Hopi thinking, Mashali was "on trial" since he was aspiring to handle ceremonial and other powers that he was not entitled to, and which might, if misused, turn on the possessor and his group. At First Mesa the Snake clans had come to control both the Antelope and the Snake societies and Mashali was Antelope chief as well as village chief. We have no information as to why he was selected, but the traditional position of the Snake clans as "warriors" may have been an important factor, along with their growing prestige. As a result, the Snake clans contested with the Bear clan for priority of traditional arrival at First Mesa, since ceremonial precedence is associated with order of arrival in Hopi thinking (cf. Fewkes, 1901, 585).

With Mashali's death at the hands of the Navaho it was evident that he had "failed"--his new powers not only had not warned and protected him, but also had allowed him and his companions to be killed or wounded. In this new crisis the village leaders turned to

another clan group, the members of the Horn phratry. This phratry
group is only found on First Mesa and is therefore, in all probability, rather recent. But it was quite large, in contrast to the Snake
clans, and had come to control the Blue Flute ceremony at some earlier time. Also, one of the lineages, at least, had close connections
with the Navaho. Simo, a young man at the time and a member of the
Millet clan, was selected as village chief. According to Stephen's
account:

> Simo's grandmother was of the Horn clan and was stolen by the
> Navajo when she was a young girl. She grew up and married a
> Navajo, and her daughter, Simo's mother, also married a Navajo.
> Simo's elder brother, Deza, had always remained with the Navajo,
> but Simo, when a young man, returned to his mother's people,
> the Horn clan of Walpi, and, his elder brother refusing to leave
> the Navajo, Simo succeeded his maternal ancestor as chief [Horn
> clan chief, Flute society chief]. (Stephen, 1936, 949-50)

The selection of Simo as village chief did lead to better relations
with the Navaho, particularly after their return from their four-year
captivity (1864-1868) at Fort Sumner. During his tenure the Blue
Flute ceremony increased in importance and its *tiponi* became symbolic
of the village chieftaincy on First Mesa. The Horn--"Flute" clans
moved up to third or fourth place in the traditional order of arrival
of clans at Walpi; and, more significant for our purposes, the drama-
tization of the mythical arrival of the Horn clan, bringing the Flute
ceremony with its ability to cause the rain to fall, was altered in
conformity. As Simo told the story to Stephen, when the Horn clan
people arrived, "the chiefs of the Bear and Snake demanded to know
where we were going and what we desired to do." After the chiefs
opened the trail, "we set up the Flute altar and sang and the rain
fell and the Bear and Snake said, 'For a surety your chief shall be
our chief'. And truly", said Simo, "I am chief (Kikmoñwi, Town chief)
this day" (Stephen, 1936, 810-11). Here we have dramatized in ritual
the changes we have outlined in the social system.

When Simo died October 18, 1892, there were a number of as-
pirants for the position but the Hopi ceremonial leaders finally
agreed on Tüinoa, a sister's daughter's son. Tüinoa was a young man
and did not wish to take on the responsibilities of the village chieftaincy. Stephen notes that "He is not very forceful, and perhaps for
that very reason is more in sympathy with the peculiar bent of these
folks. A reforming chief would be an evil" (1936: 139).

When Kotka, the last survivor of the "Bear" clan, died after
World War II, the Walpi leaders made efforts to get a Bear clan girl
from Shungopovi to revive the group but the latter village decided
against it. But other efforts undoubtedly will be made.

We might now turn to the later version of the events connect-
ed with Mashali's ill-fated expedition. In 1936 Edmund Nequatewa, a
Hopi Indian from Second Mesa, wrote "Truth of a Hopi and Other Clan
Stories of Shungopovi", in which Chapter XI, entitled "How the Hopi
Marked the Boundary Line Between Their Country and That of the Nava-
jo", is directly concerned with these events.

> Now with all this fighting and the Navajo coming in around them,
> the Hopi were always thinking of their boundary lines and of how
> they should be marked in some way. But how? What sort of a
> mark could they put that would be respected by other peoples?
> It must be something that both the Hopis and the Navajo would
> remember.

> So just at this time there were two men at Walpi who were
> rivals over a woman named Wupo-wuti. Now both these men were
> looking for a chance to show this woman how brave and strong they
> were. Finally they thought of this boundary line and the "theory"
> of their people that it should be marked in such a way that every-
> one would always remember. So these two men thought that this
> was a chance for them to prove themselves and to really do some-
> thing for their people at the same time. They thought they would
> plan a fight with the Navajos as near the boundary line as they
> could get and there they would sacrifice themselves and leave
> their skulls to mark the line. In this way they thought that
> they would prove that they were brave and good fighters and they
> would really be doing something for their people, and so it was
> agreed upon.

> Then Ma-sale (feathers crossed) said they would go to Fort
> Defiance. So they both made an agreement that they would go ear-
> ly in the fall. Ta-wupu (rabbit skin blanket) thought they were
> going alone, but later found out that there was going to be a
> party going over. He thought they were sacrificing too many
> lives, but, of course, he had made the promise to this other man
> so that he could not tell on him or give him away at that time.
> The crier made an announcement that whoever wanted to go to Fort
> Defiance with this party was welcome, and that they must prepare
> themselves and be ready to go soon. Ma-sale had a son named
> Hani and he loved him, so he thought that he would take him along.
> He figured that if he should be killed it might be best for the
> boy to die also. Of course, this being a time of war, everyone
> was asked to take his bows and arrows along. Ma-sale asked his
> boy to come along and to be sure to make some new arrows. The
> boy, of course, being ignorant of his father's plans, was glad
> to go with them.

> By this time the people had found out that the two rivals
> were going together to Fort Defiance, and they figured out that
> there was something going to happen--that they were going out to
> give themselves away, or sacrifice their lives.

> The morning of the day they were starting out, one of the
> relatives of this boy, Hani, asked him if he was going along with
> his father and he said he was. This man said to the boy that it
> would be better for him not to go with them. But Hani said he
> was all ready and the man, being his father, he was going along
> with him.

> "Well", this relative said, "if you are, I will warn you
> right now. Wherever you camp you want to be sure where you lay
> your weapons or your bows and arrows, for your life will be in
> danger." He told him never to lay his bow and arrows under his

head, but that he must lay them at his feet. "Because", this
man said, "if you are lying on your back with your bows and arrows at your feet and you are waked up suddenly you will jump up
forward. Having your weapons there at your feet you will lay
your hands on them every time." He also told him that he must
try not to sleep too soundly, that he must remember he was in
danger all the time.

Hani, after getting his warning, started out and was the last
one to leave. At that time the trail was through Keams Canyon.
When he was quite a ways through the canyon, an eagle flew over
his head and it was flying low. He thought that if the eagle
settled down somewhere on a rock he would kill it and take the
feathers along in case he wanted to make some more arrows on the
way, so he kind of hid himself in the brush. Finally the eagle
landed on top of a rock and Hani crawled toward him and took a
shot at him. He did get him and the bird fell from the rock.
Hani ran over to the place and found that his eagle was a buzzard. This seemed kind of strange, for he really had seen an
eagle. That made him sort of suspicious. He thought it might
be a warning or witchcraft, but as he was on his way already, he
couldn't very well turn back. Well, finally he came up with the
party, in the late afternoon.

That night when they made their first camp he had the warn-
ings in his mind and he couldn't sleep. Anyway, he must have
fallen asleep for awhile and when he opened his eyes he was wide
awake. He heard two men talking but he didn't make any noise
and pretended he was sound asleep. He recognized his father's
voice and also the voice of the other man, Ta-wupu. He overheard
Ta-wupu asking his father why he had brought his boy along and
his father said he couldn't very well leave him behind because
he loved him so dearly. He said that if his boy should refuse
to come along with him he would back out too and he said it would
be better for both of them if they got killed. When the boy began to move the two men rushed back and crawled into their beds.
Now, after Hani had overheard what the two men had said, he
couldn't sleep.

From then on the boy was rather uneasy every night when they
made camp. After they lay down to sleep he'd keep awake quite
awhile because he knew, then, what the two men were up to. All
the rest of the party didn't seem to know anything about it.
They were ignorant of the plans of the two men.

After several days on the road, they finally reached the
place--Fort Defiance. There they were welcomed by the white man
and were asked to stay several days with them. There were twelve
or fifteen men in the party. Four being the sacred number of
the Hopi, they decided to stay four days. On the fourth day,
when they were getting ready to go back home, the Bahana gave
them flour and sugar and coffee and different kinds of cloths,
besides yarns.

So the next morning when they were ready to leave, every burro
they had with them was pretty well packed. Before they left they
were asked if they would like to have a guard to go along with
them. In case they were in any danger, they would have someone
to show that they were the friends of the white man and they
were not to be harmed, but since they didn't see any signs of
danger when they were coming over they refused to take a guard
along. Having been granted all their wishes for things that they
had wanted for so long they were very happy when they left there.

They were two days on the road before they reached Ganado,
and the night before they reached Ganado this boy, Hani, over-

heard the two men talking with some other man. This time there were three men sitting around the camp fire quietly smoking. The boy could not really understand just what they were saying because it was all in a whisper. Then, of course, he couldn't help but move and when he did, one man rushed off and the other two men went to bed. One man was an outsider, a Navajo. The next morning the boy was more suspicious than ever, but still he could not ask his father what this night meeting was about.

So that day they traveled all day (on the other side of Ganado). On this day camp was made rather early and they said they wanted to get settled before dark. So they got everything ready before the sun went down, which was northwest of Ganado in the red hills. They said that they would have a good supper that night so they cooked a great deal of their food that they had gotten at Fort Defiance--with bacon and some beef that they had brought along. Having an early supper they said they would go to bed soon and would get up early in the morning for they figured on reaching home the next night.

This man, Ma-sale, the boy's father, seemed very happy that night. Before going to bed they cut a lot of branches off the cedars and brush that was around and put them clear around the camp, as a windbreak, you might say. Against this they put their saddles and all the packs that they had. That night Hani kept awake quite a long time, but he could not stand it very long so he finally fell asleep.

During the night some time, Hani thought that he was dreaming and that there was a heavy hail storm coming up for he thought that he heard the hail dropping. First he heard it dropping slowly and then faster. When he was wide awake he knew what was going on. They were being attacked and when he did come to, all the men were up. About this time his father spoke at the top of his voice in Apache, then in Navajo and then in Zuni. He was asking who it was that was attacking them. The boy did not forget where to have his bow and arrows every night, so when he did jump up he had his hands right on his bow. By this time arrows were coming from every direction. When Hani was well on his feet all the enemy rushed into the camp and as this was during the night he did not know who was who. Anyway, he started on a run and they chased after him. It happened that some Navajo had a corn patch near there and in the corn patch he had some squash with very long vines. Hani thought the whole country was full of enemies, so he hid under the vines, breathless and excited. He heard his father make his last groan and he was very angry. Dead or alive, he decided to go back but he found himself with only a few arrows, two or three left. So he ran back to the camp and when he got there he found his father dead, with many arrows sticking in his body. His scalp was gone. He thought that before doing anything else he must find his arrows and he found them rolled up in his blanket. This little blanket was only half the size of a double saddle blanket (a-teu-eu). Now the enemy thought that he was one of their party so he was not shot at until he had shot at them. As the enemy followed him he ran backward, holding the little blanket in front of him to stop the arrows. The moon was just going down below the horizon and it was getting quite dark.

At first he did not realize that he had been shot, for being a good runner the enemy could not keep up with him, but when he got up to the hills they were rather too steep for him to climb, because he realized then that he was shot, one arrow in his stomach, one in his hip and one between his shoulders. He pulled out two, the one from his hip and the one from his stomach, but he couldn't reach the one in his back. Well, anyway, he thought himself dead when he started to crawl up the hill. When he was halfway up the hill he cried for his dear life and prayed to his gods that if he should die, some day his skull would be found there. He didn't know how many of the party were killed or saved; he didn't know whether they were all dead or not. When he said his prayers, he cried some more, but he couldn't cry very loud, for he'd rather die in peace than have the enemy find him and use a club on him.

As he was going up, it began to show that it was dawn. He could see the daylight over the horizon and he wished that he would not die. If the sun did come up in time, he believed that it would give him strength. Of course, he couldn't help from groaning as he crawled up, and then he heard someone speak to him from the top of the hill, which scared him nearly to death and he thought some enemy had headed him off, so he did not answer. The voice came again and it was in plain Hopi. It said, "Are you hurt badly?" And he said, "Yes". And then the other said, "Will you be able to make it up here?" But he said, "No". So this other man came down and helped him up. When they got up he recognized this man and it was a man by the name of My-yaro. Well, this man said to the wounded boy that they would try to travel on together, as he was not wounded. He had been in the party, but had got away safely.

Hani told him to go on and leave him alone for he was done for and was ready to die but this other man refused to leave him. He said that if the enemy should head them off and follow them, he would be willing to die with him. So they went on walking slowly and while they were going along, another man named Tohchi (moccasin) joined them. He was hiding too. Hani asked them both again to leave him and run on home but they both refused. They asked him which of his wounds hurt him most and he said the arrow in his back hurt him the worst. So they thought they would pull this arrow out, but it was stuck fast in the bone. They tried it, but the shaft came off from the point. Then it was even harder to pull out. So they both tried their teeth on it and finally they pulled it out. One of these men was asked to scout ahead and the other to scout behind. So each man was supposed to be about one-fourth mile from the wounded man.

They were going very slowly. Finally they went down into another valley. It was about sunrise. As they were going along Hani saw a rabbit, a little cottontail on the side of the trail and he wanted to shoot this rabbit because he said he was hungry and needed something to eat. Well, the other man said not to kill the rabbit. He said, "You belong to the Rabbit Clan and you can't kill that rabbit. It might bring you luck if left alive. It might bring us both luck." So he said, "Let the rabbit live".

They thought of a spring around the point for they were both tired and thirsty. Instead of scouting ahead, the third man, Tohchi, had run home. When they got to the spring My-yaro would not let the wounded boy have a big drink, thinking that his stomach was injured. When they got kind of cooled off, My-yaro thought he would look back over the hill and see if the enemy was following. Before he left, he told the wounded man not to drink any more, for if his stomach was injured badly it would not hold water. But just as soon as he left Hani took a big drink and he felt much better.

Well, My-yaro went over the hill and as he looked down on the trail he saw a Navajo walking back and forth over the trail.

He watched this Navajo for quite awhile and he saw that he was very much discouraged. Well, finally, the Navajo turned back, so My-yaro went back to the spring and when he got there Hani told him he had had a big drink and felt better and he asked to have some more.

Then they both started back for the trail. This man, My-yaro, said he would go back to the trail and see what the Navajo was doing. When he got there where they had seen the rabbit he found that the rabbit was gone. So he investigated there and found that the rabbit had gone over their tracks three times. So this rabbit had disappointed the Navajo who thought the man had passed them in the night long before daylight.

It was about the middle of the day, and it was hot, so they got in among some rocks. Hani was pretty well tired out and he said he would like to lie down for awhile and cool himself off. So he did lie down under one of the rocks and fell right asleep and the other man kept awake. Well, this man on the watch would close his eyes every little while and as he was doing this, he saw the shadow of a little bird on top of a rock. It was a little rock sparrow and it was very much excited about something. The man thought this was a warning to them, so they got right up and started on.

As they were going along it began to show signs that it was going to rain. Clouds were coming up. When it did cloud up they felt very much better, for they were cooled off. Then it started to rain. They thought they would not stop for shelter, but kept right on going while it rained. Finally, it poured down on them and there was a regular cloudburst. It rained so hard on them that it washed all the blood off Hani. He said that he felt very much better, so My-yaro asked him to try himself out on a trot.

The man asked him if he felt his wounds hurting him and he said, "No". Then he asked him to go a little faster, and then he asked him again how he felt. Hani said that he felt all right, so My-yaro asked him to run as fast as he could. Then he asked him again if the wounds hurt him. Hani said, "No", and thought that he was well, so My-yaro said, "Let's go then".

Now when Tohchi reached Walpi and told the people what had happened, Hani's mother heard that he had been wounded badly and might die, so she wrapped up some piki and some sweet corn meal and she started out to look for him, all by herself. Now this was a very brave thing for a Hopi woman to do. She thought that she might find him dead somewhere and if she did she would roll his body under a ledge of rock or a bank of earth and cover him up with heavy stones and she would leave the piki and the sweet corn meal there for him.

But near the head of Jeddito Canyon she saw two men coming and then she recognized them for it was her boy Hani and My-yaro with him. And when they met they could not help but cry for joy. They hurried on home from there and when they came to the edge of the mesa south of Walpi, they saw clouds of dust in the valley coming toward them. They wondered what it was and thought it was an attack on the mesa. So they said to themselves, if there was an attack they would go on and meet the Navajo. So they went on and were met halfway and they found that this was a war party sent out to help them. When they met the whole party hurried back to the mesa and there at the foot of the mesa the whole village was crying for they found that only six men were saved out of the party that went to Fort Defiance.

Hani chose his godfather at the foot of the mesa, and of

course it was My-yaro who was the first one to find him wounded,
so instead of going to his own house he went with this man to be
washed up and cared for the next day. When this was done he
fasted four days. On the fourth day he was given his new name,
"Hani". From then on he always had in mind to get even with the
Navajos in that part of the country, and so he did, for later
he led war parties to that country often and brought back a scalp
every time. He was considered one of the greatest and bravest
men of the Walpi villages. (Nequatewa, 1936, 52-59)

This account, which is interesting in its own right, gains in significance when it is compared with Djasjini's eyewitness acount.
The personnel and the outline of events are similar, *but the whole
motivational structure is changed, and the account is on its way to
becoming tradition and myth.*

In Hopi belief important events are predestined, but the individual
is thought to be responsible for the decision as to how and when the
they will take place. Here Masale (Mashali) and Tawupu are cast as
rivals over a woman, and their motive for the journey is to "commit
suicide" by arranging for the Navaho to kill them, thus showing the
woman how brave they are and sacrificing themselves for the benefit
of the people by leaving their skulls to mark the boundary line.

     Rivalry over women, usually involving adultery with the wives
of chiefs, is a recurrent theme in Hopi mythology, beginning even
while the Hopi were living in the Underworld. When a chief is thus
wronged he leads his followers elsewhere, or arranges for his own
death, or those of his followers, at the hands of the enemy. Thus
in the tradition of the destruction of Awatovi (c. 1700-1701), the
village chief is said to have called on the people of Oraibi and
Walpi to destroy his fellow villagers because they had seduced his
wife (Parsons, 1921, 213, fn. 2.) Voth records a Shipaulovi tale
in which the Oraibi chief punished his people by arranging with the
Walpi chief to kill them during a raid. And in the Oraibi account
of "The Last Fight with the Navaho" a number of Hopi are reported as
going secretly to the Navaho camp the night before and arranging with
individual Navaho to kill them in the next day's battle. (Voth,
1905, 255-56, 258-66.)

     Mary-Russell Colton, the editor of Nequatewa's account, notes
that the Hopi idea of "sacrificing themselves" is difficult for a
white man to understand. "If a Hopi has enemies, or there is someone
who is causing him great misery, he becomes so unhappy that he wishes
to destroy himself. But he cannot do away with himself without 'losing face' as the Chinese say, or in other words losing his reputation
as a brave man. Therefore, he looks about for someone, or some other
tribe, who may be bribed to make a sham attack upon him or upon his

village during which he will be killed. . . . And so it is that the Hopi suicide makes a glorious end!" (Nequatewa, 1936, 107 fn. 32.)

In Nequatewa's account, Hani is made the son of Masale, and the latter's love for his "son" is his reason for taking him along on the fated journey. In the Hopi social system a father has no authority over his son, and Hani's maternal kinsman warns him of danger, but he decides to go anyway. The pattern of boy heroes who survive various dangers, with the help of animals or supernaturals, is characteristic of Pueblo and Hopi tales. Here we find a warning from an eagle who turns into a buzzard, a bird of ill omen; and, later, a rabbit whom Hani spares aids him by obliterating his trail and thus confusing the pursuing Navaho. Hani was of the Tobacco clan which is closely affiliated with the Rabbit clan, and the rabbit was thus a clan *wuya*, or totem, aiding him in emergency.

Nequatewa mentions from twelve to fifteen men in the party, but the editor, in a footnote, lists nine names, evidently secured from Nequatewa: Masale, Hani, Tawupu, Tohchi, My-yaro, Chihi (a Navaho adopted by the Hopi), Chongoh, Tavaco, and Tamoah. The Hopis killed in the battle were Masale, Tawupu, Chihi, and one other Hopi adopted Navaho. The Hopis saved were: Chongoh, Tavaco, Tamoah, Tohchi, and My-yaro, plus Hani, whom the editor doesn't mention but who is the protagonist (Nequatewa, 1936, 107 fn. 33). The last two lists give us ten men as participating in the journey.

Between the earlier and the later lists there is very considerable agreement, not only in number but also in names, and it is possible to account for most of the discrepancies. Hopis change their names after acquiring a new social status--hence Lesma was given a new name, Hani, after being initiated into the War Society by his "ceremonial father". Djasjini ("Black Ears") was a nickname given to Tanyemo, a Tewa from Hano, who may well be the same as Tamoah. My-yaro may have been added to the later account as a "participant" since he became Hani's "ceremonial father" and restored him to health. The "Uncle of Hili" and Chongoh are possibly the same individual, but I have been able to find nothing further on either. With regard to those killed, Mashali and Tawupu are on both lists and Lemoa may be the unnamed Navaho in the later account. Only Wiki is not accounted for, possibly because another Wiki, nephew and successor to Mashali in the Antelope Society, was active long after the latter's death.

The events of the journey are modified in a number of directions. The agent at Fort Defiance is identified with the *bahana*, the white elder brother of the Hopi who went off to the east after the emergence from the underworld but promising to return and help the

Hopi in time of need. The agent gives them gifts of food and cloth
and offers them a guard. They had stayed four days because four is
"the sacred number".

The events of the Navaho attack, as "seen" through the eyes
of Hani, are radically modified. The boy returns to get additional
arrows and finds his father dead and scalped. He continues the fight
and only retreats when he is outnumbered and full of arrows. This
is the kind of behavior that one expects from the little Twin War
Gods in mythological accounts, and is designed as a model for Hopi
young men to follow. The scalping is suspect in that neither Hopi
nor Navaho usually took the other's scalps, but it would intensify
the motive of revenge.

The events of the escape from the Navaho and return to the
village involve the intervention of animals and birds, as well as a
refreshing fall of rain. His courageous mother and the war party on
the way to help are added items to encourage young men to emulate
him as "one of the greatest and bravest men of the Walpi villages".

Hani lived to become chief of the Singer's Society, and of
the whole Wuwutcim ceremony, as well as participating regularly in
the Snake and Flute ceremonies, and did not die until 1923. He undoubtedly repeated the account of his experiences on numerous occasions, but no direct record survives so we can't be sure whether he
or others are responsible for the innovations. But the account as
reported by Nequatewa is clearly in the Hopi tradition and well on
the way to becoming myth.

Nequatewa's account, however, ends without any further reference to the boundary line between the Hopi and the Navaho that the
fight was supposed to establish. Mrs. Colton, the editor, in her
notes to the text gives the following additional information:

> For years it is said that the skulls of the victims of this foray
> were visible near the roadside between Ganado and Keams Canyon.
> . . .
>
> Edmund Nequatewa relates that in 1904 he passed along the old
> trail in the red hills near Ganado where the battle occurred.
> At that time one of the two Hopi skulls placed there to mark the
> boundary after the battle, was still in place on top of a small
> hill.
>
> It was the custom of both Navajo and Hopi who happened to be
> passing on the old trail, to pause and place a daub of red paint
> on the skulls, as a mark of respect for the departed heroes. He
> said further, that the spot where the skulls rested was somewhat
> northeast of the boundary as claimed by the Hopi. (Nequatewa,
> 1936, 107-108, fn. 33)

It seems evident from these notes that the boundary line is a separate problem which was added to, but not fully integrated into Nequatewa's account of the fight. We find a further reference to this

boundary line in a memorandum on Hopi land claims prepared by Gordon
MacGregor, at that time Anthropologist for the Bureau of Indian Affairs, and addressed to John Collier, Commissioner of Indian Affairs
under date of August 6, 1938. One of the paragraphs on First Mesa
claims is as follows:

> The First Mesa or Walpi people made an agreement with the Navajo
> some time about 1850 establishing a boundary line. The Navajo
> were to cross it only on condition of good behavior. As a sign
> of good faith the Navajo are said to have presented a feather
> shrine or symbol, which First Mesa still preserves. A pile of
> rock some distance west of Ganado and on the old road once marked
> this line. First Mesa, of course, would like to see this line
> form the eastern limit of the reservation. (MacGregor, 1938, 2)

Confirmation of these statements came in dramatic fashion when a delegation of Hopi Indians from First Mesa appeared at Prescott, Arizona,
during the Federal Court hearings on the dispute between the Hopi and
Navaho over the ownership of the Hopi reservation. The leader of the
delegation was from the Walpi Snake clan and had in his possession a
crude *tiponi*, or feather emblem, composed of ancient eagle feathers
wrapped in cotton string. The story he told--along with the *tiponi*--
had been handed down from his old uncles, and was concerned with earlier disputes between the Navaho and Hopi. The substance of his account was to the effect that, after a period of "troubles", the Navaho had agreed to be peaceful and had promised not to come into Hopi
territory except for trade and other friendly purposes. As a mark
of their sincerity, they had presented the feather symbol to his clan
ancestors with the injunction to show it to the Navaho if they ever
transgressed on Hopi territory. The Snake clan leaders wondered if
this was not the time to bring the *tiponi* forth. They identified
the marked boundary as west of Ganado, near the present junction of
the road to Canyon de Chelly.

We do not as yet have the full details of this account, but
it is evident that here is one key to the entire story. Mashali's
death led to a period of intensified hostility between the Hopi and
their allies on one side and the Navaho on the other at a time when
the Navaho were facing U.S. troops for the first time. The "peace
treaty" with its marked boundaries freed their rear from attack and
restored mutually advantageous trading relations with the Hopi. And
with the cessation of war the Hopi were able to return to the condition of peacefulness which had marked earlier Pueblo life and which
characterizes them today.

In this larger context we can see some of the reasons for the
coalescence of these separate events and their condensation into myth
form. But we can also see from this example that it may be possible
to reverse the process--to unravel the traditions and myths and iso-

late the historical events embedded in them from the motivational and other patterns that have been added. This will tell us a good deal about Hopi history and character, and help us to understand the changes they have undergone. Such a procedure may well be valid for the Pueblos as a whole, since they share to a remarkable degree a common ethos. The Navaho have a different pattern of mythmaking and it would be interesting to record their reactions to the events described above, if they survive. Ultimately we should gain a greater understanding of myth and mythmaking in general, as a mode of language use.

One example does not allow us to generalize very far, but it does demonstrate that it will be profitable to reanalyze Hopi mythology for its historical content, as well as for other purposes. The critical cases will, of course, be those traditions for which we have no possibility of discovering independent accounts and which don't fall into type situations such as we have described above. These will have to be handled in terms of other objective criteria, as yet only partly worked out. Time perspective will have to come from archeology and from comparative studies, since the Hopi are relatively unconcerned with absolute time. We can now handle changes in social structure with greater sophistication than did Fewkes and Mindeleff and thus correct their analyses and interpretations. We will need to carry out the comparative studies that Lowie demanded and will rely on their internal consistency rather heavily, to begin with. Eventually we may be able to develop rough scaling techniques for different classes of events. But these are tasks for the future.

Returning to Lowie's dictum as to the lack of value of oral tradition, we can see that, with regard to the Hopi at any rate, he is too severe in his judgment. In this case the Hopi have not only remembered historical events with considerable accuracy, but have remembered *significant* happenings. Although Lowie was willing to ascribe psychological and cultural values, but not historical values, to oral traditions, I think that we can now accept all three. The Hopi have a different world view from ours and a different conception of human nature. B. L. Whorf (1956) has opened one door to an understanding of the Hopi universe through his ethnolinguistic studies; and Stephen's remarks on Hopi conceptions of time suggest that there is much for the ethnologist to investigate. We want to understand history in Hopi terms as well as in those of the objective world.

BIBLIOGRAPHY

Benedict, Ruth
1935 *Zuni mythology* (=*Columbia University Contributions to Anthropology*, vol. 21) (New York, Columbia University Press).

Colton, M. F.
1936 *See* E. Nequatewa.

Cushing, F. H.
1896 "Outlines of Zuni creation myths", *Bureau of American Ethnology, Annual Report*, no. 13 (Washington, D.C., Smithsonian Institution), pp. 321-447.

Dixon, R. B. and J. R. Swanton
1914 "Primitive American history", *American Anthropologist*, 16: 376-412.

1915 "Reply [to R. H. Lowie]", *American Anthropologist*, 17:599-600.

Eggan, Fred
1950 *Social organization of the Western Pueblos* (Chicago, University of Chicago Press).

Fewkes, J. W.
1901 "Tusayan migration traditions", *Bureau of American Ethnology, Annual Report*, no. 19 (Washington, D.C., Smithsonian Institution), pp. 577-633.

Kroeber, A. L.
1917 "Zuni kin and clan", *American Museum of Natural History, Anthropological Papers*, vol. 18, pt. 2 (New York), pp. 39-204.

Lowie, R. H.
1915 "Oral tradition and history", *American Anthropologist*, 17: 596-599.

1917 "Oral tradition and history", (Presidential address, American Folk-Lore Society), *Journal of American Folklore*, 30:161-167.

MacGregor, G.
1938 "Memorandum on Hopi land claims", dated Aug. 6, 1938, reproduced as Plaintiff's Exhibit 55, *Indian Claims Commission Docket* No. 196 (Hopi), Vol. II, Mimeographed, 1962.

Nequatewa, E.
1936 "Truth of a Hopi and other clan stories of Shungopovi", edited by Mary-Russell F. Colton, *Museum of Northern Arizona, Bulletin* No. 8, Flagstaff.

Parsons, E. C.
1921 "The Pueblo Indian clan in folk-lore", *Journal of American Folk-Lore*, 34:209-216.

1936 *See* A. M. Stephen.

Stephen, A. M.
1936 "Hopi journal of Alexander M. Stephen", edited by E. C. Parsons, *Columbia University Contributions to Anthropology*, vol. 22. (New York).

Underhill, R.
1956 *The Navajos*, Norman (Oklahoma, University of Oklahoma Press).

Vansina, Jan
1965 *Oral tradition: a study in historical methodology*, translated by H. D. Wright (Chicago, Aldine Publishing Company).

Voth, H. R.
1905 *The traditions of the Hopi* (=*Field Columbian Museum Publication* 96, Anthropological Series, vol. 8) (Chicago).

Whorf, B. L.
1956 *Language, thought and reality. Selected writings of Benjamin Lee Whorf*. Edited by John B. Carroll (New York, John Wiley and Sons, Inc.).

16

LEWIS HENRY MORGAN'S SYSTEMS: A REEVALUATION

1972

I

It seems quite appropriate in a centennial program in commemoration
of Lewis Henry Morgan's publication of *Systems of Consanguinity and
Affinity of the Human Family* (1871) to attempt a reevaluation of his
contributions to the study of kinship.   The Morgan lectures at the
University of Rochester are evaluating Morgan's work more generally;
but recent critics have called into question the procedures initiated
by Morgan for the study of kinship, and the question is being asked
whether a unified approach to the study of kinship will be possible
in the coming decade and whether it is desirable.

To answer this latter question it is important to consider
Morgan.   One hundred years ago he published a volume which initiated
a unified approach to the study of kinship in relation to society.
What Morgan's *Systems of Consanguinity and Affinity of the Human Family* led to has been expounded in Meyer Fortes' *Kinship and the Social
Order, The Legacy of Lewis Henry Morgan* (1969), an excellent and far-
reaching account of modern structural-functional theory and method
as it applies to the study of kinship and social organization.   From
Fortes' view this theory and method "stems directly from Morgan's
work," and he sets out in detail the steps by which it has been developed.

In the meantime, there have been counter-movements in social
anthropology which threaten to make this elaborate structure of method and theory obsolete, or at least old-fashioned.   Let us look at a
recent review of Fortes' monograph from the *Times Literary Supplement*:

If the study of kinship is the peculiar preserve of social
anthropology, then it is safe to assume that the progress made

in this area will give some indication of the state of the whole discipline. Earlier this year, at the annual conference of the Association of Social Anthropologists, a strong current of dissatisfaction with this progress was revealed, and the feeling was expressed by some of the participants that social anthropologists should put their house in order by spring-cleaning the cherished but exhausted categories with which they habitually approach kinship [Anonymous 1970:880].

The anonymous reviewer goes on to note that Professor Fortes' recent contributions "are good sources of ammunition for the proponents of this view."

I happened to be at the Bristol meeting of the Association of Social Anthropologists referred to, where Edmund Leach was chairman and Rodney Needham the organizer of the program, and the forthcoming volume of papers will confirm these statements. But the new chairman of ASA--in the peculiar British method of succession to office-- is none other than Meyer Fortes, so the next meeting should be even more interesting.

Those who know Thomas Kuhn's *The Structure of Scientific Revolutions* (1962) will recognize in this situation the outlines of a possible case of the rise and decline of a scientific paradigm, in which the assumed inadequacies of structural-functional theory to account for change, or to develop an adequate explanation for similarities and differences in social structures, require a different method and approach.

In this country the opposition to Morgan was early and radical. Kroeber, in a now classic paper on "The Classificatory Systems of Relationship" (1909), rejected Morgan's distinctions and argued that "terms of relationship reflect psychology, not sociology. They are determined primarily by language and can be utilized for sociological inferences only with extreme caution." With the development of modern linguistics and information theory, there has been a return to Kroeber's position, even though Kroeber himself had partly abandoned it, and some anthropologists in this country have developed componential analyses of kinship terminologies or have attempted formal or "generative" accounts by which models are constructed which replicate the empirical data.

Across the Atlantic, Lévi-Strauss' *Elementary Structures of Kinship* ([1949] 1969) proposes "a general theory of kinship systems" based on exchange and provides a set of abstract models for various systems of preferential marriage which can be subjected to mathematical formulation.

In another direction, there has been renewed interest in the nature of kinship and the cultural assumptions concerning its basic features. This has led both to new procedures for collecting information on kinship systems and to a major interest in the native or "folk" model, best represented by David M. Schneider's *American Kinship: A Cultural Account* (1968).

II

What have all these developments to do with Lewis H. Morgan? In the 1930's it was possible to say that he was neglected, but today his fame is secure. In addition to the devoted services of Leslie A. White, Carl Resek has written an excellent biography entitled *Lewis Henry Morgan: American Scholar* (1960), and most of his books have been reprinted in several forms. In the Marxist world Engels' version of Morgan still reigns supreme, though there has been some rearrangement of the evolutionary sequences in recent years. Lévi-Strauss dedicated *The Elementary Structures of Kinship* "to the memory of Lewis H. Morgan . . . to pay homage to the pioneer of the research method modestly adopted in this book" (1969:xxvi). And we have already mentioned Meyer Fortes' *Kinship and the Social Order, The Legacy of Lewis Henry Morgan* (1969).

In our efforts to restore Morgan to his rightful place in the history of anthropology, it is possible that we have overdone the praise and attributed to Morgan virtues which he did not actually possess. As I read over my earlier contributions, "Lewis H. Morgan in Kinship Perspective" (1960) and my own "Morgan Lectures" (1966), I am aware that a historian of science would demand a more balanced account. For there are deficiencies as well as virtues in Morgan's pioneer efforts, and our failure to recognize and remedy them will delay modern developments.

The controversies over Morgan's contributions to social and cultural evolution have largely died down, but there is still much to be learned. Leslie A. White, in "The Concept of Evolution in Cultural Anthropology" (1959), notes that Morgan's theory of cultural evolution "had been developed in outline in *Systems of Consanguinity and Affinity* (1871) as part of his interpretation of systems of kinship nomenclature" (1959:107). White further states that "Morgan's promiscuity theory was not merely the fruit of his 'creative imagination'; it was derived from and based upon a great mass of *facts*--kinship nomenclatures--which he had gathered *himself* by *fieldwork*" (1959: 123-124, White's italics).

Carl Resek's biography shows clearly that the basic evolutionary hypothesis was provided to Morgan by his friend, the Reverend J. H. McIlvaine. Morgan had completed a first draft of *Systems* in

1865, but Joseph Henry, Secretary of the Smithsonian Instituion, refused to publish the manuscript on the grounds that "in proportion
to the conclusions arrived at, the quantity of your material is very
large" (Resek 1960:97). As Resek notes, "Morgan pondered the Reverend McIlvaine's hypothesis for three years before he used it, and
he might have withheld it longer had McLennan not been establishing
his priority in the field" (1960:96); but in May, 1867, Morgan sat
down and "constructed a conjectural history of the human family from
the 'primitive horde,' exercising complete sexual promiscuity, through
fifteen stages of evolution of the laws of incest, to the modern monogamous family" (Resek 1960:97). When he read his account before
the Academy of Arts and Sciences in Boston a year later, his distinguished audience received his paper in complete silence, and Morgan
left the hall convinced of failure; but the Academy had merely been
stunned, and soon requested his paper for publication and elected
him to membership. With the revision of the manuscript of *Systems*,
it was accepted for publication by the Smithsonian in 1868 and came
out early in 1871.

The particular sequences which Morgan set forth have long
been abandoned by most scholars, though they have survived in the
Soviet Union through being enshrined in Engels' *The Origin of the
Family, Private Property and the State, in the Light of the Researches
of Lewis H. Morgan* (1934). Recent Soviety social scientists have
reorganized Morgan's sequence for the development of kinship and the
family by shifting the Hawaiian or Malayan type from an initial to a
later stage, *not* because of a new analysis of the kinship system but
because "Morgan's assumption that the Polynesians were a primitive
people has proved to be erroneous" (Olderogge 1961:105). We will return to the Malayan systems later.

III

As is well known, *Systems* developed out of Morgan's initial interest
in the Iroquois and his researches among the Seneca in particular.
In modern perspective, we see *The League of the Iroquois* (1851) not
only as a pioneer ethnological monograph, but as a contemporary classic in political anthropology. Morgan's account of the structure of
the League with its balanced oppositions, and his account of the matrilineal clan system and its relevance to the unity of the tribal
confederation still are valid. But his account of kinship occupied
only two pages, and the terms themselves were relegated to a footnote.
Even so, the broad outlines were clear:

The Iroquois mode of computing degrees of consanguinity was unlike that of the civil or canon law; but yet a clear and definite system. No distinction was made between the lineal and collateral lines, either in the ascending or descending series [1962:85].

Morgan went on to point out that only a portion of Ego's relatives were in the same matrilineal clan, but that the members of each clan were all relatives and their relationships easily traced. Since the clans were exogamous, marriage united different clans in the family. Likewise, since a similar clan system was found in each of the Iroquois tribes, the League "was in effect established, and rested for its stability, upon the natural faith of kindred" (1962: 90).

With regard to the classification of kinsmen, Morgan did not follow up these leads; rather, he emphasized the bilateral and balanced character of the terminological system, which contrasted sharply with the pattern of descent. When Morgan returned to the Iroquois for additional data as a basis for the comparative studies of terminological systems which resulted in *Systems of Consanguinity and Affinity of the Human Family*, he never resolved this apparent contradiction, so that his conception of the Iroquois remained incomplete. I have discussed some of the results elsewhere (Eggan 1960), but since then additional information has come to light.

Most recent field research on the Iroquois has been concerned with the larger aspects of their social structure, but Merlin Myers, a student of Professor Fortes, has looked at lineages and household structure as well. On the Grand River reserve in Canada, where many of the Iroquois went to reside after the Revolutionary War, the longhouse (or traditional) group has maintained much of Iroquois society and culture, despite efforts of the government to modernize them and bring them under Canadian laws. The matrilineal lineage is still the key group in Iroquois society, with corporate functions and control of political and ritual offices. Each lineage has a set of names which objectify and maintain the internal structure and establish identity in the cosmos.

Within the lineage are smaller segments, usually of three generations, composed of an older woman, her daughters, and grandchildren. While residence is no longer matrilocal, many of the conservative families still are extended in terms of the matriline, or live close enough for the women to cooperate in household and lineage tasks.

The father's matrilineage is also an important group and is referred to as "people of my father's sister"; any member of the lineage may be addressed as such. The spouse's lineage is also important, especially in the funeral rituals. The surviving spouse "releases" the corpse to the lineage members, who make all the arrangements and carry out the mourning rituals and the funeral feast, releasing the spouse after ten days and distributing the effects of the deceased. The dead person joins his lineage ancestors in the "world beyond the sky," where he continues to influence the well-being of the living members.

Within the family and household, the terminological structure is bilateral, but the weighting of relationships is toward the matriline. The father provides the substance from which the body is formed, but the mother supplies the blood which contains the life or spirit, so that the mother is the closest and most important relative. For some Iroquois groups, the father's sisters may also be called "little mother" and are entitled to the same deference, but they do not receive the same affection or have the same moral position.

The father is socially recognized in the naming ceremony and ideally *pater* and *genitor* should be the same. In addition to the ties with the father's matrilineage, there is a cognatic extension of kinship for certain purposes, and at present the term "mother's brother" sometimes is used for the father's brother. The mother's brother today has little control over his sister's children unless he is the lineage chief; even here, titles to office are vested in the women of the lineage. Marriage within the lineage is likened to marriage with oneself: there would be no "father" and the child might have no bones or be otherwise deformed (summarized from Merlin Myers n.d.).

Traditionally, according to Morgan, the founders of the Iroquois confederacy rested the League on the system of clans. In each of the five tribes there were originally eight clans, which were grouped into two exogamous divisions. Each set of four clans were in the relation of "brothers" to one another and "cousins" to the opposite set, so that one married a conceptual cousin. It is possible that the Iroquois who resided on the St. Lawrence River in the sixteenth century may have had bilateral cross-cousin marriage at the time the League is thought to have been formed, but no documentary evidence has appeared so far. Today lineage exogamy is still strong; there are no specific rules as to spouses otherwise. However, Merlin Myers' genealogies show that marriages between cross-cousin are relatively common, at least among the longhouse group. It would be worthwhile to reexamine Goldenweiser's extensive genealogies, gathered on the same Reserve in 1912-14, from the standpoint of preferential marriage.

Today in Canada, there are *four* longhouse ritual and political groups in place of the original one. Each has a dual organization, with the lineages generally belonging to one side or the other.
Each "side" is a corporate group, with a set of officers hereditary
in the associated lineages. The reciprocal activities between the
two sides are not much changed from Morgan's time: each longhouse
has its own building, burial ground, and ritual paraphernalia, and
each carries out a ceremonial cycle and takes charge of funeral activities.

The contradictions between the kinship terminology and the
lineage organization are partly resolved by the recognition that *both*
the mother's and the father's lineages were important and that Ego
was related to both, although in somewhat different ways. The behavior patterns and obligations between relatives were also different
in degree, even though similar terms were utilized. If cross-cousin
marriage were once a part of Iroquois culture, as is true of their
northern Algonkian-speaking neighbors, a bilateral bifurcate-merging
kinship terminology might be maintained despite the matrilineal emphases. One important question has been: Why didn't the Iroquois
develop a Crow system of kinship? The answer is that they did in
part, since members of the father's lineage might be addressed as
"father's sisters," symbolizing the jural unity of the father's matrilineage. The Iroquois, during much of their recorded history, were
engaged in warfare with other Indian tribes and with the whites.
Their strength lay in their unanimity of decision, but continued warfare took a heavy toll. The losses were replenished by the adoption
of war captives, who were given names from the clan set and became
members of Iroquois society. It is probable that women came more
and more to carry the task of maintaining both society and culture
at the same time that Iroquois men were reduced to a common denomina-
tor through warfare and raiding.

Iroquois social institutions have also changed over time. It
has been over 400 years since Jacques Cartier first sailed up the St.
Lawrence River and found the Iroquois in possession of the region.
When Champlain founded Quebec a few decades later they were gone,
perhaps to join their relatives to the south and west. Somewhere
around this period the League was put together and the set of fifty
sachems hereditary in particular lineages was established. The fur
trade, the French and Indian Wars, and finally the Revolutionary War,
all had important effects. The longhouse, as a residence for women
of the lineage and their spouses, gave way to smaller units, and the
longhouse as a conceptual symbol of the whole tribe--and group of
tribes--took its place.

After the above had been written, Anthony F. C. Wallace's article on "Handsome Lake and the Decline of the Iroquois Matriarchate" (1971) appeared. Here Wallace outlines the classical Iroquois patterns of social organization and notes the drastic changes in the character of the Iroquois "matriarchal" institutions under the conditions of reservation life. The code of Handsome Lake, the Seneca prophet who founded a new religion in the early nineteenth century, emphasized changes in kinship behavior, along with the practice of agriculture by males and the abandonment of witchcraft.

The changes in kinship behavior were designed to strengthen the nuclear family and the husband-wife relationship at the expense of the lineage and mother-daughter ties. "Men were supposed now to assume the role of heads of families, being economically responsible for their wives and children, and not frittering away their energies on strong drink, gambling, dancing and philandering nor in mother-in-law trouble" (1971:373). Wallace sees these changes as Iroquois adaptations to their new technological and political circumstances rather than the copying of European institutions.

Despite Handsome Lake's reforms, the longhouse groups in Canada show strong matrilineal emphases, and we look forward to Merlin Myers' monograph on the Grand River Iroquois, as well as to further ethnohistorical research.

IV

When Morgan, in 1858, discovered that the Ojibwa had a set of kinship terms substantially similar to those of the Iroquois, and set out to collect the terminologies found in *Systems*, his primary interest was in the bearing these might have on the problem of the historical origins of the American Indian. Hence he developed a simplified "model" for American Indian terminological systems, contrasting it with the model he was most familiar with. As he began to gather further data from the rest of the world, he attempted to fit them into his two basic types, the "classificatory" and the "descriptive," and to arrange them into a developmental order. But some of his patterns of terminology seemed intermediate or aberrant and proved difficult to place.

Morgan's initial procedures involved filling out a large schedule covering over 200 separate relatives, consanguineal as well as affinal, but for comparative purposes he reduced the data to some ten "indicative features" primarily concerned with the consanguineal core. He accepted the conventions with regard to kinship prevalent in mid-nineteenth century American folk-culture, tempered by his knowledge of law, but made little effort to inquire into the possibly different conceptions of the Iroquois and other tribes he investigated. He did, however, attempt to see the terminology as a systematic whole.

Since Morgan's time there have been numerous attempts to provide a more adequate classification and conceptualization. Kroeber, Rivers, Lowie, Kirchhoff, Spier, Radcliffe-Brown, and Murdock have all concerned themselves with the typology of kinship systems, and in that process have raised more problems than they have solved. Ward Goodenough has recently dealt with various attempts to describe, type, and compare kinship terminologies in his *Description and Comparison in Cultural Anthropology* (1970), including componential analysis and transformational analysis. He notes that the comparative study of kinship terminology rests on the assumption that genealogical space is a cross-societal constant with reference to which kinship phenomena in all cultures can be defined, described, and compared, and he goes on to conclude:

> We anthropologists have assumed that kinship is universal, that all societies have kinship systems. If we are correct in this assumption, if every society does have some set of relationships whose definition involves genealogical considerations of some kind, then genealogical space must be constructed of things that are common to all mankind. These, we have seen, are parenthood and socially recognized sexual unions in which women are eligible to bear and from which women and especially men derive rights in children and thus establish parent-child relationships. If we cannot find a satisfactory way to conceptualize these things so that they withstand the test of cross-cultural application, we shall be unable to make meaningful comparison of the many ways in which people handle the classification of siblings and cousins [1970:97].

Anthropology, which developed as a comparative study of culture, thus faces a crucial decision. If it is concluded that kinship systems are not comparable, then much of the work of the past century is valueless or mistaken. Classification, which involves discrimination of the general from the particular, is difficult, and some of our colleagues dismiss such efforts, preferring to keep their analysis within the confines of a single society and culture.

The analogy with the biological world may be relevant. Early classifications in botany and zoology were made before the development of modern evolutionary biology and in fact contributed to that development. If it can be done for the biological world, it might be possible in the social world. One difficulty is that we do not as yet know the full dimensions of the latter world. While Murdock, our most assiduous collector, now has over a thousand complete systems of kinship terminology in his files, he has so far presented patterns for only eight sets of kinsmen: grandparents, grandchildren, uncles, aunts, nephews and nieces, siblings, cross-cousins, and siblings-in-law.

The patterns of classifications of kin terms are given for the major world geographic regions, but no attempt is made to classify in terms of whole systems, although presumably that is now possible. And Murdock notes that "the more interesting problem of ascertaining the extent to which the several patterns correlate with particular features of social organization or other elements of culture must be postponed for further consideration" (1970:181).

The kin term patterns for cross-cousins, which have been the basis of so many systems of classification, show a number of surprises. The Iroquois pattern, Morgan's archetype for the American Indian, makes a poor showing in North America when compared with the Hawaiian type, though on a world-wide basis the two are neck-and-neck, with the Eskimo pattern a poor third. Morgan's Descriptive pattern, on the other hand, is completely absent from North America and the Pacific, although well represented in Europe and the Mediterranean. It is clear that a classification in terms of total pattern is practical, and we can hope that Murdock will give it some priority.

In this volume, Harold Scheffler proposes a general structural typology for systems of kin classification in terms of the nature of the extensions which are utilized, though a full exposition is yet to come. Scheffler's conclusion is worth noting: "It is both possible and a relatively simple matter to demonstrate the structural similarities and differences between systems as wholes and, thereby, to set the stage for a more productive, because more realistic, sociology of kin classification" (1970:24; also this volume 128-129).

V

Morgan's most surprising discovery was that of the Hawaiian terminological system, which was "classificatory" to a much greater degree than the American Indian system he was in the process of defining. Here kinship was organized in terms of generations, with each term widely extended without collateral modification. He could see how the addition of clans to such a system might bring about an Iroquois type but could think of no adequate explanation for the Hawaiian system itself, until the Rev. McIlvaine suggested a possibly earlier state of promiscuous intercourse. Some notes from the Rev. Artemus Bishop with regard to Hawaiian society apparently confirmed this: "This confusion of relationships is the result of the ancient custom among relatives of the living together of husbands and wives in common."

With the acceptance of this hypothesis, Morgan became a social evolutionist and went on to write *Ancient Society* (1877), which made him world famous. With the downfall of classical evolution, interest in Malayan systems dwindled and has been revived only in recent years as non-unilineal or cognatic systems became of interest. We might look briefly at some of the current research to see whether *comparative* studies of kinship systems are still worthwhile and, if so, under what conditions.

Vern Carroll's recent study of Nukuoro, one of the Polynesian Outliers, has provided an excellent account of kinship (1968) in which nothing is taken for granted. He isolated lexical sets in terms of linguistic frames and found an overall set of lexemes which he labeled "interpersonal relationships" and which included, in addition to kinship terms, such terms as leader, servant, deity, enemy, chief, etc. Within this set he found that a further linguistic division could be made in terms of the prefix, *hai* ("to be in the relationship of"). These terms included, among others:

> dinana--"female elder"
> damana--"male elder"
> daina--"sibling"
> bodu--"spouse"
> soa--"friend"

The word for child (dama) was not included in this set, however, since it took a slightly different linguistic frame.

Informants would almost invariably suggest that "spouse" and "friend" belonged with *dinana, damana, daina, dama*, etc. but rejected any suggestion that the word for "relatives" (*hai dangata*) defined a domain which included these terms. "Relatives" in Nukuoro "are those with whom one shares rights in land" and are not necessarily kinsmen at all. Even the term "real relatives" or "close relatives" did not include any of the relatives listed above. The latter are even "closer" and can be considered as "relations" *sui generis*.

The Nukuoro thus have no native category of "kinsman" or "relative" comparable to ours, nor do they have "kin types" defined by reference to genealogical relationships. How, then, is such a system to be analyzed and compared with other systems? Carroll proposes to discover "the common core of *cultural meaning* in the entire lexical set" in terms of behavior. Sex and aggressiveness seem to be opposed to responsibility and cooperation, and they provide a subset of "friend" and "spouse" which contrasts with "elders" and "siblings." He finds no clear basis for predicting which individual will fill the assumed "kinship" categories: assignment of individuals is largely on the basis of performance.

Nukuoro terminology is thus "quite atypical in its relationship to the genealogical counting which has been reported for most societies," and Carroll hopes his results will encourage "anthropologists to look again at their data to assess whether their 'kinship terms' are really as wedded to genealogy as we think our own are." He also suggests that every anthropologist who offers a terminological analysis should hereafter explain "how he has decided which native terms are to be considered 'kinship terms'" (summarized from Carroll 1968; see also Carroll 1970.)

This is fair enough, since Nukuoro, on the evidence, does not seem to have a kinship terminological system in the generally accepted sense of that phrase. If Nukuoro is an exception to the assumed universality of kinship, then perhaps other systems are also. But there is another alternative which Carroll does not sufficiently consider: Nukuoro may have changed its kinship system in recent times.

The evidence for such a suggestion is contained in Michael D. Lieber's paper on "Kapingamarangi Kinship Terminology," presented at the same symposium in Seattle. Since he requested that it not be quoted I can only summarize his contribution, but it is particularly relevant to Carroll's major thesis. Kapingamarangi is not too far away from Nukuoro and is likewise a Polynesian Outlier, closely related in culture and language.

Lieber agrees in general with Carroll's procedures and is concerned with applying some of Goodenough's distinctions concerning identity, status, and role. He finds that the Kapingamarangi "system of categorizing relatives" is of the Hawaiian type and uses five main terms:

> tamana--male relative in an ascending generation
> tinana--female relative in an ascending generation
> tuahina--relative in speaker's generation
> tama--relative in a descending generation
> roto--spouse

Here, all of these, including *tama* ("child"), are included under the category *hai tangada*, and most of the terms are precise cognates of the Nukuoro series. Furthermore, these terms have consanguineal and affinal referents as well as more general applications, although the term *roto* refers only to one's own spouse. Lieber finds that these terms also designate statuses, involving rights and duties: anyone who plays the role of a particular relative also has that status, regardless of genealogical relationship.

With regard to land rights, these generally are limited to

kinsmen. Any person exercising his rights to the *use* of land refers
to the relative owning the land as *tamana* or *tinana*, since the latter
is acting like a parent in "feeding" his "child." Lieber concludes
that the meaning of any Kapingamarangi kin term includes genealogical
categories, but these do not comprise all the designata of the terms
(Lieber 1968, 1970).

On the basis of the data available, it seems clear that the
two systems are genetically related and that Nukuoro has shifted further away from the ancestral model, whatever that may turn out to be.
The treatment of the term for "child" is illuminating. In Kapingamarangi, it is classed with the parental relatives in linguistic treatment, as we would expect from Sol Tax's logical rules for reciprocals;
in Nukuoro, "child" is slightly separated. Only in Nukuoro is the
term for "friend" included in the group of relatives. And genealogy,
which is still significant in Kapingamarangi, has almost disappeared
as an important factor in Nukuoro.

Current controversies over emic and etic concepts are relevant here. Ward Goodenough has stressed the importance of etic concepts for general science. Too exclusive a reliance on linguistic
frames and native concepts may obscure some of the things we want to
know, particularly the nature and directions of social and cultural
change.

Within the Oceanic region, at least in the portions speaking
Malayo-Polynesian languages, genealogies of one kind or another are
often of great significance. If Murdock is correct in his comparative study of Malayo-Polynesian groups, his reconstructions "provide
overwhelming support for the hypothesis that the original Malayo-
Polynesian speech community had a social organization of the Hawaiian
type" (1949:350).

Several thousand miles to the west, the pagan populations of
the Mountain Province, Philippines, exhibit kinship systems that conform to the Malayan type, in part at least, and this is true of many
of the populations of the Indonesian region. All of the Mountain
Province groups have kinship systems built precisely on genealogy
and generation. The Ifugao, who are well-known through the researches
of Barton and others, array their kindred in generations and control
them through strict genealogical reckoning. All kin of the same generation as one's father and mother are *ama* and *ina*, who are identifiable cognates of Kapingamarangi and Nukuoro "relatives" in ascending
generations. While only the limitations of memory inhibit the extension of kinship within the generation, the extension of obligations
and rights is strictly controlled. Marriage within the range of

"third cousins" is taboo; this is also the extent of obligations to revenge injuries or the right to share in wergelds. Hence every Ifugao has to know his own as well as the kindred of others, since his very life may depend on that knowledge. Marriage, on the other hand, merely allies two kinship groups, and the ties that bind each partner to his own kindred are much stronger than those that bind them together. Only when a child is born is the alliance more than tentative. Furthermore, all the people in a district are encompassed in a genealogical network based on descent from founding ancestors or other cultural heroes.

Neighboring groups, such as the Bontok, Kankanay, and Kalinga, as well as the lowland Ilocano, have developed a referential system which is closer to our own, the Ilocano even having terms for first, second, third, fourth, etc., cousins; but in direct address, these and most other Philippine systems utilize the Hawaiian patterns of terminology. As I have noted elsewhere, these facts might have prevented Morgan from establishing his evolutionary sequences, since here the "earliest" and the "latest" patterns occur side by side in the same groups.

Returning to the Polynesian region, there is considerable variation among different island groups in the utilization of kinship terms in daily life. In some instances, kin terms are used in addressing elders; junior relatives are addressed by personal names or nicknames. In other instances, kin terms are only utilized on formal occasions, as when requesting the fulfillment of obligations or duties resident in kinship.

Thus Raymond Firth has noted, in a recent article on "Sibling Terms in Polynesia" (1970) that, with regard to kinship terminology, it is enough for social purposes that it "provides a frame of reference for categories of social action . . . In many Polynesian societies, kinship terms are mainly terms of reference and even people of senior status are addressed by personal names" (1970:272). He suggests, with reference to sibling terminology that "Only a very few societies, small in geographical range and in population, and remote from larger centres, have the simpler sibling patterning. That their ecological relationships have not demanded any more elaborate differentiation was my initial hypothesis, and this still seems plausible, if one reckons that the smaller the community, in numbers and in geographical circumscription, the more face-to-face contact is likely to obtain, and the less need for more complex forms of identification" (1970:275).

It is possible that on the smaller islands every individual

is related to all others in a variety of ways, so that one can either select an appropriate relationship or make new distinctions on the basis of social identity, status, and role, depending on the context or situation. With regard to size and simplicity, both Nukuoro and Kapingamarangi are at one end of the scale.

On other islands genealogy provides the major basis for relationships, and marriage is usually with a distant "relative." In many cases there is a clear extension of kinship, as Scheffler and others have demonstrated. Roger Keesing's conclusion to the Seattle symposium on "Kinship Terminology in Oceania" is relevant here:

> Kinship terms denote genealogical positions in that the classification of close kin is not contingent on their assuming the social identities connoted by them, or enacting their roles. When a kin term is used to label a pattern of role behavior by someone not meeting these genealogical criteria, it *is* contingent on that social identity being relevant in the context of the moment; it may also be contingent on alter's enacting that role, or of ego's attempt to shape alter's behavior [1968:12].

These few comments suggest that comparative studies of kinship systems are still worthwhile and that Oceania offers an opportunity not only to study a whole range of variants of a basic type but to put them in some developmental order, utilizing both linguistic and socio-cultural comparisons. In this endeavor, we will find some of Morgan's observations still useful and relevant.

VI

We might now return for a few minutes to the general question: Will a unified approach to the study of kinship be possible in the coming decade and is it desirable? My tentative answer to the first part of this question is that we will *not* develop a unified approach in the 1970's. I see this decade as one of keen competition between rival techniques for the study of kinship, based on different conceptions as to the relations between society and culture and on different philosophical positions as well.

The linguistic approach to kinship, initiated by Kroeber, has been developed in a number of new directions. Componential analysis as such has not led to much in the way of new insights into kinship and will probably give way to formal or "generative" models, as developed by Lounsbury, which are more dynamic and closer to the data. Formal accounts are said to be distinguished both by "sufficiency" and by "parsimony," but no one so far can write a formula for "all the women of the father's matrilineal clan and phratry are called 'father's sister.'" It would seem relevant for linguists to expand their models to take account of sociological factors. Where this has been done, the models are both more sufficient and simpler, although the "logics" may be less elegant.

The important role that Lévi-Strauss has played in kinship studies is too well known to summarize here. He has made his own assessments of "The Future of Kinship Studies" in his Huxley Memorial Lecture, 1965. The problems concerned with handling marriage choices in Crow-Omaha and "complex" structures in mathematical terms are sufficiently difficult that Lévi-Strauss believes the study of kinship will "mark time" until the theory of games is further developed (1969:xlii).

Edmund Leach, in *Rethinking Anthropology* (1961) also has argued for a mathematical approach to the study of society, but he recommends topology. He rejects the functionalism of Malinowski and Radcliffe-Brown in favor of functionalism in a mathematical sense, "concerned with the principles of operation of partial systems." In place of the organic analogy, he puts the analogy of a mechanism: "The entities that we call societies are not naturally existing species, neither are they man-made mechanisms. But the analogy of a mechanism has quite as much relevance as the analogy of an organism" (1961:6).

Leach is critical of comparison and classification and advocates an escape from both typology and ethnocentric bias: "Instead of comparison let us have generalization; instead of butterfly collecting let us have inspired guesswork" (1961:5). Here he is back to Malinowski and critical of Radcliffe-Brown, although he shows little evidence of having assimilated *A Natural Science of Society* (1957). In his reprinted essay on "The Structural Implications of Matrilateral Cross-Cousin Marriage," however, Leach states "an important principle of method. If anthropologists are to arrive at any valid principles of social organization, the general method must be comparative" (1961: 103). He goes on to emphasize the comparison of models rather than of "whole cultures," but insists "that the comparison must always take into account the whole range of institutional dimensions with which the anthropologist usually has to deal and must start from a concrete reality--a local group of people--rather from an abstract reality--such as the concept of lineage or the notion of a kinship system" (1961:104).

I have quoted Leach at some length because there are contradictions in his "messages" to anthropologists as well as inspiration. British social anthropologists have never been happy with kinship studies, for the most part, and, as Leach notes, are giving up the attempt to make comparative generalizations in favor of detailed historical ethnographies of particular peoples (1961:1).

The renewed interest of the last decade in kinship as culture will certainly continue in the 1970's. One aspect, represented by ethnoscience, attempts to collect better data, not by imposing a preconceived frame, but by establishing the native categories for lexical sets which include kinship terms. Another aspect is concerned with the nature of kinship as seen by the natives and with construction of a folk model which will make the terminology and behavior more intelligible. Carried to an extreme, however, this procedure suggests that the resulting "cultural systems" may be so different as not to be comparable. Since anthropology traditionally has been a comparative discipline, this would make a major change in our life style. Evans-Pritchard has been proposing a reversion of anthropology to history in recent years, but most of us, I think, have resisted Maitland's dictum: "By and by anthropology will have the choice between being history and being nothing."

The structural-functional approach, with its emphasis on the central position of social systems, will continue but will lose its distinctive position. Structural-functionalism, to the extent that it has been validated, has been absorbed in a number of social sciences, including social anthropology. Fortes and Goody have provided an enlarged dimension by considering the domestic cycle and politico-jural activities as separable domains. My own contribution has been to introduce a time dimension and to see social structures over time, as well as in ecological perspective. Here I am reasonably close to Leslie A. White's conception of social evolution as a temporal sequence of forms, except that I see recent temporal sequences as cyclical rather than developmental and can think of no adequate way to reconstruct the social systems of the distant past.

Since language is a part of culture and since society and culture are interrelated in a variety of ways, I envisage a new and broader synthesis developing, perhaps at the end of the coming decade, which will form the basis for a new paradigm to guide research. It will have a better foundation in more detailed studies of individual communities, with full attention to their uniqueness; and from these studies there will emerge more useful conceptual systems for cross-cultural comparison.

Whether a unified approach to the study of kinship is desirable depends both on the extent to which we envisage social anthropology as a discipline interested in generalizations and our view of the progress to date. My personal belief is that we will progress faster if we work within a common conceptual framework, even though periodically that framework needs to be enlarged or modified. I see no great virtue in starting completely afresh and rediscovering what we already know.

If we look back now to Morgan's *Systems of Consanguinity and Affinity of the Human Family*, we can see its importance in a new light. Many of his conclusions were wrong, but he did demonstrate the possibilities inherent in a broad and unified approach. That he went astray is less important than that he provided us with a series of problems which have occupied our attention for the past century. The amount of controversy and discussion about kinship and its relation, or lack of relation, to other aspects of society and culture is some indication of the significance of Morgan's contributions. The papers in the present volume suggest the directions in which we are moving and the ingredients which will contribute to the new synthesis.

REFERENCES CITED

Anonymous
1970   *Review of* Kinship and the Social Order, the Legacy of Lewis Henry Morgan. M. Fortes. Times Literary Supplement. London.

Carroll, V.
1968   Nukuoro Kinship Terms. Paper presented at the 67th Annual Meeting of the American Anthropological Association, Seattle, Washington, November.

1970   Adoption on Nukuoro. *In* Adoption in Eastern Oceania, ASAO Monograph No. 1. Vern Carroll, Ed. Honolulu: University of Hawaii Press.

Eggan, F.
1960   Lewis H. Morgan in Kinship Perspective. *In* Essays in the Science of Culture in Honor of Leslie A. White. G. E. Dole and R. L. Carneiro, Eds. New York: Thomas Y. Crowell.

1962   Study of Kinship Systems. Current Anthropology 3:98-99.

1966   The American Indian, Perspectives for the Study of Social Change. Chicago: Aldine. (The Lewis Henry Morgan Lectures/ 1964. The University of Rochester, Rochester, New York.)

Engels, F.
1934   The Origin of the Family, Private Property and the State, in the Light of the Researches of Lewis H. Morgan. New York: International Publishers. (First German edition 1884.)

Goodenough, W.
1970   Description and Comparison in Cultural Anthropology. Chicago: Aldine. (The Lewis Henry Morgan Lectures/1968. The University of Rochester, Rochester, New York.)

Firth, R.
1970   Sibling Terms in Polynesia. Journal of the Polynesian Society 79:272-287.

Fortes, M.
1969   Kinship and the Social Order, The Legacy of Lewis Henry Morgan. Chicago: Aldine. (Lewis Henry Morgan Lectures/1963, University of Rochester, Rochester, New York.)

Keesing, R.
1968 On Quibblings over Squabblings of Siblings: Some Reflections
on Kin Terms and Behavior. Paper presented at the 67th Annual Meeting of the American Anthropological Association,
Seattle, Washington, November. (Paper has since been published in revised form in the Southwestern Journal of Anthropology Vol. 25:207-227, 1969.)

Kroeber, A. L.
1909 The Classificatory Systems of Relationship. Journal of the
Royal Anthropological Institute 39:77-84.

Kuhn, T.
1962 The Structure of Scientific Revolutions. Chicago: University of Chicago Press.

Leach, E.
1961 Rethinking Anthropology. London School of Economics Monographs on Social Anthropology No. 22. London: Athlone.

1961 The Structural Implications of Matrilateral Cross-Cousin
Marriage. (*Reprinted in* Rethinking Anthropology.)

Lévi-Strauss, C.
1966 The Future of Kinship Studies. The Huxley Memorial Lecture
1965. Proceedings of the Royal Anthropological Institute of
Great Britain and Ireland for 1965. London.

1969 The Elementary Structures of Kinship. Rodney Needham, Ed.
Boston: Beacon.

Lieber, M. D.
1968 Kapingamarangi Kinship Terminology. Paper presented at the
67th Annual Meeting of the American Anthropological Association, Seattle, Washington, November.

1970 Adoption on Kapingamarangi. *In* Adoption in Eastern Oceania.
ASAO Monograph No. 1. Honolulu: University of Hawaii Press.

Morgan, L. H.
1871 Systems of Consanguinity and Affinity of the Human Family.
Smithsonian Contributions to Knowledge V. 17. Washington,
D.C.: Smithsonian Institution.

1877 Ancient Society. New York: Henry Holt.

1962 League of the Iroquois. New York: Corinth Books. (Originally published in 1851.)

Murdock, G. P.
1949 Social Structure. New York: Macmillan.

1970 Kin Term Patterns and Their Distribution. Ethnology 9:165-
207.

Myers, M.
n.d. Report on the Grand River Iroquois. Ms.

Olderogge, D. A.
1961 Some Problems in the Study of Kinship. Current Anthropology
2:103-107.

Radcliffe-Brown, A. R.
1957 A Natural Science of Society. Glencoe: The Free Press.

Resek, C.
1960 Lewis Henry Morgan: American Scholar. Chicago: University
of Chicago Press.

Scheffler, H.
1970 A Structural Typology of Systems of Kin Classification.
Mimeographed. (Published in revised form, this volume, pp.
113-133.)

Schneider, D. M.
  1968 American Kinship: A Cultural Account. Englewood Cliffs:
        Prentice-Hall.

Wallace, A. F. C.
  1971 Handsome Lake and the Decline of the Iroquois Matriarchate.
        In Kinship and Culture. Francis L. K. Hsu, Ed. Chicago:
        Aldine.

White, L. A.
  1959 The Concept of Evolution in Cultural Anthropology. *In* Evolu-
        tion and Anthropology: A Centennial Appraisal. Washington,
        D.C.:   The Anthropological Society of Washington.